Vi
& Budapest

Sevan Nisanyan

Prentice Hall Travel

New York • London • Toronto • Sydney • Tokyo • Singapore

THE AMERICAN EXPRESS ® TRAVEL GUIDES

Published in the United States by
Prentice Hall General Reference
A division of Simon & Schuster, Inc.
15 Columbus Circle
New York, NY 10023

PRENTICE HALL and colophon are
registered trademarks of Simon &
Schuster, Inc.

First published in the United
Kingdom by Mitchell Beazley
International Ltd, Michelin House
81 Fulham Road, London SW3 6RB

Edited, designed and produced by
Castle House Press, Llantrisant,
Mid Glamorgan CF7 8EU, Wales

© American Express Publishing
Corporation Inc. 1992

The author wishes to thank in
particular Müjde Tönbekici, who
provided essential moral support
during the researching and writing of
the text. The editor and publisher
wish to thank the Austrian National
Tourist Office, London, Danube
Travel, London, Chris Frizelle of ITEC,
Bromley, England, Mike De Mello of
Triptych Systems Ltd, Gerrards Cross,
England, and Gary Walther of
Departures, New York, for their
assistance during the preparation of
this edition. Warm thanks are due
also to Neil Hanson, David Haslam,
Sylvia Hughes-Williams, Hilary Bird,
Anne Evans, Jonah Jones, Judith
Maro, Peter Jones, Dr Maggie Smales
and Tom Mulligan.

FOR THE SERIES:
General Editor:
  David Townsend Jones
Map Editor: David Haslam
Indexer: Hilary Bird
Cover design:
  Roger Walton Studio

FOR THIS EDITION:
Edited on desktop by:
  David Townsend Jones
Art editor:
  Eileen Townsend Jones
Illustrators:
  Sylvia Hughes-Williams,
  David Evans
Gazetteer: Anne Evans
Cover photo: Europress

FOR MITCHELL BEAZLEY:
Art Director: Tim Foster
Managing Editor: Alison Starling
Production: Sarah Schuman

PRODUCTION CREDITS:
Maps by Lovell Johns, Oxford,
  England
Metro maps by TCS, Aldershot,
  England
Typeset in Garamond and
  News Gothic
Desktop layout in Ventura Publisher
Linotronic output by Tradespools
  Limited, Frome, England

Contents

Preparations

Vienna

Budapest

Maps

How to use this book

Few guidelines are needed to understand how this book works:

- For the general organization of the book, see CONTENTS on the pages preceding this one.
- Wherever appropriate, chapters and sections are arranged alphabetically, with headings appearing in **CAPITALS.**
- Often these headings are followed by location and practical information printed in *italics*.
- As you turn the pages, you will find subject headers, similar to those used in telephone directories, printed in CAPITALS in the top corner of each page.
- If you still cannot find what you need, check in the comprehensive and exhaustively cross-referenced INDEX at the back of the book.

CROSS-REFERENCES
These are printed in SMALL CAPITALS, referring you to other sections or alphabetical entries in the book. Care has been taken to ensure that such cross-references are self-explanatory. Often, page references are also given, although their excessive use would be intrusive and ugly.

FLOORS
We use the European convention in this book: "ground floor" means the floor at ground level (called by Americans the "first floor").

KEY TO MAP SYMBOLS

CITY MAPS

▨	Place of Interest or Important Building
▢	Built-up Area
▨	Park
†	Church
✡	Synagogue
⊞	Hospital
i	Information Office
✉	Post Office
♙	Police Station
⚓	Parking Lot
ⓤ	Metro Station (Vienna)
Ⓜ	Metro Station (Budapest)
←•→	Funicular Railway
→	One-way Street
⊐⊐⊐⊐	Stepped Street
╪═╪	No Entry

METROPOLITAN MAPS

▪	Place of Interest
▨	Built-up Area
▨	Wood or Park
↑↑	Cemetery
═O═	Autobahn (with access point)
═ ═	Autobahn (under construction)
━━	Main Road / 4-Lane Highway
━	Other Main Road
—	Secondary Road
SS4	Road Number
═ ═	Railway
+++++	Rack Railway
✈	Airport

Key to symbols

☎	Telephone	♿	Facilities for disabled people
Fx	Facsimile (fax)	❏	Cable TV in rooms
★	Recommended sight	❦	Garden
☆	Worth a visit	◀€	Good view
i	Tourist information	≈≈	Swimming pool
⬌	Parking	🏖	Good beach nearby
🔲	Entrance fee payable	⌂	Sauna
ƒ	Guided tour	☀	Solarium
✱	Special interest for children	℘	Tennis
❧	Hotel	☗	Gym/fitness facilities
⌂	Quiet hotel	👥	Conference facilities
⬜	Cheap	♝	Bar
⬜	Inexpensive	▣	Minibar in rooms
⬜	Moderately priced	⇶	Restaurant
⬜	Expensive	🚗	Open-air dining
⬜	Very expensive	♫	Live music
AE	American Express	❦	Dancing
◉	Diners Club	▲	Camping
◖	MasterCard/Eurocard		
VISA	Visa		

About the author

Prolific author **Sevan Nisanyan** was born in Istanbul and educated at Yale (philosophy) and Columbia (politics). His exploits include stints as the boss of a large computer firm, adventurer in the Andes, and political prisoner. Among his previous publications are *Insight Guide: Istanbul* and, in this series, *American Express Athens and the Classical Sites*. Many years of familiarity with the Austrian and Hungarian capitals form the background to this guide, which was written in Kuzguncuk, by the Asian shore of the Bosphorus.

Nicholas Parsons (who contributed EATING AND DRINKING IN VIENNA) is a widely-published writer and journalist who has lived in Central Europe for almost ten years. Currently his home is in Vienna.

A message from the series editor

In designing *American Express Vienna & Budapest* we aimed to make this brand-new edition simple and instinctive to use, like all its sister volumes in our new, larger paperback format.

The hallmarks of the relaunched series are clear, classic typography, confidence in fine travel writing for its own sake, and faith in our readers' innate intelligence to find their way around the books without heavy-handed signposting by editors.

Readers with anything less than 20:20 vision will doubtless also enjoy the larger, clearer type, and can now dispense with the mythical magnifying glasses we never issued free with the old pocket guide series.

Many months of concentrated work by author **Sevan Nisanyan** and his editor have been dedicated to ensuring that this edition is as accurate and up to date as it possibly can be at the moment it goes to press. But time and change are forever the enemies, and in between editions we appreciate it when you, our readers, keep us informed of changes that you discover.

As ever, I am indebted to all readers who wrote during the preparation of this book. Please remember that your feedback is extremely important to our efforts to tailor the series to the very distinctive tastes and requirements of our sophisticated international readership.

Send your comments to me at Mitchell Beazley International Ltd, Michelin House, 81 Fulham Road, London SW3 6RB; or, in the US, c/o American Express Travel Guides, Prentice Hall Travel, 15 Columbus Circle, New York, NY 10023.

David Townsend Jones

Vienna
& Budapest

Twin capitals of the Danube

Until 1918 — in other words, within the lifetime of people who are alive today — Vienna and Budapest were the twin capitals of a great European empire. It was one of the richest and most imperious that the Old Continent has ever known, a dynastic power that played for European supremacy for hundreds of years before it fell apart in the cataclysm of the First World War.

The Austro-Hungarian Empire infuriated its critics by its obtuse archaism: "the Habsburgs never forget and never learn" was the motto attributed to its ruling house. Yet it enchanted its admirers as the last European bastion of a gentle, aristocratic and splendid way of life, of old values that had long gone out of fashion in the modern world. The 68-year-long reign of Franz Joseph — "the last European monarch of the old school" — carried the era of counts, dukes and bishops into that of airplanes, socialism and psychoanalysis. It was a relic of the past, and it disintegrated under the onslaught of the Twentieth Century.

> In other countries dynasties are episodes in the history
> of the people; in the Habsburg Empire peoples are a
> complication in the history of the dynasty. The Habsburg lands
> acquired in time a common culture and, to some extent,
> a common economic character: these were the creation, not
> the creators, of the dynasty. The Habsburgs were the greatest
> dynasty of modern history, and the history of central Europe
> revolves around them, not they round it.
> (A.J.P. Taylor, *The Habsburg Monarchy, 1809-1918*)

Time has gone rapidly since 1918. Vienna is now the capital of a minor republic whose very existence was a matter of uncertainty until 1955. It is a beautiful city; one with a split personality. Its modern identity — as manifested in fashions, bistros, politics, rock clubs and shopping malls — is an echo of the modern German wonder, but slightly provincial in flavor, a little "southern" and sloppy in manner, less cosmopolitan than Berlin and less cockily self-assured than a Munich or Hamburg.

On the other hand is a Vienna that clings resolutely to the image of its past grandeur: the city of Strauss waltzes and Mozart operas, the Imperial Riding School, the Boys' Choir; the city of curtseying and hand-kissing, and of titled aristocrats whose daughters are introduced to society at the annual Emperor's Ball; a city that still has more palaces than banks. It is this facet of Vienna that attracts several million dazzled visitors each year from around the world.

Budapest lies a mere three hours' journey down the Danube. For many centuries it was bound up with Vienna in a symbiosis of love and hate. It rebelled against Austrian rule often and with the compulsiveness of a captive beast; yet it shared Vienna's rulers and institutions, copied its architectural styles and street names, emulated its café culture and cuisine. It never loved Franz Joseph, but it raised his queen, the tragic Elisabeth, to the status of a popular saint.

For 44 years after the Second World War the twin metropolises of the Danube were kept apart by an Iron Curtain of mutual ignorance. Vienna continued to capitalize on its history; Budapest faded in the Western imagination into the gray and indistinct universe of an alien "East." It was indeed more accessible — and more often visited — than other cities of that chill realm; all the same, it was a place of suspicion and incomprehension, of inane and menacing regulations and glassy-eyed civil servants. Unlike Vienna, it seemed to have forgotten its past: its concerns were the burning issues of today — rebellion, survival, manipulation — while history seemed hardly to matter outside a few packaged and sterile sights kept up for the sake of hard-currency tourists.

The amazing revolution of 1989-90 has now removed the Iron Curtain, and what emerges is a city groping to rediscover its past — even as it hurtles forward, exhilaratingly, to build a future. Every day brings to light some new monument or palace or old institution, rescued from abuse and restored to its ancient splendor. Rechristened city streets bristle with the names of the kings, queens and archdukes of the House of Habsburg where once the likes of "Lenin" and "Red Star" held sway. And in a supreme gesture of reversion, Otto von Habsburg, the heir to the last Austro-Hungarian emperor, is held up briefly as a candidate for the Hungarian presidency.

It is a time, in other words, when the paths of the twin cities of the Danube converge again. Vienna: the old beauty of smooth manner and tired soul. Budapest: the long-lost sister flush with the excitement of reunion. Few guides of the *American Express* series have dealt with so fascinating a pair, in so timely a fashion.

The sense of Austro-Hungarian nationhood was an entity
so strangely formed that it seems futile to try to explain it
to anyone who has not experienced it himself... the mysteries
of this dualism are at least as difficult to understand
as those of the Trinity.
(Robert Musil, *The Man Without Qualities*)

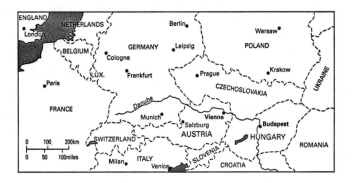

A NOTE ON ADDRESSES

Both Vienna and Budapest are divided into numbered districts, which form an essential component of every address. In Vienna, district number precedes street name, followed by a period and comma, as in:

8., Laudongasse 25.

Budapest uses Roman numerals followed by a period; thus:

VI. Téréz körút 12.

For the sake of greater clarity we give district numbers, when necessary, in parentheses. In the case of Vienna we generally omit district numbers for addresses in the Inner City (District 1.), where a large majority of sights, hotels, restaurants, cafés, shops and so on are located. Thus any Vienna address given in this book without a district number will be located in the Inner City.

The following terms and abbreviations occur in addresses:

Austria: Strasse (abbreviated Str.) = street
           Gasse = alley, lane
           Platz = square

Hungary: utca (abbreviated u.) = street
           út = road
           útja = avenue
           körút = ring road
           tér = square

HUNGARIAN NAMES

Personal names in Hungarian are customarily given surname first and given (Christian) name next. We follow the normal English order in naming persons but the Hungarian pattern in the case of streets, buildings and other items named after persons. Thus **Lajos Kossuth**, a person, but **Kossuth Lajos tér**, a square.

13

Preparations

Before you go

DOCUMENTS

Citizens of most European, North American and East Asian countries need only a valid passport to enter **Austria** for a stay not exceeding 3 months.

Hungary no longer requires a visa from US, Canadian or Western European visitors (exceptions are Ireland, Portugal and Greece); visas for visitors of other nationalities are obtainable at the main road frontier crossings and Ferihegy Airport, but not at train or river frontier crossings. Foreigners intending to remain in Hungary longer than a month are expected to register with a local police station unless they stay at hotels. Visitors who wish to extend their stay should apply in Budapest to **KEOKH** *(VI. Andrássy út 12, map 8 C4, open Mon, Thurs 2-6pm, Tues, Wed, Fri 8.30am-noon).*

Drivers arriving by car in **either country** must have a valid driver's license (an international driver's license is not required), the vehicle registration (logbook) and certificate of insurance. An international ("green") insurance card is required by Hungary in the case of certain countries, but not for cars registered in the US, UK or Canada.

TRAVEL AND MEDICAL INSURANCE

It is advisable to travel with an insurance policy that covers loss of deposits paid to airlines, hotels and tour operators, and the cost of dealing with emergency requirements, such as special tickets home and extra nights in a hotel.

The **IAMAT** (International Association for Medical Assistance to Travelers) is a nonprofit organization that has a directory of English-speaking doctors who will call, for a fee. There are member hospitals and clinics throughout the world, including four in Vienna, three in Budapest and several in other parts of Austria and Hungary. Membership is free and other benefits include information on health risks overseas. For further information, write to **IAMAT** headquarters in the US or in Europe *(417, Center Street, Lewiston, NY 14092, USA or 57 Voirets, 1212 Grand-Lancy, Genève, Switzerland).*

CUSTOMS

Austria is not — yet — a member of the EC, so there are the usual limits on the amount of tobacco, alcohol, coffee, perfumes and other items that you can bring into the country. There also exists a largely theoretical limit of US$400 on the amount of goods that can be taken out of the country without an export permit. Visitors who like to obey the letter of the law can obtain this at the shops where they buy the goods in question.

Hungarian Customs formalities have now improved to near-civilized standards. There is still an import duty on gifts brought into Hungary and an export duty on articles bought in the country, in either case over the total value of F5,000, but neither is strictly enforced in the case of foreign visitors — unless they seem to be engaging, as many do, in the cross-border trade. The import or export of Hungarian currency over the value of F500 is prohibited. In addition, it is forbidden to take out of the country any foodstuffs, groceries, medicines or laundry soaps over the total value of F500. It may be advisable to register items of value when you enter the country to avoid complications when you leave it.

Dogs and cats must have a rabies inoculation certificate no newer than 30 days but no older than 1 year. For regulations that apply to other pets, contact the nearest Austrian and Hungarian consulates.

MONEY

The **Austrian Schilling** is closely anchored to the German Mark (DM), with an average rate of AS7 to DM1 and a maximum vacillation of a half percentage point. The DM is generally accepted in all daily transactions, although most merchants will only take it at AS6.75 to DM6.90 (as opposed to banks, which offer closer to DM7.00). As of early 1992, other exchange rates were about AS11.50 per US$1 and AS20 per £1 sterling. The Schilling is divided into 100 Groschen.

The **Hungarian Forint** exchanged in early 1992 at about F75 per US$1 and F135 per £1 sterling, having lost its value by 35 percent over the previous year. Prognoses for the coming years varied wildly. The fillér, 100 of which make up one forint, has become irrelevant. Many hotels in Hungary quote prices in Western currencies, and we follow the same practice here. Forints can be bought freely in banks, hotels and private shops. Changing them back into Western currencies, however, is usually near impossible, so it makes sense to buy only as needed. Private money-changers, a throwback to old black-marketeering days, hang on at Váci utca and other tourist haunts: expect chicanery if offered more than a slight margin over the official rate.

Major charge and credit cards and **Eurocheque Encashment Cards** are accepted by most hotels, by better restaurants and by many shops in Vienna and Budapest, although the use of plastic is generally less widespread in this part of the world than it is in the main English-speaking countries.

American Express and **Eurocheque** cash machines dispensing local currency exist in Vienna; cash advances can also be obtained on these and other charge and credit cards from participating banks in Vienna and Budapest. Travelers' checks are cashed at nearly all banks in Austria (easily) and Budapest (reluctantly and minus a hefty commission). Cash can be sent easily from EC countries to Austria via any bank branch or post office, usually within 24 hours. For money transfers from North America, it is easiest to use **American Express** *(Vienna*

17

office: (1.) Kärntner Str. 21-23 ☎ *51567, map 3D3),* whose **Money-Gram**® service makes it possible to wire money worldwide in just minutes, from any American Express Travel Service Office. This service is available to all customers and is not limited to American Express Card members.

COSTS

Rents in Vienna are relatively high, and so are hotel rates. Otherwise Austrian prices are among the lowest of any major Western European metropolis.

Samples: ‡ Urban transportation ticket: AS15 ‡ Cup of coffee: AS22 ‡ Museum entrance: AS60 ‡ 2-mile taxi ride: AS70 ‡ Double room in simple suburban pension: AS700 ‡ Double room in good downtown hotel: AS1,700.

The Hungarian economy is very much in flux, so that while prices in some sectors have raced ahead to Western levels, one can still find astonishing bargains in other fields. As a rule, imported goods and services geared mainly to tourists — above all, hotel rooms — cost about the same as in the West; dinner at a good restaurant costs no more than half; and the prices of humdrum daily things (bus, bath, beer...) often cause gasps of delight.

Thus: ‡ Local phone call: F5 ‡ Bottle of Coke: F11 ‡ Museum ticket: F20 ‡ Pack of best local cigarettes: F52 ‡ Thermal bath with massage: F180 ‡ Full dinner in top-class restaurant: F800 ‡ Double room in good hotel: F10,000.

LANGUAGE

German is the language of Austria, and Hungarian (Magyar), a language unrelated to most other European speeches, that of Hungary. In Austria, nearly all people born after 1945 speak some English; printed information, as on road signs, explanatory placards and museum displays, however, is invariably given in German alone.

Hungary is more accommodating in this respect: shops, public amenities and tourist sights often advertise themselves in Magyar and — more or less — English. A majority of Hungarians speak some German, but the knowledge of English is not as widespread. The ongoing boom in foreign-language courses may begin to change this soon.

Refer to WORDS AND PHRASES (page 285) for a simple, practical guide to the basics of both languages.

CLOTHING

Vienna takes pride in its elegance, and although young Americans in sweatshirt and sneakers are now as common at the Staatsoper as galla-bieh'ed Saudis at Harrods, most others will feel more comfortable in the Austrian capital when dressed up in style and with taste.

Budapest emulates Vienna in this as in many other respects: the Hungarian in the street has not yet fully shed the drab clothes of socialism, but she/he expects a Westerner to live up to a certain image of "quality" or prosperity.

ELECTRIC CURRENT

Electricity in both Austria and Hungary is 220V (50Hz). Most North American appliances will thus require a converter, while British appliances will run on a simple adaptor plug.

TIME ZONE

Both Austria and Hungary observe Central European Time, which is 6 hours ahead of Eastern Standard Time, 7 to 9 hours ahead of the other time zones in the US, and 1 hour ahead of Greenwich Mean Time.

WHEN TO GO

The tourist season in non-Alpine Austria runs from April through October; outside this period, many hotels, museums and other tourist amenities, especially in the countryside, either shut down or operate on limited capacity.

Seasonal boundaries are less strict in Vienna, and in Hungary in general. Few hotels, for example, close down off-season, but as a rule there are fewer things to see or do or attend in winter. Late spring and early fall are the best times to travel — bright weather, beautiful nature, fewer crowds — although a majority of tourists arrive in July and August.

Vienna, located on the boundary of the Atlantic and mid-European climatic zones, has highly variable weather. Budapest is perceptibly more continental in character: hotter in summer and colder in winter.

	Vienna	Budapest
Average daily high, January	+1°C/34°F	-1°C/30°F
Average daily high, August	24°C/75°F	27°C/81°F
Annual precipitation	720mm/28ins	610m/24ins

HOLIDAYS

Public offices, banks and some museums are closed on the following days. Transportation, parks, etc. follow Sunday schedules.

Austria: January 1; January 6 (Epiphany); Easter Monday; May 1; Christi Himmelfahrt (Ascension: 40 days after Easter); Whit Monday (50 days after Easter); Corpus Christi (Thursday of the week following Whitsuntide); August 15 (Assumption of the Virgin); October 26 (National Day); November 1 (All Saints); December 8 (Maria Empfängnis: Annunciation); December 25-26 (Christmas).

Hungary: January 1; March 15 (National Uprising, 1848); April 4 (Liberation Day, 1945); Easter Monday; May 1; August 20 (Constitution Day); December 25-26.

WHAT TO READ

There is a rich literature on turn-of-the century Vienna, less on the earlier era of true Viennese splendor, and very little indeed — in English — on Austrian or Viennese affairs of more recent times. Paul Hofmann's *The Viennese* (Doubleday 1988) is a well-written and enjoyable overview of Vienna's history and culture. Frederic Morton's *A Nervous Splendor* (Little, Brown 1979, Penguin 1980) offers a fascinating chronicle of Vienna in the year 1888/89. Carl E. Schorske's *Fin-de-siècle*

Vienna (Knopf 1980, Vintage 1981) is a classic of cultural history.

Budapest is less written about than Vienna. John Lukacs's *Budapest 1900* (Grove Weidenfeld 1988) presents a nostalgic portrait of the city at its historic peak.

Of the many books on the history of the Habsburgs, A.J.P. Taylor's *The Habsburg Monarchy, 1809-1918* (The University of Chicago Press 1948) stands out as a work of uncompromising intelligence. András Gerő's fascinating and well-written book, *Heroes' Square, Budapest* (Corvina, Budapest 1990) tells the history of Hungary through the story of a monument that summarizes it all.

An avalanche of publications greeted the Mozart bicentenary of 1991. Volkmar Braunbehrens's *Mozart in Vienna* (Oxford 1991) provides an interesting counterbalance to the picture of the composer and of his era popularized by the film *Amadeus.*

FURTHER INFORMATION ABOUT AUSTRIA
The **Austrian National Tourist Office** is an invaluable source of information about holiday conditions in Austria.
US
- 500 5th Ave., #2009-2022, New York, NY 10110 ☎(212) 944-6880 ℻(212) 730-4568
- 11601 Wilshire Blvd., #2480, Los Angeles, CA 90025 ☎(213) 477-3332 ℻(213) 477-5141
- 500 N Michigan Ave., #1950, Chicago, IL 60611 ☎(312) 644-8029 ℻(312) 644-6526

UK
- 30 St George St., London W1R 0AL ☎(071) 629-0461 ℻(071) 499-6038

Canada
- 2 Bloor St. East, #3330, Toronto, Ontario M4W 1A8 ☎(416) 967-3381 ℻(416) 967-4101
- 1010 Sherbrooke St. W, Montréal, Québec H3A 2R7 ☎(514) 849-3709 ℻(514) 849-9577
- 736 Granville St., #1410, Vancouver, BC V6Z 1J2 ☎(604) 683-8995 ℻(604) 662 8528

Hungary
- VI. Váci utca 40, #20, Budapest ☎ and ℻118-7824, map **8D4**

FURTHER INFORMATION ABOUT HUNGARY
Up-to-date tourist information is difficult to obtain outside the country. **IBUSZ**, the national travel company, has offices at:
US
- 630 5th Ave., New York, NY 10111 ☎(212) 582 7412
- Airport Plaza Drive, Long Beach, CA 90846 ☎(213) 593-2952

UK
- 6 Conduit St., London W1R 9TG (Danube Travel Ltd) ☎(071) 493-0263 ℻(071) 493 6963

Austria
- Kärntner Str. 26, A-1010 Vienna ☎51555, map **3D3**

Getting there

ORGANIZED TOURS

Austria is a major holiday destination, so there exists a vast variety of packaged tours to choose from that appeal to every conceivable taste, interest and budget. In the past, such tours often combined Austria with Switzerland, Germany and/or Italy. Since the revolutions in Eastern Europe, an increasing number of operators have been offering packages pairing Vienna with Budapest and/or Prague.

The best place to shop for tours is your travel agent, where you can find such standard deals as **Austrian Airways'** 6-day Vienna-Budapest tour from New York, which includes the round-trip airfare, first-class hotels, and sightseeing. There are also specialist deals such as personalized tours by chauffeured car, art and culture tours guided by Oxbridge dons *(Swan Hellenic Tours, 77 New Oxford St., London WC1A 1PP)*; ballooning vacations *(Bombard Society, 6727 Curran St., McLean, VA 22101)*; or vacations in aristocratic castles *(Value Holidays, 10224 N Port Washington Rd., Mequon, WI 53092)*.

Among the most popular items are Danube cruises, which start at Passau or Vienna and end in Budapest or the Black Sea, using special luxury boats or standard passenger ones. They last as little as a day or as long as 2 weeks.

BY AIR

Austrian Airlines, the national carrier, fly nonstop from New York's JFK airport to **Vienna** daily except Tuesday. Alia (Royal Jordanian Airlines) offer the only other nonstop service from North America, flying twice a week late at night from New York, and once a week from Chicago. Many other carriers serve Vienna via a stopover in Western Europe. For lowest fares, try Alia, or take Virgin Atlantic or another low-price carrier to London (Gatwick airport), then Lauda Air from Gatwick to Vienna.

From Britain, Austrian Airlines and British Airways fly to Vienna daily from London's Heathrow airport. Former auto-racing star Nikki Lauda's Lauda Air departs six times a week from Gatwick, and DanAir has both scheduled and chartered flights to Vienna from Gatwick.

Budapest has fewer flights and slightly higher prices than Vienna, although the rapid pace of change in Hungary is likely to affect this soon. Malév, the Hungarian airline, used to fly twice a week from New York to Budapest; in 1991 they announced a dramatic expansion of services from New York, Los Angeles, Chicago and Toronto, and several other carriers sought to enter the field as well. Malév fly daily to Budapest from London.

FROM THE AIRPORTS TO THE CITIES

Vienna's **Schwechat airport** is located 15km (9 miles) E of the city. Express buses shuttle between the airport (every 20 minutes during the day, every half-hour at night; length of ride 20-25 minutes) and the City Air Terminal, which is beside the Hilton *(am Stadtpark, map 4D4)*. Another half-hourly express bus shuttle links the airport with the Süd-bahnhof and Westbahnhof *(map 2D4 and 1D3 respectively)*. Hourly trains between 5am and 10pm link the airport with the Wien-Mitte station *(map 4D5)*. For airport information ☎77702231.

Taxis to the city center cost about AS350. But perhaps most convenient is the minibus service, which will take you anywhere in Vienna: make a reservation in advance with your airline, at the airport, by phone or through your hotel desk.

Budapest has two airports, of which **Ferihegy I** (20km/13 miles SE of the center) serves all foreign airlines, while the new **Ferihegy II** (24km/15 miles SE of the center) is reserved for Malév. An express bus runs between both airports and the general bus terminal at Erzsébet tér *(map 8D4)* every 30 minutes from 5am to 11pm (length of ride 30-40 minutes). It is also possible to take city bus 93 to or from the terminus of the metro #3 at Kőbánya. For airport information ☎157.9133.

BY RAIL

Trains from London to the Continent seem designed exclusively for the backpacking crowd, and offer the corresponding standards of service and cleanliness. It is a different world once you reach the Germanic lands: here, there is always a train leaving to your destination in the next 15 minutes, it arrives and leaves on time, and is full of clean, polite people reading the *Frankfurter Allgemeine*. The faster IC, EC and SuperCity trains are subject to a surcharge *(Zuschlag)*, and offer on-board telephone, bar and other amenities.

The *Austria Night Express* leaves London (Victoria) daily around noon and arrives in Vienna (West) in about 22 hours. The alternative is to take the early afternoon or night train to Köln (11 hours), changing there to Vienna (11 hours) or Budapest (14$\frac{1}{2}$ hours). The one-way ticket to Vienna costs £105; for the same money you can buy a round-trip charter flight, be served decent meals on board, avoid slaving around Dover docks at 3 in the morning, and have £5 to spare into the bargain.

There are 9-10 trains daily each way between Vienna and Budapest, a ride of about 3$\frac{1}{2}$ hours. Note that some of these trains depart from/arrive at Westbahnhof station, others from/to Südbahnhof station.

The Simplon Orient Express Ltd runs a luxury train at special fares from London to Budapest via Paris-München-Vienna, departing 11am every Thursday and Sunday, February to November. For further information call in London ☎(071) 928-6000 or inquire at a travel agency.

BY CAR

Vienna is about 1,150km (720 miles) from Ostende via Brussels-Köln-Frankfurt-Nürnberg-Passau-Linz (autobahn throughout; average driving time 10 hours). For pleasant scenery, take the right-bank drive along the Danube between Passau and Linz; this is a secondary road with light traffic.

Budapest is a further 250km (155 miles) on from Vienna. An autobahn connecting the two cities is under construction; meanwhile the Hegyeshalom (frontier) to Györ section forms a massive bottleneck, so it may be advisable to use the somewhat longer route via Sopron.

Enough gas stations have sprouted along the western approaches of Budapest to give the country a definitely Western look, but elsewhere in Hungary they remain rare and far between. Fuel prices in both Austria and Hungary tend to be slightly lower than Germany, but otherwise similar to Western European levels. Lead-free fuel is common in Austria but rare in Hungary.

The speed limit in **Austria** is 50kph (31mph) in towns, 100kph (62mph) in country roads and 130kph (81mph) on autobahns, although the last figure is reduced to wishful thinking by numerous German kamikaze drivers, who have no speed limit on their own autobahns and who tend to treat Austria as a province of Bavaria. Seat belts are obligatory. Children under 12 are not allowed on the front seat.

In **Hungary** the maximum permitted speed is 50kph (31mph) in towns, 70kph (44mph) in country roads and 120kph (75mph) on super-highways (motorways). The alcohol ban is absolute; no trace of blood alcohol is tolerated. Seat belts are obligatory.

RIVER BOAT

Regular passenger ferries operate on the Danube between Passau (in Germany), Linz and Vienna from early May through September. There are two boats daily from **Passau to Linz** *(departures at 9am, 3.30pm; duration 5hrs)* and one from **Linz to Vienna** *(depart 8.05am; 12hrs)*. The combined **Passau-to-Vienna** one-way fare costs DM136, plus an additional DM95 for double 1st-class cabin, or DM62 for a double 2nd-class cabin. Or for only DM142 you can take a boat-and-train round trip from Passau to Vienna and back. For further information contact **DDSG** *(in Vienna* ☎ *266536; in Passau* ☎ *(0851) 33035* ⒻⓍ *(0851) 33032)*.

In addition to various tour and cruise boats, a twice-daily hydrofoil runs between **Vienna and Budapest** *(departures from Vienna at 8am, 2.30pm; duration 4$\frac{1}{2}$ hrs)*.

CAR RENTAL

In **Vienna**, the cost of renting an economy car for a week inclusive of unlimited mileage, minimum legal insurance and 20 percent tax varies between AS2,800 ($240) and 4,000 ($350). Prices climb quite steeply for more upscale models.

In **Budapest**, the typical rates at reputable companies vary around F15,000 ($180) for a week plus a surcharge of F15 per kilometer, although it is possible to find street-corner shops which will let you have the same car, maybe with less glitz, at less than half this price. The catch, however, is that you cannot leave Hungary in a rented car.

In the case of international companies, you can save some money by making arrangements through an agency at home prior to departure.

It may also be worth keeping in mind that **Switzerland** offers rental rates comparable to Austria, but levies no tax. You can rent a car in Switzerland and drop it in Austria and vice versa.

CAR RENTAL COMPANIES IN VIENNA

Avis   Opernring 1 ☎5876241, map **3E3**; airport ☎71110-2700
Budget   Hilton Hotel, am Stadtpark ☎756565-0, map **4D5**; airport ☎71110-2711
Europcar   Kärntner Ring 14, map **3E3**; airport reservations ☎5054166
Hertz   (3.) Ungargasse 37, map **4E5**; Kärntner Ring 17, map **3E3**; Hilton Hotel, am Stadtpark, map **4D5**; Marriott Hotel, Park Ring 12a, map **4D4**. Central reservation ☎7131596-0 Fx7127083

CUT-RATE RENTALS

Buchbinder   (3.) Schlachthausgasse 38 ☎71750-0; plus many branches in city
Rainbow   (12.) Biedermanngasse 35 ☎8498505, map **1E2**

"TOP CAR RENTALS"

Rent-A-Dream   (14.) Hadikgasse 128 ☎8245481 Fx8285481-20
Blecha   (16.) Lienfeldergasse 35-39 ☎453672 Fx468985

MOTORCYCLE RENTAL

InterCity   (5.) Reinprechtsdorfer Str. 17 ☎556186; airport ☎71110-3311

TRAILER/CARAVAN AND CAMPER RENTAL

Benkö   (4.) Rechte Wienzeile 21 ☎5711993, map **3F2**

BUSES WITH OR WITHOUT DRIVER

Rent a Bus   (12.) Assmayergasse 60 ☎833223

RENTAL COMPANIES IN BUDAPEST

Avis/Ibusz   (V.) Martinelli tér 8 ☎118-6222, map **8D4**
Budget/Cooptourist   (IX.) Ferenc Körút 43 ☎113-1466
Europcar/InterRent/Volántourist   (IX.) Vaskapu utca 16 ☎133-4783; Ferihegy I airport ☎(361) 134-2540, map **6D5**; Ferihegy II airport ☎(361) 157-8570, map **6E6**
Fötaxi   (VII.) Kertész utca 24 ☎122-1471, map **8C6**
Hertz   (V.) Aranykéz utca 4-8 ☎115-7533, map **8D4**
Hungar Motorent   Camper and minibus rentals: Budapest Airport ☎ and Fx157-8280

CONVERSION FORMULAE

To convert	Multiply by
Inches to Centimeters	2.540
Centimeters to Inches	0.39370
Feet to Meters	0.3048
Meters to feet	3.2808
Yards to Meters	0.9144
Meters to Yards	1.09361
Miles to Kilometers	1.60934
Kilometers to Miles	0.621371
Sq Meters to Sq Feet	10.7638
Sq Feet to Sq Meters	0.092903
Sq Yards to Sq Meters	0.83612
Sq Meters to Sq Yards	1.19599
Sq Miles to Sq Kilometers	2.5899
Sq Kilometers to Sq Miles	0.386103
Acres to Hectares	0.40468
Hectares to Acres	2.47105
Gallons to Liters	4.545
Liters to Gallons	0.22
Ounces to Grams	28.3495
Grams to Ounces	0.03528
Pounds to Grams	453.592
Grams to Pounds	0.00220
Pounds to Kilograms	0.4536
Kilograms to Pounds	2.2046
Tons (UK) to Kilograms	1016.05
Kilograms to Tons (UK)	0.0009842
Tons (US) to Kilograms	746.483
Kilograms to Tons (US)	0.0013396

Quick conversions

Kilometers to Miles	Divide by 8, multiply by 5
Miles to Kilometers	Divide by 5, multiply by 8
1 meter =	Approximately 3 feet 3 inches
2 centimeters =	Approximately 1 inch
1 pound (weight) =	475 grams (nearly $\frac{1}{2}$ kilogram)
Celsius to Fahrenheit	Divide by 5, multiply by 9, add 32
Fahrenheit to Celsius	Subtract 32, divide by 9, multiply by 5

Vienna
(Wien)

Culture, history and background

Capital of the Austrian Federal Republic. Settled since 1stC AD; city since c.1130. The city of Vienna is one of the nine states *(Länder)* forming the Austrian federation. It is also part-capital of the state of Lower Austria (Niederösterreich).
Municipal area: 414 square kilometers/160 square miles.
Population: 1.5 million.
Altitude at river bank: 160 meters/525 feet.

Until 100 years ago Vienna was the third largest metropolis of Europe after London and Paris, and the capital of an empire which included modern Austria, Hungary, Czechoslovakia, parts of Poland, Ukraine, Romania, Yugoslavia and Italy. Deprived of its empire in 1918, it suffered famine (1918), financial collapse (1929), civil war (1934), German annexation (1938), war damage (1944-45), foreign occupation (1945-55) and the small-country syndrome (from 1955). During this time its population declined from more than 2 million to 1.5 million.

To an extent greater than either London or Paris, Vienna's culture in its 18th and 19thC heyday was shaped by the habits and activities of its court. Its chief buildings were imperial palaces and noble residences. Its music and theater had their roots in courtly entertainment. An ancient, inbred aristocracy led social life well into the 20thC. Many traces of that aristocratic past have survived a century of misfortunes, and the nostalgia of a vanished era of pomp and elegance pervades Vienna today.

History: an overview

VIENNA
Roman legions founded the garrison of **Vindobona** on the Danube frontier of the province of Pannonia. It grew into a populous town over the next 300 years. The period of barbarian invasions (c.400-1000) is obscure, but some continuity of settlement is assumed. The inhabitants of this time were Slavs or Avars, possibly mixed with Germans. Full Germanization occurred in the 12thC.

Around the year 1000, Vienna was captured by the margraves of Austria, a small outpost of the German Empire on the locks of the middle Danube. It flourished as an important commercial and cultural center under the Babenberg dukes (c.1130-1246), King Ottokar of Bohemia

(1250-76) and the early Habsburgs (1278-1490s). It declined in importance during the religious and Turkish wars that racked Austria in the 16th-17thC, and was heavily damaged in the Turkish siege of 1683. It flourished again as the capital of the consolidated Habsburg empire after this date. A great majority of its buildings were constructed or altered in the monumental Baroque style during the first decades of the 18thC, giving the city its distinctive architectural character.

The demolition of the city walls in 1858 and the construction of the Ringstrasse in their place marked the start of a new round of expansion and architectural activity. The tenure of the populist mayor Karl Lueger (1897-1910) carried the city into the modern age. The socialist governments of 1920-34 built a series of vast housing projects, and some hasty rebuilding was done after the destruction of World War II, but overall, the outward appearance of Vienna remained little affected by the post-1918 world.

AUSTRIA

The march of Austria was founded in 803 and again in c.960 as a frontier post of the medieval Western/Germanic Empire. It consisted originally of a string of fortresses along the Danube in the district of Wachau (Pöchlarn, Melk, Krems). The name **Österreich** (*Austrie* in Old French) translates approximately as "Eastland."

Austria became a hereditary duchy under the Babenbergs, and passed to the Habsburg family in 1278. By then it covered the whole Danube basin between Passau and Vienna, the modern *länder* of Upper and Lower Austria. From the 14thC the Habsburgs also controlled the neighboring domains of Styria, Carinthia, Carniola and Tyrol, corresponding approximately to the territory of modern Austria and Slovenia.

At various times between 1477 and 1918, the Habsburgs possessed the duchy of Burgundy (modern Netherlands, Belgium, Luxemburg and northeast France); the kingdoms of Spain, Naples, Hungary and Bohemia (the Czech half of Czechoslovakia); the states of Lombardy, Tuscany, Parma and Venice in Italy; and the territories of Silesia, Galicia, Bukovina, Bosnia-Herzegovina and Dalmatia. All these places bore the vague appellation of "Austria" in the diplomatic language of their time.

THE HOLY ROMAN EMPIRE

The duchy of Austria was a vassal of the **Holy Roman Empire of the German Nation**, or the *Reich,* a loose collection of several hundred such domains. The Holy Roman Emperor was elected for life by seven of the sovereign princes of the empire who bore the title of Electors; until the late Middle Ages he was usually anointed in Rome by the pope, and claimed the heritage of the emperors of ancient Rome ("Kaiser" = Caesar).

A Habsburg, Rudolph I, was elected emperor in 1273. One of his descendants, Albrecht V of Austria, was elected again in 1438. Thereafter reigning members of the Habsburg dynasty succeeded to the imperial dignity more or less automatically for nearly 400 years.

The Reich was reduced to a largely ceremonial office by the Peace of

Westphalia in 1618, and abolished under Napoleon's pressure in 1806. After this date, Habsburg rulers bore the newly created title of Emperors of Austria.

AUSTRIA-HUNGARY

The Habsburgs acquired the bare title to the kingdom of Hungary in 1526 and its actual territories in 1683-99. The kingdom included, in addition to modern Hungary, the lands of Slovakia, Transylvania (northwest Romania), Croatia and northern Serbia; it was governed by an ancient feudal constitution of its own, and always formed a separate entity within the Austrian realms.

The Hungarians revolted against Habsburg rule in 1848. The revolution was quashed, but after a period of heavy-handed repression, the Compromise *(Ausgleich)* of 1867 granted many of the Hungarian nationalist demands, amounting to near-full independence under the Habsburg crown. Foreign and defense policies were coordinated, but two separate parliaments and two prime ministers sat in their respective capitals of Vienna and Budapest. From this date to the collapse of the empire in 1918, the Habsburg empire was known as Austria-Hungary — the Dual Monarchy.

The official terminology of the Dual Monarchy was a matter of utmost intricacy. The monarch was Emperor of Austria and King of Hungary. Those offices of government that applied to both parts of the realm were called *kaiserlich und königlich* (imperial and royal, abbreviated *k&k* or *k.u.k.*). The government of territories ruled directly from Vienna was *kaiserlich-königlich* (imperial-royal, or *k.k.*), while the government of Budapest was known as Royal Hungarian.

MODERN TIMES

Modern **Germany** (the "Second Reich") was created in 1871 under the leadership of Prussia, Austria's traditional rival in German affairs. German nationalists in Austria agitated to join the new nation, but the monarchy opted to stay out, fearing, on the one hand, subordination to Prussia, and on the other, the loss of the four-fifths of its territories that were not German.

When both the monarchy and the non-German territories were lost in World War I, the very existence of Austria as a nation became problematic. Overriding strong public sentiment in favor of union with Germany, the victorious Allies created an independent republic of Austria by the peace of St Germain (1919). The rise of the Nazis in Germany introduced bitter divisions into Austrian opinion, so the much-anticipated union *(Anschluss)*, when it came, was only accomplished by force of arms. After World War II the Allies re-established Austria as a neutral buffer between the West and the Soviet bloc.

Landmarks in Vienna's history

EARLY HISTORY

c.25000BC: Willendorf culture (early Homo sapiens). **750-400BC**: Hallstatt culture in central Europe (Iron Age). From **c.400BC**: Celtic tribes settle large parts of central Europe: the La Tène culture.

16BC: Roman conquest of Noricum, a Celtic kingdom in central Austria (Tyrol, Styria, Carinthia, Upper and Lower Austria to Vienna Woods). **15-12BC**: Roman conquest of Pannonia, the plains between the Danube bend and the Sava (Vienna, Budapest, Belgrade, Zagreb). **1stC AD**: Roman frontier consolidated at the Danube: system of frontier forts *(limes)* with major garrisons at Vindobona (on the site of present-day Vienna), Carnuntum and Aquincum (Obuda).

180: Emperor Marcus Aurelius dies in Vindobona in campaign against German tribes (Marcomanni). **193**: Septimius Severus proclaimed Roman emperor in Carnuntum. **c.280**: Emperor Probus authorizes wine-growing in the Danube area. **c.300**: St Florian, the Christian governor of Noricum, martyred near Linz.

395: Barbarian invasions force the Roman Empire to abandon the Danube frontier. Roman citizens withdraw from Pannonia by **405**. Germans (Baiuvars = Bavarians) settle Noricum. Repeated invasions in the Pannonian plain: Huns, Goths, Gepids, Langobards, Avars. Under Avar rule, Slavs settle wide area from Bohemia to the Balkans, including Austria. **8thC**: Bavarian king Tassilo reconquers Austrian uplands as far as the Vienna Woods; (re)introduction of Christianity.

791-97: Charlemagne destroys Avar kingdom. **803**: Charlemagne creates the Eastern March *(Austrie)* on the Danube. Slavs (Moravians, Bulgars) on the Pannonian plain. **883**: First known mention of Wenia (Vienna), an obscure place on the border.

896: Magyar (Hungarian) invasion devastates central Europe, destroying the Eastern March (**909**), among others. **955**: Otto I of Germany defeats Magyars, thereby saving Christendom.

BABENBERGS

c.960: Otto re-establishes the Eastern March *(Ostarrichi)*, appointing (**976**) Leopold of Babenberg as Margrave. First Babenberg seat at Pöchlarn, then Melk, Tulln and Klosterneuburg. **c.991**: Babenbergs extend their authority to the Viennese plain.

1137: First recorded mention of Vienna as a city. First church of St Stephen built. **1141-77**: Heinrich II "Jasomirgott" transfers Babenberg seat to Vienna, where he builds a castle. **1156**: Austria elevated to a hereditary duchy by Emperor Frederick Barbarossa. **1192**: Duke Leopold V "the Virtuous" captures Richard Lionheart of England, imprisoning him at Dürnstein castle. His ransom is said to have paid for Vienna's early medieval walls (**c.1200**). **1221**: Leopold VI "the Glorious" grants city charter, and builds earliest nucleus of the Hofburg. Period of prosperity.

1246: Babenbergs become extinct with the death of Friedrich II "the Quarrelsome" in battle against Hungarians. **1250**: King Ottokar Przemysl of Bohemia acquires the Babenberg lands, transferring his residence to

Vienna. City reaches peak of medieval development under his rule. **1273**: Rudolph of Habsburg elected Holy Roman Emperor. **1276-78**: Rudolph defeats Ottokar at the battle of Marchfeld, seizing the duchy of Austria for his son Albrecht. Beginning of 640 years of Habsburg rule in Austria.

HABSBURGS

1288: Uprising of Viennese burghers against Habsburg rule crushed, and civic freedoms curtailed. **1309**: Second Viennese citizens' uprising defeated. **1335**: Duke Albrecht II acquires Carinthia (Kärnten) and Carniola (Krain, modern Slovenia). **1358-65**: Rudolph IV "the Founder" adopts the title of Archduke. In rivalry with Prague, he establishes the University of Vienna and starts to rebuild St Stephen. **1363**: Countess Margaret Muzzlebag *(Maultasch)* of Tyrol bequeaths her lands to the Habsburgs.

1438: Albrecht V elected Emperor (as Albrecht II). With one interruption, Habsburgs will monopolize the imperial title until 1806. **1452**: Friedrich III crowned Holy Roman Emperor. He maintains a brilliant court in Vienna (to **1493**). **1462**: Viennese revolt. Friedrich besieged in the Hofburg by citizens. **1469**: Vienna becomes a bishopric. **1477**: Friedrich's son Maximilian I marries Mary of Burgundy, heir to the Low Countries and parts of northeast France. **1485-90**: Matthias Corvinus of Hungary captures Vienna with the support of the burghers. After this incident, the Habsburg court will generally avoid Vienna until the 1610s.

1516: Karl (Charles) V, Maximilian's grandson, inherits the kingdom of Spain with its vast American colonies. In **1519** he succeeds to Maximilian's titles in Burgundy and various German territories, and is elected Emperor. His brother Ferdinand I governs Austria, with the title of Archduke. **1521**: Luther breaks with the Roman church. Protestantism enthusiastically received in Vienna as Karl fights in vain to prevent its spread in Europe.

1526: Hungarian kingdom destroyed and partly occupied by Turks. Ferdinand, as heir to the Hungarian crown, obtains Bohemia and part of Hungary. **1529**: First Turkish siege of Vienna under Sultan Süleyman the Magnificent. Count Niklas Salm defends the city.

1556: Habsburg domains divided up on Karl's retirement: Philip II, his son, inherits Spain and Burgundy; Ferdinand takes Austria, Bohemia-Hungary and the Imperial title. Two branches of the family cooperate closely until 1700.

1545-63: Council of Trent unleashes the Catholic Counter-Reformation. Habsburgs lead the Catholic cause in Europe. **1571**: Maximilian II proclaims religious freedom: over 80 percent of Vienna is Protestant. **1576**: Return to Catholic policy under Rudolph II. Jesuits invited to Vienna. **1598-1618**: Protestantism banned and Protestant nobles dispossessed throughout Austria. Bloody repression under Cardinal Khlesl. **1607-11**: Rudolph retired by a palace coup of Catholic hardliners.

1618: Rebellion of Bohemian nobles against Habsburg rule (Defenestration of Prague) starts the Thirty Years' War. **1620**: Bohemian revolution crushed at the battle of White Mountain. Wallenstein's imperial army subdues Germany. Maximum extent of Habsburg power. **1630-48**: Swedish and French invasions devastate Germany, breaking the Habsburg grip. **1648**: Peace of Westphalia: Habsburg ambitions checked. The German Empire, deprived of authority, survives in name only.

1673-79: War with France over the Low Countries. **1679**: Plague epidemic kills more than 30,000 in Vienna. **1688-97**: War with France.

1683: Second Turkish siege of Vienna under Grand Vezir Kara Mustafa. Count Starhemberg defends the city. Turks defeated by pan-European army under Polish King Jan Sobieski. **1684**: First Viennese coffeehouse opened on Domgasse.

1683-1736: Prince Eugene of Savoy supreme commander of imperial armies and (from **1703**) president of the privy council. **1686**: Austrian counteroffensive in Hungary. Hungary and Belgrade captured. **1697**: Final Turkish defeat at Zenta. Treaty of Karlowitz (**1699**) ends the Turkish menace. **1700**: Extinction of the Spanish Habsburgs unleashes War of the Spanish Succession (**1701-14**). **1703-11**: Hungarian rebellion: Rákoczi's irregulars threaten Vienna, defeated by Prince Eugene. **1713-14**: Defeated by Austria and England, France sues for peace. End of 200 years of French wars.

1713: Pragmatic Sanction of Karl VI, the first fundamental law of Austria, establishes the unity and indivisibility of Habsburg lands. **1722**: Vienna becomes an archbishopric. Massive rebuilding and cultural vitality in Austria: **1716**, Lower Belvedere; **1718**, Melk abbey church; **1719**, Karlskirche begun; **1726**, Court Library, Upper Belvedere.

1740: Maria Theresa's ascension to the Habsburg throne unleashes the War of the Austrian Succession (**1740-48**). **1750**: Completion of the summer palace at Schönbrunn. **1753-92**: Emergence of a centralized administration under Chancellor Kaunitz.

1772: Expulsion of Jesuits from Austria. **1780-90**: Joseph II introduces radical reforms: monasteries closed, religious freedom granted, and aristocratic privileges curbed.

c.1740-1809: Haydn in Vienna and Eisenstadt. **1782-91**: Mozart in Vienna. **1792-1827**: Beethoven in Vienna. **1828**: Schubert dies in Vienna, aged 31.

1806: Abolition of the Holy Roman Empire after Napoleon's victories at Austerlitz (**1805**) and Jena (**1806**). Franz II re-styled Franz I, Emperor of Austria. **1809**: French occupation of Vienna after Napoleon's victories at Eylau and Wagram. Napoleon marries Franz's daughter Marie-Louise. **1812-14**: Austria joins Russia, Prussia and England in an alliance to defeat Napoleon.

1814-15: Congress of Vienna reshapes Europe after upheavals of the French Revolution and Napoleonic wars. Austria trades Belgium for gains in northern Italy. **1809-48**: Prince Metternich leads Austria and dominates European diplomacy. "Holy Alliance" of conservative states (Austria, Prussia and Russia, and France until 1830). Reactionary era ("Pre-March") in politics and ideas: censorship, police state. **1825**: Johann Strauss Sr. forms first waltz orchestra in Vienna. **1843**: Johann Strauss Jr. forms rival orchestra.

1848: March revolutions: Student uprising in Vienna forces the government to flee. Revolutions in Hungary, Bohemia, Italy. Ferdinand I abdicates. Vienna retaken by force (November); Hungarian independence crushed (**1849**).

1848-1916: 68-year reign of Franz Joseph I, divided into 3 periods: **1848-67**, Conservative regime of army and church; **1867-90s**, Liberal ascendancy and economic boom; **1890s-1914**, rise of nationalist, populist and socialist movements.

1859: Italian risorgimento: Austria loses Lombardy and Tuscany. **1866**: Battle of Sadova: Prussia defeats Austria and establishes hegemony in German affairs. Modern German state formed in 1871, excluding Austria. **1867**: Compromise *(Ausgleich)* of '67 grants full autonomy to Hungary, creating the Dual Monarchy (Austria-Hungary), with separate governments in Vienna and Buda-Pest.

1857-65: Building of the Ringstrasse. Its architectural monuments (completed **1861-88**) epitomize the Liberal era. **1897-1910**: Karl Lueger mayor of Vienna. Era of populist politics and urban modernization. **1895**: Theodor Herzl founds the Zionist movement. **1897**: Group of progressive artists (Klimt, Otto Wagner) form the Secession. Gustav Mahler appointed director of the Vienna Opera. **1899**: Freud publishes *The Interpretation of Dreams*. **1907**: Arnold Schönberg composes atonal music. **1907-13**: Adolf Hitler lives in Vienna as aspiring artist.

1887: Suicide of Archduke Rudolph at Mayerling. **1898**: Assassination of Empress Elisabeth. **1914**: Assassination of Archduke Franz Ferdinand in Sarajevo precipitates World War I. **1916**: Karl I succeeds Franz Joseph.

1914-18: Austria-Hungary joins Germany in World War I. German defeat in October **1918**. Czechoslovakia declares independence (October 28). Revolution in Hungary brings Socialists to power (October 31). Austrian Assembly deposes Karl I (November 11), declaring Austria "a constituent part of the German Republic." Hungary declares independence (November 16). Serbian troops occupy Croatia, Slovenia and Bosnia.

THE AUSTRIAN REPUBLIC

1918-19: Socialist government of Dr Karl Renner. Anarchy and famine in Vienna. **1919**: Treaty of St Germain creates independent Austria, overriding Austrian wishes for union with Germany.

1920-38: Social Christian (Catholic-conservative) rule in Austria; Marxists control Vienna city government ("Red Vienna") until 1934. **1929**: Collapse of the Creditanstalt: economic depression and political chaos follow. **1933**: Chancellor Dollfuss (Social Christian) dissolves parliament, establishes a clerical-fascist regime under Mussolini's tutelage, but resists Hitler's pressures. **1934**: February: "4-day War" — government forces destroy "Red Vienna." July: Nazis assassinate Dollfuss in coup attempt.

1938: March 9: Chancellor Schuschnigg announces referendum on union with Germany *(Anschluss)* for following week. March 11: Schuschnigg resigns after German ultimatum; Nazi leader Seyss-Inquart appointed chancellor. March 12: German troops occupy Austria.

1943: Moscow Declaration: US, UK and USSR agree to re-establish Austria after the war. **1945**: March 12: Allied air raid causes heavy damage in Vienna. April 10: St Stephen's cathedral gutted by fire. April 13: Soviet troops liberate Vienna. April 27: Coalition government under Dr Renner proclaims the rebirth of an independent Austria.

1945-55: 4-power occupation of Austria. **1955**: State Treaty grants Austrian independence under condition of "perpetual neutrality."

1970-83: Chancellor Bruno Kreisky plays active role in international politics and Middle Eastern affairs.

1986: Election of Kurt Waldheim to the Presidency causes diplomatic furor. **1987**: Election successes of Freedom Party compel coalition government of mainstream parties, Socialist Party (SP) and People's Party (ÖVP, Catholic), under Franz Vranitzky.

1989: Revolutions in Eastern Europe enhance Austrian influence in Hungary, Czechoslovakia, Slovenia and Croatia.

The Habsburgs: Empire as family business

The Habsburgs ruled over a hodgepodge of states separated by geography, language, tradition and legal status. They acquired kingdoms by marriage, bequest, barter, blackmail and conquest. They ruled in different lands as Emperor, King, Duke, Margrave or Voivode; here with absolute right and hereditary title, there with parliament and ancient constitution. All the great families of the realm were upstarts promoted and enriched for their loyal service to the dynasty. Chief ministers were recruited from outside (Prince Eugene was French, Metternich a Rhinelander from Köln) to manage the family holdings. A unified administration was created by the reforms of Maria Theresa and Joseph II; but even in the age when the nation came to be regarded everywhere as the basis of the state, it was the dynasty alone that held the Habsburg domains together.

The history of Austria is their family history, permeated with their victories and defeats, their quirks and character traits, their tangled web of brothers, uncles, marriages and mistresses. Visitors to Vienna are reminded of this at every turn.

ORIGINS
The counts of Altenburg (in Swabia, southwest Germany) acquired Castle Habsburg (near Bad Schinznach in Aargau, Switzerland) in 1173 and adopted its armor. Their marriage in 1216 to the heirs of the county of Kyburg earned them respectability and a strong position in Swiss affairs. By 1273 they owned the bishoprics of Säckingen and Muri, the landgraviate of Alsace and the county of Zürichgau. That year Rudolph I of Habsburg was elected Holy Roman Emperor.

FRIEDRICH III *(1440-93)*
The founder of Habsburg greatness was the first of his family to be anointed Holy Roman Emperor in Rome, and first to cultivate the Roman connection, which would remain a pivot of Habsburg policy

35

until the days of Joseph II. He was credited with the maxim: *Bella gerant alii tu felix Austria nube* ("Let others wage war; you, happy Austria, marry!"). His magnificent tomb in the Stephansdom bears the cryptic inscription AEIOU: his successors took it to mean *Austriae Est Imperare Orbi Universo* ("Austria must rule the entire world") and duly obeyed. His son married the heiress of Burgundy to inherit a flourishing duchy stretching from Switzerland to Flanders and Holland. His grandson wed Mad Joanna of Spain, sole heiress to the crowns of Castile, Aragon and Naples, and his great-grandchildren's double marriage to the heirs of Hungary and Bohemia yielded half of central Europe.

MAXIMILIAN I *(archduke 1477/emperor 1493-1519)*
In childhood, Maximilian saw his father besieged in his palace by a furious Viennese mob, and he never forgave the city for this. He lived in Innsbruck and Flanders, where his court formed the breeding ground of the northern European Renaissance. His descendants mistrusted and often avoided Vienna for more than a century.

KARL V *(archduke 1516/emperor 1519-56)* and FERDINAND I *(archduke 1526/emperor 1556-64)*
While the dark, brooding, suspicious figure of Karl towered over Europe through the epic days of the Renaissance and Reformation, his younger brother Ferdinand held the ramparts in Vienna against the Turkish and Protestant menaces. A grim and fortified palace, the Hofburg, protected him from the burghers of Vienna, whose last vestiges of civic independence he abolished in 1526. The Swiss Court of the Hofburg bears his inscription.

MAXIMILIAN II *(1564-76)*
The first and only Protestant to ascend the Austrian throne ruled at a time when nearly all of Austria's ancient nobility and a majority of Vienna's citizens had converted to the Lutheran creed. His *Assekuranz* of 1571 kept Roman Catholicism as state religion, but guaranteed the rights of the schismatics. His memory was erased from the annals of the later Habsburgs, and his favorite palaces were turned into horse stables or a stone quarry.

RUDOLPH II *(1576-1612)*
Rudolph withdrew from the bitter world of the religious wars to the seclusion of Prague's Castle, where he gathered the greatest geniuses and cranks of the waning days of the Renaissance to brood over the arcane sciences of alchemy. His advisers sought the elixir of life and the philosopher's stone, attempted to resurrect mummies and to produce men in the laboratory. He was also a compulsive collector of the rare, the curious and the extraordinary: the greatest treasures of Vienna's Art Historical Museum and much of the best art in Prague and Budapest owe their origin to his private menagerie.

Meanwhile in the real world, Jesuits let loose the full fury of the Catholic Counter-Reformation against the recusant subjects of the kaiser.

Protestantism was defeated, the old nobility of Austria was persecuted and its estates confiscated, and there emerged the mixture of absolutist state, boastful church and servile aristocracy that would remain the Habsburg hallmark for many generations.

FERDINAND II *(1619-37)*

Ferdinand attempted 250 years before Bismarck to turn Germany into a real state with iron and fire. His success in Bohemia reduced that once rich and flourishing land into a poor backwater of Europe. His failure in Germany left behind a smoldering heap of ruins after 30 years of warfare in which nearly half the population of central Europe perished.

The great aristocratic families of the later Habsburg monarchy, the Liechtensteins, Lobkowitzes, Schwarzenbergs, Salms, Czartoryskis, Colloredos, Waldsteins and Rakoczys, emerged from the turmoil of the Thirty Years' War. They came from a variety of ethnic backgrounds and rose through their loyalty to the emperor alone. They helped extinguish the old Protestant nobility of Austria and Bohemia, and were rewarded with their titles and estates.

LEOPOLD I *(1657-1705)*

The extraordinary chin of the first Baroque emperor, Leopold I, juts up in supplication to Christ, Mary, the Holy Trinity and various saints in the altarpieces of a dozen Viennese churches, and most prominently at the base of the Plague Column on Graben, the greatest monument of his overblown and Jesuit-fed piety. His long reign marks the transition of Austria from the obsessive religiousness of the 17thC, through the disasters of plague and Turkish siege, to its rebirth in the rich, frivolous and theatrical world of the 18thC.

Leopold himself took an active part in the artistic side of the revival: he composed musical plays and directed an operatic extravaganza in which it is on record that 1,000 members of the imperial court and dynasty acted and sang.

KARL VI *(1711-40)*

Karl was trained to succeed to the throne of Spain, where his Habsburg cousin would die heirless. The War of the Spanish Succession deprived him of Spain, and the untimely death of his brother Joseph brought him Austria instead. But his love of things Spanish stayed on. His courtiers wore the black Spanish habit (hence Schwarzspanier Str. — "Blackspaniards"), and his pet project, never finished, was to build at Klosterneuburg a replica of the Escorial. To this day, horsemen of the Spanish Riding School doff their hats before each performance to a portrait of their imperial patron.

Nearly all the great Baroque palaces and churches that define Vienna's skyline today were built or rebuilt in the reign of Karl VI, many in the splendid decade of the 1710s. The greatest of them, Belvedere, belonged to Prince Eugene of Savoy, the enigmatic bachelor who fed lions in the gardens of his palace and held the courts of Europe in terror with his personal network of agents and spies.

MARIA THERESA *(1740-80)* and **FRANZ I** *(1743-65)*

When Karl died without a male heir, the Powers of Europe ganged up on his daughter, a seemingly helpless girl of 23, to solve the matter of Austria once and for all. She proved a shrewder player than them all, and survived to become the mightiest monarch of the house of Habsburg. Her husband, the plump and bewigged Francis of Lorraine, bore the title of emperor as Franz I; but it was she who ran the affairs of state with the pluck and verve of a Viennese *Geschäftsfrau*.

She raised spectacle and stagecraft into instruments of highest policy. The imperial theater — the famous Burgtheater — was launched in 1751, and became under her guidance "the nexus between the palace and the people." She produced 16 children; their births, parties, affairs and marriages became the chief events of the royal calendar. At Schönbrunn palace, family rooms mingled with cabinets of state and gilded halls where splendid festivities (no less than 40 balls a year) kept the country spellbound and submissive.

JOSEPH II *(co-emperor 1765/emperor 1780-90)*

Far from being the vacuous fool portrayed in *Amadeus,* Joseph was perhaps the most radical reformer to have ascended a European throne. "The people's emperor" walked alone and in simple garb, stayed in country inns, flirted with peasant girls, and boarded up the Hofburg to live in the simplicity of his country house at Augarten. His Patent of Tolerance proclaimed the freedom and civil equality of all religions. He expelled the Jesuits after 200 years of overbearing presence, and ordered some 700 monasteries dissolved. Pope Pius VI rushed to Vienna to reason with his prodigal son, but he was politely ignored.

Joseph's reforms also attacked the nobility's special privileges, abolished serfdom, prohibited torture and the death penalty, and all but eliminated censorship. His surviving monuments are the parks of the Prater and Augarten, former imperial preserves that the emperor threw open to the public, and the General Hospital, which was Europe's first and remains its oldest.

The French Revolution of 1789 showed where such dangerous ideas could lead. Within two years of his death Joseph's reforms were quietly shelved, and Austria became the purest bastion of European conservatism for a half century afterwards.

FRANZ I *(1792-1835: Holy Roman Emperor as Franz II 1792-1806; Austrian Emperor as Franz I 1804-1835)*

The epic struggle against Napoleon, his nemesis and son-in-law, occupied the first half of Franz's reign and cast a shadow over its remainder. After a crushing defeat at Austerlitz, he was forced to relinquish the last residue of Habsburg claims on Germany: his title was reduced from Holy Roman to Austrian emperor, and his number was cut in half accordingly.

After the disasters of Eylau and Wagram, he suffered the indignity of giving his daughter Marie-Louise in marriage to the Corsican upstart. She

and her son, the unfortunate Napoleon II, the Duke of Reichstadt, lived at Schönbrunn as sad ghosts of an exorcised past for many years after Bonaparte was gone from the scene.

Austria won the fight, at least in the short run. Archduke Karl stopped the French armies at Aspern; Schwarzenberg was one of the allied generals who dealt them the finishing blow at Leipzig and Dresden; Metternich shaped, at the Congress of Vienna, a new Europe that tried to bury what the French Revolution and Napoleon had unleashed. The extravagant manners of the congress, its lavish entertainment and un-abashed aristocratism harked back to an age that the fall of the Bastille (perhaps even the reforms of Joseph II) had forever undermined. It inaugurated an era in which the state lived in a constant, paranoid fear of revolution. The terms "reaction" and "reactionary" entered the political vocabulary; public life turned inward, and poets sang the nostalgia of ancient, vanished beauties.

FERDINAND I *(1835-1848)*
A mild and friendly man, Ferdinand was certified mad and deposed in 1848 by the conservative military clique that controlled the state. His number, like that of his predecessor, is confusing: the counter was reset for the emperors of Austria when that title was invented in 1804.

FRANZ JOSEPH *(1848-1916)*
A man of narrow imagination and a bureaucrat's sense of duty, Franz Joseph nevertheless managed to hold together the empire by the sheer force of his personality for 68 years. His first years in office were

marked by the desperate effort to cling to the Austria of Prince Eugene and Maria Theresa ("the Habsburgs never learn and never forget"); his last years stretched into the world of Freud and Schönberg, Churchill and Lenin.

Along the way, his dashing looks, his unquestioned integrity, his immense personal tragedies transformed him from the oppressor of Budapest into the beloved father of his people, the one focus of sentimental attachment that joined the warring Croats and Magyars and Czechs, the Marxists and anti-Semites, the aristocrats and proletarians of the creaking Habsburg monarchy. At some point in the 1890s it dawned upon many observers that the monarchy could not survive his death; it did, by just two years.

Since then, there has been a tendency to summarize the entire Habsburg legacy in the image of Franz Joseph. His mutton chops dominate every bookstore and souvenir shop in Austria, and his stamp is evident in every edifice that carried Vienna from the Baroque era to the eve of the socialist 1920s.

His brother Maximilian was involved in the mad project to become emperor of Mexico, and was executed by Benito Juárez's firing squad in the Mexican town of Querétaro in 1867. His wife Elisabeth, a woman of astonishing beauty and an independent mind, abandoned Franz Joseph early on for a life of restless wandering; she was murdered in Geneva by an Italian anarchist in 1898. Their only son, the dashing and romantic Rudolph, committed suicide at Mayerling in 1889 after shooting his 17-year-old girlfriend. A nephew, the petty, illiberal Franz Ferdinand, was made heir to the throne in his place; his assassination by a Serbian patriot in Sarajevo at last broke the old kaiser's poise and set loose the avalanche that would bring his empire to end.

KARL I *(1916-1918)*

A distant grandnephew who rose to the throne through accident and was toppled and exiled before he could make his mark, "Karl the Sudden" makes a sad close to the Habsburg saga. The new state of Hungary recognized him as king, but twice arrested and expelled him when he tried to enter the country. He died a penniless exile in the island of Madeira in 1922. His wife, Empress Zita of Bourbon-Parma, was permitted to visit Austria in 1980 and became the last Habsburg to be buried in the Imperial Crypt on her death in 1989. Their son, Mr Otto von Habsburg, is a citizen of Germany and an active member of the European Parliament. He played an important role in the secret negotiations that opened Hungary to the West in 1989, and was briefly considered as a candidate for the Hungarian presidency.

All Habsburg properties within the Austrian Republic were seized without compensation by a law passed in 1918, and the family was expelled in perpetuity from Austria. The exile law was relaxed somewhat in 1961, but the Habsburgs are still excluded from Austrian citizenship. Habsburg possessions in Hungary were seized by the Communist regime in 1948. Nevertheless several branches of the family continue to live in Hungary.

Culture

"Austrian civilization, like the buildings which it created, was grandiose, full of superficial life, yet sterile within; it was theatre, not reality.... At its heart was a despairing frivolity: 'hopeless, but not serious' was the guiding principle which the age of Baroque stamped upon the Habsburg world.... The Habsburgs learned from the Jesuits patience, subtlety and showmanship; they could not learn from them sincerity and creativeness."
(A.J.P.Taylor, English historian)

"I could not live in this city alone or for long; earnest men and serious matters are here neither valued nor understood. The beauty of the surroundings is a substitute."
(Robert Schumann, German composer)

For many, Vienna is a byword for charm and cultured elegance: the city of gilded cafés and waltzing horses. It is an image cultivated with care: the main park of the city is reserved nightly for crowds waltzing to the lilt of Johann Strauss; ancient palaces offer champagne and Mozart; coffeehouses train their waiters in the idiom and manners of an aristocratic butler; men kiss the hands of women and address each other in full and florid titles.

The image goes deep enough to be part of the city's living culture: Viennese German — nasal, sardonic, sophisticated — relates to the Teutonic mainstream as upper-class Londonese to Californian. Viennese social life revolves around the annual coming-out ball at the imperial palace. And a net majority of Vienna's inhabitants do dress up each evening to take their coffee and cake under the solicitations of their favorite mock-aristocratic butler. Vienna, it seems, has combined German sentimentality with a typically Italian sense of style.

The reverse of the coin, however, is no less conspicuous. Vienna has suffered Europe's highest suicide rate ever since such statistics have been compiled; and every commentator on the city has been moved to remark on the undercurrent of melancholy and despair that seems to lurk in the Viennese soul. Mozart has become a symbol of the city, all sweetness and light: yet every true lover of Mozart knows that a tragic, almost demonic strain lies under the unflappable surface of his music.

More recent products of Viennese culture have allowed that demonic strain to go unchecked: Karl Kraus, the most cynical of all writers; Arnold Schönberg, the inventor of toneless music; Adolf Loos, the father of modern architecture; Sigmund Freud, who discovered the dark continent beneath the surface of civilized life; and Adolf Hitler, who unleashed the passions of that continent.

The Habsburgs were once known as the nastiest and most autocratic of Europe's ruling families. Throughout the closing centuries of the Middle Ages they fought to suppress the civic freedoms of the inhabitants of their capital; then they fought a relentless battle to impose Catholicism on their rebellious subjects. After 1683, they possessed the riches to buy loyalty. They still distrusted intellectual or political strivings, so offered splendor and entertainment instead. The architecture that emanated from their court made their capital one of the most beautiful in Europe. The creative genius of the Viennese was given ample outlet in music, the least political of all the arts. Literature and philosophy, by contrast, stagnated until the closing days of the monarchy.

Art and architecture

Sightseeing in Vienna is strolling through the history of European architecture: few cities are so aware and so proud of their architectural heritage. A triumphant church put its stamp on the city in the 17thC; a triumphant aristocracy reshaped it in its own image in the 18th. Later periods imitated, reacted to, or tried to improve on that legacy, and even the most aggressive novelties of the 20thC have carried on a subtle dialogue with their Baroque surroundings.

MEDIEVAL VIENNA *(11th-15thC)*
The **Romanesque** style dominated church architecture until the late 13thC, longer than elsewhere in Europe.

The best surviving specimen is Ruprechtskirche, Vienna's oldest church; at Michaelskirche, too, the cross-shaped, late-Romanesque core shows through layers of later alterations.

Gothic was brought to Vienna around 1220 by the mendicant orders, although none of their early churches survives. There are several specimens of the early 14thC (such as the Augusti-nian, Minorite and Teutonic Knights' churches, and Maria am Gestade). But the supreme example of Viennese Gothic architecture is the great cathedral of St Stephen, which took its present form between 1365 and 1511.

Although many houses in the Inner City possess medieval sections and substructures, few fully fledged relics of civil architecture still survive in Vienna from the Middle Ages.

Stephansdom

Among them are parts of Altes Rathaus (beneath a 17thC facade) and the Griechenbeisl house.

RENAISSANCE *(16thC)*

With few exceptions, the architecture of the Renaissance is mostly absent from Vienna. The imperial court was often away in the 16thC from its sullen and religiously suspect capital, while a weak and conservative church prevented the search for new paths in church architecture: as late as the 1610s, the Franciscans would build their church in an imitation of the Gothic. Among specifically Renaissance works of architecture are the two oldest wings of the Hofburg, Stallburg and the Swiss Court, and the forlorn but impressive hulk of the ruined Neugebäude. Several private houses are dated to the 16thC (for example, Bäcker Str. 7).

The so-called **Danube School** of painting (a term of convenience for a number of artists who worked independently) flourished in Vienna for a brief period at the turn of the 16thC. It was patronized by the city fathers, who were then on adverse terms with the Habsburg court. The main exponents of the school were Albrecht **Altdorfer** (active c.1500-38), the young Lucas **Cranach** the Elder (in Vienna 1500-4) and Wolf **Huber** (1484-1553). Their work is characterized by its dramatic intensity and convoluted expressionism.

BAROQUE *(1620-1780)*

Early: The bold, extravagant, theatrical manner of the Baroque entered Vienna with the final defeat of Protestantism in 1620. Its early monuments were the churches of the various orders of the Catholic Counter-Reformation (Jesuits, Piarists, Servites) and the palaces of the new aristocracy that emerged from the looting of Protestant estates (Liechtenstein, Starhemberg).

Nearly all the architects, sculptors and painters of this period were Italians (Burnacini, Canevale, the Carlone brothers, Martinelli, Tencala) who arrived with the priests and the inquisitors to proclaim the triumph of the Roman church.

High: The Turkish siege of 1683 occasioned considerable destruction; the end of the Turkish menace in 1697-99 introduced a new confidence; and the final conquest of Hungary in 1711 created immense sources of new wealth. From this point to the end of the reign of Karl VI in 1740, a stupendous building boom changed the face of the Habsburg capital and established the Baroque, now somewhat moderated by the less flamboyant and more sentimental imagination of native Austrian masters, into the architectural signature of Vienna.

Three architects set the tone of the era with their splendid designs. Johann Bernhard **Fischer von Erlach**, whose work was continued after his death in 1723 by his son Josef Emanuel, designed the extraordinary Plague Column of Leopold I, the Karlskirche (illustrated on page 116), the Winter Riding School, the Great Hall of the Court Library, the Bohemian Chancery, and several aristocratic palaces among which the winter palace of Prince Eugene and Palais Trautson take first rank. Johann Lucas von **Hildebrandt** (1666-1745) was the creator of the Piarist and St Peter's churches, the Kinsky, Schwarzenberg and Schönborn palaces, and above all Prince Eugene's summer palace at Belvedere. Jakob **Prandtauer** (1660-1726) built the exquisite abbey churches of Melk and St Florian as well as numerous other edifices of great delicacy in the province of Lower Austria, but nothing in the city of Vienna itself.

The painting and sculpture of the Baroque remained ancillary to architecture. The native masters Michael Rottmayr, Daniel Gran, the two Johann Georg Schmidts ("Wiener Schmidt" and the more important "Kremser Schmidt") and the Italian Martino Altomonte filled the new churches with cascading angels and soaring saints, and enriched aristocratic palaces with playful gods and voluptuous goddesses; the Strudel brothers, Balthasar Moll, Zauner, and above all Georg Rafael **Donner** (1692-1741), adorned their altars, niches, portals, architraves, pools and gardens with their highly rhetorical sculpture.

Late: The flamboyance of the Viennese Baroque was muted further in the thriftier and more delicate era of Maria Theresa. The supreme product of this period was the Schönbrunn palace, a work of the Italian Nicolaus **Pacassi**.

Schönbrunn palace

The light playfulness of the late 18thC style that the French called Rococo found little echo in Viennese architecture, but it reached a zenith in the astonishingly light and fanciful frescoes and altarpieces of Franz Anton **Maulbertsch** (1724-96), perhaps the best of Austrian decorative painters.

CLASSICISM *(1770s-1848)*

A revival of interest in the unadorned lines and noble proportions of Classical Greek and Roman architecture emerged under the patronage of Joseph II, but never took firm root in the pomp-and-spectacle-loving soil of Vienna. The Gloriette (1775), the Josephine medical complex and Palais Pallavicini (both 1783) employed a Classicizing manner, while the fake Roman ruins of the Schönbrunn gardens (1778) foreshadowed the historicism of the later 19thC.

In the 1820s, architects Peter von **Nobile** and Josef **Kornhäusl** adorned the city with temples and colonnades that copied the newly rediscovered monuments of Greek Antiquity. A high point of Classicism was reached in the masterpieces of the Italian sculptor Pietro **Canova**, who worked in Vienna from 1805-9: most notable is his marble pyramid in the Augustinian Church.

BIEDERMEIER *(1815-48)*

The name of the satirical character Gottlob Biedermeier ("Praisegod Dogood") was first applied to the slender and unassuming style of furniture that became fashionable in the 1810s. It then expanded to include all branches of art that shared the sentimental, unheroic, inward-looking world of the *Vormärz,* the period preceding the March revolutions of 1848. The genre painters Friedrich von **Amerling** and Ferdinand Georg **Waldmüller** painted charming scenes of domestic bliss, country days and innocent love. Franz **Grillparzer** brought the same themes to poetry, and Franz **Schubert** sang them in music, with a wounded and nostalgic spirit lurking beneath their seemingly uncomplicated surfaces.

A few buildings of small size and great charm (Dreimäderlhaus in central Vienna, Schloss Pötzleinsdorf in district 18.) pursued a similar sensibility in architecture.

HISTORICAL ECLECTICISM *(1858-1918)*

The aristocracy and the church built everything of note until the end of the 18thC. The middle class that replaced them built small charming homes in the Biedermeier era, and loud temples to Science, Art, Liberty and Progress in the second half of the 19thC. The era of the triumphant bourgeoisie affected the art of past ages with tremendous overstatement; its buildings "did not content themselves with being Gothic, Renaissance or Baroque, but made use of the possibility of having all of them simultaneously" (Robert Musil).

This phenomenon, sharing traits with England's Victorian mentality and Germany's Gründerzeit, took in Vienna the name of **Ringstrasse architecture**, from the new boulevard which was overlaid, under the guiding hand of Franz Joseph himself, with a Neoclassical parliament, a Neo-Byzantine arsenal, a Neo-Gothic cathedral and city hall, a Neo-Early-Renaissance opera, a Neo-Late-Renaissance university and a Neo-Baroque Neo-Burgtheater.

In the property boom that accompanied the expansion of the city, substandard tenement houses *(Rentenpalais)* were built behind the facades of aristocratic palaces, and shopping arcades were designed in the shape of larger-than-life Venetian palazzi. For some reason, however, the eclecticism of late-imperial Vienna never matched the reckless flamboyance of Budapest, the rival capital of the Dual Monarchy, which experienced its great flowering days at this time.

The leading Viennese architects of the period were Teophil Hansen, Eduard van der Null, August von Siccardsburg, Heinrich Ferstel, Karl Hasenauer and Gottfried Semper. The painter Hans **Makart** (1840-84) produced vast and pretentious historic tableaux which made him a darling of court and society.

45

SECESSION AND MODERNISM *(1897-1918)*

In a dramatic move that jolted Vienna's artistic establishment, a group of young artists, architects and intellectuals broke with the official artists' association (the *Künstlergenossenschaft*) in 1897 with a manifesto that spelled out their modernist creed.

Their leader was the painter Gustav **Klimt** (1862-1918), whose brash, shockingly beautiful and heavily mannered art epitomized turn-of-the-century Vienna. The work of architects Otto **Wagner** (1841-1918) and Adolf **Loos** (1870-1933) moved the city to the vanguard of a worldwide movement, which was known in Paris by the name of *Art Nouveau* and in the German-speaking world as *Jugendstil*.

The **Karlsplatz tram station**, designed by Otto Wagner in 1898.

Secessionism, however, was a short-lived phenomenon that had already exhausted its creative spark before 1910. Loos declared in 1908 that "ornament is crime" and became a founder of the most chilling dogmas of 20thC architecture. Painting passed rapidly from Klimt's elegance to the screaming colors of Oskar **Kokoschka** (1886-1980) and the sexual perversity of Egon **Schiele** (1890-1918).

SOCIALIST ARCHITECTURE *(1918-34)*

The socialists who controlled Vienna's city government from the end of World War I to the civil war of 1934 regarded the city's chronic housing shortage as their first priority. A tax was imposed on anything considered as luxury, and its proceeds financed vast housing projects where Vienna's working classes found inexpensive lodging. To this day, the proud red phrase *Wohnhausanlage des Gemeinde Wien* (Housing Compound of the Commune of Vienna, with date of construction) marks many buildings throughout the city.

The great socialist compounds of the 1920s and '30s, such as the 1,400-unit Karl-Marx-Hof or the much smaller George-Washington-Hof, combined residential units with social facilities, reflecting the endeavor to create a "new human" who was to be "honest, selfless, community-minded, industrious and soberly joyful." Their architecture carried an odd echo of Vienna's age-old preoccupation with theatrical effect.

RECENT TRENDS

After World War II, Vienna's efforts to maintain its stature as a world-class city often clashed with the realities of a declining population and an impoverished City Hall. Several white elephants like the vast office-and-residence complex of the UNO-City and the Haas Haus on Stephansplatz were born of that tension. Two prominent sculptors, Fritz **Wotruba** (Holy Trinity church in district 23.) and Alfred **Hrdlicka** (War monument at Albertinaplatz), maintained the grim traditions of modernism, while more recently, the works of the painter-architect Friedensreich **Hundertwasser** marked a return to the spirit of frivolous, decorative fancy (see the illustration on page 114).

Music

From the middle of the 18th to the end of the 19thC, Vienna was the unquestioned capital of European music. Mozart, Haydn, Beethoven, Schubert, Brahms, Bruckner, Mahler and Richard Strauss spent all or most of their creative career in the Austrian capital; the waltzes of father and son Johann Strauss entertained the Viennese public, and 19thC musical comedy reached its pinnacle in the operettas of Suppé, Lehár, Millöcker and Kálmán.

EARLY MUSIC
The Babenberg court of the 12th-13thC was one of the most prominent centers of medieval German minstrelry *(Minnesang)*. Walther von der Vogelweide, Ulrich von Liechtenstein and the demonic Tannhäuser sang at the ducal court (Am Hof). The next significant musician to make his appearance in Vienna was Christoph Willibald von **Gluck** (1714-1787), who was employed as *Kapellmeister* in Maria Theresa's court.

CLASSICAL MUSIC
Josef **Haydn** (1732-1809), the first great master of Viennese classicism, started his career as a Vienna Choirboy. As music director for the Esterházy princes, he spent a lifetime commuting between their palace in Eisenstadt (50km/30 miles s of Vienna), their country home in Esterháza (now across the border in Hungary), and their town house on Naglergasse. In 1790 he retired to Vienna, where he lived surrounded with a reverent halo as the grand old man of European music. His death coincided with Napoleon's occupation of Vienna, and occasioned a majestic funeral honored by the conqueror and the defeated emperor alike.

Wolfgang Amadeus **Mozart** (1765-91) performed as a child prodigy at Schönbrunn palace in the presence of Maria Theresa, then returned to Vienna at the age of 27 to spend there the final, and most creative, nine years of his life. The apartment on Domgasse where he spent three years and composed the *Marriage of Figaro* is preserved as a museum; the house on Rauhensteingasse where he wrote his unfinished *Requiem* and died has become a department store.

Ludwig van **Beethoven** (1770-1828) was a native of Bonn who adopted Vienna at the age of 22 as the proper setting for his genius and ambition. Throughout his life he moved restlessly between various addresses in town and the then-rural villages of the Vienna Woods. In 1802, his increasing deafness moved him to the edge of suicide in Heiligenstadt; later on he composed some of his greatest symphonies in the same village. In the 1820s he began spending an increasing amount of time in the spa of Baden, where he composed his last string quartets, perhaps the profoundest works of Western music. He died in his last home at Schwarzspanier Str. 15.

Franz **Schubert** (1797-1828), the only native Viennese among the great composers, was born at Nussdorfer Str. 54, and spent his short life practically without a fixed address, drifting from home to friendly home, falling in love often and paying his compliments and debts in music. The court and the great nobility had by then ceased to maintain full musical establishments, and the publicly-supported philharmonic and operatic societies of the late 19thC were yet to come. His music was therefore performed in homes, cafés, inns and wine gardens, among friends rather than at public concerts, with small ensembles rather than full orchestral resources. Its intimate spirit prefigured the era of Romanticism.

Johannes **Brahms** (1833-97), by contrast, arrived in Vienna at the peak of his career and as the uncrowned king of the city's musical establishment. As the guiding spirit of the Vienna Philharmonic Society, he promoted perfection over sentiment, and elegance of idiom over warmth of expression. His great antagonist was Anton **Bruckner** (1824-96), whose massive tonal structures formed an exact counterpart to the grandiose style of contemporary architecture. Bruckner's greatest admirer was none other than Franz Joseph, who permitted the bumbling provincial bachelor from Linz to reside in a garden house of the Belvedere palace.

If Bruckner belonged to Ringstrasse, then the mannered elegance of Gustav **Mahler** (1860-1911) had much in common with the Secession. As director of the Philharmonic and of the Opera, Mahler embodied the musical culture of Vienna's final decade of glory. His *Lied von der Erde* of 1907 was a deeply lyrical farewell to the centuries-long quest for beauty in music. From then on, "serious" music — as in the atonal works of Arnold **Schönberg** (1874-1955) and Alban **Berg** (1885-1935), leading members of the Second Viennese School — became increasingly divorced from popular tastes, while audiences turned to "popular" music for entertainment.

WALTZ AND OPERETTA

The appearance of an "entertainment" music as distinct from "art" music went back to the years following the Vienna Congress (1815), and in this field, too, Vienna led European fashions. "The Congress danced" to the minuet, the polka and the *laendler*.

A few years later, Joseph **Lanner** (1801-43) and Johann **Strauss** (1804-49) started the waltz craze during a summer's contract as bandleaders at Dommayer's casino in Hietzing, a stone's throw from the

Schönbrunn palace. Waltz orchestras proliferated, and before the decade was over every casino, park and public garden in town claimed its own band. The most popular of them belonged to the son of Strauss, Johann **Strauss Jr** (1825-99), who made his debut as his father's rival in 1844. The younger Strauss fell out of favor for his involvement in the revolution of 1848, but by the '50s he was back in fashion, and reigned until his death as the undisputed king of Vienna's entertainment world.

The operetta emerged as a genre in Paris, but reached the peak of its popularity in Vienna, where it grew into a craze in the "golden age" of the 1870s. Strauss himself produced some of the most popular operettas of all time with his *die Fledermaus* (1874) and *Gypsy Baron* (1885), while Franz **von Suppé** (1820-95) rivaled him with his sparkling tunes. The "silver age" of the Viennese operetta opened after 1900 with the works of Franz **Lehár** (1870-1948, *The Merry Widow*) and Emmerich **Kalman** (1882-1953, *Csardas Fürstin, Countess Maritza*).

Many representatives of the Viennese musical theater emigrated to the United States after 1918 and 1938, becoming the founding fathers of the Broadway musical and Hollywood film music.

Intellectual life

During the centuries in which Vienna was the capital of a powerful empire, it produced hardly any writer, poet, humanist, historian, philosopher or political thinker of note. Then, in the span of a single generation — from the 1890s till after World War I — there occurred an extraordinary intellectual flowering which took place against the darkening political background of the dying Habsburg empire. Nearly all the major figures of this generation were Jewish. They dealt mainly with the darker aspects of the soul and society, in sharp contrast with Vienna's culture of elegant superfice.

Sigmund **Freud** (1856-1939) developed the theory and practice of psychoanalysis from around 1895; he lived and worked at Berggasse 19 until forced to flee Austria by the Nazi takeover in 1938. The writers Arthur **Schnitzler** (1862-1931), Karl **Kraus** (1874-1936) and Robert **Musil** (1880-1942) presented a despairing, cynical vision of man. Stefan **Zweig** (1881-1942) tried to rise above despair through moral vision, while Hugo von **Hoffmansthal** (1874-1929) took refuge in a world of artificial elegance. Theodor **Herzl** (1860-1904) was a fashionable columnist and a café dandy before he converted to the Jewish cause and formed the Zionist movement. Georg von **Schönerer**, by contrast, became the founder of modern anti-Semitism and influenced the young Adolf Hitler. The Viennese journalist and feminist Bertha von **Suttner** became the first woman to receive the Nobel peace prize in 1905.

No writer or thinker of international renown has emerged from Vienna since 1938.

Vienna today

Some 82 percent of the urban population is registered as Roman Catholic. There are some 6,000 Jews (there were about 180,000 in 1938), and 60,000 Muslims, mostly Turkish "guest workers." Nearly a third of the inhabitants are descendants of Slavic (Czech, Slovak, Slovene, Croat) and Hungarian immigrants who settled in the imperial capital in the 19thC.

The three most recent prime ministers of the republic (Kreisky, Sinowatz, Vranitzky) have been of Czech descent. The recent sudden increase in immigration from Eastern European countries has created alarm and political tension, fueling a sharp growth in the votes of the anti-immigrant Freedom Party.

The two dominant political groups of modern Austria were born in 1888-89. The Christian Social Party was founded by Karl Lueger on the basis of a Catholic, at least initially anti-Semitic, "little man" ideology; since 1945 it has changed its name to People's Party (ÖVP). The Austrian Socialist Party (founders Viktor Adler, Otto Bauer, Karl Renner) was Europe's leading Marxist organization before the rise of Lenin's Bolsheviks. Followers of the two parties fought a civil war in the 1930s, which led to the "clerico-fascist" dictatorship of the Christian Socials. Both groups evolved toward a moderate stance during their joint resistance to Nazi rule.

An ÖVP-SP grand coalition governed Austria after the end of World War II, and a complicated power-sharing system has been the basis of the republic since then. The coalition was revived in 1987 in response to the alarming growth of Jörg Haider's far-right Freedom Party.

The Soviet collapse and the reunification of the two Germanies has again sparked an old debate on the Austrian identity. Is there an Austrian nation? Is there a justification for its separate existence? The predominant opinion in the west and south of the country seems to be negative, as reflected in the meteoric rise of the Freedom Party, which advocates closer ties with Germany.

Most voters in Vienna, by contrast, seem pulled to the idea of *Mitteleuropa,* a code word for regrouping Austria, Hungary, Czechoslovakia, Slovenia and Croatia — the old Habsburg lands — in a new cultural-economic zone.

Practical information

On-the-spot information

TOURIST INFORMATION

Official **tourist information bureaux** supply free of charge an excellent selection of maps, listings and brochures, as well as a full **hotel catalog**, which lists everything, including prices, that anyone is ever likely to want to know about Vienna's hotels. They also provide a **room referral** service.

The main downtown bureau is at **Kärntner Str. 38** *(map 3 E3, open daily 9am-7pm).*

There are additional offices at **Schwechat airport** arrivals hall *(open June-Sept 8.30am-11pm, Oct-May 8.30am-10pm)* and at two rail stations, **Westbahnhof** *(open 6.15am-11pm, map 1 D3)* and **Südbahnhof** *(open 6.30am-10pm, map 2 D4).*

On autobahn approaches to Vienna, there are offices at the **Wien-Auhof** exit on the w Autobahn *(open 8am-10pm)* and the **Triester Str.** exit on the s Autobahn *(open 9am-7pm).*

Refer written requests for information to **Wiener Fremdenverkehrsverband** *(write to A-1095 Wien or ⒻⓍ 433292).*

GUIDED TOURS

Various firms conduct sightseeing tours by bus and boat, including:
Cityrama   Departures from Stadtpark/Johannesgasse, map 4E4 ☎534130
City Touring Vienna   Hotel pickup service ☎89414170
Corso Sightseeing   ☎5123337
Vienna Sightseeing Tours   Central Bus Terminal Wien-Mitte ☎7124683, map 4D5

Boat tours of the Danube embankment are offered by **DDSG** *(at (1.) Schwedenbrücke ☎2181896, map 4 C4).* The daily tour departs from April to October at 1pm.

The **Stattwerkstatt** offers **"alternative" tours** of Vienna, in part by bicycle, and is among other things a good way of meeting interesting young people *(☎343384).*

City tours by **old-timer tram** depart from Karlsplatz *(map 3 E3)* from May to September every Saturday at 1.30pm, and on Sunday at 11am and 1.30pm. The tour costs AS150 for adults, AS50 for children *(☎5873186).*

A more intimate way of getting to know Vienna is to participate in the great variety of **walking tours** that are organized around specific themes.

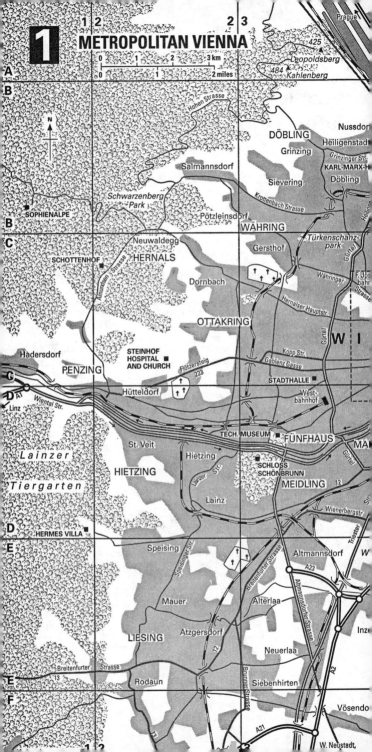

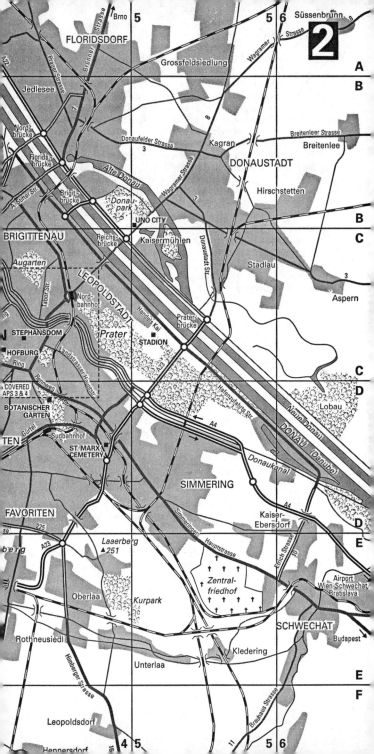

Listings are available at any tourist information bureau and in hotel lobbies. Each tour costs AS100, and departs with a minimum of 3 participants, regardless of weather. Unfortunately, many are available in German only. Some examples: Death in Vienna; Freud and Jewish Vienna of the Turn of the Century; Jugendstil — Then and Now; Medieval Vienna Above & Below Ground; Old Houses — Silent Courtyards; The Power and Wealth of the Habsburgs; Vienna Legends and Crime Mysteries; The Viennese Coffeehouse.

Tours and activities associated with the 200th anniversary of the death of **Mozart** mushroomed in 1991, and did not seem likely to vanish soon. Among the more interesting ideas was a walking tour of Mozartiana accompanied by a cello-and-guitar duo and featuring a course in dancing the menuet at the Figaro house. Departures every Saturday at 2.30pm from the main gate of Stephansdom *(map 3 D3* ☎ *316580)*.

Licensed **private guides** charge AS900 for a half day, and AS1,800 for a full day (8 hours). They can be engaged through various agencies, including those below:

Charlotte Speiser   (2.) Rennbahnweg 24/43/1 ☎2592535
Travel Point   (9.) Boltzmanngasse 19 ☎314243, map **3A1**
Vienna Guide Service   (11.) Geiselberg Str. 36/2a/69 ☎745202

PUBLICATIONS

A variety of brochures are obtainable free of charge at hotel lobbies and information bureaux. Best of all is the official *Vienna A to Z* published by the Tourist Office, sold for AS30 at all Tabak-Trafik kiosks. For people younger in age or tastes the Tourist Office also publishes an excellent brochure named *Jugend-Szene,* free of charge but in German only.

Vienna's five daily newspapers carry listings of movies, concerts, exhibitions and so forth. The *Kronenzeitung* and *Kurier* are tabloids, although they do not quite sink to the level of their Anglo-American or German counterparts. The conservative *Presse* and *Standard* and the leftish *Neue AZ* are more serious.

Wiener, an unconventional weekly, is a good source of information about the latest developments in town.

MONEY AND BANKING

Banks are open from Monday to Wednesday and on Friday from 8am to 3pm, and on Thursdays from 8am to 5.30pm. Branches in the outer districts (but not those in the Inner City) close for a lunchtime break from 12.30-1.30pm.

Off-hour and weekend exchange facilities exist at the following points (closing hours are indicated within brackets): the **airport** (Arrivals 11.30pm, Departures 9pm), the **City Air Terminal** (6pm, Sunday 1pm), the **Westbahnhof** and **Südbahnhof** (10pm), and the **Opera Passage** (7pm, Sunday 1pm).

There are exchange automats for the major Western currencies at three points along **Kärntner Str.** *(#7, #51 and Stephansplatz)* and at **Michaelerplatz** *(at the Loos-Haus).*

POSTAL ADDRESSES

Addresses are written with their Bezirk (district) number first, followed by the street name and number. This is the form in which they appear throughout this book. Thus:

(1.) Kärntner Strasse 12

(8.) Laudongasse 25

To find the postal code of each Bezirk, multiply the district number by 10, then add 1,000. Some districts are subdivided into smaller postal units by varying the last digit. This is how letters are supposed to be addressed:

A-1015 Wien, Kärntner Strasse 12

A-1080 Wien, Laudongasse 25.

POSTAL SERVICES

Post offices open Monday-Friday 8am-noon and 2-6pm, Saturday 8-10am. The Main Post Office at (1.) Fleischmarkt 19, and post offices at the Westbahnhof and Südbahnhof stay open round the clock. The Main Post Office handles **poste restante (general delivery)**: mail should be marked *Hauptpostlagernd* and sent to A-1011 Wien. 1992 **postage rates** for mail sent abroad were AS5 for postcards, AS7 for letters weighing up to 20 grams, and AS12 for letters over 20 grams.

For **postal information** call ☎832101.

TELEPHONE SERVICES

To make an **international phone call**, dial 00, the country code, the city/area code and the number. The country code for the US and Canada is 1; the UK is 44. To call Germany or Switzerland out of Austria, you have to dial, respectively, 060 or 050 followed by the city code (without a zero).

The city code for Vienna is **0222** when dialed long-distance from within Austria, **1** when dialed from outside the country. The country code for Austria is **43**.

For **directory assistance**, call ☎16 for numbers in Austria and ☎08 for numbers worldwide.

Telegrams can be sent via telephone ☎190.

USEFUL SERVICES

Airport   Arrivals and departures ☎77702231 (24 hours)

Austrian Airlines ☎71799, Monday-Thursday 7.30am-6pm, Friday-Sunday 8am-5pm

Interpreters/translators   ☎5139128

Lost and Found   (9.) Wasagasse 22 ☎313440, map **3**B2, open Monday-Friday 8am-noon

Wake-up service   ☎18

Weather   ☎1566

CONSULATES

Vienna has a full complement of embassies, but most tourist affairs are handled at consulate level if such a separate section exists.

55

Australia (4.) Mattielli Str. 2-4 ☎5128580, map **3E3**
Canada Embassy at (1.) Dr-Karl-Lueger-Ring 10 ☎5333691, map **3C2**
Ireland (3.) Landstrasser Hauptstrasse 2 (in the Hilton hotel)
☎754246, map 4D5
South Africa Embassy at (19.) Sandgasse 33 ☎326493, map **1B3**
UK (3.) Jaurèsgasse 10 ☎7136117, map 4F5
US (1.) Gartenbaupromenade, Parkring 12a (in the Marriott Hotel)
☎51451, map 4D4

RELIGIOUS SERVICES

A predominantly Catholic city, Vienna offers religious facilities for various other Christian denominations and non-Christian groups as well. The brochure *Grüss Gott,* available in churches and tourist bureaux, has a comprehensive listing of services in downtown churches.

Vienna's English-speaking Catholic Church holds Holy Mass Saturday and Sunday at 5.15pm in the Teutonic Knights' Church (Deutschordenskirche) at (1.) Singer Str. 7 *(map 3 D3).* A multilingual Mass (including English) is celebrated every Saturday at 6pm in the **Votive Church** *(map 3 C2).*

Services at other churches:
Anglican/Episcopal Church (3.) Jaurèsgasse 17-19. Map 4F4. For information in English call Monday to Friday ☎7131575.
Baptist Church (6.) Mollardgasse 35 ☎8049259. Service in English on Sunday at 11.30am.
Community Church (interdenominational) (1.) Dorotheergasse 16. Map 3D3. Service in English on Sunday at 11.30am.
The International Chapel (5.) Blechturmgasse 11/4 ☎550557. Services on Sunday at 9.30 and 11am.
Methodist Church (15.) Sechshauser Str. 56. English service on Sunday at 11.15am.
Synagogues (1.) Seitenstettengasse 4, map 4C4 ☎53104 and (2.) Tempelgasse 1, map 4C5.

The **Islamic Center and Mosque** are located in district 22. near the UNO-City *(map 2 B4; take commuter train from Wien-Mitte to Floridsdorf, then bus 20B to Islamic Center).*

The **Matsumae Buddhist Temple** is in the industrial 10. district, off Triester Str.

The **Samaritans** provide religious counsel and aid in English daily from 6.30-10pm and also from Monday to Friday between 9.30am and 1pm ☎7133374.

SOCIAL CENTERS
Afro-Asiatic Mensa A meeting place (self-service restaurant) of students from the Third World *(9., Türken Str. 3 ☎344625, map 3 B2).*
Amerlinghaus The core institution of the revived Spittelberg historic district. Activities and "events" organized mostly by Green/Alternative groups. Popular snack-restaurant, live music, courtyard garden *(open Mon-Fri from 2pm at (7.) Stiftgasse 8 ☎936475, map 3 E1).*

Emergency information

EMERGENCY SERVICES
In emergency, dial any of the following from anywhere in Austria:
Fire ☎122
Police ☎133
Emergency medical aid ☎141
Ambulance ☎144

MEDICAL HELP
Call ☎1550 for a taped list of pharmacies on duty and ☎5122078 for off-hours and weekend dentists.

The **American Medical Society of Vienna** can be of help to those who speak no German—☎424568.

If you are a member of the **IAMAT** (International Association for Medical Assistance to Travelers) you will already have contact details in Vienna for medical assistance involving English-speaking doctors. See page 16 of this guide for details of the scheme.

CAR BREAKDOWN
Two separate automobile clubs provide emergency road service. Call **ARBÖ** on ☎123 or **ÖMATC** on ☎120, both from anywhere in Austria.

RAPE
The **Rape Emergency Center** answers calls on ☎932222 in Vienna, Monday 9am-noon and Tuesday, Thursday 6-9pm.

Frauencafé Men are not welcome at the café (*open Mon-Fri from 7pm, Sunday brunch from 11am*), but they may enlighten themselves at the adjoining **Frauenzimmer** bookstore (*both at (8.) Lange Gasse 11* ☎*438678, map3 D1*).
Homosexuelle Initiative Wien (HOSI) The leading organization for gay men and women in town (*at (2.) Novaragasse 40, Map 8 B5*); **Rosa telefon** for information and counseling (☎*266604, Tues, Fri 6-8pm*); **Gay Pride Palace** (disco) on Saturday from 7pm.
Mensa der Katholischen Hochschulgemeinde Cafeteria and social center for younger Catholics (*cafeteria open Mon-Fri 10.30am-2pm, closed July-Sept, at (1.) Ebendorfer Str. 8* ☎*483587-39, map 3 C2*).

VIENNA U-Bahn & S-Bahn system

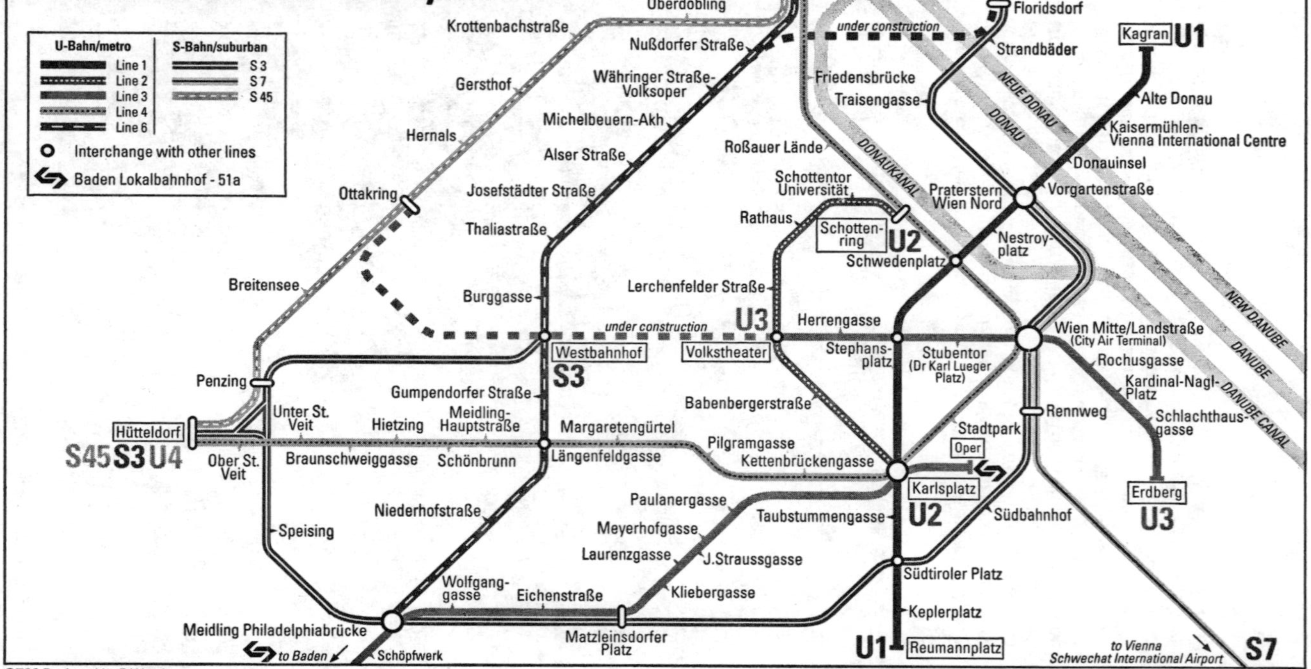

©TCS Designed by R.Woods

Map authorised user number D/CAS/WW/AM/1013

WUK   A huge ex-school building taken over by a self-governing cooperative of more than 40 radical and "alternative" groups, a mecca of Vienna's underground culture: punks, bicycle workshop, concerts and **Lila Löffel** women's café *(all at (9.) Währinger Str. 59* ☎ *438220, map 3 A1).*

Getting around in Vienna

See EXCURSIONS, page 173, for travel outside Vienna. See page 23 for CAR RENTAL information.

PUBLIC TRANSPORTATION
Vienna has enjoyed one of Europe's best-integrated public transportation systems since the seminal days of Mayor Lueger at the turn of the century.
Metro   Construction of the metro (subway) network was started in 1969 and continues to the present day. There are now five metro *(U-Bahn)* lines including the brand-new U3 and the renamed U6 (formerly the *Stadtbahn)* — there is no U5 as yet.
Trams and buses   A majority of the tram *(Strassenbahn)* and bus lines spread out from end-stations on either the Ring or the Gürtel — the two semicircles that girdle the Inner City — toward outer districts. Trams 1 and 2 circle the Ring in opposite directions (Tram 1 clockwise, Tram 2 counterclockwise), and the CityBuses 1A, 2A and 3A circulate within the Inner City.
Trains   There are express and local commuter trains *(S-Bahn* and *R-Bahn)* running from Vienna's five major rail stations. The narrow-gauge **Badner Bahn** operates between its terminal on Kärntner Ring *(map 3 E3)* and the spa of Baden with intermediate stops along the way.
Information   System maps and timetables are available at Tabak-Trafik kiosks, tourist bureaux and Transport Authority *(Verkehrsbetrieb)* offices in major metro stations.
Tickets   A one-way ticket allowing transfers is valid in all components of the system. This costs AS20 when purchased singly, or AS15 per ticket when purchased in packages of 4, 5 or 8. Unlimited-travel cards *(Netzkarte)* valid for 24 hours, 72 hours or 8 days cost AS35, 45 and 115, respectively. Two or more tickets are needed if you cross the city boundaries of Vienna.
Night services   The metro, trams and most buses operate between about 5am and midnight. Special buses marked **N** serve several key routes at nighttime out of the night bus terminal at Schwedenplatz.

TAXIS
Taxis are not permitted to cruise for passengers. You may get a cab at a taxi stand — there are five of them along the Ring, but only one in the inner Inner City, at Hoher Markt *(map 3 C3)* — or by calling ☎1712,

31300, 40100, 60160 or 91011 (English is usually understood). Day fares are AS22 to start, plus about AS15 per kilometer. Extras: AS10 call-up fee, AS10 for night travel (11pm-6am) and Sunday rides, AS10 or 20 for luggage.

Chauffeured limousines are provided by **Avis-Adler** *(☎334327)*, **Mazur** *(☎6042233)* and **Peter Urban** *(☎7135255)*, among others.

HORSE CARRIAGES

A considerable fleet of horse carriages *(Fiaker)* stands at the disposal of sightseers at various points around the Inner City. The main terminals are at Albertinaplatz, Heldenplatz and Stephansplatz. A city tour costs AS500 or AS300 depending on its extent. For those who wish to pursue this interest further, there exists a **Fiakermuseum** *(17., Veronikagasse 12, open first Wed in each month 10am-1pm)*.

DRIVING IN TOWN

Try to avoid entering the maze of the Inner City. Remember that the Ring runs one way: clockwise. Those two warnings apart, Vienna traffic is no better and no worse than any big city.

Public **parking garages** in the city center are prominently signposted and marked *frei* or *voll*. They cost from AS15 to AS35 per hour and **close at 10pm**. There are no street parking meters: in order to park in restricted areas, obtain a parking ticket *(Parkscheiben)* at banks, post offices or Tabak-Trafik kiosks, and display it visibly on the windshield. If you don't, chances are your car won't stay long where you left it. In case disaster strikes, call the aptly named **Abschlepp-Platz** at ☎6042392 and be prepared to pay about AS1,700. The platz in question is at (10.) Eibesbrunnergasse, about 5km (3 miles) sw of the center.

The gas station at **Franz-Josefs-Kai/Morzinplatz** *(on the Danube Canal, map 4 C4)* stays open all night. All-night gas stations ring the city, on **Neubau-Gürtel** *(w)*, **Heiligenstadter Str.** *(N)*, **Hadikgasse** *(sw)* and **Triester Str.** *(s)*.

Planning and walks

When to go

Vienna is at its best in the early summer and fall: May and June, when the chestnut trees are in bloom, and September and October, when the air is crisp and luminous and the ivies begin to turn. Most visitors nevertheless arrive during high summer — July and August — which is the very moment that several leading Viennese attractions, including the Spanish Riding School, the Boys' Choir, the Opera and the Philharmonic, close down for their summer vacation.

Or consider "high winter." The city comes alive before Christmas, celebrates New Year's Eve in grand style, and puts on its highest spirits in the run-up to the Carnival. A drawback, though, is that winter will restrict your opportunity for walking in a leisurely fashion, in a city where strolling, feasting the eye and soaking up the atmosphere is a primary function for the visitor.

You might wish to target specific days of the week to be in Vienna, in which case be aware of several important points. Most museums, including the Art History Museum and the Belvedere collections, are closed on Monday. The Hofburg museums, including the Treasure Chamber, are closed on Tuesday, the National Library and Albertina on Sunday, and the Hofburg Imperial Apartments on Sunday afternoon. The Spanish Riding School holds public exercises Tuesday through Saturday except in July and August. And the Boys' Choir sings at mass every Sunday morning in the Hofburg chapel except July to mid-September.

Weekends present two attractive occasions: the Naschmarkt flea market on Saturday, and the crafts fair which is held along the Danube Canal promenade every Saturday and Sunday.

TRADITIONAL CELEBRATIONS

In every great city's annual calendar there are special moments of collective celebration. The locals take their city over, and the visitor can almost disappear into the crowd. Many discerning travelers pick these times precisely for that reason. Vienna has several such annual occasions that are particularly attractive or moving.

Vienna's **Carnival**, although not as spectacular as those of Venice or Rio, is lively enough to merit an adjustment of your vacation plans. Parades and processions take place throughout February, reaching a climax on the Monday and Tuesday preceding Ash Wednesday (40 days before Easter, in late February or March).

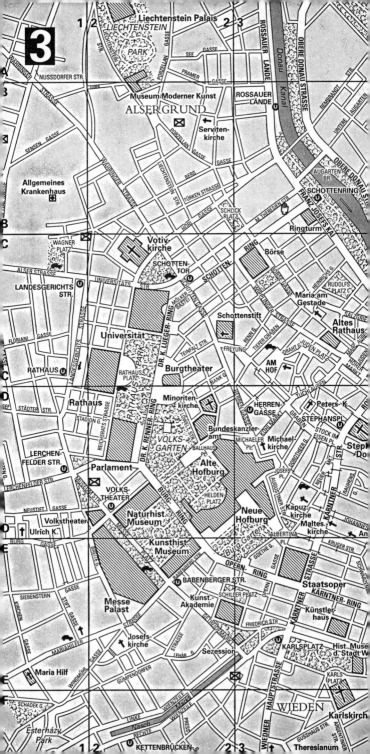

CENTRAL VIENNA

4

0 100 200 300 400 500m
0 100 200 300 400 500yds

AUGARTEN

AM TABOR

DARWIN GASSE

NORDBAHN STRASSE

LASSALLE STRASSE

Leopold-kirche

LEOPOLDSTADT

NOVARA GASSE

HEINE STRASSE

ROTENSTERN GASSE

PRATERSTERN

Wien-Nord Bahnhof

AUSSTELLUNGS STR.

Riesenrad

Karmelkirche

FRANZENSBRÜCKEN

VIVARIUM STR.

PRATER STRASSE

CZERNIN

NESTROY PLATZ

FRANZENS BR.

GROSSE ANDREAS GASSE

ZIRKUS GASSE

UNTERE DONAU STRASSE

DAMPFSCHIFF STRASSE

WEISSGERBER LÄNDE

Donau Kanal

SCHÜTTEL STRASSE

MARIEN-BR.

SCHWEDEN BR.

ASPERN BR.

uprechts K.

FRANZ-JOSEF KAI

SCHWEDEN-PL.

JULIUS RAAB PL.

RADETZKY STR.

FLEISCHMARKT

Haupt-postamt

KRIEGLER G.

OBERE VIADUKT GASSE

UNTERE VIADUKT GASSE

Othmarkirche

Jesuiten-kirche

ROSENB. STR.

DOMINIKANER BASTEI

ZOLLAMTS STR.

HINT. ZOLLAMTS STR.

NETZ GASSE

KEGEL GASSE

UNGER GASSE

KEGEL GASSE

Dominik.-kirche

BÄCKER STR.

WOLLZEILE

STUBEN TOR

STUBEN RING

MARXER GASSE

MARXER GASSE

ROTUNDEN BR.

Museum für angew. Kunst

STADT PARK

INVALIDEN STRASSE

LANDSTRASSE (WIEN-MITTE)

ERSTE PLATZ

SAAM GASSE

SUMOSKY GASSE

ERDBERGER LÄNDE

Franziskkirche

PARK RING

LANDSTRASSE HAUPT STRASSE

City Air Terminal

Kursalon

SCHUBERT RING

STADT-PARK

BEATRIXG.

RECHTE BAHN G.

UNGAR G.

ERDBERG

ROCHUS GASSE

WASSER GASSE

Beethoven-PLATZ

ROCHUS GASSE

Konzert-haus

LOTHRING. STR.

Am Modena Park

SALESIANER GASSE

LANDSTRASSE

SEBASTIAN PLATZ

Arenberg Park

HAUPT STRASSE

SCHWARZEN-BERG PL.

NEULING GASSE

Serb.- kirche

NEULING GASSE

UNGAR GASSE

Palais warzenberg

STROH GASSE

GASSE

Orangerie

RENNWEG

JUCH GASSE

Unteres Belvedere

Austria's chief religious celebration since time immemorial has been the **Corpus Christi procession**, which is celebrated in every town, with the active participation of various religious orders and large crowds of people. This event takes place on the ninth Thursday after Easter, in late May or June.

St John's Day (Johannisfest) is marked on June 21 with country fairs and firework displays throughout the country.

St Martin's Day on November 11 is comparable in significance to the American Thanksgiving, except that goose *(Martinigansl)* rather than turkey is the fowl of tradition, and the rule is to eat out at inns and country taverns rather than in the privacy of the home. Four days later, **St Leopold's Day** on November 15 is honored with festivities in the state of Lower Austria, whose patron saint it commemorates, and especially in the town of Klosterneuburg, where he is buried.

In the German-speaking lands, **St Nicholas' Day**, honoring the patron saint of children (December 6), takes up some of the traditional significance attached to Christmas in other Western countries. Open-air markets selling toys, handicrafts and candies are set up a few days before this date — for example, in Spittelberg — and usually remain open until Christmas.

Christmas mass is said in St Stephen's cathedral at midnight on December 24, with the cardinal-archbishop of Vienna officiating. This is an extremely popular event, so it is a good idea to obtain an entrance pass in advance.

Where to go

Six "must-visits" stand out on any Vienna checklist. Allow at least a day for the **Hofburg** complex: you will need to line up several times, and plenty of time to browse. The **Belvedere** and **Schönbrunn** palaces and the **Art History Museum** each deserve a minimum of half a day. The **Stephansdom** cathedral can be combined with a walking exploration of the historic **Inner City**.

An essential component of the Vienna experience is **music**, whether your tastes run to Strauss' waltzes or Mozart's operas — or even if they don't. So, set apart an evening or two for a concert and a waltz-out.

Finally, reserve at least one long evening for the extraordinary charm of the *Heurigen*, the wine gardens of Vienna's suburban villages. Go to **Grinzing** if you like to be with the majority. Or try **Stammersdorf** or **Sievering** if you prefer the simple and authentic.

A three-day program might then look like this:
DAY 1
- Hofburg: morning exercise of the Spanish Riding School, followed by the Imperial Apartments, Treasury and National Library.
- Lunch at Sacher or Café Griensteidl. The Imperial Crypt. Walking tour of Kärntner Str., Stephansdom, Graben and Kohlmarkt.
- Evening at the Opera, or at a café in the Bermuda Triangle.

DAY 2
- Several hours at the Art History Museum.
- Then a long walk: Mariahilfer Str., Spittelberg, Rathaus, Votive Church; the back streets of the Inner City from Herrengasse to Schönlaterngasse; and if you have energy remaining, Naschmarkt, the Secession building and Karlskirche.
- Evening: wine and waltzing at the Stadtpark.

DAY 3
- Schönbrunn. Upper and Lower Belvedere.
- Early evening: to Grinzing or another *Heurigen* village.

Omitted from this basic schedule are such important highlights as the museums of the newer wing of **Hofburg**, the **Albertina** art collection, the **Dorotheum** auction rooms, the **Hundertwasser houses**, the **Imperial Furniture Collection**, the **Josephinum** anatomical cabinets, the modern art museums of the **Stallburg** and the **Liechtenstein Garden Palace** — or a leisurely day visit to the villages of the **Vienna Woods**. And dinner (budget permitting) at such culinary temples as the **Hilton** hotel restaurant or the one at **Hotel/Palais Schwarzenberg**.

Reserve these for an extended stay or a subsequent visit. Above all never try to cram all into a short time, for a cultural overdose — a real risk in cities like Vienna — is as tiresome in its results as the intemperate enjoyment of any other delight.

Walking tours

The famed "short circuit" of the Inner City around KÄRNTNER STRASSE–STEPHANSPLATZ–GRABEN–KOHLMARKT–MICHAELERPLATZ–AUGUSTINERSTRASSE–ALBERTINAPLATZ — follow the "Short walk" route on the WALK 1 map overleaf — is the almost inevitable sightseeing itinerary that every visitor is bound to follow at least once during his or her visit. With more time and/or greater curiosity to discover the less obvious sights of the Inner City, you can follow the "Long walk" route on the same map. This route is described below as WALK 1.

The outer city does not lend itself as easily to walking as the old center. Distances are considerable; in addition, all important thoroughfares are oriented outward from the center like the spokes of a wheel, making it hard to combine them on a single itinerary. WALKS 2 and 3 seek to cover as many points of interest as possible in 6-8 hours each: how far you get depends on your energy and curiosity. Both walks exclude anything beyond the Gürtel — above all, the palaces of SCHÖNBRUNN and LAXENBURG; GRINZING and other vineyard suburbs; and the graveyards of ST MARX and CENTRAL CEMETERY — which are all excursions in their own right.

WALK 1: THE INNER CITY
Allow 4-6 hours.

Start at MICHAELERPLATZ and proceed to BALLHAUSPLATZ, a large open space dominated by the Baroque palace of the Prime Minister of Aus-

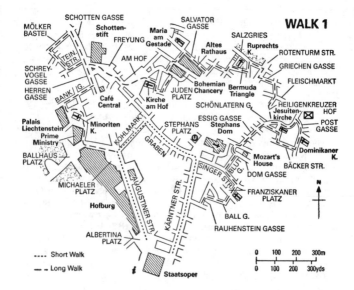

WALK 1

tria. Follow the main facade of the Prime Ministry into Minoritenplatz, where a series of stately historic edifices surround the Gothic church of the Minorites. Take the narrow Abraham-a-Sancta-Clara-Gasse, squeezed between the Starhemberg Palace on the right and the Liechtenstein Palace on the left, to emerge on Bankgasse. Turn right here, but only after observing the imposing main portal of the **Liechtenstein Palace**, which remains on your left.

Bankgasse takes you onto HERRENGASSE, which deserves to be explored along its whole length to observe its full architectural wealth. And you could pay a quick visit to the Museum of Lower Austria, located at #9.

Make a detour toward the N end of Herrengasse, turning left on Teinfalt Str., right on Schreyvogelgasse (note the Dreimäderlhaus at #10), right on Mölker Bastei (**Beethoven's apartment** is at #8), and right again on Schottengasse. Where Schottengasse, Herrengasse and Freyung intersect stands the **Schottenstift**, the church and abbey of the Scots. Visit it, then take a coffee break at the legendary **Café Central**, located in the arcade of Palais Ferstel, the mock-Venetian edifice on Freyung.

Continue via Heidenschuss to the square AM HOF, trying to imagine how nice it might be without car traffic. Observe the triumphal majesty of the old Jesuit Church, then follow the alley of Schulhof on the left to explore the maze of ancient lanes behind the church where two landmarks — the **Clock Museum** at Schulhof 2 and the newly discovered **medieval frescoes** at Tuchlauben 19 — deserve visits. End up, after many wrong turns, at Juden Pl., where you will notice the **Bohemian Chancery**, a work of the Baroque master Fischer von Erlach, and behind it, across Wipplinger Str., the medieval ALTES RATHAUS, the former City Hall of Vienna.

The street to the left of the Rathaus, called Stoss-im-Himmel ("Shot-in-the-Sky"), leads to the graceful Gothic church of **Maria am Gestade**. Visit it, noting the broad staircase in front, which once led down to the river embankment. Then follow Salvatorgasse behind the Rathaus, turn left on Marc-Aurel-Str., and immediately right on Sterngasse to emerge into the so-called BERMUDA TRIANGLE.

The triangle, defined by Seitenstettengasse, Judengasse and Salzgries, is interesting enough by day, although it really blooms in the evening. Its central feature is the modest church of St Rupert, the oldest in Vienna. There are enough restaurants, taverns and snack bars near it to tempt anyone, but you may consider continuing across Rotenturm Str. and on to Griechengasse, where the historic **Griechenbeisl**, the oldest tavern in Vienna, provides a more memorable choice for a lunch break.

Griechengasse abuts onto Fleischmarkt. Several apparently dead-end alleys off the right of this street give access to the lovely courtyard of the **Heiligenkreuzer Hof**, a historic residential complex which on certain weekends becomes the setting for a lively handicrafts market.

The main exit from the courtyard is onto SCHÖNLATERNGASSE, perhaps the most lovely of Vienna's old streets. Follow this narrow lane left, turning right on Postgasse where you see the 17thC church of the Dominicans, and right again on Bäcker Str. to end up on Dr-Ignaz-Seipel-Platz, a cozy space dominated by the Old University Church (now the **Jesuit Church**) and the former **University Aula** (now the Austrian Academy of Sciences).

Turning left on Essiggasse and continuing on Strobelgasse across Wollzeile now takes you into the deeply historic area behind STEPHANS-DOM. On Domgasse, where Strobelgasse eventually leads, are Mozart's house and the semi-legendary site of Vienna's oldest coffeehouse. **Blutgasse**, a medieval-looking alley, has been fully renovated and offers a series of ancient buildings with interesting inner courtyards. It leads on to Singer Str., where a left and then a right turn brings you to another intensely pleasing corner of Vienna, the FRANZISKANERPLATZ.

Narrow Ballgasse curves off Franziskanerplatz to debouch on Rauhensteingasse, where a large department store now occupies the site where Mozart died in 1791. Finish at Vienna's oldest continuously operating café, the **Frauenhuber**, at the corner of Rauhensteingasse and Himmelpfortgasse, a half block away from the crowds of Kärntner Str.

WALK 2: SOUTH OF THE RING
Allow 6-8 hours.

Start your day with the visual delight of the HUNDERTWASSER HOUSE, not neglecting to visit also the KunstHaus, which is located a few blocks away on Untere Weisgerber Str. Continue to the end of Löwengasse, turn right onto Rasumofskygasse and stay on that street when it immediately forks to the left. You will admire the palatial splendor of the **Geological Institute**, formerly Palais Rasumofsky.

Having walked to the end of Rasumofskygasse, turn right on Land-

WALK 2

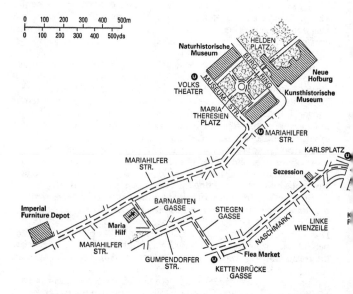

strasser Hauptstrasse and walk two blocks until you reach the covered passage of **Sünnhof**, a lovely Biedermeier period piece, on the left. The Hotel-Gasthaus inside the passage is a good place to stop for breakfast. Alternatively, emerge at the other end of Sünnhof and continue down Ungargasse to **Stadtpark**, where you can sip Viennese coffee against the **monument of Johann Strauss** on the terrace of the Kursalon.

Leave the Stadtpark on Lothringer Str., walking past the **Beethoven Monument**, to Schwarzenbergplatz. Turn left, then follow Rennweg, the left-hand of the two major avenues branching off Schwarzenbergplatz, to the lower entrance of BELVEDERE. The two palaces and three museums of Belvedere will probably take up the rest of the morning.

Emerge from the upper exit on Prinz-Eugen-Str. It may be time to consider lunch — perhaps in the beautiful (but far from inexpensive) garden of Belvedere Stöckl, or even the luxurious surroundings of HOTEL IM PALAIS SCHWARZENBERG.

Walk back down on Prinz-Eugen to Schwarzenbergplatz, observing the now so ironic Soviet Monument and the majestic portals of the French Embassy on your left. Then follow Bruckner Str. and the complicated intersection that follows it, to emerge opposite the Baroque grandeur of the KARLSKIRCHE. Karlsplatz, the square/park named after the church, offers, counterclockwise, the HISTORICAL MUSEUM OF VIENNA, the Philharmonic Hall

(Musikverein), the **Exhibition Hall** (Künstlerhaus), the Art Nouveau **tram stations** of Otto Wagner, and the gold-crowned SECESSION building.

The broad, covered-up course of the Wien stream, starting from the vicinity of the Secession, is occupied by the NASCHMARKT produce market. Here your route suddenly plunges away from Viennese grandeur into the sounds and smells of the Third World. Stroll up the market, noticing the graceful apartment houses of Linke Wienzeile on your right, until you reach the open area where the Saturday flea market is held. Then turn right into the tricky uphill-and-downhill streets that separate the depression of the Wien stream from Mariahilf.

By now it is probably too late to visit the IMPERIAL FURNITURE DEPOT at #88 Mariahilfer Str., but the right time to observe the crowds that swarm around the shops and department stores of Vienna's principal everyday shopping zone.

As evening falls, walk down Mariahilfer Str. toward Maria-Theresien-Platz and impress yourself with the illuminated facades of the museums of ART HISTORY and NATURAL HISTORY, with the monument of Maria Theresa rising in their midst. Cross the Ring to **Heldenplatz** to conclude your tour at Vienna's most magnificent open space.

WALK 3: NORTH OF THE RING
Allow 6-8 hours.

The ART HISTORY MUSEUM opens only at 10am on weekdays (9am on weekends), so early risers could use the first part of the morning for viewing the most important RINGSTRASSE monuments. Drop in for coffee at one of the quintessentially academic cafés near the UNIVERSITY. Then visit the VOTIVKIRCHE, which is quite impressive albeit a complete fake.

Walk along Reichsrats Str., one of Vienna's most elegant streets, to the RATHAUS, then across the statue-lined Rathauspark to the BURGTHEATER, and then back across the Ring to the PARLIAMENT. Don't try in one day to visit both of the great museums, the Naturhistorische (NATURAL HISTORY) and Kunsthistorische (ART HISTORY): limit your curiosity to the latter.

Afterwards, go around the **Messepalast**, observing the noble beauty of its frontage, then turn left on Burggasse and continue two blocks to the historic district of SPITTELBERG, whose two main pedestrian-only streets, Gutenberggasse and Spittelberggasse, offer a rich menu of pleasant cafés and small restaurants to choose from for a lunch break.

The afternoon itinerary will be determined by whether you wish to catch either the FREUD MUSEUM or the JOSEPHINUM, both of which close at 3pm. If you decide to miss them out, take time instead to explore the Josephstadt district.

Leave Spittelberg via Burggasse and turn left on Museum Str. (**Palais Trautson** is on your left), which turns into Auersperg Str. (**Palais Auersperg** is on your left). Veering left onto Josefstadter Str., walk up three long blocks to Lederer Str., then turn right to visit the PIARIST CHURCH, memorable for its frescoes by Maulbertsch.

Go back downtown via Laudongasse, noticing on your right — and possibly visiting — the **Austrian Folklore Museum** housed in the former Palais Schönborn. Turn left where Laudongasse ends, right on Alser Str., and left on Garnisongasse to reach Schwarzspanier Str., the scene of Beethoven's death (at house #15, no longer extant). Then continue onto Berggasse, where Freud discovered psychoanalysis (at #19) and Herzl founded the Zionist movement.

Turn left on Servitengasse for a quick look at the **Servite Church**, then continue via Grünentorgasse and Porzellangasse to the LIECHTENSTEIN GARDEN PALACE, which offers Vienna's Museum of Modern Art as well as a lovely park. Both remain open until 6pm.

Climbing the quaint turn-of-the-century stairway of Strudlhof to Währinger Str., consider your choice for the evening. You can either return to the city, a 15-minute walk down Währinger Str., or take a tram to HEILIGENSTADT (noticing the workers' fortress of KARL-MARX-HOF on the right), where you can find one of the sweetest wine taverns of Vienna in the parsonage on Pfarrplatz that was once Beethoven's home.

WALK 3

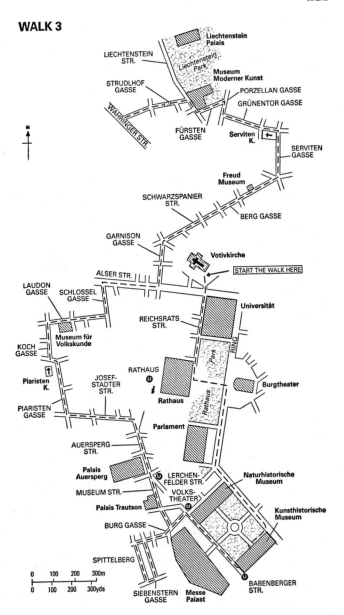

Sights and places
of interest

Introduction

In this chapter, we have divided Vienna into its three natural areas for sightseeing: the INNER CITY, the HOFBURG and the OUTER CITY. Each section has a slightly different structure, for reasons that will become clear in the following explanation.

The **Inner City** lends itself naturally to walking tours, and is memorable more for its overall wealth of historic and architectural interest than for any individual monuments. Our organization of this section therefore follows, by and large, **streets and neighborhoods** rather than specific sights. Arranged alphabetically, most of them include several subentries describing specific sights in the neighborhood.

The **Hofburg**, a vast conglomerate of imperial apartments, government offices, museums, libraries, horse stalls and public spaces, deserves to be treated as a town-within-a-town rather than a single sight. Thus it receives a section to itself, arranged alphabetically.

The **Outer City** is too large and bustling immediately to reward idle strolling, hiding its points of interest in an often unexciting spread of city streets. Its more prominent landmarks and museums are therefore listed singly in the traditional style of the *American Express Travel Guides*.

The **Vienna Woods** lie in part within the boundaries of metropolitan Vienna and in part outside them, in the land of Lower Austria. Following this — admittedly artificial — distinction, we treat the nearest of their villages as part of the OUTER CITY, while the farther villages appear under EXCURSIONS, starting on page 173.

PALACES

The history of Vienna was shaped by the imperial dynasty and the two dozen or so noble families that served it through many generations. Their palaces are the most prominent sights of the city. The **Hofburg** was the principal residence of the Habsburgs, and **Schönbrunn** their summer home; various members of the family also lived in the **Belvedere**, **Alte Favorita** (Augarten), **Neue Favorita** (Theresianum), **Neugebäude**, **Laxenburg** and **Hermes Villa**.

Aristocratic families followed the imperial example by maintaining a *Palais* in town and another in what used to be the suburban countryside but now has become part of the city; they might also have a manor house *(Schloss)* and a castle *(Burg)* in the provinces of the empire. Many of these residences have become offices of the Austrian government, and "their rooms now resound to rubber stamps rather than noble quadrilles" (Richard Bassett). Several are at least partly accessible to the public as venues for concerts and exhibitions, one is a hotel, and a few have been converted into museums.

CHURCHES

The other major formative factor in Vienna's past was the Catholic Church, which held sway with Baroque pomp from the final victory of the Counter-Reformation around the year 1620 to the end of the 18thC. All churches of the Inner City have roots going back to the Middle Ages, although many were either thoroughly refurbished or rebuilt in the Baroque fashion. The area outside the city walls was destroyed during the second Turkish siege, so with one exception — the **Servite** — all churches in district 2 and higher belong to a date later than 1683.

MUSEUMS

Of the more than 120 museums that exist in Vienna, four — the **Art History Museum**, the **Albertina**, the Austrian collections of the **Belvedere**, and the **Treasury of Hofburg** — must count among Europe's most important repositories of art.

Many other museums specialize in objects of art and beauty from the era of Austrian greatness (16th to 19thC); thus the **Hofburg** collections of armor, musical instruments and tableware, the treasury of the **Teutonic Knights**, the **Schönbrunn** carriage collection, and indeed the **Capuchin** crypt. The modern period is rather thinly represented.

PARKS

The parks of the **Belvedere** and **Schönbrunn** are masterpieces of 18thC landscaping art, and the **Augarten** nearly so. The **Prater** is closely followed in popularity by the various natural and recreational parks along the **Old Danube** and on the **Danube Island**.

The most attractive stretches of nature — of nature improved by human hand, to be precise — will be found in the **Vienna Woods**, a broad chain of hills, forests, parks and vineyards which embrace Vienna a short distance w and make it one of the greener cities of Europe.

HOW TO USE THIS SECTION

In this chapter, look for the ★ symbol against the outstanding, not-to-be-missed sights. The ☆ symbol indicates sights we consider particularly to merit a visit if you are in the neighborhood. Places of special interest for children (✸) and with outstanding views (◀≤) are also indicated. For a full explanation of symbols, see page 7.

Some lesser sights do not appear under their own headings but are included within other entries: if you cannot find them readily in the text, look them up in the INDEX.

Places mentioned without addresses and opening times are often described more fully elsewhere in this chapter. Check whether they are **cross-references**, which are in SMALL CAPITALS. If they are, they have their own heading and description.

The Inner City (Innenstadt)

The fortified Roman *campus* of Vindobona occupied a rectangular area defined today by Tiefer Graben, Naglergasse/Graben, Rotenturm Str. and the Danube Canal. The city grew under the Babenberg dukes as far as the Dominican church in the E and Michaelerplatz in the S (c.1200), and was enlarged again under King Ottokar (1250-76), who built a second line of medieval walls enclosing an area slightly smaller than the current Inner City.

The full extent of old Vienna was reached just before the first Turkish siege of 1529. The modern defensive walls built then and rebuilt before the second Turkish siege of 1683 defined the limits of the city until their demolition in 1858.

Apart from a few modern buildings occasioned by the wreckage of World War II, the architecture of the Inner City consists of a harmonious mix of 17th, 18th and 19thC structures. No building is higher than 5 or 6 stories, and the medieval spire of the **Stephansdom** presides over a uniform spread of red tile roofs and bronze cupolas — a historic small town, whose survival in the heart of the big metropolis adds considerably to its charm.

Unlike many other historic cities, the Inner City of Vienna is by no means a museum piece but remains very much the administrative, commercial and social center of the Austrian capital. The three-part "Main Street" of **Kärntner Str.**, **Graben** and **Kohlmarkt** continues to form the principal promenading, café-going and shopping axis of the city, as it has since the days of Maria Theresa. The offices of the Austrian government cling to the skirts of the Hofburg as if old Franz Joseph still sat at his desk. And the elderly dames of Viennese society still descend to "the city" to catch a whiff of the vanished imperial air.

ALBERTINAPLATZ
Map 3D3-E3. Bus 3A to Albertinaplatz.
The irregularly shaped space between the OPERA and HOFBURG forms an assembly point for Vienna's considerable fleet of horse carriages *(Fiaker)*, and is thus popular with tourists. It takes its name from Palais Albertina, the Neoclassical residence of Duke Albert of Saxe-Teschen (1738-1822), who was the husband of Marie-Christine, one of Maria Theresa's eleven daughters. The mounted statue of *another* Albert, the archduke who ordered the massacre of the revolutionaries of March 1848, looks down from a raised platform (the **Albrechtsrampe**), which once formed part of the city's bastions.

Albertina Collection ★
Albertinaplatz 1 ☎528683 ▥ Open Mon-Thurs 10am-4pm; Fri 10am-2pm; Sat-Sun 10am-1pm. Closed Sun in July and Aug.
The Albertina houses what is generally recognized as Europe's most important collection of Old Master graphics and watercolors. The full extent of the collection consists of 44,000 drawings and 1.5 million

sheets of copper-plate or wood prints, representing virtually every major artist from the 15thC to the present day. Only a small and circulating selection is exhibited in the display hall, but the rest is accessible by permission.

The core of the Albertina holdings comes from the private collection of Prince Eugene of Savoy, which was acquired in 1795 by Duke Albert and expanded by later additions. The palace was constructed in 1781. It was heavily damaged by Allied bombing in 1945 and subsequently restored.

Highlights of the Albertina are the famous prints and watercolors of Albrecht **Dürer**, of which Vienna possesses the world's most complete selection. The German Renaissance is represented further by the works of Holbein, Lucas Cranach the Elder, Altdorfer, and the 60 splendid miniatures of the anonymous *Triumph of Kaiser Maximilian I.*

From Italy comes a large selection of Raphael drawings, including the famous *Madonna with Pomegranate,* as well as works by Leonardo, Michelangelo and Tintoretto. The Dutch and Flemish section contains masterpieces by Brueghel, Rubens and van Dyck, and nearly all the extant sketches of Rembrandt. French masters include Poussin, Fragonard and Géricault as well as several modern classics. There are English watercolors by Gainsborough and Reynolds and a wealth of cartoons by Hogarth. Notable among the moderns are a series of watercolors by Egon **Schiele**, which were painted while the artist was in jail on charges of molesting a prepubescent girl.

A particularly interesting section is devoted to **architectural drawings**, among them original sketches by the Baroque architects Hildebrandt and Fischer von Erlach.

Located within the same building are two special collections of the Austrian National Library, both with public exhibits. The **Papyrus Collection** holds several brilliantly illuminated scrolls from pharaonic Egypt, as well as the world's earliest musical manuscript, a 2ndC BC text with notes of a chorus from the *Orestes* of Euripides. The **Music Collection** possesses autograph copies of some of the greatest works of European music, including Mozart's unfinished Requiem, and illuminated volumes of medieval and Renaissance musical works.

World War II Memorial (Mahnmal gegen Krieg und Faschismus)

A controversial monument by the Austrian artist Alfred Hrdlicka was placed in 1988 at the center of Albertinaplatz to commemorate "victims of war and fascism." This is the site of the tragedy of March 12, 1945, in which a British-American air raid killed or buried alive several hundred civilians in the bomb shelters of the Philipp-Hof, the Jockey Club headquarters which used to stand here. The bodies of the victims were never recovered and presumably lie under the ground.

A first group, entitled *Portals of Rage,* represents the victims of war and of Nazism, respectively, on two pillars mounted on granite blocks which were cut by inmates of the Mauthausen concentration camp; a prostrate, barely noticeable Jew offers sacrifice. A second unit commemorating the victims of Philipp-Hof shows *Orpheus Entering Hell* (or perhaps leaving it). The third piece, a rough stele, carries the text of the declaration of the provisional government which announced the rebirth of Austria on April 27, 1945.

The monument is in part a modern reinterpretation of the Plague Column on Graben, to which it makes many formal references.

Hotel Sacher
Philharmoniker Str. 4.

From its founding by Eduard Sacher in 1876 through the reign of his legendary, cigar-smoking widow Anna, Hotel Sacher was a hallowed institution of the Austro-Hungarian monarchy, a virtual adjunct of the imperial court. Its private dining rooms, the famous *separées,* formed the venue of many a royal visit and high-society tryst, including the last social dinner together of Archduke Rudolph and Countess Mary Vetsera before their joint suicide.

The famous *Sacher Torte,* the mother of all chocolate cakes, was said to have been invented by an ancestor of Eduard. A celebrated legal battle has now resolved that the two-word spelling of the cake is a trademark of the hotel, while lesser establishments can go on serving the humble *Sachertorte.* A sales outlet on Kärntner Str. sells the official product in every imaginable quantity and packaging.

ALTES RATHAUS AND VICINITY (Old City Hall)
Map 3C3. Bus 1A, 3A to Schwertgasse or Hoher Markt.

The neighborhood of Altes Rathaus corresponds to the heart of Roman Vindobona. The fortified garrison of Trajan's XIII Legion had its *forum* at HOHER MARKT, an old Vienna square now abused as a parking lot. Wipplinger Str. and Mark-Aurel Str./Tuchlauben formed the principal cross axes of the *campus,* and Emperor Marcus Aurelius died 1,800 years ago possibly within sight of the street that now bears his name.

Tiefer Graben ("Deep Ditch") was dug by the Romans as a defensive moat, and remained filled with water until the late Middle Ages: the stairs in front of the church of MARIA AM GESTADE ("Mary-by-the-Embankment") are a reminder of the time when Danube boats could sail up the channel to debark their wares below the church.

Altes Rathaus, which retains its medieval structure intact beneath a 17thC facade, was originally the home of a patrician family by the name of Scheibenböck. Built in the late 13thC, it was confiscated in 1309 following an unsuccessful burghers' conspiracy against the Habsburgs, led by a member of the family. It was then granted to the City in one of those exquisite gestures that have always been a Vienna hallmark: the city fathers — traditionally a source of resistance to arbitrary authority — would thereafter meet in the shadow of their executed leader.

When the City regained its former political status some 550 years later, it moved on to its neo-medieval castle on the Ring. The old building now houses a **Museum of the Austrian Resistance**, containing displays covering the periods 1934-38 and 1938-45 respectively.

The Baroque structure across the road from the Rathaus is the **Böh-**

mische Hofkanzlei, built by Fischer von Erlach in 1714 to house the royal administration of Bohemia (now the Constitutional and Administrative Court). It faces **Judenplatz** ("Jews' Square" ★), a calm, pleasant space containing several open-air restaurants, which during its medieval heyday in 1294-1421 formed the center of the Jewish ghetto of Vienna. The house "Zum grossen Jordan" still carries an inscription which proclaims that, as Christ was purified by his baptism in the river Jordan, so the city purified "the terrible sin of the Hebrew dogs" in a flood of fire anno 1421. A subtler symbolism is involved in the newly installed statue of Gotthold Ephraim Lessing, an assimilated Jew and one of the founders of the German Enlightenment.

Jews were invited to Vienna by the Habsburg dukes as a counterweight to the recalcitrant citizenry; but the pogrom of 1421 ended their presence in the city for more than 250 years. Jewish financiers began to play an important role in the court of Leopold I (after 1683), and the Toleration Edict of Joseph II (1781) again turned Jewish citizens into loyal subjects of the supranational Habsburg monarchy. The center of Jewish life in this later period was the district of **Leopoldstadt**.

Maria am Gestade (Mary-by-the-Embankment)

The purest specimen of Gothic church architecture in Vienna originated in the 14thC, although its purity is actually the product of later restoration. The interior contains some admirable medieval paintings, which lose only a little of their impact when one realizes that they mostly date from 1901-3. Among the few original pieces of the church are the foundations of Roman defensive walls, on which part of the N side rests.

An attractive chapel on the right contains the **tomb of Klemens Maria Hofbauer**, the patron saint of Vienna (1751-1820). He was a pastor who fought Enlightenment and "Josephinism" — the secular reforms of Joseph II — and was canonized in reward.

AM HOF

Map 3C3. Bus 1A to Heidenschuss/Am Hof.

The largest and potentially most beautiful of old Vienna's squares lies grimy and quite derelict, a parking lot for cars and tourist buses. The name ("by the court") derives from the castle of the Babenberg dukes, which once stood where the Länderbank building now flaunts its mediocrity.

One of the legendary festivities of the European Middle Ages took place at the square Am Hof on the occasion of the departure of the Third Crusade. Emperor Frederick Barbarossa, who personally led the German knights, was entertained by duke Leopold V (1177-94) to two weeks of tournaments, chivalrous deeds, minstrelry and music. The great minnesinger Walther von der Vogelweide was there, as was perhaps the demonic Tannhäuser. The gathering also provided an opportunity to massacre Vienna's Jews.

Long after the Babenberg castle was gone, the same spot was occupied by the Austrian Ministry of War. Here in October 1848 a revolutionary mob lynched Count Latour, the Minister of War, and hanged him from a lamppost outside his office.

The E side of the square is occupied by various institutions of the Jesuit order, while attractive patrician houses, with roots going back to the Middle Ages, surround it on the remaining three sides. The **Kattus house** *(#8),* dating from the 16thC, is one of Vienna's oldest; the **Märklein** *(#7)* and **Urbani houses** *(#12)* are attributed rather doubtfully to Hildebrandt. The former **City Arsenal** raises an ornate Baroque facade (1732) at the NW corner. Next door at #9 is the entrance to the underground excavations, where archeologists have revealed considerable Roman ruins.

At the center of the square, **Mary's Column** (by Martino Carlone, 1667) shows the Virgin trampling upon a snake, a dragon, a basilisk and a panther, the symbols of plague, war, hunger and heresy — four woes that often afflicted Vienna in the 17thC.

The Church am Hof (Kirche am Hof)
E side of Am Hof.

The former Jesuit church is among the most imperiously theatrical of Vienna's Baroque temples. It dates from 1607, a high point in the Jesuits' triumphant attack on the Protestant peril in Habsburg lands. Antonio Carlone's facade with its unusual balcony was added in 1667 to fit the majesty of an institution which at that time effectively held the reins of the monarchy. From this balcony in 1782 Pope Pius VI delivered his famous Easter homily, which in vain implored Joseph II and the people of Vienna to stick to the path of true Catholicism.

The interior follows the "Jesuit style," with four deep chapels to each side of the nave. A giant altarpiece (1798) occupies the oddly elongated choir, and paintings by the leading Austrian masters of the 16th-18thC fill the chapels. Notable are a fresco of the *Elevation of the Saints* by Maulbertsch (2nd chapel on the left), and a magnificent *Crucifixion* with a portrait of Leopold I by a Flemish master (3rd chapel on the left).

The Society of Jesus was founded in 1540 by St Ignatius Loyola with the task of promoting reform in the Catholic church and fighting the Protestant heresy. Its power spread in the 17thC from its triple strongholds of Rome, Madrid and Vienna, and the Jesuits were often accused of a sinister influence across Europe. The order was banished from Austria in 1773, but was permitted to return after 1814.

Vicinity
A curious detail attaches to the house at Drahtgasse 9. This was once the home of one Mr Rosenbaum, secretary to the Esterházy princes, who stole Joseph Haydn's skull a few days after the composer's internment and kept it in his study until his own death in 1829.

The narrow alley of **Schulhof** leads from one side of the Church am Hof to several back lanes of great age and character. The **Clock Museum** (Uhrenmuseum) (☆ *Schulhof 2* ▨ *open daily except Mon 9am- 12.15pm, 1-4.30pm* ☎ *5332265)* contains a fascinating collection of antique and modern timepieces, some splendid work in gold, ivory and enamel, a gigantic astronomical clock of the 18thC, and a country clock with a pendulum made of a cow's tail.

A small **chapel** at Steindlgasse 6 marks the site of the martyrdom of St Stanislaus Kostka *(open every Tues except July-Aug)*. When the saint, who was a poor Polish student of solid Catholic faith, fell mortally ill in 1567, his evil Protestant landlord refused him the comfort of a priest, whereupon St Barbara appeared in person to administer the last rites. The miracle was noted by the Jesuits, and became a *cause célèbre* in the religious conflicts that peaked around this time.

The house at Tuchlauben 19 (**▧** *open Tues-Sun 9am-12.15pm, 1-4.30pm, closed Mon)* is interesting for a series of medieval frescoes from c.1400, which were accidentally discovered in 1979 beneath many centuries of plaster and paint. The pictures depict festive scenes and apparently belong to the guild hall of the cloth merchants (Tuchhändler) who lent their name to the street.

AUGUSTINERSTRASSE
Map 3D3. Bus 3A to Michaelerplatz or Albertinaplatz.
Augustinerstrasse clings to the walls of the Hofburg between **Albertinaplatz** and **Michaelerplatz**. At its middle is the attractive space of **Josefsplatz** embracing a statue of the reforming emperor Joseph II.

Three palaces of the empire's prominent servants surround the square: **Palais Palffy**, with a Renaissance core (1575) hidden from sight by a rather drab 19thC facing; **Palais Pallavicini** (1784), distinguished for its magnificent Neoclassical portal; and **Palais Lobkowitz** (1687), which owes the design of its equally impressive portal (1711) to Fischer von Erlach. Concerts are still given in the ballroom of the Lobkowitz palace, where Beethoven's Third *("Eroica")* symphony received its first performance in 1804.

Augustinian Church (Augustinerkirche)
The Gothic church of the Augustinian Fathers was built in 1339 (the belfry was added in 1652), and served the wedding and coronation ceremonies of many members of the Habsburg dynasty. Among the more memorable occasions celebrated here were the marriage by proxy of Marie-Antoinette, a daughter of Maria Theresa, to the future Louis XVI, her companion at the guillotine (1770); the wedding of Napoleon to Marie-Louise, a daughter of Franz I of Austria (1810); and that of Franz Joseph to Elisabeth of Bavaria (1854).

A crypt off the graceful Gothic **St George's Chapel** contains in silver urns the hearts of 54 members of the Habsburg dynasty, which by family tradition were interred separately from the bodies (in the Capuchins' Crypt) and the entrails (Stephansdom).

The more memorable treasure of the church, however, is the extraordinary **Tomb of Marie-Christine** (★), a masterpiece of Classical sculpture by Antonio Canova, commemorating the wife (died 1801) of Albert of Saxe-Teschen of ALBERTINA fame. A pyramid of white marble forms the centerpiece, into whose dark vault Virtue and Charity carry the ashes of the deceased; a Lion, heraldic symbol of the duke's Saxon lineage, crouches in deep sorrow, while a Warrior averts his eyes. The perfect balance of the composition, the delicacy of the workmanship, and the noble and tranquil sadness that pervades the whole thing, combine to create a deeply moving work of art.

Dorotheum ☆
Main showroom at Dorotheergasse 17; **Kunstpalais** at Dorotheergasse 11
☎515600. Both open Mon-Fri 10am-6pm, Sat 8.30am-noon; closed Sun.
Auctions Mon-Fri 2pm, Sat 10am: special emphasis on Mon is silver; on Wed, furniture and carpets; on Thurs, jewelry ✗ in German only: apply at tourist bureau for times.

Founded in 1707 by Joseph I as a public pawnshop, the imperial institution which the Viennese know by the affectionate name of "Tante Dorothee" has grown into the largest auction house on the European continent, rivaling Christie's and Sotheby's of London. Today it still helps common people to pawn household goods, and the ancient families of Vienna to sell the heritage of empire. Four major art auctions in March, June, September and November attract investors and experts from around the world.

The main showroom, devoted to furniture and *"pretiosen"* (precious objects), occupies a Neo-Baroque palais, while paintings and sculpture are shown at a separate house (the Kunstpalais) farther along the street. The value and beauty of some of the materials on display never fail to astonish, and overall the Dorotheum impresses the visitor with the mildewed grandeur of the capital of the Habsburgs as effectively as any of its museums and palaces.

BALLHAUSPLATZ AND MINORITENPLATZ
Map 3D2. Metro U3 to Herrengasse. Bus 3A to Michaelerplatz.
Two attractive and surprisingly calm squares off the NW corner of Hofburg bracket the offices of the federal Prime Minister. A medieval church stands in their midst, surrounded by the Baroque edifices of the Austrian government.

Prime Ministry (Bundeskanzleramt)
The former **Geheime Hof- und Staatskanzlei** (Privy Court and State Chancery) was built in 1719 by Hildebrandt, and expanded to its present proportions in 1766 to the design of Pacassi. Kaunitz, the chancellor of Maria Theresa and her sons (in office 1753-92), and Metternich, chancellor from 1809 to 1848, had their offices here. The plenary sessions of the Congress of Vienna were held in this building, and World War I was hatched in its corridors at the time when it served as the Foreign Ministry of Austria-Hungary.

On July 25, 1934, a band of Nazis broke into the Prime Ministry and shot Chancellor Dollfuss in hopes of a coup d'etat. The dictator was left to bleed to death on his office couch. Four years later in the same room,

Chancellor Schuschnigg announced to the world the German ultimatum and Austria's defiance.

The **State archives** adjacent to the building *(closed to the public)* contain some of the most important documents of European history, including the original copy of Luther's *95 Theses,* whose posting on a church gate of Eisenach in 1517 inaugurated the Protestant reformation.

Minorite Church (Minoritenkirche)

The austere exterior of the church reflects the traditions of the Fratres Minores, the stricter branch of the Franciscan order, for whom the late-Gothic edifice was built between c.1300 and 1447. The pure and powerful lines of the **main portal** on the NW (c.1350) nevertheless form a worthwhile sight. The roof and steeple were shot away by a Turkish mortar in 1683, and subsequently replaced with the curious tent-like structure that covers the building today.

The sparse interior contains a mosaic copy of Leonardo's *Last Supper,* and the **tomb** of Pietro Metastasio, the poet laureate of Maria Theresa's court. The Leonardo copy was commissioned by Napoleon during his occupation of Vienna. It was intended as a replacement for the original at Milan, which the conqueror planned to remove to Paris. After his fall, the outstanding salaries of the artists were paid from the purse of Franz I, and the work was locked up in the cellars of Belvedere until its rediscovery in 1845.

Vicinity

Several of the noblest buildings of Vienna surround Minoritenplatz. **Palais Starhemberg**, built in 1650-61 as one of Vienna's earliest Baroque palaces, now houses the Ministry of Education. To its W, **Palais Dietrichstein** raises its graceful Rococo facade (1755); on the E is a Gothic chapel (1516) attached to the Landhaus (see under HERREN-GASSE). The cool and arrogant **Palais Liechtenstein** (by Martinelli, built 1695-1706) has a portal by Fischer von Erlach on Minoritenplatz, and a mightier one on Bankgasse.

The palace was built for Prince Johann Adam of Liechtenstein, a friend and ally of Prince Eugene, and founder of the first state bank of Austria. He shares with Ibn Saud the distinction of being one of two men after whom a sovereign nation has been named in modern times. Two small domains that he bought in the Alps and joined under his name were declared an independent state during the Napoleonic wars, and confirmed in his family by the Congress of Vienna. The principality of Liechtenstein, which flourishes as the home of the world's offshore banks, still owns the palace. The current prince is also called Johann Adam.

"BERMUDA TRIANGLE" ☆

Map 3C3-4C4. Tram 1,2 to Salztor Brücke. Bus 3A to Salzgries.

The triangle circumscribed by Seitenstettengasse, Judengasse and Salz-gries, one of the oldest parts of the Inner City, was rescued from its dilapidated state in the 1980s and converted into an area of trendy cafés and night spots favored by the young and fashionable. Three establishments formed the anchor of the revival: **krah krah**, a mix of old-fashioned beer cellar and student pub, **Rote Engel**, a "wine and song bar" in fancy architecture, and **Kaktus Bar**, the classic new-German *in-treff* (fashionable pub), with occasional live jazz. Nearly twenty others have opened since.

Art galleries followed the lead of Elisabeth Schaumberger's **Neue Galerie**, a pioneer of Vienna's artistic avant-garde. A lovely strawberry-and-cream palais was recently renovated as the MERCURE hotel (see WHERE TO STAY), and the former **Salzamt** (Salt Authority) was remodeled by the prominent architect Hermann Czech into a cultural center and meeting point for Vienna's smart people.

An inconspicuous facade on Seitenstettengasse hides the leading 19thC **synagogue** of Vienna, the only one of 42 to survive the Holocaust. The temple was built in 1826 by the prominent Neoclassical architect Josef Kornhäusl in keeping with a law that required all synagogues to be hidden from street view.

Ruprechtskirche

The modest church of St Rupert is Vienna's oldest. The Romanesque structure that survives today was first recorded in 1137, and probably goes back to the previous century. Its interior, decorated in the 15thC, was funded by the salt merchants' guild, whose members inhabited this neighborhood. The area fell upon hard times in later centuries, and the church was on the verge of collapse when a restoration saved it in the 1930s.

St Rupert, the first bishop of Salzburg, was a student of the Irish missionaries who converted many German tribes to Christianity in the 8thC, and was possibly Irish himself. According to tradition, his disciples founded a church in 740 where Ruprechtskirche now stands, the first Christian place of worship in what was then the territory of the pagan Avars.

A **memorial** in Morzinplatz, a vacant lot below Rupert's church, identifies the site of the former Hotel Metropol, the Gestapo headquarters in 1938-45.

CATHEDRAL   See STEPHANSDOM.

DANUBE CANAL (Donaukanal)
Map 3A3-4D6. Metro U2 to Schottenring, U4 to Schottenring, Schwedenplatz, U1 to Schwedenplatz. Tram 1, 2.
Roman and medieval Vienna stood directly on the bank of the Danube and waxed strong on the control of this important trade and strategic route. To stop the flooding of the city, the main channel of the river was diverted in 1598, and the former riverbed was turned into a regulated side-arm, which now goes by the name of the Danube Canal.

The main channel was again shifted from its irregular course (Alte Donau) to its current bed in 1868-76. A parallel overflow channel (Neue Donau) was dredged in recent years. The Danube is thus split into four branches at Vienna.

Few other historic cities of Europe have so neglected their riverbank as Vienna. The Inner City embankment of the Canal is occupied by a chaotic multilane thoroughfare called **Franz-Josefs-Kai**, and generally fails to excite the imagination despite a few moderately good-looking buildings on the opposite bank. More recently, a lively craft bazaar has started to bring some color every weekend to the Canal promenade between Schottenring and Schwedenplatz.

Schwedenbrücke, one of the four bridges connecting the Inner City and Leopoldstadt, commemorates the Swedish attack of 1645 during the Thirty Years' War. Thorstensson's troops had devastated Germany and Bohemia, but they withdrew from Vienna after camping several days across the channel.

FRANZISKANERPLATZ ★
Map 4D4.
The intimate little square forms a picturesque corner of old Vienna with its church and varied collection of historic houses. The **Moses Fountain** at the center dates from 1798, and shows the prophet striking a fountain from the rock of Sinai. The delightful **Kleines Café** at #2, created recently as a token of Vienna's renewed interest in pleasing architecture, adds considerably to the coziness of the place.

The **Franciscan Church** and **Abbey** were built in the early years of the 17thC in a style that combines elements of the Gothic and German Renaissance, two architectural idioms that had long fallen out of fashion by that time. Inside, an altar by Andrea Pozzo (1707) and a beautiful Baroque organ of 1642 evoke admiration.

A passage through the house at #5 gives access to **Ballgasse**, a small lane with an unspoiled 18thC appearance. Ballgasse 8 has been the guild hall of Viennese carpenters continuously since 1772. Around the block at Rauhensteingasse 8 is the **Steffel Department Store**, which honors the spot where Wolfgang Amadeus Mozart worked feverishly on the final bars of his *Requiem* and expired on December 5, 1791 with a small memorial gracing its bicycle-and-sneaker department on the 5th floor.

FREYUNG   See HERRENGASSE.

GRABEN ★
Map 3D3. Metro U1, U3 to Stephansplatz. Bus 1A, 2A, 3A to Petersplatz.
Half street and half square, the broad, gracefully proportioned space of Graben has been the main evening promenade and most elegant address of Vienna since the 18thC.

The name Graben ("ditch") derives from the moat that once existed outside the old Roman walls. This was filled up c.1225 by orders of Duke Leopold VI, and served for centuries as Vienna's grocery and vegetable market. Aristocratic homes and the notorious *Glückshäfen* — silver and tableware shops, which also served as gambling houses — moved in around 1700. In Maria Theresa's reign, the ladies of the capital's *demimonde* began to be known as "Graben nymphs." The first *Rentenpalais* of Vienna, palatial buildings subdivided into rental apartments, appeared on Graben in the 1720s.

A majority of Graben's buildings date from the late 19thC or the turn of the 20th. An exception is **Palais Bartolotti-Partenfeld** *(#11),* which was built in 1720 as Vienna's first Baroque apartment building. The ornate **Grabenhof** complex at #14-15 is, surprisingly, a work (1876) of Otto Wagner, who afterwards became one of the founding fathers of 20thC architecture; the **Ankerhaus** at #10 represents the mature style of the same architect. The **Knize** tailor shop was decorated by Adolf Loos, Wagner's colleague in the Secessionist movement, while the underground **public toilet** (★) was built in the 1980s as a modern tribute to the Secession.

Graben's shops are expensive and highbrow, those nearest to KOHLMARKT most of all. The **Augarten Porcelain** outlet has its roots in the imperial workshops established in 1704, and the **Albin Denk** glassware and silver store traces them to the first *Glückshäfen* opened in 1702.

But their windows somehow seem stuck in the wooden esthetics of the 1970s; the fashion stores lack the verve of a Milan or London, or even the spotless prosperity of the German cities, and the visitor is left with that faint taste of mustiness and neglect that seems to pervade everything in the old capital of the Habsburgs.

The Plague Column (Pestsäule) ★

At the center of Graben stands the most extravagant monument of the Viennese Baroque, the memorial column which Leopold I erected in fulfillment of a vow he had made during the plague epidemic of 1679. The overall conception of the work belonged to Fischer von Erlach, who also fashioned the base with its convoluted symbolism of the Holy Trinity, while Lodovico Burnacini created the fantastic pillar of cloud in which scores of cherubs frolic in the most improbable poses. Leopold is shown praying at the foot of the column to scenes which refer to virtually every facet of Christian iconology, interweaving them with the arcane symbols of the Habsburg monarchy.

Two monumental **fountains**, dedicated respectively to St Joseph (the husband of Mary) and St Leopold (Duke Leopold III of Babenberg), were placed in 1804 on either side of the Plague Column.

Peterskirche ★

A short alley separates Graben from Petersplatz, whose center is occupied by the largest Baroque church of the Inner City. The domed church of St Peter was designed in 1702 by Gabriele Montani in the purest Roman style, and finished 30 years later by the hand of Hildebrandt. The interior, with its bold oval structure and rich gold-ocher stucco work, is among the most impressive in Vienna. A splendid group of sculptures in the high altar (Lorenzo Mattielli, 1729) depict St John of Nepomuk being thrown into the Moldau.

HERRENGASSE
Map 3C2-D3. Metro U3 to Herrengasse. Bus 1A to Teinfalt Str., 3A to Michaelerplatz.

Herrengasse ("Lords' Lane") and its immediate vicinity are filled with the aristocratic homes that once furnished virtually all the highest officials of the Habsburg monarchy: no other street in Europe has ever had a comparable ratio of titled nobility per square foot. Descendants of the same families still own several of the palaces, while others return to the homes of their ancestors as high officials of the republic.

The palaces span architectural history from the late 17thC to the turn of the 20thC. **Palais Wilczek** at Herrengasse 5 was the home of Count Hans Wilczek, leader of the famous Austrian North Pole expedition of 1899 (he failed to reach his goal, but discovered a previously unknown archipelago, which he named Franz-Joseph Land.) **Palais Mollard-Clary** (1760) houses the **Museum of Lower Austria** (Niederösterreichisches Landesmuseum), which possesses a considerable painting gallery (🖼 *open Tues-Fri 9am-5pm, Sat 9am-2pm, Sun 9am-noon, closed Mon).* Next along is the **Landhaus**, the seat of the duchy (now *land*) of Lower Austria since the 16thC. Beneath its Classical exterior (1837-48) the building retains many Renaissance and Baroque elements, including a series of magnificent assembly halls, which can be visited by prior arrangement (☎ *635711).*

Two imposing Baroque palaces face each other where Herrengasse widens to form the Freyung: seen as a pair, **Palais Harrach**, built before 1700 by Domenico Martinelli, and **Palais Kinsky**, a masterpiece of Lukas von Hildebrandt (1713-16), permit an interesting comparison of the majestic "Italian" school and the softer, more playful "Austrian" manner.

Palais Ferstel (★), on Herrengasse and Freyung, is not a palace at all but a 19thC bank and shopping complex built in the style of a Venetian *palazzo* by Heinrich Ferstel, one of the leading names of the historicist school. Within its arcade is **Café Central**, which served as the headquarters of literary Vienna from the 1890s to the 1930s. It has recently been revived in its original decor, complete with a life-sized model of the essayist Peter Altenberg occupying the table where he spent effectively his entire life.

Lev Davidovich Bronstein, alias Leon Trotsky, was a habitué of the Central during his Vienna exile. When warned of the danger of a revolution in Russia shortly before 1917, von Berchtold, the foreign minister of Austria-Hungary, is said to have guffawed, "And who will make that revolution? Herr Bronstein of the Café Central?"

Vicinity
Bankgasse, off the w side of Herrengasse, is lined wholly with palaces (see also under BALLHAUSPLATZ). A particularly attractive example is the

INNER CITY / HERRENGASSE

Hungarian Embassy *(#6)*, which occupies the former **Palais Windischgrätz** — the home, ironically, of the Austrian general who drowned the Hungarian revolt of 1848 in blood and fire.

One block farther N and also to the left of Herrengasse, **Teinfalt Str.** separates the palace district from the area of the former city ramparts, a quiet neighborhood favored by academics from the nearby UNIVERSITY (see page 91). The **Dreimäderl house** at Schreyvogelgasse 10 (turn right off Teinfalt Str.) is a delightful piece of Biedermeier architecture (1803), named after the three sisters whom Franz Schubert is said to have courted simultaneously and successively.

A small **Beethoven museum** can be visited next door at Mölker Bastei 8, an apartment building of the 1790s where the composer lived on several occasions, and where he composed his Fourth, Fifth and Seventh symphonies (**☎** *open daily except on Mon 10am-12.15pm, 1-4.30pm).*

Café Landtmann, a Vienna landmark located on the Ring below Mölker Bastei, counted Dr Sigmund Freud among its regular customers. Unlike many others, Landtmann has been continuously in business since the turn of the century.

Schottenstift
On the N side of Freyung.

The dominant institution of the NW corner of old Vienna obtains its name — "Scottish abbey" — from the *Irish* monks (sic) who were invited to Vienna in 1161 by Duke Heinrich Jasomirgott to civilize the still imperfectly Christian inhabitants of his new capital. Benedictine fathers have since then maintained here an abbey and a famous **school**, whose pupils have included Johann Strauss Sr, the father of the waltz, Viktor Adler, the founder of Austrian socialism, and Karl I, the last kaiser.

The abbey **gallery** contains a 15thC altarpiece and a small selection of Old Master paintings *(visits by permission only).*

The abbey church of the Scots, the **Schottenkirche**, whose exterior on Freyung is one of the more attractive sights of Vienna, dates in its present form from 1634-48. The impressive **Starhemberg Memorial** by Fischer von Erlach makes a visit to the interior worthwhile. Starhemberg himself is buried in the crypt, along with Duke Heinrich, the man who first made Vienna into an important center.

Count Rüdiger von Starhemberg commanded the 16,000 defenders of Vienna during the 2 months in which a Turkish army under Grand Vezir Kara Mustafa, estimated liberally at 150,000 or 200,000, besieged the city. Just when the situation seemed hopeless, a combined Christian force under the Polish king Jan Sobieski appeared over the hill of Kahlenberg with banners unfurled, and a joint attack on September 3, 1683, scattered the Turkish camp.

Rüdiger, the seventh Prince of Starhemberg, was the leader of the fascist militia of the *Heimwehr* and interior minister of the Dollfuss dictatorship in the 1930s. Later he joined the anti-Nazi resistance, and fought in Africa with de Gaulle's Free French forces.

HOHER MARKT   See ALTES RATHAUS.

JUDENPLATZ   See ALTES RATHAUS.

KÄRNTNER STRASSE ☆
Map 3E3-D3. Metro U1 to Opera, Stephansplatz. Bus 3A to Kärntner Str.
Named after the great road that once led from here to the southern county of Carinthia (Kärnten), the High Road of Vienna bustles with chic and pseudo-chic shops, opulent old hotels, outdoor cafés and fast-food franchises, peddlers of suspicious watches, Bolivian folk singers, disdainful old dames and hordes of camera-toting tourists.

Starting out from the OPERA and walking toward **Stephansplatz**, you will note the **Hotel Bristol**, which along with the Sacher and Imperial formed Vienna's elegant trio in the *belle époque* of the turn of the century; the former **Palais Esterházy**, now a gambling casino; and the small **Church of the Maltese Knights** (Malteserkirche, 14thC), with its Neo-classical facade of 1808.

Annagasse leads to the attractive **Church of St Anne** (Annakirche, 1714), with a beautiful ceiling fresco by Daniel Gran. On Himmelpfort-gasse is the imposing **Winter Palace of Prince Eugene** (☆), on which the two masters of the Viennese Baroque, Hildebrandt and Fischer von Erlach, collaborated from 1697 to 1724. The building houses Austria's Ministry of Finance; its spectacular stairwell and some of its halls, with gilded and painted ceilings, can be toured by application (☎ *523511).*

In a glassed-in niche at the corner of Kärntner Str. with Graben is the **Stock-im-Eisen**, a wooden stump with an iron band and an "unpickable" lock. A legend first recorded in 1533 attributes the lock to a locksmith's apprentice who built it after making a pact with the devil. For many centuries, every Viennese locksmith would hammer a nail into the trunk on his passage from apprentice to journeyman to signify his disapproval of devilish practices.

KOHLMARKT ☆
Map 3D3. Bus 1A to Michaelerplatz or Bognergasse, 2A to Michaelerplatz.
The best and most elegant shops of Vienna crowd the narrow pedestrian lane of Kohlmarkt ("Coal Market"), cultivating the custom of the Viennese aristocracy and high echelons of government. The epitome of it is no doubt the **Demel** confectionery, where waiters continue to address guests in noble forms of speech long disappeared from the German vernacular.

The stationers **Huber & Lehrer** print (and display) the visiting cards of "Le prince de Starhemberg," letterheads for Graf und Gräfin Kinsky, and wedding invitations for Archduke Joseph Arpád von Österreich, resident in Estoril, Portugal. The art and music publishers **Artaria**, although taken over since 1935 by the publishing house Freytag & Berndt, still occupy the offices which Haydn, Mozart and Beethoven visited to read galley proofs of their works. **Parfümerie Douglas** maintains its Jugendstil interior designed by Adolf Loos. Many shops bear a discreet sign identifying them as *ehemaliger k.u.k. Hoflieferant,* former suppliers to the imperial and royal court of Austria-Hungary.

MARIA AM GESTADE   See ALTES RATHAUS.

MICHAELERPLATZ
Map 3D3. Metro U3 to Herrengasse. Bus 1A, 2A to Michaelerplatz.
An open **excavation** has occupied the center of Michaelerplatz for some years, baring up several layers of Vienna's past in fascinating conjunction: the ground floors of the villas of Roman civilians who lived outside the garrison of Vindobona; parts of a garden palace of the 16thC; and the foundations of the old Burgtheater, symbol and epitome of Maria Theresa's court, which used to stand here until it was torn down in 1888 to make way for the elaborate **portals** of the new Michael's Wing of the Hofburg.

The **Church of St Michael** (Michaelerkirche), built probably under King Ottokar around 1275, is one of the oldest churches of the city, although its original Romanesque core lies hidden under Gothic, Baroque and Classical additions. Its tremendous **altar** (★), depicting the fall of Lucifer, is Vienna's last (1781) and perhaps most impressive piece of Baroque sculpture.

The **Loos Haus**, designed in 1910 by Adolf Loos as a deliberate insult to the Viennese love of ornament, is considered one of the pioneering works of modern architecture; Franz Joseph, whose office faced Michaelerplatz, regarded the "house without eyebrows" as an abomination.

The old emperor also found reason to dislike **Café Griensteidl**, the birthplace of the intellectual and artistic counterculture of the 1890s. Having been demolished in 1896, the house was recently revived at the same address for the benefit of tourists.

MINORITENPLATZ   See BALLHAUSPLATZ AND MINORITENPLATZ.

NEUER MARKT (New Market)
Map 3D3. Bus 3A to Plankengasse.
This hectic square off Kärntner Str. is distinguished by the magnificent **Donner Fountain** (★), a monument executed by the Baroque master Georg Rafael Donner (1739). The statue of Providentia represents the city of Vienna surrounded by the rivers Enns, Ybbs, Traun and March. The bold nudity of the figures so scandalized Maria Theresa that the fountain had to be mothballed until Franz II agreed to reinstate it in 1801.

The composer Antonio Salieri lived at Göttweihergasse 1, off the N end of the square. Contrary to legend, he did not poison Mozart, with whom he maintained a respectable professional relationship. At #9 on the same street, Schubert composed his Eighth (Unfinished) Symphony.

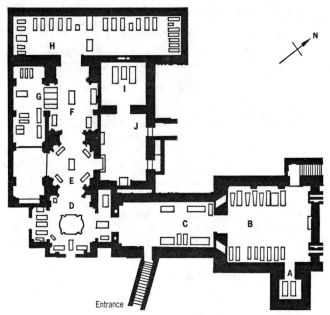

IMPERIAL CRYPT: KEY **A** Founder's crypt, 1632 **B** Leopoldine crypt, 1657 **C** Karl's crypt, 1720 **D** Maria-Theresa crypt, 1753 **E** Franz crypt, 1824 **F** Ferdinand crypt, 1842 **G** Toscana crypt, 1842 **H** New crypt, 1960 **I** Franz Joseph crypt, 1909 **J** Chapel

Imperial Crypt (Kaisergruft) ★

The sober **Capuchin Church** (Kapuzinerkirche, 1622-33) houses in its crypt *(separate entrance next door)* the bodies of 138 members of the Habsburg dynasty, including those of 12 emperors and 15 empresses. Their metal caskets sum up the political and artistic history of the Habsburg monarchy, and their combined presence, with its strange and morbid glorification of death, forms one of the more memorable images of the old Habsburg capital.

The oldest coffins belong to Emperor Matthias (died 1618) and his wife. The increasingly elaborate sarcophagi of the Baroque emperors Leopold I (1705), Joseph I (1711) and Karl VI (1740) culminate, at the borderline between genius and absurdity, with the cherub-and-trumpet infested double-bed of Maria Theresa and her consort Franz I. A stark metal coffin reflects the Enlightenment rationalism of their son Joseph II (1790), while his 19thC successors return to elaborate forms with a certain self-conscious hesitation. The newest casket holds the body of Empress Zita, the widow of Karl I, whose death in 1989 occasioned the first fully fledged public display of Habsburg nostalgia in Vienna since the founding of the republic.

Franz Joseph was the last kaiser for whom the ancient Habsburg burial rites were enacted in full. A chamberlain knocked on the gate of Stephansdom, announcing His Majesty Franz Joseph I...

...by Grace of God Emperor of Austria, King of Hungary and Bohemia, of Illyria, Croatia, Slavonia, Galicia, Lodomeria and Illyria; King of Jerusalem, etc.; Archduke of Austria; Grandduke of Toscana and Cracow; Duke of Lorraine, Salzburg, Styria, Carinthia, Carniola and Bukovina; Grand Prince of Transylvania; Margrave of Moravia; Duke of Upper and Lower Silesia, Modena, Parma, Piacenza and Guastalla, of Auschwitz and Zator, of Teschen, Friuli, Ragusa and Zara; Count of Habsburg and Tyrol, of Kyburg, Görz and Gradisca; Prince of Trient and Brixen; Marquis of Upper and Lower Lausitz and in Istria; Count of Hohenembs, Feldkirch, Bregenz; Lord of Trieste, of Cattaro, and over the Wendish Mark; Grand Voivode of the Voivodeship of Serbia etc. etc....

A priest responded, "We know him not." The chamberlain knocked again, this time for "His Majesty Franz Joseph I." Once more the priest answered, "We know him not." Finally, entry was begged for "Franz Joseph, a poor sinner," and the church opened its gates to admit the body.

POSTSPARKASSE (Postal Savings Bank)
Dominikaner Bastei/Dr-Karl-Lueger-Platz. Map 4C4-D4. Metro U3 to Stubentor. Tram 1, 2, N to Julius-Raab-Platz.
The headquarters of the Postal Savings Bank, a work of Otto Wagner (1906), is generally considered the greatest masterpiece of the Secessionist movement, indeed of modern architecture, in Vienna. To the untrained eye it looks as exciting as any post office building in the world. The aluminum nails garnishing its surface possess historic significance as the first recorded use of this metal in a construction.

SCHÖNLATERNGASSE ★
Map 4D4.
"Fair Lantern Alley," along with the old university district adjoining it, forms one of the most pleasant corners of old Vienna. The houses along the narrow lane date from various periods, but all seem to be based on earlier medieval structures: thus, among others, the **Heiligenkreuzer Hof**, a residential property owned since the 13thC by the abbey of Heiligenkreuz near Vienna, with its attractive courtyard and hidden Baroque chapel. Small art galleries and a historic smithy, now converted into an art and lecture center (**Alte Schmiede**), complete the "old world" charm of the area.

The **Basilisk House** at #7 owes its name to a famous Vienna legend. The story goes that in the days of Duke Leopold the Glorious (1198-1230), a basilisk leapt out of a hen and hid itself in the fountain that used to be under this house. Countless people who drank from the fountain died or were sickened by its poison. A solution was finally found after many years: a mirror was held to the grotesque creature, who was so overcome with despair that it turned to stone and died. The petrified monster can be seen incorporated in the house wall, which was rebuilt in the 17thC.

OLD UNIVERSITY
✗ in German only, each Wed at 10.30am at Lugeck, under the Gutenberg Monument.
The university of Vienna was founded by Duke Rudolph the Founder in 1365, to form the second university in the German-speaking lands after that of Prague. In 1623 it was placed under the control of the Jesuits. In 1753 a reformed university was inaugurated by Maria Theresa, along with the French-Rococo **Lecture Hall** (Aula) on Ignaz-Seipel-Platz, which now houses the Austrian Academy of Sciences.

On March 13, 1848, a group of university students demonstrated outside the Aula against the autocratic regime of Metternich. Within days the aged chancellor was forced to escape the city hidden in a laundry cart, and incidents grew into a massive revolution. For 7 months, revolutionaries held the city effectively in their control. In October, the troops of Felix von Schwarzenberg besieged the capital and opened artillery fire across the Glacis; 2,000 people lost their life in the fighting, and countless others were executed after the capture of the city. In November, the feeble Ferdinand I was deposed in favor of the 18-year-old Franz Joseph.

The **Jesuit Church** (Jesuitenkirche) — formerly University Church — facing the Aula was built in 1627 and redecorated by Andrea Pozzo in 1705. The interior combines Jesuit themes (Sts Francis Xavier, Ignatius Loyola, Aloysius) and academic allegories (Philosophy and Theology).

Monsignor Ignaz Seipel, a Jesuit and a person of fanatical convictions, was prime minister of Austria in 1921-29. An attempt was made on his life in 1924 in the square that now bears his name.

Vicinity
On Postgasse, behind the massive bulk of the former Jesuit abbey, is the small 17thC **Church of St Barbara** (Barbarkirche), and the **Dominican Church** (Dominikanerkirche), built in 1632 and considered to be one of the finest early Baroque churches of Vienna. 346 angels made of stucco flutter around its soaring mock-Gothic vaults, and its superb Baroque organ is often used for recitals.

SCHOTTENSTIFT   See HERRENGASSE.

STEPHANSDOM (St Stephen's Cathedral) ★
✗ every Mon at 2pm, at Riesentor.
The great Gothic cathedral of St Stephen, one of Europe's most important medieval churches, marks the geographical center of Vienna. Its spire (see the illustration on page 42) has dominated the city's skyline since the 14thC.

History

A first church of St Stephen was consecrated in 1147 over the site of a pagan shrine that lay outside the city walls. It stood under the authority of the bishops of the Bavarian city of Passau to whom Vienna was then subject in ecclesiastical matters, and was dedicated to the first Christian martyr, the patron saint of Passau. Destroyed by a fire in 1258, the church was rebuilt gradually over the next three centuries.

The massive **main portal** *(Riesentor)* and two Romanesque **towers** flanking it *(Heidentürme)* date from the first phase of reconstruction in the reign of King Ottokar (c.1263). The Gothic **body** belongs to Rudolph the Founder, who took over the project from the Passau bishops and relaunched it on a more ambitious scale in 1359. The **s steeple**, a masterpiece of the Gothic, was begun under Rudolph but only finished in 1433; its N counterpart was never completed, and was finally abandoned with the addition of an octagonal cap in 1579.

The cathedral was hit in the Allied air raid of March 12, 1945, and severely damaged during the battles that accompanied the Soviet occupation the following month. Repairs were completed in 1962.

Exterior

The Riesentor is decorated with sculptures dating from the 13thC, and reliefs and epitaphs from all ages encrust the outer surface of the church. Their full history is detailed in various publications that are on sale inside. Of some interest is the figure **05** carved near the main portal: this became a secret symbol of the Austrian resistance to the Nazis during the German annexation, as the number 5 was taken to stand for E, the fifth letter of the alphabet, and the combination gave the abbreviation for the forbidden word OEsterreich (Austria).

The **Tirna chapel**, to the left of the main portal, contains the tomb of Prince Eugene, as well as a crucified Christ who wears a long black beard of human hair. The beard is believed to grow with time.

The best angles from which to view the cathedral as a whole are obtained from the corner of Graben with Spiegelgasse, from the courtyard of the Archepiscopal Palace, and along Churgasse.

Spire ☆ ◁€

No fewer than 343 stairs lead to the **observation platform** of the "Steffl," the single spire of St Stephen, which at 137 meters (449 feet) forms the third-highest medieval tower of the European continent (▨ *open daily 9am-4.30pm, closed Nov 15 through Feb)*. The view extends on clear days from the Semmering Alps in the sw to the hills of Czechoslovakia in the NE. Count Starhemberg (see page 86) is said to have climbed to this platform daily during the siege of 1683 to look out for the rescue party, which failed to materialize for two excruciating months. The **bench** where he sat is shown to visitors.

The golden imperial **apple** that crowns the tower was for two centuries the coveted prize of the expansionist dreams of the Ottoman Turks, for whom it symbolized the power and pride of the hated Austrian Caesar. Equally symbol-conscious, the Viennese melted the captured Turkish cannon of 1683 to cast the **Pummerin**, the 20-ton bell of St Stephen's. This hung in the tower until 1945, when an Allied bomb hurled it down to smithereens. It was recast from fragments after the war, and placed lower down in the stump of the incomplete N tower.

The devil was responsible for the incompleteness of this N spire. Master Hans Puchsbaum was commissioned to build the tower in 1450, and for a couple of years construction went so fast that everyone knew some devilry was at work. The price that the Prince of Darkness had exacted, however, was that Puchsbaum should never utter a holy name. To be sure, his beloved Maria walked one day past the building site, the master shouted out her name, and his work was doomed instantly.

Interior

The interior of Stephansdom has been criticized for lacking stylistic integrity, but it is nevertheless an attractive space when not overwhelmed by sightseeing crowds. Two rows of piers along the nave are richly sculpted with a combination of Gothic (15th-16thC) and Baroque (18thC) statuary. Note especially the **chancel** (★ — third pier on the left), a work of lace-like intricacy by Master Anton Pilgram (c.1515), who portrayed himself admiring his own work from a half-open window below the stairs. A **Madonna** immediately next to the chancel has served since c.1320 as the protectress of housemaids falsely accused of theft. Farther on to the left one can see the image of **Zahnwehherrgott** ("Toothache Lord God!"), which brings relief to those suffering from tooth pain.

The most imposing work of art in the cathedral is undoubtedly the **Tomb of Friedrich III** (died 1496), a giant sarcophagus of red marble with the celebrated inscription AEIOU, which is believed to signify the Latin equivalent of "Austria shall inherit the earth." The same cryptic letters appear also on the beautiful **Wiener Neustadt Altar**, a work dating from the reign of the same emperor.

Catacombs

✗ of parts (but not all) of the catacombs, daily 10-11.30am and 2-4.30pm.

An entrance below the N tower leads to an extensive network of underground chambers, which contain the remains of tens of thousands of Viennese who chose to be buried in the cathedral. The practice originated in the Middle Ages and continued until prohibited by Joseph II in 1783.

The centerpiece of the catacombs is the **Dukes' Crypt**, where members of the Habsburg dynasty were interred until the founding of the **Imperial Crypt** of the Capuchins. Even after that point, the entrails (minus the hearts) of the imperial family were preserved for posterity here in the company of their ducal ancestors.

STEPHANSPLATZ

Map 3D3. Metro U1, U3 to Stephansplatz. Bus 3A to Brandstätte.

The space surrounding the cathedral suffered considerable damage in World War II, and has not fully regained the charm that is so characteristic of similar squares elsewhere in Europe. Prominent buildings include the **Archiepiscopal Palace** (1641) and adjoining **Zwettlhof** (1842), which contains a **Cathedral Museum** (Dom- und Diözesanmuseum) *(⊠ open Wed-Sat 10am-4pm; Sun 10am-1pm; closed Mon, Tues).*

The modern shopping and leisure complex of **Haas Haus**, completed in 1990, has been hailed as an epoch-making work of architecture, but it hardly soars in comparison to any decent-sized suburban mall. Its 2nd-floor café and 7th-floor restaurant are both good places to enjoy a full view of Vienna's central hub.

An underground chapel, the **Virgilkapelle**, was discovered beneath Stephansplatz during the construction of the metro in the 1970s. The 13thC structure has been glassed off inside the metro station, and is used for various exhibitions.

Behind Stephansdom

For ✗ apply at tourist bureau for details of two walking tours: "Old Houses — Silent Courtyards" and "The Blutgasse Quarter".

On Singer Str. immediately behind the cathedral is the Gothic **Church of the Teutonic Knights** (Deutschorderkirche, 1395) and the adjoining abbey (Deutschordenshaus), which houses the small but extraordinary **Treasure of the Teutonic Knights** *(✰ ⊠ open daily 10am-noon, and Tues, Wed, Fri, Sat 3-5pm),* the third-best collection of elaborate and fantastic objects in Vienna after the ART HISTORY MUSEUM and the IMPERIAL TREASURE.

The charitable and military order of the Teutonic Knights was founded during the Third Crusade (1190), and later set up its own sovereign state on the Baltic coast (1226-1561). After the fall of that state, various Habsburg rulers continued to support the Knights as an aristocratic fraternity, and several members of the dynasty served as High Master. The High Master's residence, the **Hoch- und Deutschmeisterpalais**, a grand Ringstrasse palace of 1868, faces Park Ring not far from the church.

Blutgasse (✰), an attractive old alley, was the site in 1317 of the bloody massacre of the Templar knights, whose headquarters used to stand at the site of the historic complex of **Fähnrichshof** *(#3-9).*

A sunnier occasion is commemorated on Domgasse, where Mozart spent the happiest and most creative 3 years of his life in 1784-87. The house at #5, an apartment building from the 1720s, has been renamed "Figaro House" after the opera *The Marriage of Figaro*, which Mozart composed here, and the composer's home has been converted into an impeccably re-created **Mozart Museum** (✰) *(☎ 5240722 ⊠ open Tues-Sun 10am-12.15pm, 1-4.30pm, closed Mon).*

In his less than 10 years in Vienna, Mozart moved house at least nine times. His first room was at Graben 17, not far from the home of his future wife Constanze Weber on Petersplatz. They married at a house on Wipplinger Str. (on the corner of Färbergasse), then lived in Baron Wetzlar's house at #14 on the same street, and at Judenplatz 3 where their first son was born, before moving to the prestigious Trattnerhof on the Graben (on the corner of Trattnergasse). After the Figaro House, the Mozarts moved in rapid succession to Landstrasser Hauptstr. 75, Tuchlauben 27,

Währinger Str. 26, Judenplatz 4, and finally Rauhensteingasse 8, where Wolfgang Amadeus died at the age of 36.

A plaque at Domgasse 8 identifies the site where a Pole, Franz Georg Kolschitzky, is said to have opened the first coffeehouse in Vienna, and thus in Europe, shortly after the Turkish siege of 1683. A popular Viennese legend attributes the founding of the first café to a store of coffee beans rescued by Kolschitzky from the loot of Kara Mustafa's camp. In reality, the first commercial coffeehouse of Vienna appears to have been opened several years before this date by an Armenian named Diodato (literally, "God's Gift").

The Hofburg

Map 3D2-3.

The principal residence of the Habsburg dynasty consists of more than a dozen interconnected buildings, which took their present shape over the course of 800 years. It houses the offices of the President of the Republic of Austria, several federal ministries including that of Women's Affairs, the headquarters of the UN Atomic Energy Commission, as well as public showrooms, numerous museums based on the possessions of the imperial family, the world's leading collection of Esperanto books, the National Library of Austria, the performance halls of the famous Lipizzan horses, and a chapel where the famous Vienna Choirboys sing.

A full tour of those parts of the Hofburg that are accessible to the public involves buying at least ten different tickets, and standing in the line for the Lipizzan show, which on a good day may approach the population of a small town. In addition, it is only on three days of the week (Wednesday, Thursday, Friday) that all the main attractions are simultaneously open to the public, so sightseeing is almost inevitably spread over two or more days.

Those who lack the time, or who feel oppressed by too much imperial pomposity, may prefer to limit their visit to the **Treasury**, a truly overwhelming collection of gold-and-precious-stone extravagance, and the Great Hall of the **Library**, the dream room of every book lover. The **Imperial Apartments** are indeed memorable, but not so very different from SCHÖNBRUNN, nor as impressive. And the **horses**, while admirably behaved, may not always justify the effort of getting to see them.

HISTORY
A fortified castle was built at the site of the **Swiss Court** (Schweizerhof) by the Babenberg duke Leopold VI in 1221, and withstood three attacks by the Hungarians (in 1252, 1291 and 1490) and two armed risings of the Viennese populace (in 1287 and 1462). Ferdinand I converted this oldest core of the palace to its present appearance, and added a colorful **portal** in 1552. Maximilian II built the **Stallburg**

95

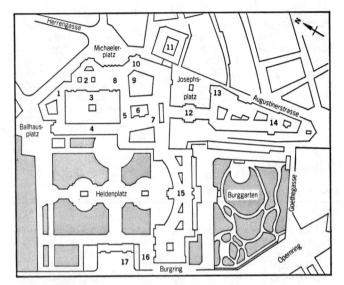

THE HOFBURG: KEY **1** Amalienburg **2** Reichskanzlei **3** Imperial Apartments **4** Leopoldinischer Trakt **5** Treasury **6** Schweizerhof **7** Chapel **8** Michaelertrakt **9** Silver and Tableware Collection **10** Winter Riding School **11** Stallburg **12** National-bibliothek **13** Augustiner Kirche **14** Albertina **15** Neue Hofburg **16** Ethnographical Museum **17** Burgtor

(1565), the most important work of Renaissance architecture in Vienna, and began a wholly new castle to the NW of the old. Perhaps to exorcise the memory of this Protestant renegade, his successors used the former as a stable for their horses, and the latter was renamed **Amalienburg** to honor a wholly unrelated lady.

Elegance and comfort replaced defense as overriding concerns in the reign of Leopold I, who gave his name to the **Leopoldine Wing** (Leopoldinischer Trakt, 1666), which joined the Swiss Court with Amalienburg. This residence of the great Baroque emperors and empresses of the 17th and 18thC now serves as the offices of the president of the republic, and is not accessible to the public. The building boom of the reign of Karl VI (1711-36) enlarged the Hofburg further with the **Chancellor's Wing** (Reichskanzleitrakt), the **Winter Riding School** (Winterreitschule) and the magnificent halls of the **Court Library**, now called the National Library.

After a century and a half with few major additions, the palace was visited in the second part of Franz Joseph's reign by the boastfulness of the Ringstrasse style. The old Burgtheater was razed in 1888 to build the dome of **Michael's Wing** (Michaeler Trakt), and a Wagnerian **New Palace** (Neue Burg) was completed on Ringstrasse in time for the 65th jubilee of the kaiser in 1913.

BURGGARTEN   See PARKS.

HELDENPLATZ ★

The vast and stately space of "Heroes' Square" was designed for the requirements of large-scale military parades, an urban tradition that began with Napoleon's Paris and may have ended with Moscow's Red Square. It is entered through the **Burgtor**, a mighty propylon in the Classical style (1824) erected by Franz I of Austria, the victor and father-in-law of Napoleon, but later refurbished as a memorial to the heroes of World War I.

Equestrian statues of the two greatest military men of Austrian history dominate the square — **Prince Eugene** (1663-1736), who laid the foundation of Austria's 18thC prosperity with his victories against the Turks and the French, and **Archduke Karl** (1771-1849), a brother of Franz I, who defeated Napoleon at Aspern on May 21-22, 1809. His brother, who started his career as Franz II of the Holy Roman Empire but was bullied by Napoleon into reducing his claims, is depicted in the garb of a Roman Caesar in an imposing monument (1846) in the courtyard behind the Leopoldine Wing.

The most famous triumph of the history of Heldenplatz, one that has made its name a by-word in Austrian politics, was celebrated in this century. On March 15, 1938, three days after the Anschluss that seemed to have ended forever the independent existence of Austria, Hitler promised here to a delirious crowd estimated at one million that he had "set the pearl of Vienna in a fitting frame."

As a provincial youth from Upper Austria, Hitler had spent six miserable years in the imperial capital before World War I, seeking employment unsuccessfully as an artist or architectural draftsman. The Heldenplatz rally was his first occasion to return to the city that blighted his youth.

HOFBURG CHAPEL

Mass with Vienna Choirboys every Sun at 9.15am.

The private chapel of the palace, entered through the Swiss Court, was built in the 13thC, rebuilt in 1449, and redesigned internally in the Baroque manner in the 18thC. It is considered to be Vienna's most prestigious venue for weddings. The chapel orchestra consists of members of the Vienna Philharmonic, and the chapel choir — the world-famous **Vienna Choirboys** — takes part in mass every Sunday.

The Court Boys' Choir was founded by Maximilian I in 1498 and maintained as a palace institution until 1918. After the fall of the monarchy the group was barely saved from disintegration, renamed Vienna Choirboys (Wiener Sängerknaben), and relocated to the former palace of Augarten. The boys are selected at the age of six on the basis of musical talent, and undergo a course of training that has been perfected over 500 years. They leave the choir when their voice changes at adolescence, but continue their secondary education at Augarten and often end up with elite careers in all areas. The staged sweetness of their concert appearances may not be to everyone's liking, but the purity and precision of their voices makes the Hofburg masses a stirring occasion indeed.

Sängerknaben jokes are among the less elegant aspects of Viennese popular culture.

IMPERIAL APARTMENTS (Kaiserappartements/Schauräume der Hofburg) ★
📷 *Open Mon-Sat 8.30am-4pm; Sun 8.30am-12.30pm.*

The section of imperial residences that is open to visitors comprises the apartments of Franz Joseph, his wife and his successor, covering one whole floor of Reichskanzleitrakt and Amalienburg. The rooms display overwhelming opulence, touched by more than a hint of age and neglect.

The **Franz Joseph apartments** consist of a train of rooms which progress from the relatively public — dining and smoking rooms of the kaiser's staff officers — to the most private. Some gobelins are the work of Flemish masters of the 17thC, and the chandelier of the Audience Hall is a masterpiece of Bohemian crystal, but the overall impression that the furnishings convey of the man who called himself "the first civil servant of the state" is the stiffness of a Victorian banker, not the exuberance of a lord of the manor.

The room where he is calculated to have received more than a million petitioners, and the desk where he ministered to the minutest details of the administration of his empire for 68 years, have been kept in their original shape. On display are the legendary iron cot in which the old soldier preferred to sleep, and the portable washstand which he kept on using long after everyone else in town had installed running water and modern facilities. His walls are filled with paintings of the battles in which his generals defeated the rebellious Hungarian, Italian and Austrian subjects of his empire in the traumatic early years of his reign, and various portraits of his wife, who abandoned him and probably detested him, but to whom he went on being attached with dogged devotion.

The **apartments of Empress Elisabeth** are much more attractive, in part because of the many pictures of the breathtakingly beautiful woman who owned — but rarely occupied — them. Among the exhibits is a lovely statue of Pauline Bonaparte, by Canova, which belonged to the empress, and memorabilia related to her assassination in 1898.

Elisabeth ("Sissi"), a princess of the Bavarian royal house, disliked the stiff formality of the Habsburg court, and spent most of her married life traveling. She often lived on the Greek island of Corfu or in various country estates near Vienna and Budapest, or stayed in hotels where she would sign herself as Countess Hohenembs. She was a supporter of Hungarian causes, and rumor supposed her to be romantically involved with the prime minister of Hungary. She was murdered by an Italian anarchist while visiting Princess Julie Rothschild in Geneva.

The **Alexander apartments** are named after the Russian czar who lived in them for nearly a year during his attendance at the Congress of Vienna (1814-15) and nearly bankrupted the Austrian exchequer in the process. They were used again by Karl I and his wife Zita during his brief imperial career in 1916-18. The "Red Hall" is decorated with French gobelins that were a gift of Marie Antoinette to her brother Joseph II.

NATIONAL LIBRARY (Österreichische Nationalbibliothek) ★
Prunksaal 🖾 *open May-Oct Mon-Sat 10am-4pm; Sun 10am-1pm; Nov-Apr Mon-Sat 10.30am-noon. Manuscript Collection open Aug Mon-Fri 9am-1pm; closed Sept 1-21; open rest of the year Tues and Thurs 1-6.45pm.*
The former court library was designed by Fischer von Erlach Sr and realized by his son in 1723-26. Its famous **Great Hall** (Prunksaal), one of Europe's most extraordinary Baroque interiors, houses the 15,000 gold-bound volumes of Prince Eugene's private library. Ceiling **frescoes** by Daniel Gran (1730) represent the apotheosis of Karl VI, the emperor who commissioned the library, while statues by Peter and Paul Strudel depict 16 of his predecessors on the Habsburg throne.

The library itself, which spreads into several buildings stretching from the Neue Burg to Albertinaplatz, contains 2 million printed volumes, 38,000 manuscripts, 224,000 maps, 500,000 portraits of famous people, a 400,000-item photographic archive, and a theater collection which boasts some 600,000 historic theater tickets (see also the ALBERTINA COLLECTION, under ALBERTINAPLATZ, pages 74-5).

The **Manuscript Collection** *(entrance right of the Prunksaal, 2nd floor)* displays some unique treasures such as the oldest illuminated Bible manuscript in existence (from Antioch, 6thC), an ancient Roman road map, and various manuscripts dating from the Renaissance, from the library of Maximilian I.

NEUE BURG ★
Ethnographical Museum 🖾 *open Mon, Thurs-Sat 10am-1pm; Wed 10am-5pm; Sun 9am-1pm; closed Tues. Other museums 🖾 open daily 10am-4pm except Tues.*
The planners of Ringstrasse proposed to rebuild the imperial palace on a scale that would put other European capitals to shame, but only a fragment of their project was approved by Franz Joseph. Construction went on from 1881 to 1913, and was finished just in time before the monarchy went out of business. Four moderately interesting museums based on former Habsburg heirlooms are now housed in Gottfried Semper and Karl Hasenauer's monumental halls. The first three are visited on a combined ticket.

The **Ephesus Museum**, centered on Classical fragments from the excavations of the Austrian Archeological Institute at Ephesus (Turkey) and Samothrace (Greece), is interesting for visitors who are familiar with these sites, but otherwise rather lean. Highlights include a monument erected to commemorate the Parthian Wars of AD161-65, and a fine bronze athlete from the Roman period.

The **Weapons Collection** contains the world's largest selection of ancient armor, including some truly magnificent pieces collected by Ferdinand I (1526-64), as well as parts of the inexhaustible Turkish booty of 1683.

The **Musical Instruments Collection** offers many beautiful and a few extraordinary instruments of various historical periods, including a memorable cister — a stringed instrument — in the shape of a cuddlesome woman, which was made for a son of the same Ferdinand.

A separate entrance leads to the **Ethnographical Museum** (Museum für Völkerkunde). This centers around three permanent displays: the art of the African kingdom of Benin, the collections of the English explorer James Cook, and Aztec treasures, including the feathered crown of Moctezuma that the conquistador Hernán Cortés sent as a gift to Karl V, the Habsburg king of Spain (brother of Ferdinand I). There are also circulating exhibits.

PARKS: BURGGARTEN AND VOLKSGARTEN

Of the two palace parks, one that came to be known as People's Garden (Volksgarten) was opened to the public in the 1820s while the other (the Burggarten) remained a private preserve of the court until 1918. The major sight in the former is a replica of Athens' Theseus Temple (Theseum), built by Peter von Nobile in 1820-23 at the height of the Europe-wide infatuation with Greek antiquities. The same architect is responsible for the **Corti Coffeehouse**, which has survived to the present day without much change. The monument of **Elisabeth**, the assassinated wife of Franz Joseph, was unveiled in 1909.

Burggarten, landscaped in the romantic "English" manner, contains the monuments of Mozart, Franz Joseph and Franz I of Lorraine, the consort of Maria Theresa. The **Mozart Monument** (1896) represents the composer as a sweetened cherub in the manner of the 19thC; one of the more popular tourist sights of Vienna, it affords good photographs against the rich green backdrop of the park. The modest, pigeon-encrusted monument of **Franz Joseph** was inaugurated in 1957 as an historic act of detente with Austria's past: there had been no statues of the kaiser in his lifetime, and under the republic, both the left and the Nazi right regarded him as a villain.

SILVER AND TABLEWARE COLLECTION (Hoftafel- und Silberkammer) ★
▓ *Open Tues-Fri, Sun 9am-1pm. Closed Mon, Sat.*
The gala and everyday tableware of the imperial household are displayed in six rooms of the Michaeler Trakt. Displays include splendid pieces of Oriental and Sèvres porcelain, "panorama plates" decorated with Austrian landscapes, and a Vermeil set of gold-plated silver for 140 persons.

Habsburg table etiquette was a science unto itself, which Vienna's elegant restaurants still aspire to follow with varying degrees of rigor. Among its peculiarities was the "Spanish" tradition of placing all silver on the left, and a special technique of folding napkins that was kept as a court secret.

SPANISH RIDING SCHOOL   See WINTER RIDING SCHOOL.

STALLBURG (Neue Galerie)
▓ *Open Sat-Mon, Wed-Thurs 10am-4pm. Closed Tues, Fri.*
The formerly graceful and now forlorn Renaissance quadrangle known as Stallburg (loosely translated, "Horse Palace") was built for the residence of Maximilian II in 1558-65, but used as a stable through

most of its career. Converted into a painting gallery in the reign of Maria Theresa, it now combines both functions: the stables of the Lipizzan horses of the SPANISH RIDING SCHOOL occupy the lower floor, while the modern classics collection of the ART HISTORY MUSEUM are displayed on the upper floors. The latter contains several mildly interesting pieces by French and German romantics of the 19thC, as well as some works of Manet, Monet, Renoir, Degas, van Gogh, Cézanne, Rodin and Munch.

TREASURY (Weltliche und Geistliche Schatzkammer) ★
☎5337931 🚇 Open Apr-Oct Mon, Wed-Fri 10am-6pm, Sat-Sun 9am-6pm, closed Tues; Nov-Mar Mon, Wed-Fri 10am-4pm, Sat-Sun 9am-4pm, closed Tues ✗ (apply at tourist bureau for hours).

The "secular and spiritual" treasures of the Habsburgs are stored in 21 rooms in the vaults of the Swiss Court, recently reopened to the public after several years of repairs. They form a most remarkable collection of ceremonial objects, symbols of empire, unicorns, saints' bones, and emeralds and opals the size of bricks.

The "secular" treasure is organized around the symbols and paraphernalia of various monarchical titles that the Habsburgs held. By far the most important of these are the **regalia of the Holy Roman Empire** (Reichsinsignien and Reichsreliquien, rooms 9-12), which for nearly 900 years conferred on whoever possessed them the right to claim the heritage of the Roman Empire and a dominion extending over half the continent of Europe. Highlights are the **Imperial Crown (★)**, a heavy, primitive diadem that was originally made for the coronation of Otto the Great in 962; the Sword of Empire, which is said to have belonged to Charlemagne; the Imperial Apple and scepter; the Mantle of Empire that Roger of Sicily obtained as booty from the Arabs in the 12thC; and the Seven Holy Relics, which include a tooth of John the Baptist and a piece from the crib of Jesus.

Also displayed here (room 9) is the magnificent **coronation robe of Bohemia**. As Kings of Bohemia, one of the seven historic Electors of the Holy Roman Empire, the Habsburgs were entitled to one vote in the imperial election. The elections took place in Frankfurt, while the regalia were traditionally kept in the imperial treasury at Nürnberg. Left — illegally — in Habsburg possession after the abolition of the reich in 1806, they were brought back to Nürnberg by the Nazis after 1938, but returned to Austria by the US Congress in 1945.

The reich was an elective office which the Habsburgs held in trust; other symbols belonged to the family itself or to various crowns it held by hereditary right. Room 1 contains insignia of the Austrian Archduchy, the ancient core of the Habsburg patrimony. Rooms 2-3 exhibit the paraphernalia of the hereditary Austrian Empire which was created in 1804, including a magnificent **crown** that was originally fashioned for Rudolph II in 1602. Another **crown** of stupendous worth and barbaric splendor (room 7) was presented by the Ottoman Sultan in 1605 to the rebel Hungarian king István Bocskai, but inherited by the Habsburgs when they conquered Hungary.

A separate section (rooms 13-16) exhibits the inheritance of the Duchy of Burgundy, including the exquisite **Treasury of the Order of the Golden Fleece**, a knightly fraternity created by Duke Philip the Good in 1429 and passed to the Habsburgs in 1477.

In room 5 are memorabilia of the son of Napoleon, among them an over-rich **crib** made by Milanese artists. Napoleon II was proclaimed King of Rome at his birth, and was believed to be destined to unite under his rule the two formerly rival empires of Europe, France and Austria. He lived instead to become a consumptive youth, renamed Duke of Reichstadt and semi-imprisoned with his mother Marie Louise at Schönbrunn palace. He died in 1832 at the age of 21.

Room 8 possesses two unusual items which constitute the so-called inalienable heirlooms of the House of Habsburg: an extraordinary **bowl** of agate that was believed to be the Holy Grail that held the spilled blood of Christ (in fact a work of Constantinople from the 4thC), and a **unicorn's horn** of great beauty, which formerly constituted the chief proof of the existence of this fabulous animal.

The "spiritual treasures" (rooms I-V) comprise Europe's second largest amassment — next to Rome — of holy relics, housed in reliquaries of incalculable value and most extraordinary workmanship. The documentation is laconic, making it impossible to know who all the scores of saints are who are represented in their various bits and pieces; but they certainly include each of the twelve Apostles and St Paul, all the Jesuit greats, St Francis of Assisi and St Theresa of Avila. A graceful sudarium features a drop of St Veronica's milk. The Savior is present with a drop of His blood, as well as numerous thorns from the crown of thorns, the holy lance that pierced His side, the nail that transfixed His right hand, and a piece of the Holy Cross itself that miraculously failed to burn in the Hofburg fire of 1668 — all embedded in enough gold and silver to balance the payments of a small state.

VOLKSGARTEN   See PARKS.

WINTER RIDING SCHOOL (Winterreitschule) ★
*Performances Mar-June, Sept-Dec Sun 10.45am; Sept-Oct Wed 7pm. **Short program** Mar-June, Sept-Dec Sat 9am. **For tickets** write at least 3mths in advance to Spanische Reitschule, 1010-Wien, Josefsplatz 1. Prices AS135-600. Tickets (▨) for morning exercise available Mar-June, Sept to mid-Dec Tues-Sat 10am-noon (☎5339031-0).*

The pirouetting, pesading, courbetting and caprioling stallions of the **Spanish Riding School** represent the quintessence of aristocratic Vienna and thus form one of the most popular tourist attractions of the city. Performances follow palace etiquette, with riders wearing the court livery of black boots, white tights, brown frac (dress-coat), and a gilded *bicorne* (2-cornered hat), which they doff for Emperor Karl VI at the start and end of each session. The Baroque white hall in which all shows take place, the Winter Riding School, built in 1729-35, is in its own right an admirable masterpiece by Fischer von Erlach Jr.

The regular Sunday performances, however, are for all practical purposes inaccessible to ordinary mortals unless they reserve tickets many months in advance or can pull influential strings. The alternative is to attend the morning exercises, held five days a week (except from July to August and in mid-winter), to which spectators are admitted on a first-come first-serve basis. The line for this starts forming around 9am, and moves after 10am only as fast as people who arrived first choose to leave.

The tradition of breeding "Spanish" horses in Vienna goes back to Maximilian II, who developed the habit around 1560, but Karl VI is credited with instituting the elaborate code of training and performance that raised the Spanish Riding School into an essential component of court ceremonial. The Lipizzan stallions, which receive their name from the farm near Trieste where they were bred until 1918, are descendants of Spanish and North African "Berber" ancestors that can be traced back many centuries. They are born brown or mouse-gray, and only at the end of 4 to 10 years develop the spotless white fleece that has made them famous. Since 1918, the Styrian village of Piber has been their home.

During World War II the horses were evacuated to a village in Czechoslovakia where they faced a grim future as farm animals or worse. General George S. Patton of the US army is credited with discovering them and negotiating with Soviet occupation authorities their return to a nobler career.

The Outer City

A broad green belt called the Glacis separated the walled city of Vienna from its suburbs, which until the middle of the 19thC consisted of idyllic little villages and vineyards alternating with the country estates of the nobility. After the demolition of the walls in 1858, the Glacis was built over with a series of public and private edifices in the grandiloquent style of the late 19thC, and suburbs became quickly integrated with the rest of the city as new residential quarters. Only the names of the former villages now survive as the designations of districts which spread out fan-fold from the core of the Inner City.

Ringstrasse, the principal boulevard of modern Vienna, circumscribes the Inner City on three sides. A second semicircle, the Gürtel ("Belt"), runs parallel to the Ring at a distance of about 1.5km (1 mile). Districts 3.-9. lie between the Ring and the Gürtel, forming a first loop around the center, while district 2. faces the Inner City across the Danube Canal. A second loop, spreading beyond the Gürtel and the main Danube branch (districts 10.-23.), starts out as a dull urban sprawl in which old palaces and the historic cores of former villages stand out as islands of interest. It then rises, in the N, W and SW, to a string of unspoiled villages of great beauty and "old world" charm.

In this alphabetical section, districts are indicated in bold parentheses — e.g., **(9.)** and **(11.)** — preceding the address, map reference, opening times etc. At the end of the chapter, on page 132, a section titled OTHER

SIGHTS describes numerous points of interest scattered around the 22 outlying districts of Vienna. On page 133 there is a useful outline **map** showing the districts.

ACADEMY OF FINE ARTS (Akademie der Bildenden Künste)
(1.) Schillerplatz 3. Map 3E2-3 🔲 *Open Tues, Thurs, Fri 10am-2pm; Wed 10am-1pm, 3-6pm; Sat-Sun 9am-1pm. Closed Mon. Metro U1, U2, U4 to Karlsplatz.*

The Academy, built in the Renaissance style by Theophil Hansen, a leading figure of "Ringstrasse" architecture (1876), houses a painting collection second in importance only to the ART HISTORY MUSEUM. Among the highlights are Hieronymus **Bosch**'s fantastic *Last Judgment* (☆), one of the most reproduced paintings in history, and several masterpieces by Lucas Cranach the Elder. *Tarquinius and Lucretia* by Titian and a *Madonna with Angels* from the workshop of Sandro Botticelli are among the memorable possessions of the gallery.

A large part of the collection is devoted to Flemish and Dutch masters of the 17thC, among them several Rubenses and Rembrandts. One room contains a selection of recent Austrian artists.

ART HISTORY MUSEUM (Kunsthistorische Museum) ★
(1.) Maria-Theresien-Platz ☎ *934541. Map 3E2* 🔲 *Open Apr-Oct Tues-Fri 10am-6pm, Sat-Sun 9am-6pm, closed Mon; Nov-May Tues-Fri 10am-4pm, Sat-Sun 9am-4pm, closed Mon* ✗ *Metro U2 to Babenberger Str. Tram 1, 2 to Burgring.*

Vienna's Kunsthistorische Museum rivals the Louvre, the British Museum, the Uffizi and the Metropolitan as one of the world's great repositories of European art. Its painting gallery (on the first floor) is not unduly large, but presents without dilution the very best work of the greatest pre-modern masters. Its too often ignored collection of sculpture and *objets d'art* (on the mezzanine floor) holds an altogether unique assemblage of things of beauty and virtuosity. In addition, the museum has first-rate collections of Egyptian and Graeco-Roman art (on the mezzanine floor) and an important numismatic section (on the second floor).

History
The museum's holdings derive almost exclusively from the collections of the Habsburg family, four of whose members stand out as great acquirers.

Ferdinand I (1526-64) and his son, Archduke Ferdinand of Tyrol, assembled at Schloss Ambras near Innsbruck a fabulous collection of historical portraits, armor, rhinoceros horns, seashells and curiosities, which form the basis of several Viennese museums. To Rudolph II (1576-1612) the museum owes its wealth of Brueghels and Dürers as well as the psychedelic fantasies of Arcimboldo who, among others, painted a portrait of the emperor out of cereals and crops. Archduke Leopold William, a son of Ferdinand II (1619-37) who was governor of the Low

Countries, was a leading patron of 17thC art. A painting by David Tenier in the Kunsthistorische shows him in the midst of his vast assemblage of Veroneses, Tintorettos, Titians, Rubenses and van Eycks, many of which can be seen to this day in the museum.

It was Joseph II (1780-90) who first made an inventory of the family's scattered artworks, selling off large chunks and placing the rest on display at BELVEDERE, where they can still be seen. The non-Austrian works of the collection were moved to their present location when the museum was completed in 1891.

Maria-Theresien-Platz

A small formal park separates the twin museums of Art History and NATURAL HISTORY, with the **Monument of Maria Theresa** at its center. Kaspar Zumbush's group (1888) shows the empress enthroned in majesty among the mounted figures of four of her generals (Laudon, Daun, Traun and Khevenhüller) and four leading statesmen of her court on foot (Swieten, Haugwitz, Kaunitz and Liechtenstein). Wisdom, Strength, Justice and Mercy support her throne, and medallions depict illustrious contemporaries (Gluck, Haydn and the child Mozart).

The building

Karl Hasenauer and Gottfried Semper built both museums, the most elaborate of Ringstrasse edifices, in a Neo-Baroque idiom. The great central hall of the Kunsthistorische is decorated by a ceiling fresco *(The Apotheosis of Art)* by Mihály Munkácsy, the leading Hungarian artist of the day, surrounded with 12 lunettes of famous painters by Hans Makart, his Austrian counterpart. Between the columns are Gustav Klimt's smaller compositions, which shine forth with their sassy self-confidence.

The main stairway climbs to Canova's powerful statue of *Theseus Vanquishing a Centaur* (1819), said to represent Austria's victory over Napoleon. Theseus, the mythological king of Athens, defeated the Centaurs, uncouth half-humans who tried to kidnap the bride at a wedding. Franz I of Austria who commissioned the work was an ardent Philhellene, in part because of his active interest in promoting an independent Greek state in the Balkans. Napoleon had married his daughter.

Painting collection

The painting gallery covers European art of the 16th through 18thC arranged by national schools. **Halls I-IV** are currently closed for restoration, so the placement of some of the paintings may differ from the normal order followed here. In the text, hall and room numbers **in bold** refer to the plan of the first floor of the museum, overleaf.

WEST WING: This is devoted mainly to Italian masters. **Raphael** is represented by his superb *Madonna in Green* (**hall I**), and **Titian** by several of the his best-known works including the *Danae* and *Ecce Homo* (**hall II**). Other Italians progress from the Renaissance clarity of Mantegna, Bellini and Antonello da Messina, through the increasingly convoluted Mannerism of Correggio, Parmigianino, Veronese, Bassano,

105

FIRST FLOOR

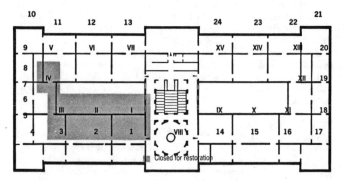

Tintoretto, Caravaggio and Carracci, to the late-Baroque idylls of Tiepolo and tourist panoramas of Canaletto. **Room 10** holds **Velázquez**'s famous portraits of various members of the Spanish branch of the Habsburgs.

EAST WING: Here are housed the works of Northern European masters, above all of the Flemish, Dutch and North German schools. One of the most interesting rooms (**hall X**) (★) is devoted to the fanciful canvases of Peter **Brueghel**, with such well-known masterpieces as *Children's Plays, The Massacre of the Innocents, The Meeting of Carnival and Lent, The Tower of Babel* and *Village Wedding*. Albrecht **Dürer** is present with eight works (**room 15**) which include the magnificent *Martyrdom of 10,000 Christians* and the *Portrait of Maximilian I*, one of the greatest portraits of all time.

Rooms 16 and **17** contain several beautiful pieces by **Lucas Cranach the Elder**, spanning the period from his early work in the Danube School to the more accomplished manner of his later output. Hans **Holbein**'s portraits in **room 18** include *Jane Seymour*, the third wife of Henry VIII of England, and *John Chambers*, the physician of the same king.

Halls XIII and **XIV** house a large collection by Peter Paul **Rubens**, among them an excellent *Self-Portrait*, the *Woman with a Cloak* which features his second wife, and two magnificent compositions depicting the miracles of the Jesuit saints Francis Xavier and Ignatius Loyola. **Room 23** holds two splendid self-portraits and other works by **Rembrandt**, and **room 24** offers **Vermeer**'s celebrated *The Artist in his Workshop*.

Mezzanine

The lower floor of the museum is reserved for three specialized collections of ancient and European art, each of which deserves quite as much time and admiration as the paintings upstairs.

The **Egyptian and Oriental Collection** (halls I-VIII ★) is the richest of its kind in Europe after that of the British Museum. The **Classical Antiquities Collection** (halls IX-XVIII ★) possesses a superb selection of Greek vases, a series of Greek and Roman statues of the highest quality, and above all the famous **Gemma Augustea** (★), a 1stC cameo of

Arabian sardonix, which is among the finest masterpieces of carved stone created by man.

The **Collection of Statues and Objets d'Art** (halls XIX-XXXVII ★), covering European 3-dimensional art from the Middle Ages through the 18thC, is a treasure-trove of every sort of item on which beauty and mastery could be brought to bear. Among its prized possessions is Benvenuto Cellini's golden **salt cellar** (hall XXVII ★), one of the great artworks of the Renaissance.

The Middle Ages are represented by some **locks** of extraordinary artistry. A tremendous wealth of Renaissance jewelry, cameos, crystal and enamel works, ivory or rhinoceros-horn statuettes, magnificently worked-out playing tables, clocks, mechanical globes, toys — even a mechanical Turk — reflect the exuberant taste of the courts of Ferdinand I and Rudolph II. Also on temporary display in this section are the works of the Milanese **Arcimboldo** (✩), who painted *trompe-l'oeil* portraits made of fruits, flowers and fish, and the 16thC **Mömpelgard Hexaptych**, composed of 158 smaller paintings.

Second floor

The uppermost story of the museum holds the so-called **Secondary Gallery** of paintings, which does not hide any undiscovered gems, as well as a fascinating series of historical **portraits** made for Ferdinand of Tyrol, and a **numismatic collection**.

AUERSPERG PALAIS See under SPITTELBERG.

AUGARTEN

(2.) Map 4A4. Tram 21, N to Heine Str.; 31, 32 to Obere Augarten Str. Bus 5A to Obere Augarten Str.

One of the finest achievements of formal gardening in Vienna, the ex-imperial park of Augarten bears comparison with the great gardens of Schönbrunn and Belvedere. Its geometric chestnut and linden alleys are tours de force of the topiarist's art — although republican neglect has now introduced too many bald spots for comfort.

A dominant feature of the park are the pair of **flak towers** rising surrealistically over the landscape. These are two of the six that were built in 1942 against Allied air raids (the others are at Esterházy Park in Mariahilf and Arenberg Park in Wieden). Dismantling them is unfeasible, as the amount of explosive required to demolish them would also demolish the entire neighborhood.

The history of Augarten is intimately connected with the name of Joseph II, whose decision to open the former imperial preserve to the public was seen in 1775 as a pointed symbol of the end of an era, comparable to the fall of the Berlin Wall in our time. The entrance still bears a dedication from the People's Emperor: "To The People, From Their Admirer." At Joseph's orders, the **Alte Favorita**, the garden palace of his great-grandfather Leopold I, was converted into a public hall where at different times Mozart, Beethoven and J. Strauss Jr conducted summer concerts.

Joseph himself usually lived at the small, attractive **Augartenpalais** (built c.1700 to plans by Fischer von Erlach), which is now used as a boarding school for the Vienna Choirboys and is not normally accessible to the public. The modest **Josephsstöckl** adjoining Augartenpalais serves today as the Mutantenheim, where choirboys whose voice changes in teenage ("mutants") reside till the end of their studies.

The famed **Imperial Porcelain Manufactory** of Augarten was founded in the 18thC in an annex of the Alte Favorita as the second-oldest porcelain maker in Europe (after Meissen in Saxony). Revived by the city of Vienna in 1924 after a break of 80 years, it manufactures a line of exceedingly popular tourist items.

BELVEDERE ★
(3.) *Lower Belvedere:* *Rennweg 6. Map **4F4**. Tram 71 to Unteres Belvedere.*
Upper Belvedere: *Prinz-Eugen-Str. 27. Off map **4F4**. Tram D to Schloss Belvedere.* **Museums** 🖼 *open Tues-Sun 10am-4pm, closed Mon.* **Light and sound show** 🖼 *daily at 9.30pm in summer.*

The twin palaces of Belvedere, the most impressive secular works of Baroque architecture in Vienna, were built not for the imperial family but for Prince Eugene of Savoy, the French soldier of fortune who became the empire's most powerful man during the early part of the 18thC. Acquired by Maria Theresa after the prince's death, they were used to house various members of the dynasty, including Archduke Franz Ferdinand prior to his famous assassination at Sarajevo. They now form a museum in which the Austrian collections of the ART HISTORY MUSEUM are displayed in separate medieval, Baroque and 19th/20thC divisions.

History
Prince Eugene of Savoy (1663-1736) was the son of a prince of the French royal blood. His mother Olympe Mancini, a niece of Cardinal Mazarin, became a mistress of Louis XIV, then wrote a scandalous memoir of her life at court, and ended up being banished to Brussels. Young Eugene applied for a post in the French army and was turned down by the king. Storming out in a rage, he showed up as a volunteer at the siege of Vienna, and rose in the ranks during the conquest of Hungary and the Balkans.

He was made commander-general in 1697 when a policy of Catholic bigotry had sparked a revolt in the "liberated" territories and revived the Turkish threat. He successfully ended the war in the east, defeating also the Hungarian rebellion of 1703-11, and amassing great wealth along the way. In the west, he joined forces with England's Marlborough to defeat the French at Blenheim and Ramillies. After 1703, he dominated the empire's policies through his personal network of agents and spies. He owned Europe's most valuable art and book collections, remained a lifelong bachelor, and was reputed to be gay.

Lower Belvedere ★

The main residential wing of the palace was built in 1714-16 by Lukas von Hildebrandt and forms the appropriate setting for the **Museum of Austrian Baroque** (Österreichisches Barockmuseum) which it hosts. Resist the temptation to mock if the exhibits, with their florid rhetoric of gods and saints, appear at first sight an easy target of ridicule. On second thoughts they are liable to reveal themselves as the most unexpectedly gratifying works of art in Vienna. This is the place to seek inspiration if the Baroque pomp of the capital of the Habsburgs does not immediately appeal: the extraordinary range of human gesture represented, the wild, at times perverse imagination restrained by the rigid formality of idiom, will stimulate thought, and perhaps pleasure too.

All the masters whose work fills the palaces and churches of 18thC Vienna are present at the museum. Whole rooms are devoted to Rottmayr, Troger, Gran, the Kremser Schmidt, and especially **Maulbertsch**, who achieves the most extraordinary sense of winged, weightless splendor in his saints. The **frescoes** of the halls themselves, notably those of rooms 8 and 10, belong to Martino Altomonte. Room 16 contains an unusual series of **grotesques** by Franz Xaver Messerschmidt.

Orangerie

The winter garden building outside Lower Belvedere houses the **Museum of Medieval Austrian Art** (Museum mittelalterlicher österreichischer Kunst), the most important collection of its kind in Austria. The majority of works date from the second half of the 15thC and include several fine representatives of the Danube School.

Upper Belvedere ★

The upper palace, completed in 1723, crowned the life's work of Hildebrandt with what is generally recognized to be his most perfect monument. The building was designed primarily for balls and receptions, although its rooms also served the needs of the Prince's complex political dealings. Its two floors now house the **Austrian Gallery of 19th and 20thC Art** (Österreichische Galerie des 19. und 20. Jahrhunderts). Each floor is dedicated to one century.

The 19thC gallery is of limited interest except for the Biedermeier idylls of **Waldmüller** and **Amerling**, and what might very well be the most erotic picture of a woman hanging in a major museum, by one Hans Canon (room 10). The second half of the century is characterized by unbearable bombast, culminating in the cliché-ridden canvases of Hans **Makart**. The 20thC collection offers the best-known works of Gustav **Klimt**, including *The Kiss, Judith I,* and the portraits of Fritza Riedler and Adele Bloch-Bauer (rooms 17-18). The Expressionist works of Oskar **Kokoschka** and Egon **Schiele** are also reputed to have their admirers.

Gardens ◄€ ★

The Belvedere Gardens cover a gently sloping hill in what once was open country, and offer the best panorama of the center of Vienna that is available anywhere. Their combination of splendid architecture and formal landscaping produces one of Vienna's esthetically most satisfying environments.

The park was designed by the French landscapist Dominique Girard according to an elaborate symbolic code. The wooded lowest level has statues of Pluto and Proserpina, god and goddess of the underworld, and is filled with symbols of the Elements and the Seasons. The central area below the monumental fountain holds statues of Apollo and Hercules; they were embodiments of Art and War, two areas in which the Prince claimed distinction. The sunny upper garden — the domain of the immortals — is protected by rows of mysterious sphinxes, and contains many references to the Olympian gods.

The Prince kept in his gardens several free-roaming lions, his heraldic symbols. The beasts were later moved to Schönbrunn to form the nucleus of the imperial zoo.

Vicinity
Rennweg ("Runway"), the street below Lower Belvedere, is named after the foot race that used to be run at Vienna's annual market, with a length of scarlet cloth as the traditional prize of the winner. It is lined with several attractive churches — the **Salesian Church** (Salesianerinnenkirche) of 1717 is a fine example — and other buildings: note the **State Printing House** (Staatsdruckerel), which has a lovely **botanical garden** behind.

At #27 is **Palais Metternich** (now the Italian Embassy), home of the man who shaped European politics for nearly half a century until his overthrow in 1848. Prince Wenzel von Metternich, whose palace was on the wrong side of the street that divides Landstrasse from Wieden, is credited with the quip: "Asia begins at Landstrasse." He also said: "Austria had to be invented if it did not exist." He meant in both cases that the multinational Habsburg state was a necessary bulwark of the West against the chronic mess of Eastern Europe. His thoughts, unfashionable for 140 years after his fall, have begun to seep back into currency today.

At the upper end of Belvedere, the building at Prinz-Eugen-Str. 22 was the site of Adolf Eichmann's infamous Bureau of Jewish Emigration, which "processed" over 200,000 Viennese Jews in the years after 1938.

BURGTHEATER ☆
(1.) Dr-Karl-Lueger-Ring 2. Map 3C2. Outside show times, sightseeing is by permission only (☎514440). Tram 1, 2, D to Rathausplatz.

The Hofburgtheater was established by Maria Theresa and cultivated by Joseph II as a showcase for the imperial court, "the nexus between court and people", performing a role not unlike the circus of the ancient Romans or the Hollywood of modern times. Thanks to it, Vienna became the undisputed theatrical capital of the German-speaking world. Private theaters proliferated after the 1780s, but they continued to take their cue from the imperial stage, and the "Burg" remained to the present day the most prestigious dramatic institution of central Europe. Several contemporary movie stars, such as Klaus Maria

Brandauer, have made their way into cinema from the Burgtheater.

The old Burgtheater on Michaelerplatz was connected by a passage to the imperial quarters, allowing members of the court to take their boxes without leaving the palace. Once, when Maria Theresa broke into tears praising the performance of an actress, her husband Franz I of Lorraine was heard to comment, "I know no actress greater than you, Madame."

The new Burgtheater was completed in 1888 as the showiest of the Ringstrasse buildings. The architects were Carl Hasenauer and Gottfried Semper, who chose the style of the French Baroque to underline the 17thC origins of modern high drama. The magnificent **stairwell** was gilded, painted and statued with great abandon. The ceiling **frescoes** illustrating the history of theater were done by young Gustav Klimt (with his brother Ernst and friend Franz Matsch) before his Secessionist period; one composition depicting Shakespeare's Globe Theatre shows the painter himself in Elizabethan courtier's attire, leaning on a column on the right.

CENTRAL CEMETERY (Zentralfriedhof)
(11.) Simmeringer Hauptstrasse 234. Map 2E5. Tram 71, 72 (main gate at Zentralfriedhof 2. Tor).

The largest cemetery of Vienna was consecrated in 1874, and an ambitious project was undertaken to transfer the bodies of great men, including those of Beethoven, Schubert and Johann Strauss Sr, to a specially designed pantheon within it. They were later joined by Brahms, Strauss Jr, Lehár, Suppé, Millöcker and the prominent architects and painters of the Ringstrasse era. Mozart, too, although untraceable, was given an extra tomb.

The **monuments** *(Ehrengräber)* occupy a stately circle half-way between the main cemetery entrance and the elephantine but strangely melancholy **Church** of Karl Lueger (1910). A crypt in front of the church contains the tombs of all presidents of the Austrian Republic. Elsewhere, as you stroll along, you will discover the collective tomb of the founding fathers of Austrian socialism, as well as various plots dedicated to the martyrs of February 1934, to the concentration camp victims and to fallen Soviet soldiers of 1945. An inconspicuous monument at the far end of the cemetery honors the Austrian losses of World War II.

A forlorn piece of history lies in the gardens facing the cemetery across Simmeringer Hauptstrasse: the **Neugebäude**, the great Renaissance palace of Maximilian II (built 1569-76), left to decay for many centuries and systematically robbed of its materials, but now reportedly slated for restoration. The **Crematorium**, a pioneering work of modern architecture by Clemens Holzmeister (1923), is located in the palace grounds.

FREUD MUSEUM
(9.) Berggasse 19. Map 3B2 🖼 *Open daily 9am-3pm. Tram D to Schlickgasse. Bus 40A to Berggasse.*

A typical 19thC upper-middle-class apartment building within walking distance of the UNIVERSITY served Dr Sigmund Freud as residence and psychoanalytical practice from 1891 to 1938. A memorial museum has been set up in his consulting rooms on the mezzanine (one flight up); his home on the second floor is privately owned. Displays include Freud's hat, his books and his famous collection of antiquities, which were returned to Vienna by Anna Freud in 1971. But his legendary couch remains in London.

The house was raided by some Nazis a few days after the Anschluss. The arrangements of Princess Marie Bonaparte allowed the evacuation of the Freuds to London on June 4, 1938. Freud died a year later.

Opposite the Freud apartment, at **Berggasse 6** (privately owned), Theodor Herzl wrote the seminal texts of Zionism in the 1890s.

GRINZING AND HEILIGENSTADT ★

*5-6km (3-4 miles) NW of center. Map **1**B3. **For Grinzing:** tram 38 from Schottentor. **For Heiligenstadt:** metro U4, U6 to Heiligenstadt terminal or tram 37 to Hohe Warte or D to Grinzinger Str. **For Nussdorf:** tram D to Nussdorf. Bus 38A runs from Heiligenstadt terminal to Grinzing, Kahlenberg and Leopoldsberg. For ✗ apply at any tourist bureau for walking tours of Grinzing or Heiligenstadt.*

The presence of a ring of immensely attractive villages within Sunday-outing distance has always been one of the great advantages of Vienna as a city. The quaintest of them, Grinzing, has been developed — perhaps too systematically — into a tourist attraction with scores of wine gardens serving Vienna's characteristic fresh wine *(Heurige)*, while neighboring Heiligenstadt attracts nearly as many visitors with its memories of Beethoven.

The **Vienna Woods** (Wienerwald), a ridge of thickly wooded hills running from the edge of the city to the Semmering Alps in the SW, is dotted with scores of villages of similar character: Sievering, Pötzleinsdorf, Salmannsdorf, Neustift am Walde, Hietzing, Speising and Rodaun within a 10km (6-mile) radius of the center. There are many others (see the chapter on EXCURSIONS, on page 173) farther to the W and SW. Wine-growing (and wine drinking) has been the specialty of the region ever since Probus, the Roman emperor, enjoined the planting of vines in the Danube area by a celebrated decree dated around AD280. The vineyards survived the barbarian invasions and the Middle Ages.

Vienna's elite began building estates in the wine country when pastoralism became fashionable in the age of Maria Theresa. But the Viennese countryside had its true heyday a generation or two later, in the age of the Romantic reaction which enveloped Europe after the collapse of the French Revolution. Beethoven and Schubert, Grillparzer and Waldmüller voiced the spirit of the times when they left the city for the pastoral idyll of the villages. Charm rather than glory, nature rather than culture, innocence rather than lust (and love rather than war) became, briefly, the cherished values of the day. In their architecture, music, traditions and memories, the villages of the Vienna Woods carry above all else the legacy of that era — the early 19thC.

Grinzing is memorable enough for its many wine-and-music gardens lining the main (and more or less only) street, so there is little need to sauce it up further by dumb-man's gimmicks, such as wine stocks individually owned and signed by Sophia Loren or other important personalities.

Heiligenstadt's main street is somewhat more citified, but its secluded little Pfarrplatz remains as idyllic as it probably was when Beethoven spent a summer in the *Pfarrhaus* (parish house, now a tavern). In another house on Probusgasse, nearly defeated by advancing deafness, Beethoven wrote the 1802 suicide note known as the Heiligenstadt Testament ("O men who think or say that I am malevolent, stubborn or misanthropic, how greatly do you wrong me ..."). In a happier summer 6 years later he was lodged next door to the poet Grillparzer at Grinzinger Str. 64; his daily walks to the lovely valley behind Pfarrplatz (now called Beethovengang, in neighboring Nussdorf) inspired that year his Sixth ("Pastoral") symphony.

The two northernmost hills of the Vienna Woods (and thus of the Alpine system) rise immediately behind Grinzing and Nussdorf. **Kahlenberg** (484 meters/1,588 feet) offers a superb view, an 18thC church and a large garden restaurant. **Leopoldsberg** (423 meters/1,388 feet), named after Margrave Leopold III of Babenberg, the patron saint of Lower Austria (ruled 1095-1136), who built himself a castle here, rises straight from the bank of the Danube. A church built in 1683 commemorates the Turkish victory of a different Leopold.

HIETZING   See under SCHÖNBRUNN.

HISTORICAL MUSEUM OF THE CITY OF VIENNA (Historisches Museum der Stadt Wien)

(4.) Karlsplatz 8. Map 3E3 🚇 *Open Tues-Sun 9am-4.30pm (2nd floor closed noon-1.30pm). Closed Mon. Metro U1, U2, U4 to Karlsplatz.*

Located next to KARLSKIRCHE, the museum documents the history of Vienna from prehistoric times to the present. Various historic plans and panoramas help visualize the development of the city over centuries. The first floor holds Baroque art and parts of the Turkish loot of 1683. The second floor offers a series of beautifully re-created rooms from different historical periods, including the living rooms of the poet Franz Grillparzer and the architect Adolf Loos.

HUNDERTWASSER HOUSE ★

(3.) Hundertwasser House: On Kegelgasse corner of Löwengasse, map 4D6 🚇 *information office open daily 9am-12.30pm, 1-7pm. **KunstHaus:** Untere Weisgerber Str. 11-13. Metro U3, U4 to Landstrasse/Wien-Mitte. Tram N to Hetzgasse.*

The fairy-tale housing complex designed by the painter and anti-architect Friedensreich Hundertwasser was completed in 1985 and instantly became one of the most popular tourist attractions of Vienna. Its playful, imaginative, undogmatic fun has been condemned by the archi-

tectural establishment near-unanimously as kitsch.

The building is a low-income public housing project owned by the municipal government. The design deliberately avoids all straight lines and attempts to give each apartment an individual character, combining Mediterranean village architecture with bits of a 19thC Viennese facade, and pasting it over with onion-bulb domes, Classical fragments, a London telephone booth, a Habsburg eagle, Michelangelo's *David* and trees growing out of windows. Sightseers are not allowed inside, but an information office on the ground floor offers literature and various exhibits.

Hundertwasser, a child of the 1960s hippie movement, conceived his work as an attack on the "criminal sterility" of modern architecture. Architecture, according to him, "has become a farce and is no longer suitable for human beings. Architects build prison cells in which human souls wither and die. We face a great emptiness, the desert of uniformity and creative impotence."

In 1989, Hundertwasser converted a former tire repair shop facing the building into the shopping arcade of **Kalke-Village**. His newest creation, the **KunstHaus** (Art House) (★), was opened in 1991 three blocks away. It features a permanent exhibition of the artist's work, circulating exhibits, art galleries, and an attractive café that is relatively free of tourist crowds.

IMPERIAL FURNITURE AND MATERIALS DEPOT (Bundesmobilien- und Materialdepot) ★

(7.) Mariahilfer Str. 88. Open Tues-Fri 9am-4pm, Sat-Sun 9am-noon ✗ on the hour. Tram 52, 58 to Zieglergasse.

The Federal Collection of Old Furniture (its official name) is one of the lesser known wonders of Vienna and an apt symbol of the city itself: a dusty warehouse full of the memorabilia of vanished "imperial and royal" splendor. The depot was established by Maria Theresa to store materials being held from the scores of palaces and residences of the Habsburg household — in effect, as an imperial attic. The most valuable items were sent after 1918 to museums, while the rest remained here as an inexhaustible grab-bag to garnish state receptions and decorate Austrian government offices, embassies and, it is alleged, the homes of influential people. A Kafkaesque bureaucratic domain until a few years ago, it has now been opened to the public as a museum, and attracts a small stream of fascinated visitors.

The collection is a labyrinth of mind-boggling extent: it contains perhaps 60,000 antique chairs, 150,000 pieces of tableware, an entire floor full of imperial dress cabinets, a large room filled with historic clocks, hundreds of formal portraits, scores of k.u.k. spittoons, a mirror room, a vase room, a room for official souvenirs, a vast collection of imperial busts, everyday crowns made of base material, Franz Joseph's stuffed canaries, the hats of Maximilian of Mexico, and postcards written by Empress Elisabeth. Its collection of Biedermeier furniture is said to be the world's largest.

JOSEPHINUM ☆
(9.) Währinger Str. 25. Map 3B1 🚊 *Open Mon-Fri 11am-3pm. Tram 37, 38, 40, 41, 42 to Sensengasse.*

The small museum of the Josephine Medical Academy holds a collection of unusually fascinating nature: a series of more than a hundred wax studies of human anatomy, which combine technical mastery with a sense of beauty matching the highest art. One particularly unsettling statue shows a reclining woman of cool and classical beauty, naked except for a pearl necklace, with her entrails exposed across the abdomen. Another presents a man in noble athletic pose, minus his skin. The collection was prepared by Florentine artists for Joseph II when a shortage of cadavers, caused in part by the opposition of the church, hampered instruction at his newly established School of Surgery (1783-85).

Joseph was the first to remove surgery from its traditional classification as a manual trade and have it taught at the university. Vienna led world medicine through the 19thC, introducing epoch-making advances in surgery (Billroth), immunology (Semmelweis) and anatomy (Rokitansky). The US medical profession was deeply indebted to the Viennese tradition via the two-way flow of students in the 1920s and refugees in the 1930s.

The mammoth 18thC complex of the **General Hospital** (Allgemeines Krankenhaus) stretches behind the Josephinum. With the completion of new hospital buildings, parts of the antiquated complex will be converted into a university campus.

KARL-MARX-HOF
(19.) Heiligenstädter Str. 82-92. Map 1B3. Metro U4 to Heiligenstadt. Tram D to 12 Februar-Platz.

A city within a city, with apartments for 5,000 inhabitants, parks, communal baths and kitchens, a library, conference rooms and shops, Karl-Marx-Hof was the epitome of the nearly 400 communal housing projects built by the socialist governments of "Red Vienna" between

1919 and 1934. The program was financed through a draconian property tax that ruined the Viennese aristocracy, and through luxury levies on such items as housemaids, automobiles and champagne.

Some of these "workers' fortresses," especially the Karl Marx complex that lay astride the strategic northern road into the city, were accused of being designed for a military role in a future communist revolution. On February 12, 1934, the fascist militia of the Heimwehr attempted to storm Karl-Marx-Hof; they were repulsed, leading to a bloody battle of four days in which the federal army pounded the complex with heavy artillery.

The architecture of Karl-Marx-Hof belongs fully with the fascist-socialist esthetic of the 1930s, although it still carries traces of Jugendstil themes. Surprisingly, its overall impact is somewhat pleasing to the eye.

KARLSKIRCHE ☆
(1.) Karlsplatz. Map 3E3-F3. Metro U1, U2, U4 to Karlsplatz.

The domed church of St Charles Borromeo is the largest, boldest and most majestic of Vienna's Baroque churches. The masterpiece of father and son Fischer von Erlach was erected in thanksgiving for the end of the plague epidemic of 1713, the sixth to strike Vienna in less than a half century, and consecrated in 1737. Part of the financing was met by the city of Hamburg in payment of penalties incurred during the War of the Spanish Succession.

The church is preceded by a Classical **portico** bearing the Latin inscription, "I have fulfilled my vow in the eyes of those who fear God," a reference to a pledge made by Karl VI during the epidemic. Two mighty **pillars** based on Trajan's column in Rome depict the life and miracles of St Charles Borromeo, a Milanese bishop (1538-84) who performed exemplary deeds during an earlier plague epidemic, which had the incidental effect of helping to keep the flame of Counter-Reformation alive in Protestant Vienna. The interior of the dome is decorated with frescoes by Michael Rottmayr.

Karlsplatz

The church is flanked to either side by the 19thC building of the **Technical University** and the HISTORICAL MUSEUM OF THE CITY OF VIENNA. Facing them across the shapeless square-park-intersection of Karlsplatz are the edifices of the "officially approved" arts of the Ringstrasse era: the **Künstlerhaus** and the **Musikverein**. The former, designed as the guild hall of the Artists' Society against which Secessionists rebelled in 1897, continues to function as Vienna's leading exhibition gallery. The latter has been the home of the Vienna Philharmonic Society since its construction in 1870. Its **Golden Hall** (✗ *every Sun at 1.45pm)* hosts the concerts of the **Vienna Philharmonic Orchestra**, including the famous New Year's gala concert, which is broadcast across the world.

Johannes **Brahms** was the guiding spirit of the Musikverein for a quarter century until his death in 1897. He lived opposite the square at **Karlsgasse** 4. The Philharmonic has been led by such legendary names as Gustav Mahler, Felix von Weingartner and Herbert von Karajan. Its most recent director was Carlo Maria Giulini.

The twin **stations** of the former Karlsplatz tram line (illustrated on page 46), designed by Otto Wagner in 1898 in the graceful style of the Secession, have recently been declared historic landmarks, and renovated, respectively, into a café and a metro entrance doubling up as an art gallery. The SECESSION building itself stands a few blocks away at the w end of the square.

KUNSTHAUS   See under HUNDERTWASSER HOUSE.

LAINZER TIERGARTEN

*9km (5½ miles) sw of center. Map 1D1. **Park** open Apr-Oct Wed-Sun 8am till dark; a small part of it is open year-round. **Hermes Villa** ▩ open Wed-Sun 9am-4.30pm; closed Mon-Tues. Train S3 from W Bahnhof or S15 from S Bahnhof to Speising, then bus 60B to Lainzer Tor.*

A stone wall, 23km (14 miles) long, was built under Joseph II surrounding this magnificent nature reserve where hikers can theoretically meet foxes, deer and wild boars in the course of their perambulations. About 10 minutes by foot from the outer entrance is the **Hermes Villa**, a residence built for Empress Elisabeth in 1886 and decorated with frescoes by Hans Makart and Gustav Klimt. It hosts visiting exhibitions.

LAXENBURG ☆

15km (9 miles) s of center. Franzensburg open Easter through Oct daily 10am-noon, 2-5pm. Train R61 from Südbahnhof to Laxenburg/Biedermannsdorf. Bus from district 3., Marxergasse 4-6.

One of the most attractive of the many imperial summer palaces and the finest example of 19thC "romantic" landscape gardening in Austria, the Laxenburg château remains largely ignored by visitors on account of its distance from the city center. The complex consists of **Altes Schloss**, built in the 14thC and altered in 1682, now housing a film

117

museum, and **Neues Schloss**, which was built for Maria Theresa by Pacassi in 1752 and served as the residence of Karl I in 1916-18.

An islet on an artificial lake bears **Franzensburg** (✪), a delightful mock-medieval castle built between 1798 and 1836 for Franz I of Austria. This contains an unexpectedly interesting museum displaying artwork from various Austro-Hungarian palaces, as well as Habsburg memorabilia, such as some cookie cutters that once belonged to Maria Theresa.

Not far from the palace at Laxenburger Str. 365 is Vienna's vast and colorful **Wholesale Flower Market** *(retail sales after 9am).*

LEOPOLDSTADT
(2.) Map 2C4. For ✦ *of Jewish memorials, apply at tourist bureau for details. Metro U1 to Schwedenplatz, Nestroyplatz, Praterstern.*

District 2. of Vienna, across the Danube Canal from the Inner City, was the hub of the city's Jewish life for 100 years preceding the Holocaust. Now reduced to a grimy area of cheap shops, questionable bars and many immigrants, it holds few sights of real interest apart from the parks of AUGARTEN and PRATER.

Jews settled in Leopoldstadt after 1683, but it was from the middle of the 19thC that they began to play a large role in the social life of Vienna. From c.1880 to 1938 they accounted for some 10 percent of the city's population but produced a disproportionate number of prominent people, including Freud, Herzl, Hoffmansthal, Loos, Mahler, Max Reinhardt, Schnitzler, Schönberg, father and son Johann Strauss, Zweig, nearly all the leaders of Viennese socialism, and many who achieved fame in the US as immigrants, like violinist Fritz Kreisler and film makers Billy Wilder and Otto Preminger. Today, Vienna has less than 10,000 Jewish inhabitants.

LIECHTENSTEIN GARDEN PALACE (Gartenpalais Liechtenstein)
(9.) Fürstengasse 1. Map 3A2 ▦ *Open daily except Tues 10am-6pm. Tram D to Fürstengasse. Bus 40A to Bauernfeldplatz.*

The summer palace of Prince Liechtenstein (compare the reference to Palais Liechtenstein on page 81) was built in 1698-1711 on the bank of the now-vanished Als stream. The architect was Domenico Martinelli. An attractive **park** where Mozart gave many concerts separates the N Wing, now an office building, from the main palais, whose frescoed Baroque halls hold Vienna's **Museum of Modern Art** (Museum moderner Kunst), devoted to works of the period after World War II. The emphasis of the museum is on Austrian artists, among whom the Surrealist paintings of Arik Brauer and Rudolf Hausner stand out.

Vicinity
A short stroll s of the museum leads to the **Servite Church** (Servitenkirche), built in 1651-70 by Carlo Carlone and the only suburban church of Vienna to survive the destruction of 1683. It contains the tomb of Octavio Prince Piccolomini, familiar as the nemesis of Wallen-

stein to readers of Schiller's great drama of the same name.

As a mercenary general in the service of Austria, Wallenstein formed what was then the most powerful army yet seen in Europe, and used it to subjugate the German princes during the Thirty Years' War. In 1637 he was accused of conspiring against the Habsburg crown and murdered in Bohemia by Piccolomini's men.

In the opposite direction lies **Nussdorfer Str. 54**. Franz Schubert was born in this idyllic little house of the late 18thC. Arranged as a **Schubert Museum (★)**, it is perhaps the most attractive of Vienna's many homes of famous people.

MUSEUM OF MODERN ART See LIECHTENSTEIN GARDEN PALACE.

NASCHMARKT

(5/6.) Map 3F2-E2. **Market** open Mon-Fri 6am-6.30pm, Sat 6am-1pm. **Flea market** open Sat 8am-6pm. Metro U1, U2, U4 to Karlsplatz, U4 to Kettenbrückengasse. Bus 59A to Pressgasse, Bärenmühl.

Naschmarkt is by far the largest and most interesting of Vienna's 20-odd produce and grocery markets, all of which have lately undergone a degree of revival. Its stalls stretch half a mile along the paved-up course of the Wien stream. By ancient custom, those nearest Karlsplatz (downtown) are better and more expensive, while a Third World flavor becomes noticeable farther upstream. Most of the marketeers are Turkish, although Arabs, Greeks, Serbs, Romanians and Czechs are also present.

A fascinating **flea market**, one of Europe's best, operates every Saturday in the open area at the upper end of the market. It has bloomed since 1989 with an inexhaustible flow of junk from the former socialist bloc.

The left bank of the Wien (**Linke Wienzeile**) was among the most prestigious residential addresses of the first decades of the 20thC, as its row of ornate apartment buildings bear witness. Notable among these are **#38** and **#40**, Secessionist masterpieces of Otto Wagner dating from 1898. Several blocks below them is the **Theater an der Wien**, representing one of the oldest dramatic traditions of Vienna. Built in 1801 by Emanuel Schikaneder in place of his own earlier outdoor stage (where Mozart's *Magic Flute* had received its first performance), the theater counted among its box office hits the first performances of Beethoven's *Fidelio*, Johann Strauss Jr's *Fledermaus* and the most famous operettas of Vienna's "golden" and "silver" ages.

NATURAL HISTORY MUSEUM (Naturhistorisches Museum)

(1.) Maria-Theresien-Platz. Map **3D2** 🖾 Open Wed-Mon 9am-6pm. Closed Tues. Metro U2, U3 to Volkstheater. Tram 1, 2 to Dr-Karl-Renner-Ring.

Housed since 1889 in the twin building of the ART HISTORY MUSEUM, the mineral, fossil, plant and animal collections of the Natural History Museum derive originally from the private collections of Franz I of Lorraine, the husband of Maria Theresa, who was an avid naturalist.

Noteworthy items include a 117kg (258-pound) topaz (in room 4), the so-called *Venus of Willendorf*, a statuette from c.25000BC (in room 11), and a skeleton of the extinct Steller's seacow (in the rotunda).

OPERA (Staatsoper) ☆
(1.) Opernring 2. Map 3E3 ✗ *July-Aug daily at 10am, 11am, 1pm, 2pm, 3pm; Sept-June on demand. Metro U1 to Oper. Tram 1, 2 to Oper*

When completed in 1869 as the first great showcase building of the RINGSTRASSE development, the Court Opera (originally called the Hofoper; it was renamed Staatsoper in 1918) was ridiculed for looking like "an elephant sitting down to digest its food." Eduard van der Nüll, one of the co-architects of the Neo-Renaissance structure, committed suicide when Franz Joseph voiced some mild criticism on opening night. His colleague August von Siccardsburg died of a heart attack some weeks later.

Intrigue and tragedy have since then been the opera's hallmark. Gustav Mahler, director from 1897-1907, was driven to his death by incessant criticism. Lorin Maazel, an American who was made director in 1981, was forced to leave town with the equivalent of tar and feathers when he attempted to breathe some life into the staid institution. Claudio Abbado, his successor, met the same fate in 1991.

The Opera was destroyed by American bombs in 1945. Its reopening in 1955 after 10 years of restoration became a symbol of Austria's rebirth from the ashes of war. The famous **Mahler bust** by Rodin, incidentally, escaped destruction thanks to the Nazis, who had removed it from display because of the composer's Jewish background.

The bloodiest battles of the first Turkish siege of 1529 took place at the bastions that at one time existed on the site of the Opera. At the end of a 3-week siege on October 15, the 120,000-strong army of Sultan Süleyman the Magnificent launched a final all-out attack at this point. Count Salm, commanding the defenders, was wounded in the ranks, but the city held and the Turks withdrew the following day.

PARLIAMENT (Parlament) ☆
(1.) Dr-Karl-Renner-Ring 3. Map 3D2 ✗ *Mon-Fri 9am, 10am, 1pm, 2pm except during sessions. Metro U3 to Dr-Karl-Renner-Ring. Tram 1, 2, D to Stadiongasse/ Parlament.*

An imperial parliament — *Reichsrat* — was promised during the revolutions of 1848 and finally established in 1867; mired in the multiple national rivalries of the Austro-Hungarian monarchy, it never played a serious role. The decision was nevertheless made to endow it with a building worthy of its hypothetical dignity. Theophil Hansen's design, realized in 1873-83, chose the architectural idiom of ancient Athens to honor a democratic tradition that had never been a strong suit of the Austrian capital. The front of the edifice was peopled with life-sized statues of scores of Greek and Roman sages (a row of Classical historians sit along the entrance ramp to warn politicians of the future verdict of history), and a substantial **Monument of Athena**, the Greek goddess of wisdom, was placed over a fountain in the front plaza. She carries in her right hand Nike, the winged goddess of victory.

The Federal Parliament today consists of a *Bundesrat* representing the 9 federal states and a *Nationalrat* of 183 directly elected members. Two parties, the Socialists (SPÖ) and People's Party (ÖVP, Christian Democratic), have shared a near-monopoly since 1945, governing in coalition most of the time (most recently since 1987) and otherwise sharing power according to a complex system known as *Proporz*. The steady rise of a third group, the right-nationalist Freedom Party of Jörg Haider, has caused alarm since the mid-1980s.

Dr-Karl-Renner-Ring and **Dr-Karl-Lueger-Ring** commemorate, respectively, the less controversial founding fathers of the two rival traditions of modern Austrian politics. Renner, a socialist, was called twice at moments of national crisis (1918 and 1945) to be president of the republic. Lueger, the populist founder of the Christian Social movement (the predecessor of the ÖVP), was mayor of Vienna from 1897-1910.

PIARIST CHURCH (Piaristenkirche Maria Treu)
(8.) Jodok-Fink-Platz. Off map 3C1. Tram J to Lederergasse. Bus 13A to Lederergasse.
The Baroque church of Patres Scholarum Piarum, an order founded in the 17thC to promote popular Catholic schools in Protestant-threatened lands, was built in stages between 1716 and 1771. It is worth visiting on account of the particularly beautiful **frescoes** (1752-53 ☆) by Maulbertsch, which decorate its ceiling. The monks of the Piarist Abbey run an attractive **wine cellar** and restaurant in keeping with ancient tradition.

Vicinity
Behind the abbey at Piaristengasse 44 is the **Theater in der Josefstadt**, which under the direction of Hugo von Hoffmansthal and Max Reinhardt became one of the seminal institutions of modern drama at the turn of this century. At **Kochgasse 12**, a commemorative plaque marks the home of the writer Stefan Zweig. **Palais Schönborn**, designed by Hildebrandt in 1706-11 as summer palace for the chancellor of Joseph I, houses a nicely organized **Museum for Austrian Folklore** (Österreichisches Museum für Volkskunde) *(Laudongasse 15-19, open Tues-Fri 9am-4pm, Sat-Sun 9am-noon, closed Mon* 🖭 *but free entry Sept-Apr on weekends).*

PRATER
(2.) Map 4B6. Metro/S-bahn U1, S7 to Praterstern/Wien Nord. Tram 5, 21, 0 to Praterstern, N to Prater Hauptallee. Bus 80A and 77A serve points inside the park.
"This is as jolly as the Prater," says Goethe's Faust of the Witches' Sabbath. Opened to the public by Joseph II, the former imperial game

preserve on the Danube banks became a byword for popular outdoor fun in the age of Mozart and Beethoven. It still offers an odd mixture of aristocratic elegance and democratic shabbiness.

The 4km/2½-mile-long, chestnut-lined Hauptallee begins at **Wurstel-prater**, an old-fashioned amusement park. This is dominated by a giant ferris-wheel, the **Riesenrad** (✷), one of the oldest and largest in the world and a revered symbol of the city. The **Lilliput-Bahn** miniature railway appears to cause equal joy to parents and kids.

Near the E end of the park is the **Lusthaus** (it means Fun House), an outdoor café-restaurant which has existed since the 16thC and assumed its present form under Joseph II. Here in 1814 the Congress of Vienna celebrated the fall of Napoleon with a dinner party attended by three monarchs, countless sovereign princes and ministers, and no less than 18,000 veteran soldiers.

RATHAUS (City Hall) ★
(1.) Rathausplatz. Map 3C2 ✗ *Mon-Fri at 1pm (no fee). Metro U2 to Rathaus. Tram 1, 2 to Rathausplatz.*

Under the ascendancy of the Liberals, who took over the administration of the capital in 1861, the City Hall of Vienna became the most influential political forum of the Austro-Hungarian empire while PARLIAMENT sat paralyzed by ethnic factionalism. A colossal New Rathaus (see ALTES RATHAUS, page 76) was built in 1872-83 to reflect the regained clout that the city had lost to the Habsburgs 600 years earlier. The Gothic style symbolized the medieval autonomy of Europe's cities — a tradition that Vienna had enjoyed less than any other major city in central Europe.

The Rathaus continued to play a dominant role under the populist administration of Mayor Karl Lueger (1897-1910). From 1919-34 it was the preserve of Marxists, during the "Red Vienna" period, who often governed in defiance of the national government across the avenue. In 1922 it became the seat of the federal *Land* of Vienna, when socialists voted to detach the city from the traditionally conservative state of Lower Austria.

Lueger was the son of a Viennese janitor who emerged as a fiery antisemitic orator in the 1890s. Elected four times but vetoed by Franz Joseph each time, he was finally allowed to take office in 1897. A pragmatic and immensely popular mayor, he installed electricity and gas works, developed Vienna's public transportation system into the best in Europe, opened more than 100 schools, and built an aqueduct from the Alps which still furnishes Vienna with the purest tap water enjoyed by any major metropolis. His deeply Catholic "little-man" ideology formed the basis of the Christian Social Party, the predecessor of today's ÖVP.

The public **showrooms** of the building are among the most richly appointed in Vienna and thus deserve a tour *(✗ compulsory)*. Concerts are held in summer in the arcaded **main courtyard**. As in all cities in the German lands there exists a municipal restaurant/beerhall — **Ratskeller** — in the cellar, a den of red-cheeked *gemütlichkeit.*

The monuments lining **Rathauspark** are better appreciated with reference to their political symbolism, which hints at servers of the city as opposed to the crown, and Liberal ideals as opposed to Habsburg conservatism. They comprise three rulers (Heinrich Jasomirgott, Leopold the Glorious and Rudolph the Founder) of whom only one is a Habsburg; three defenders of Vienna (Salm, Starhemberg and Kollonitsch); an architect (J.E. Fischer von Erlach); and the man (Sonnenfels) who persuaded Maria Theresa to abolish judicial torture.

RINGSTRASSE ✫

Clockwise with metro stations: **Stubenring** *(U4: Julius-Raab-Platz);* **Park Ring** *(U3: Stubentor);* **Schubertring, Kärntner Ring, Opernring** *(U1: Oper);* **Burgring, Karl-Renner-Ring, Dr-Karl-Lueger-Ring** *(U3: Dr-Karl-Renner-Ring);* **Schottenring** *(U2: Schottentor, Schottenring; U4: Schottenring). Tram 1 (clockwise) and 2 (counterclockwise) circle the Ring.*

"The Ringstrasse affected me like a fairy tale out of the Arabian Nights," said Adolf Hitler of his days as a wide-eyed youth in the imperial capital. "The new style is clumsy and flashy, it is full of pretension, that is, ordinary and vulgar," said the critic Alfred Polgar about the phenomenon which came to be known as "Ringstrasse architecture." Few other European avenues bring together so many buildings designed mainly to impress. Yet Ringstrasse lacks both the aristocratic elegance of Old Vienna and the self-confident vigor of Victorian London or Haussmann's Paris. Its disjointed lumps of architectural glory are like the dying gasps of an empire that never quite made it to the modern world.

Between 1858 and 1867, the advocates of Liberty, Progress and Wealth defeated the archaic bloc of Army and Church that had held the empire in its grip for over a half century. Conservatives had opposed demolishing Vienna's walls on security grounds, recalling with terror that the revolution of 1848 had only been defeated by artillery firing across the Glacis. In 1858, their objections were finally overridden by Franz Joseph himself. The Ring road itself was completed in 1865, but the construction of the buildings that line it, which involved the Austrian state in partnership with private developers, ran on into the 1910s.

Road traffic on the Ring runs clockwise. Following its course from the intersection with Franz-Josefs-Kai, two monumental buildings attract notice on Stuben Ring. The **Regierungsgebäude**, now housing various branches of government, was built in 1909-13 as the Imperial War Ministry; thus it is the monument of Field Marshall Radetzky, a hero of the conservative military faction, immortalized by Father Strauss's *Radetzky March*. The **Museum of Applied Arts** (Museum für angewandte Kunst, also called Kunstgewerbemuseum) holds an altogether fascinating collection of textiles including the world's most important assemblage of antique Oriental rugs, besides various other crafts such as glass and porcelain (📷 *open Wed-Mon 11am-6pm, closed Tues).*

The **Stadtpark** is liberally furnished with statues of famous Austrians, including a highly romantic **Monument of Johann Strauss Jr** (✫), the waltz king. In summer an orchestra performs his works daily at the outdoor café of the nearby **Kursalon** *(dancing 4-11pm)*.

The stretch from Park Ring to Opernring is lined with the prestigious apartment buildings of the 19thC bourgeoisie, which often imitate — in their outward appearance if not interior division — the aristocratic palaces of the previous century.

The hybrid *Rentenpalais* of the 18thC often had the landlord's residence on the *Nobeletage* (one floor up), while upper stories were subdivided for rental. Many 19thC apartment buildings maintain the illusion of a *Nobeletage* by their external decoration. To increase the value of the upper stories, the first floor is often called a *Mezzanine;* some buildings also have a *Hochparterre,* so "first floor" may actually mean three floors up.

The great public monuments of the Ringstrasse — the Museums of ART HISTORY and NATURAL HISTORY, the new wing of the HOFBURG, PARLIAMENT, RATHAUS, BURGTHEATER, UNIVERSITY and VOTIVE CHURCH — dominate the boulevard past Babenberger Str. Somewhat farther on is the Stock Exchange (**Börse**), built in the Italian Renaissance style by Theophil Hansen in 1874-77. The mammoth **Rossau Barracks** were built in a style sometimes called Neo-Byzantine as a concession to the militarist party, which otherwise opposed the Ringstrasse project.

ST MARX CEMETERY

(3.) Leber Str. 6-8. Map 2D5. Open Apr-Oct. For ✗ apply at tourist bureau for times. Tram 71, 72 to Litfass Str. Bus 74A to Hoffmansthalgasse.
Wolfgang Amadeus Mozart was buried in an unmarked grave in this cemetery on a stormy winter day of 1791. Disused for over 100 years, the cemetery now exudes the deeply romantic air of the early 19thC.

An attractive little **monument** at some arbitrary point commemorates Mozart. Mozart's funeral was not accompanied by any of his friends or family, and the location of his grave remained unknown. The melancholy circumstances, however, were not unique to him. In a spirit of radical secularism, Joseph II's Burial Decree of 1783 removed cemeteries from the jurisdiction of the church, banished them outside the city limits, prohibited burial in private coffins, and discouraged all forms of funeral pomp. Leopold II rescinded the order some months after Mozart's death.

SCHÖNBRUNN ★

Map 1D3. Obligatory ✗ of 45mins' duration, Apr-Sept from 8.30am-5.30pm, Oct from 8.30am-5pm, Nov-Mar from 9am-4pm. Park open daily 6am till dark. Metro U4 to Schönbrunn or Hietzing. Tram 58 to Schloss Schönbrunn.
Louis XIV of France moved his court from the cramped medieval lanes of Paris to the modern suburb of Versailles in 1682, and for a century afterwards every European monarch worth his penny felt the urge to follow his lead. Leopold I built Alte Favorita (at AUGARTEN) and Neue Favorita (now the Theresianum Academy: see OTHER SIGHTS, page 132). He also began building a country palace at the place called Fair Fountain (Schönbrunn), but this was soon given up. Equally abortive were

Karl VI's grandiose projects at Neubau (now the Messepalast: see SPIT-TELBERG) and KLOSTERNEUBURG (see page 181). The Habsburg response to the château of Versailles was not achieved until the reign of Maria Theresa some 70 years later.

History
Maria Theresa entrusted the project to Nicola Paccassi, who was instructed to build a palace at Schönbrunn on the basis of Fischer von Erlach's unrealized plans of the previous reign, but with minimum expenditure. The result, finished in 1750, was a building which combined majesty with an altogether pleasing simplicity of line (see the illustration on page 44). The favored color scheme of the empress — ocher and dark green — set a norm that was copied in countless buildings throughout her empire; it remains today a trademark of the older towns of Austria, Hungary, Czechoslovakia, Croatia, southern Poland, western Ukraine and northern Romania.

Schönbrunn embodied Habsburg court life in its most frilly epoch: the 18thC world of powdered wigs, masked balls and erotic sophistication. After that, it never fully recovered a role. Joseph II shunned palaces in general. Franz I preferred the Biedermeier charm of Baden for his summer repose while his daughter and grandson, the widow and son of Napoleon, lived as semiprisoners at Schönbrunn. Franz Joseph brought his homework to Schönbrunn for a couple of months each summer, so parts of the palace bear the stamp of his moldy Victorian taste.

Neglect and decline set in after 1918. The palace was hit repeatedly during air raids in February 1945, and its half-demolished hulk served after the war as the headquarters of British occupying forces. Now it processes over 2 million tourists each year with assembly-line efficiency.

Schlosstheater
The Schönbrunn theater, in the outer courtyard of the palace, was furbished in 1767 with late-Baroque frivolity, and remains the oldest stage in Vienna still to retain its original decoration. Chamber operas — mostly Mozart — are performed here during summer months *(mid-July to mid-Aug daily at 9.30pm, except on Sun)*.

The outer palace gates are flanked by two obelisks bearing the French imperial eagle, reminders of Napoleon's residence at Schönbrunn during his occupation of Vienna in 1809.

The château
Guided tours of the imperial quarters cover some 40 rooms, which are among the most luxuriously appointed anywhere in the world. The first few rooms belong to Franz Joseph and are rather similar to his quarters in the Hofburg (see IMPERIAL APARTMENTS, page 98). His **bedroom** has been kept as it was when he died on November 30, 1916.

Throughout his 68-year-long reign, the kaiser woke up regularly at 4.30am to do his paperwork. On the last day of his life he went to bed earlier than usual, telling his attendant to wake him at 3.30am because "there is so much work to be done." He died in his sleep.

The living quarters of Empress Elisabeth and the so-called Guest Apartments largely retain the original Rococo decoration of the reign of Maria Theresa, all pastels and frippery. Many rooms, notably the delightful **Breakfast Room**, hold mementoes of her 16 children (portraits of them and of favorite nannies, and suspiciously well-drawn childhood doodles). The **Mirror Room** is the setting of the famous episode where the child-wonder Mozart played the harpsichord for the little princesses, then climbed into the lap of their mother to kiss her on the cheek. Practically next door, in the **Round Chinese Cabinet**, she held her daily conference with Privy Chancellor Kaunitz to decide matters of war and diplomacy.

Beneath this veneer of domestic bliss, however, a disturbing undertone of tragedy is present: reminders of Marie Antoinette, one of the 16 children, who was guillotined in Paris; portraits of Franz II/I with his grim, set jaws; the death mask of the 21-year-old Duke of Reichstadt, Napoleon's son; the portrait of Archduke Rudolph which his mother kept after his suicide; and mementoes of Empress Zita, who was condemned to 50 years of desperate wandering because her husband had the evil luck to be thrust onto and then off the throne.

Pride of place among the various rooms goes to the **Great Gallery** and **Little Gallery**, interconnected into a single magnificent reception hall. The ceiling of the former is decorated with three vast frescoes by Gregorio Guglielmi, depicting the Habsburg Crown Lands, at the center, flanked by the Glories of War and the Blessings of Peace. The Peace composition (now fully restored) was ripped through by an American aerial bomb in 1945. In 1961, President Kennedy and Khrushchev met under it for a summit conference.

Wagenburg ✰
The former coach house of the château is now used to display a fascinating **Collection of Imperial Carriages**. The highlight of the show is the gilded and jeweled coronation car of Karl VI, which displays an almost childlike delight in finery. Also exhibited are the gala sedan-chair of Maria Theresa, the funeral coach of emperors, a child-buggy that belonged to the Duke of Reichstadt, and scores of other fantastic vehicles.

Gardens ★
See map opposite.
A splendid vista taking in the palace and a distant panorama of Vienna opens up at the **Gloriette**, a colonnade combining the style of early Classicism with a typically Baroque flourish (1775). The park calls for several hours of strolling to discover all its hidden gems: several fountains of striking beauty, some fake **Roman ruins** (built by von Hohenberg, 1778) as powerfully evocative as the real thing, an Egyptian obelisk, a charming Tyrolean Garden, and a topiary maze.

The **Schönbrunn Zoo**, established in 1752 by Franz I, the consort of Maria Theresa, is the oldest animal park functioning in Europe. It lost all its denizens in a frightful bloodbath in the Allied bombing of 1945, but

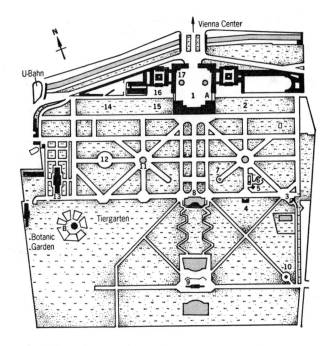

SCHÖNBRUNN PALACE GARDENS: KEY **1** Court of Honor **2** Crown Prince Garden **3** Obelisk **4** Roman Ruins **5** Beautiful Fountain **6** Angel Fountain **7** Dove House **8** Neptune Fountain **9** Gloriette **10** Little Gloriette **11** Star Basin **12** Rosarium **13** Palm House **14** English Garden **15** Chamber Garden **16** Wagenburg **17** Schlosstheater **A** Palace Restaurant **B** Zoo Restaurant

now contains about 760 species. The centerpiece of the zoo is a sumptuous Rococo pavilion, where once the imperial couple liked to take breakfast surrounded by the animals.

Hietzing ☆
Hietzing, which rivals GRINZING as one of the sweetest of Vienna's suburban villages, clings to the w edge of the palace grounds, and justifies a leisurely stroll if you have time. Particularly attractive are **Trautmansdorffgasse** and **Gloriettegasse**, full of country houses of the Biedermeier era. In one of these, at **Maxinggasse 18**, J. Strauss Jr lived and composed *die Fledermaus* at the peak of his fame in the 1870s. A few blocks away is the celebrated Dommayer casino, where a half century earlier Strauss' father and J. Lanner had started the Viennese craze for the waltz.

The highly evocative old **cemetery** of Hietzing contains the tombs of the poet Franz Grillparzer, the painter Gustav Klimt and the composer

Alban Berg. Adjacent to it and forming part of the Schönbrunn gardens is **Maxing**, the residence of Maximilian of Mexico, the fusilladed brother of Franz Joseph.

SCHWARZENBERG PALACE/HOTEL
*(3.) Rennweg 2. Map **4**F4. Tram D, 71 to Lothringer Str. Bus 4A to Lothringer Str. See also page 136 of WHERE TO STAY.*

Palais Schwarzenberg was designed by Hildebrandt in 1711. Father and son Fischer von Erlach directed its interior decoration, and Daniel Gran, the chief painter of the Viennese Baroque, executed its frescoes (destroyed in World War II but recently re-created). It has now been converted into a hotel by an heir of the Schwarzenbergs, who continues to live in part of the palace. The vast **garden** (✰), one of the most enticing parks of Vienna, is filled with allegories of Seduction and Abduction by Lorenzo Mattielli (c.1700).

Georg Ludwig, the founder of Schwarzenberg fortunes, entered the Austrian imperial service in 1617 as a penniless adventurer of 31, and distinguished himself in the suppression of the Bohemian revolt. He was granted immense estates in Bohemia, which he supplemented by marrying a five-times widowed heiress. Prince Karl Philipp, a descendant, led the Austrian armies to victory against Napoleon at Leipzig (1812) and Dresden (1813). His son Felix reconquered Vienna from the revolutionaries of 1848, and then became a byword for reactionary policies as Franz Joseph's chancellor.

At the time of writing, Karl, the current prince, is the influential chief of staff of Vaclav Havel, the president of Czechoslovakia.

Below the palace on Schwarzenbergplatz is the semicircular colonnade of the **Red Army Memorial**, featuring Soviet soldiers in heroic pose heeding the precepts of Joseph Stalin. The monument was erected in the Soviet occupied zone of Vienna after World War II, and is maintained by the terms of the 1955 treaties setting up the Austrian state.

SECESSION (Sezession) ✰
*(1.) Friedrich Str. 12. Map **3**E3 ☎ Open Tues-Fri 10am-6pm; Sat-Sun 10am-4pm. Closed Mon. Metro U1, U2, U4 to Karlsplatz.*

The exhibition hall-cum-temple of the last significant esthetic movement to emerge from Vienna, now reopened after many years in repair, was built in 1897-98. Its style has been mocked as Neo-Assyrian, and its extravagant crown of gold-plated leaves has earned the name of "golden cabbage," although none of this detracts from its cool and mesmerizing elegance. The motto engraved over the entrance, "To the Age its Art — to Art its Freedom," expresses the Secessionist program, if somewhat vaguely.

In addition to visiting exhibits, the hall offers Gustav Klimt's **Beethoven Frieze**, a vast composition in three parts that ranks among the chief works of Jugendstil/Art Nouveau. It was created for the event/show held in 1902 on the occasion of the dedication of Max Klinger's **Bee-**

thoven Monument (now at Beethovenplatz on Lothringer Str., seven blocks away to the E). The elegant bronze group of **Mark Antony** was made by Artur Strasser for the 1901 World's Fair in Paris, and shows the triumvir riding a chariot drawn by lions.

Other classics of the Secession, the **Linke Wienzeile** apartments of Otto Wagner (see under NASCHMARKT) and the **Karlsplatz tram stations** (see under KARLSKIRCHE), are within short walking distance.

SPITTELBERG ✩

(7.) Map 3E1. Metro U2 to Volkstheater. Tram 49 to Stiftgasse. Bus 48A to Breite Gasse.

The revitalization of the 5-block historic area between Burggasse and Siebensterngasse behind the Messepalast has been one of the City Council's success stories in recent years. Nearly all houses in the area date from 1683-1706 and provide an unpompous counterpart to Vienna's era of glory. Freshly repaired, painted in candy colors, filled with knickknack shops, whimsical cafés and student locales, they give a feeling of what Vienna *could be* with more public money and fewer illusions of past grandeur.

Before 1683, the Spittelberg quarter was a notorious slum of immigrant Croats, Wends (Slovenes) and Hungarians. Like everything else outside the city walls, it was demolished before the Turkish siege — *not* by the Turks, but by the defenders who wanted to deny cover to the enemy. Kara Mustafa is said to have had his tent pitched at the site of Kellermanngasse 1.

The area offers several of the most enticing little restaurants in Vienna. Try the modest **Zu ebener Erde und erster Stock** ("Ground Floor and First Story") at Burggasse 13 for their "old Viennese" specialties.

Vicinity

The **Messepalast** *(Messeplatz 1)* is a relic of the never-completed palace of Karl VI, which was originally meant to cover all of the 7. district (Neubau = "New Building") but was given up in 1725 when funds ran out. Used as horse stables for many years, the building — with its 19thC additions — now houses the year-round exhibits of the Vienna Commercial Fair (Wiener Messe).

Facing it to the N is the Neo-Renaissance edifice of the **Volkstheater**, Vienna's second most important house of drama after the BURGTHEATER.

Behind this on Neustiftgasse is the **Palais Trautson**, considered by many to be the chief secular masterpiece of Fischer von Erlach Sr. Completed in 1712, the palace was later acquired by Maria Theresa to house her famous Hungarian Guard; it now serves as the Ministry of Justice.

Next to it, the **Mechitarist Abbey** of Armenian monks offers an interesting museum of Near Eastern antiquities.

Another imposing Baroque palace, **Palais Auersperg**, rises at the corner of Lerchenfelder Str. and Auersperg Str. Its hidden **garden** (✩), used for daily Mozart and Strauss concerts, is perhaps the most elegant

129

of the publicly accessible spaces to be found in Vienna *(Mozart trio Tues, Thurs, Sat, Sun 4.30pm; coffee and cake served. Strauss waltzes daily at 7, 8, 9pm; champagne served. Both* ▨ *AS140* ☎ *40107).*

In Maria Theresa's time the Auersperg palace belonged to Count Rofrano, the hero of Hugo von Hoffmansthal's *Rosenkavalier* and Richard Strauss's opera of the same name.

STADTPARK   See under RINGSTRASSE.

STEINHOF

(14.) Baumgartner Höhe 1. Map 1C2 ⚹ *every Sat at 3pm: meet at Hospital entrance, or* ☎ *949060. Bus 47A, 48A to Psychiatrisches Krankenhaus.*

The church of the psychiatric institute of Steinhof, built by Otto Wagner and Kolo Moser in 1904-7, represents one of the genuine masterpieces of the Viennese Jugendstil. It is a rare example of the successful application of 20thC esthetics to religious art.

Another prominent Secessionist work, the **Otto Wagner Villa**, which the architect designed for his own residence, is within a long (40-minute) walking distance sw in the suburb of Penzing. The house is in private possession but can be toured by appointment *(at (14.) Hüttelberg Str. 26* ☎ *948575; from city, take tram 49 to last stop; from Steinhof, take bus 47A to tram 49).*

The long-neglected Jugendstil theater at **Baumgartner Höhe**, within the premises of the Psychiatric Institute, reopened in 1991-92 as the home of **Neue Oper Wien**, Vienna's newest opera company.

UNIVERSITY (Universität)

(1.) Dr-Karl-Lueger-Ring. Map 3C2. Metro U2 to Schottentor. Tram 1, 2 to Schottentor.

The University was designed by Heinrich Ferstel in the style of Italian Renaissance and finished at the height of the "Ringstrasse" era in 1883.

The University of Vienna was founded to rival that of Prague during the reign of Rudolph IV "the Founder" (1358-65). Relegated to a political limbo after the revolution of 1848, its return to this prestigious location on the Ring represented a victory for the Liberals.

The university flourished between the 1890s and 1930s. The "Vienna School" of economics (Karl Menger, Böhm-Bawerk) introduced the concept of marginal utility, one of the key ideas of 20thC economics. The "Vienna Circle" of philosophers (Carnap, Schlick, Wittgenstein, the young Popper) developed logical positivism, and later as refugees formed the core of Cambridge University's philosophical school. Gödel revolutionized 20thC mathematics. The psychoanalytical teachings of Freud, Adler and Frankl, meanwhile, found limited acceptance in the halls of academic psychology.

The philosopher Moritz Schlick was murdered in 1936 by a deranged student on the outer steps of the university.

UNO-CITY

(22.) Wagramer Str., 4km (2½ miles) NE. *Map* **2B4** ⚔ *and film Mon-Fri at 11am and 2pm. Metro U1 to Kaisermühlen/VIC. Bus 391, 590.*

After World War II, Vienna tried hard to compensate for its lost status by seeking a role in international organizations. Several UN agencies (the UN Industrial Development Organization, Atomic Energy Agency, the Palestinian refugee council and others) set up their headquarters in the city, allowing Vienna the consolation of naming itself the third UN center after New York and Geneva.

Kurt Waldheim, who had earlier run unsuccessfully for the Austrian presidency, became the UN's Secretary General in 1971. He promoted the gigantic office and residential complex of the Vienna International Center (popularly known as UNO-City), which nearly bankrupted the Austrian treasury and did not, for all that, necessarily please the UN functionaries who were asked to leave the gorgeous halls of the Hofburg for the marshy wastes of "Transdanubia."

The **Austria Center**, claimed to be the largest convention center in Europe, was added to the complex in 1987. A newer **Islamic Center**, consisting of a mosque and meeting facilities, underlined Vienna's ambitions to refurbish its cosmopolitan image.

UNO-City now features a revolving tower-restaurant, shopping centers and an excellent park (❀). Behind it, a series of immensely popular parks line the banks of the **Alte Donau**, a lazy branch of the Danube, offering beaches, boating clubs, swimming pools and aquatic sports. The newly created park of the Danube Island (**Donauinsel**), a 20km/13-mile-long sliver of green between Neue Donau and the main branch of the river, has also become a popular summer destination with its beaches, roller-skating rinks and bicycle routes. Nudist swimmers who at one time almost took over the island are now confined to its southern and northern extremities.

VIENNA WOODS   See GRINZING AND HEILIGENSTADT.

VOTIVE CHURCH (Votivkirche zum göttlichen Heiland) ★

(9.) Rooseveltplatz. Map **3C2.** *Metro U2 to Schottentor. Tram 1, 2 to Schottentor.*

The sumptuous Gothic cathedral of Franz Joseph was built many hundreds of years after the close of the Middle Ages, following a failed attempt in 1853 on the life of the kaiser. Archduke Maximilian, the future emperor of Mexico, organized the mass campaign to build a church of thanksgiving on the spot. Heinrich Ferstel, then aged 25, won the competition for its design. His work was the first important monument of the historicist craze that gripped Vienna in the second half of the 19thC.

Politically, Votivkirche represented a dying victory for the military-conservative party. The public subscription drive whipped up much patriotic frenzy, and it was claimed that the successful outcome expressed "the unbreakable unity of Throne and Altar against the mortally wounded tiger of Revolution."

In purely architectural terms the church is a very effective copy of the great French cathedrals of the 13thC. The interior contains several original pieces transferred from elsewhere, including the elaborate 16thC **Tomb of Count Niklas Salm**, the savior of Vienna in the first Turkish siege of 1529. The rich **glasswork**, destroyed in 1945, is still being restored.

The **Sigmund-Freud-Park** outside the church was named to commemorate the founder of psychoanalysis, who presumably crossed it often on his way between home and university.

OTHER SIGHTS

DISTRICT MUSEUMS: Each of the 22 outer districts of Vienna boasts a municipal museum. Some of them are devoted to a specific theme, and a few merit a visit. Among the more interesting ones is that of **Leopoldstadt** (district 2.), which features a **Clown and Circus Collection** *(Karmelitergasse 9, open Wed 5.30-7pm, Sat 2.30-5pm, Sun 10am-noon, closed Mon-Tues, Thurs)*, and that of **Hietzing** (13.), which possesses an important collection of Ethiopica *(Am Platz 2, open Sat 2.30-5pm, Sun 10am-noon, closed Mon-Fri)*.

Other points of interest worth seeking out are the following:

LANDSTRASSE (3.): The district hides several attractive palais, including **Palais Rasumofsky**, home of the celebrated Russian nobleman and ambassador for whom Beethoven composed his great string quartets. It is now the Federal Geological Institute.

WIEDEN (4.): Leopold I's summer pavilion, the Neue Favorita, was converted by Maria Theresa into the **Theresianum Academy** for the children of aristocratic families. It continues to be a prestigious school whose alumni dominate many areas of Austria's civil service. The huge **Museum of Military History**, a monument of the military-authoritarian era that followed Franz Joseph I's accession to the throne in 1848, contains relics of the Turkish siege of 1683 *(🔳 open Sat-Thurs 10am-4pm, closed Fri)*.

MARIAHILF (6.): The summer palace of Prince Kaunitz, the chancellor of Maria Theresa and Joseph II, once covered a large part of the district and hosted such illustrious guests as Casanova and the Pope. Acquired by the Esterházy family at a later date, it survives only in a fraction of its gardens, which go by the name of **Esterházy Park**.

The nearby **church of Mariahilf** possesses an icon of the Virgin which since time immemorial has been Vienna's most popular object of pilgrimage. In the former village of Gumpendorf, not far away, one can visit the **Haydn Museum** *(Haydngasse 19 🔳 open Tues-Sun 10am-12.15pm, 1-4.30pm, closed Mon)* in an attractive house where the composer spent his final years.

SIMMERING (11.): About halfway to CENTRAL CEMETERY on the main street of Simmering, a graceful Gothic tower stands in a desolate environment of grimy buildings, cheap bars and gas stations. Legend has it that the **Spinnerin am Kreuz** ("Spinster-at-the-Cross") was built in

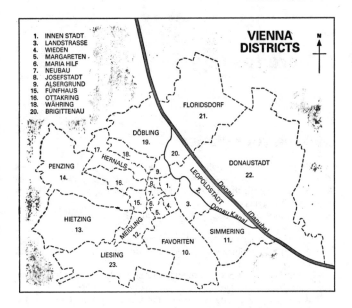

1451-52 to commemorate the wife of the knight Hintberg, who waited at the crossroads many years for the return of her husband from a crusade.

WÄHRING (18.): Here are some of the grandest garden suburbs of Vienna. The largest concentration of expensive villas is found around **Türkenschanz Park**, in the area known as Cottage. Farther up in the hills is the wine-growing village of **Pötzleinsdorf** with its delightful 18thC château *(Geymüllergasse 1),* which has a fine public park. The château was once purchased by the banker Geymüller for his mistress Maria Preindl, the most gossiped-about beauty of the Vienna Congress.

In nearby **Neuwaldegg** it is possible to see — but not enter — **Schloss Lacy**, where Maria Theresa's minister of war built one of Europe's most famous Baroque gardens, complete with a Dutch-rustic village. The property was later acquired by the Schwarzenberg family and is now a private park.

DÖBLING (19.): The district museum housed in **Villa Wertheim-stein** is a pretty Biedermeier house full of period objects, with a splendid English garden and a wine cellar next door *(Döblinger Hauptstrasse 96, entrance free, open Sat 3.30-6pm, Sun 10am-noon, closed Mon-Fri).*

LIESING (23.): The far half of the district consists of a series of sleepy wine-growing villages. In one of these, **Mauer**, the prominent sculptor Fritz Wotruba has designed the futuristic **Church of the Holy Trinity** (Zur Heiligsten Dreifaltigkeit) *(St-Georgen-Berg, open Mon-Fri 2-6pm, Sat 2-8pm, Sun 9am-5pm),* which consists of a number of vertical concrete slabs.

Where to stay

Making your choice

Austria is awash with idyllic little country inns whose very name —
Gasthof, a guest court — connotes homey ease and flower pots. Not
Vienna. In general, though with certain exceptions, the capital offers
the following styles of accommodation:

- A handful of *grands hôtels* of palatial splendor and old-fashioned
  luxury
- Some two dozen others that try to emulate them (oodles of Mozart
  and Franz Joseph, cheap crystal, piped-in waltz, Sachertorte) — and
  charge a fortune for the privilege
- About a hundred old apartment building-hotels of routine and weary
  standards
- And — a precipitous step down the ladder — moth-eaten hovels
  filled with desperate East Europeans

Prices often border on the outrageous, and many amenities you might
be forgiven for taking for granted in less ex-imperial parts of the world
— such as color TV, functioning telephones, maybe even a fitness room
— are here still considered things of expensive luxury. One saving grace
is that Viennese hotels usually serve good food. And even the lowliest of
them feels obliged to own a chandelier or two and a few pieces of period
furniture.

As a rule: the chances of discovering something oh-so-nice at an
acceptable price is near-nil within the inner districts; there are indeed a
few, but they get booked up months in advance. So either resign yourself
to basic amenities and sour service, or go directly for the palatial. The
alternative is to move out to one of the outlying villages, where there are
a few — too few — places of unimpeachable loveliness that charge
reasonable prices.

The **Vienna Tourist Board** publishes an admirably comprehensive
hotel list, available in all tourist information bureaux. Many of the bureaux
also offer a reservation service — but at a cost.

Many hotels offer package deals designed to attract customers in the
low season (November to March, except Christmas week). One such
arrangement involves a night's free stay for anyone who spends at least
three nights in a hotel over a weekend in the low season. Another
money-saving tip: never make your long-distance phone calls from your
hotel unless you find out about charges beforehand. The same call made
from a post office may cost you several times less.

LOCATION

Many hotels, including most of the classics, are located along **Kärntner Str.-Graben** and the **Ring**. About two dozen others are found scattered evenly through the northern and eastern half of the **Inner City** (although there is nothing at all in the Herrengasse area). Large concentrations of middling-to-better-class hotels exist to the sw of **Karlsplatz**, near **Mariahilfer Str.** and throughout the district of **Josefstadt**. Cheaper accommodations cluster near the main rail stations: Südbahnhof, Westbahnhof and Wien Nord.

District numbers in the Inner City (1.) are not given for hotels described in the following pages.

PRICES

As a guideline, our price categories are based on charges for two in a **double room** with private shower/bath, inclusive of breakfast and Value-Added Tax (*Mehrwertsteuer* in German, shortened to MWST). Prices given below are **winter rates** (valid October 1991 to March 1992): expect a markup of 25 to 40 percent in summer and during Christmas/New Year vacations, although relative ratings are hardly affected. Hotels indicated with a double price class (for example ▦ to ▦) offer rooms in both price categories.

Although actual prices will inevitably increase, our relative price categories should remain stable and accurate.

Symbol	Category	Current price	(Dollar amount)
▦	very expensive	AS3,000-5,000	($275-450)
▦	expensive	AS1,800-2,999	($160-275)
▦	moderate	AS1,100-1,799	($95-160)
▢	inexpensive	AS600-1,099	($55-95)
▢	cheap	under AS600	(under $55)

LUXURY HOTELS

The classic trio of Vienna's stately hotels (the **Bristol**, **Imperial** and **Sacher**) has been more recently joined by one genuine palace (**Hotel Im Palais Schwarzenberg**) and several others emulating the grand style of the older establishments (**SAS-Palais**, **Plaza Hilton**, **Hotel de France**). In addition, there is the usual complement of American chains (**Hilton**, **Inter-Continental**, **Marriott**, **Ramada**) offering smooth and reliable standards. One old-fashioned country hotel (**Clima Villenhotel**) and one very new-fashioned vacation complex (**City Club Vienna**) offer space and relaxation as quid for the quo of an inconveniently faraway location.

In the following selection, the absence of symbols does *not* imply any lack of facilities. **All** hotels in this category possess one or more restaurant and bar, have color TV and direct-dial telephone in each room, and accept major charge and credit cards. **All** offer conference facilities, although the capacity of such facilities may vary from tiny (30 persons in the case of the Hotel Ambassador) to huge (1,000 each for the Hilton and Inter-Continental).

BRISTOL
Kärntner Ring 1 ☎*51516-0*
🖷*51516550.* Map *3E3* ▥ *146 rms* ▣
▢
Location: Central, near the Opera. This has been called "a gem among the great hotels of this world," although its relatively humdrum exterior does not betray the elegance of its inner decor. Theodore Roosevelt, Enrico Caruso, Giacomo Puccini and John Galsworthy rubbed shoulders at the Bristol during the legendary days of the turn of the century. The Duke of Windsor would always take the same apartments, while Leonard Bernstein insisted on hauling in his own grand piano. The top floor is organized as a private club for select guests. Politicians and diplomats hobnob at the restaurant **Korso bei der Oper** (SEE WHERE TO EAT).

CITY CLUB VIENNA
In Vösendorf, Parkallee 2 ☎*693535*
🖷*693392.* Map *1F3.* ▥ *471 rms* ♿ ❦
⇌ ☲ ▽ ▣▢ ➹ ❦ ℘ ○ ⍩
Location: 10km (6 miles) s of the center. A brand-new vacation complex managed by Club Méditerranée near Shopping-City Süd, in Vienna's newest suburban shopping center. An ultramodern glass pyramid encloses a tropical garden and swimming pool. There is also an outdoor swimming pool, plus tennis, aerobics, fitness club, animation, and all else that one associates with Club Med except the sound of breaking surf. Day visitors pay AS290 to use the facilities.

CLIMA VILLENHOTEL 🖴
(19.) Nussbergasse 2c ☎*371516*
🖷*371392.* Map *1B3* ▥ to ▥ *30 rms*
❦ ⇌ ▣ ➷ ○
Location: In Nussdorf, 7km (4 miles) N of the center. A lovely garden house in the middle of a quiet neighborhood of prosperous villas, with a view extending over the Danube and Vienna Woods. Although somewhat far from the center at the northern edge of suburban Vienna, it is within strolling distance of the valley that inspired Beethoven's Sixth.

HILTON
(3.) am Stadtpark ☎*71700-0*
🖷*7130691.* Map *4D4* ▥ *600 rms* ▣
▢ ➷ ➹ ○ ⍩ ♿
Location: Near the center, on the N edge of the Stadtpark. The older and bigger of Vienna's two Hiltons boasts a world-famous temple of *nouvelle cuisine*, the **Prinz Eugen** restaurant. Proximity to the next-door City Air Terminal is a plus, but otherwise this is no different from any Hilton anywhere in the world.

IMPERIAL
Kärntner Ring 16 ☎*50110* 🖷*50110410.*
Map *3E3* ▥ *152 rms* ▣ ▢
Location: Right by the Opera. Inaugurated personally by Franz Joseph and boasting a star-spangled roster of celebrity guests, the Imperial unsurprisingly fails to advertise its biggest catch ever: Adolf Hitler, who would stay here whenever he came to town. The building, one of the finest *Bürgerpalais* on Ringstrasse, was originally built as the residence of Duke Philipp of Württemberg. The polished but surprisingly inexpensive **Café Imperial** serves a first-rate lunch.

SACHER
Philharmoniker Str. 4 ☎*51456*
🖷*51457810.* Map *3E3* ▥ *123 rms* ▢
Location: Across the street from the Opera. Synonymous with *fin de siècle* Viennese elegance since the days of Franz Joseph and Archduke Rudolph, Vienna's most prestigious hotel offers splendidly appointed rooms and one of Europe's top restaurants. It is a star item in its own right on Vienna's sightseeing list (see page 76).

HOTEL IM PALAIS SCHWARZENBERG
🖴
(3.) Schwarzenbergplatz 9 ☎*784515*
🖷*784714.* Map *4F4* ▥ *38 rms* ❦ ⇌
➹ ➷
Location: Within 10 minutes' walk of the Opera. Housed in a *real* Baroque palace as opposed to a 19thC emulation (see page 128), Vienna's newest luxury hotel offers access to the most seductively beautiful garden in town. Service

is impeccable, unspoiled by hype. The restaurant ranks among the top five for cuisine (see page 149). Special touches include a full selection of international newspapers, jogging in the palace park, and wall decorations by Daniel Gran.

OTHER LUXURY-CLASS HOTELS

AMBASSADOR
Neuer Markt 6 ☎*51466* ✉*5132999. Map 3D3* ▥ to ▥ *106 rms* ❤ ▣ 🔗
Centrally located on Kärntner Str., with an excellent restaurant.

HOTEL DE FRANCE
Schottenring 3 ☎*343540* ✉*315969. Map 3C2* ▥ to ▥ *217 rms* ▣ ☐ ➽ ✧ ⚲ 🔗
An elegant Ringstrasse hotel.

INTER-CONTINENTAL WIEN
(3.) Johannesgasse 28 (s edge of Stadtpark) ☎*71122* ✉*7134489. Map 4E4* ▥ to ▥ *498 rms* ▣ ➽ ➽ ✧ ⚲ 🔗
Imitation-Vienna ambience with fake-crystal chandeliers. The 6th floor is reserved for nonsmokers.

MARRIOTT
Park Ring 12a ☎*51518-0* ✉*51518-6736. Map 4D4* ▥ to ▥ *310 rms* ≋ ▣ ☐ ➽ ✧ ⚲ 🔗
Dramatically designed modern hotel.

PARKHOTEL SCHÖNBRUNN
(13.) Hietzinger Hauptstrasse 10-14
☎*822676* ✉*8284282. Map 1D3* ▥ to ▥ *435 rms* ❤ ≋ ▣ ➽ ➽ ✧ ⚲ 🔗
"The guesthouse of kaisers" is a large complex with both classical and modern wings and one of the most fashionable bars in Vienna. It faces the main entrance of Schönbrunn Palace.

RAMADA
(5.) Linke Wienzeile/Ullmann Str. 71
☎*8504-0* ✉*8504100* ▥ to ▥ *309 rms* ≋ ▣ ☐ ▣ ➽ ✧ ⚲
The least expensive of Vienna's luxury hotels.

PLAZA HILTON
Schottenring 11 ☎*31390-0* ✉*31390160. Map 3C2* ▥ *223 rms* ▣ ☐ ➽ ➽ ✧ ⚲ 🔗
Smaller, more luxurious than the other Hilton, with an excellent restaurant.

SAS-PALAIS
Weihburggasse 32 ☎*515117-0* ✉*5122216. Map 4D4* ▥ *155 rms* ▣ ☐ ✧ ⚲ 🔗
A stately palais on the Ring: the most expensive hotel in town.

MEDIUM-TO-BETTER-CATEGORY HOTELS
The official register lists some eighty 4-star and fifty 3-star hotels in Vienna, as well as some fifty 4- and 3-star pensions, which often differ from hotels in name only. Buildings vary from impeccably restored Baroque and Biedermeier mansions to prewar apartment houses adapted more or less successfully to the needs of the modern tourist business. There are some hotels, even, that occupy several floors of an apartment building otherwise filled with ordinary homes or offices. There are few modern hotels specifically built for the purpose.

BEETHOVEN
(6.) Millöckergasse 6 ☎*5874482* ✉*5874442. Map 3E3* ▥ *37 rms* AE ◑ ▥ ⚥ ☐
Location: Off Karlsplatz. A pleasant, family-run hotel, next to the famous **Theater an der Wien** where Beethoven stayed as a live-in guest during the first performance of his only opera, *Fidelio.*

BIEDERMEIER ⌂
(3.) Landstrasser Hauptstrasse 28
☎*755575* ✉*755575503. Map 4E5* ▥

204 rms ⒜⒠ ▣ ⊡ ▦ ☙ ⇌ ♈ ⬛ ➴
🛥 Metro U3 (Rochusgasse). Bus 74A
(Weyrgasse). On bus route to airport.
*Location: Within 20 minutes' walk of
the center.* An impeccable period-piece
with everything that the name implies:
nostalgic charm, period furniture, flag-
stone-paved courtyard, enclosed garden, vaulted wine cellar and pink-faced
waitresses in starched collars. The hotel
occupies part of historic Sünnhof, a narrow passage which connects Landstrasser Hauptstrasse with Ungargasse.
One of the best buys in town.

CAPRICORNO

Schwedenplatz 3-4 ☎5333104-0
⒡⒳53376714. Map *4C4* ▦ *46 rms* ⒜⒠
▣ ▦ ➡ ⬛ ➴ *Metro U1*
(Schwedenplatz).
Location: On the Danube Canal. A
clean, modern, efficient hotel with polite personnel — a refreshing touch for
a Viennese hotel outside the luxury
class. There is a nice broad view across
the river. The same company owns
Hotel am Parkring *(Park Ring 12,
map 4D4* ▦ ☎ 514800).*

HOHE WARTE ⌂

(19.) Steinfeldgasse 7, Heiligenstadt
☎373212 ⒡⒳375949. Map *1B3* ▦ *38
rms. No cards* ☙ ➴ ♿ *Tram 37 (from
Schottentor) directly to hotel, or take metro
to Heiligenstadt and walk 10mins.*
*Location: Within walking distance of
central Heiligenstadt.* A total delight,
and inexpensive too, for those who
seek peace and don't mind being a little
far from the center. Buried in greenery
with a large park behind and a smaller
one across the street, the Hohe Warte
offers a pleasant garden, a slow tempo,
and a slightly dusty 1960s ambience. A
2-minute walk across the park brings
you to the indoor public swimming
pool of Döbling — a considerable advantage after a hectic day in the city.

K+K HOTEL MARIA THERESA

(7.) Kirchberggasse 6-8 ☎52123
⒡⒳5212370. Map *3E1* ▦ *to* ▦ *123 rms*
⒜⒠ ▣ ▣ ▦ ⇌ ♈ ⬛ ➴ ♿
Location: In Spittelberg, two blocks from

the Art History Museum. Of the army of
Franz Joseph clones guarding the gates
of Austria's hotels, this one has the most
authentic-looking specimen. The ex-
ploitation of Viennese clichés is relentless, but the level of *ersatz* luxury must
be deemed admirable.

KÖNIG VON UNGARN

Schuler Str. 10 ☎51584-0 ⒡⒳515848.
Map *3D3* ▦ *32 rms* ▣ ▦ ⇌ ♈ ⬛ ♿
*Location: Centrally located on
Stephansplatz, right around the corner
from the cathedral and Mozart's house.*
The "King of Hungary" is a Vienna classic: an early 16thC building with beautiful old furniture in the rooms, not just
in the lobbies. Hand-painted doors bear
the names of illustrious guests of the
past, among them that of Schubert, who
often played and sometimes stayed in
the hotel. But don't expect any joy unless you reserve several months in advance.

MERCURE

Fleischmarkt 1a and 2 ☎53460-0
⒡⒳53460233. Map *4C4* ▦ *50 + 105 rms*
⒜⒠ ▣ ▣ ▦ ♈ ⬛ ⬛
*Location: In the "Bermuda Triangle,"
10 minutes' walk from the center.* The
old Mercure branched out in 1991 into
a nicely restored pink-and-cream historic house across the street, in the heart
of the trendy nightlife zone of the Old
City. This subscribes to the crisp, modern chic of the 1990s — as opposed to
the stiff grandeur of the *1890s*
preferred by Vienna's other hotels —
with modern rooms, and a stylish bar
and café. A special touch is the fax
connection in every room.

PENTA

(3.) Ungargasse 60 ☎71175-0
⒡⒳7117590. Map *4F5* ▦ *342 rms* ⒜⒠
▣ ▣ ▦ ⇌ ♈ ☙ ⊯ ⬛ ⬛ ➴ ☞ ♈
♿
*Location: 20 minutes' walk from the
center.* Somewhat off-center, in fact,
but this is an attractive, unusual, colorful building with its very own onion-
domed Russian church next door.
Modern and airy, it has good amenities,

RÖMISCHER KAISER
Annagasse 16 ☎5127751-0
Fx512775113. Map *3D3* ⬛ *24 rms* AE
⬛ ⬛ ⬛ ⬛ ⬛ ⬛
Location: Off Kärntner Str. This ornate Baroque mini-palace in the heart of the Inner City, built in 1684, has a cozy atmosphere and nicely furnished rooms of widely varying sizes. One major drawback is that there is no restaurant.

WANDL
Petersplatz 9 ☎53455-0 Fx5345577.
Map *3D3* ⬛ *138 rms* ☛
Location: Close to the cathedral. An ancient building with vaulted basements dating from the 12thC, its past career included stints as a monastery and as a dormitory for Vienna's prostitutes. Some rooms face the cathedral, others the Peterskirche. Reservations are essential.

OTHER MIDDLE-CATEGORY HOTELS

ALTWIENERHOF
(15.) Herklotzgasse 6 (in Gumpendorf, metro U6) ☎837145 Fx85982532 ⬛ to ⬛ *23 rms* ⬛ ⬛ ⬛
Famous above all for its gourmet restaurant (see page 149), with a few cozy rooms upstairs for those who wish to stay overnight. Good value for money.

AM STEPHANSPLATZ
Stephansplatz 9 ☎53405-0
Fx53405711. Map *3D3* ⬛ to ⬛ *62 rms* ⬛ ⬛ ⬛
This is as centrally located as you can get, facing the main gate of the cathedral. Otherwise it is routine. Parking will be a problem if you bring a car.

ARABELLA HOTEL JAGDSCHLOSS ⬛
(13.) Jagdschlossgasse 79 ☎8043508
⬛ to ⬛ *48 rms* ⬛ ⬛ ⬛ ⬛
The perfect old hunting estate in the Vienna Woods, not far from the LAINZER TIERGARTEN (see page 117). Quite far out, but on the train and tram line.

HOTEL-PENSION ARENBERG
Stubenring 2 ☎5125291 Fx5139356.
Map *4D4* ⬛ to ⬛ *25 rms* ⬛ ⬛ ⬛
Hides a surprisingly elegant, clubby atmosphere on the 3rd and 4th floors of an otherwise nondescript building.

ASTORIA
Kärntner Str. 32 ☎51577-0. Map *3D3* ⬛
5157782 ⬛ to ⬛ *108 rms* ⬛ ⬛ ⬛
⬛ ⬛ ⬛ ⬛ ⬛ ⬛ ⬛
An old hotel successfully furnished with Jugendstil and 19thC furniture.

CHRISTINA
Hafnersteig 7 ☎5332961
Fx533296111. Map *4C4* ⬛ *33 rms* ⬛
A centrally located, charming, unpretentious pension.

ERZHERZOG RAINER
(4.) Wiedner Hauptstrasse 27-29
☎50111-0 Fx50111350. Just off map
3F3 ⬛ to ⬛ *84 rms* ⬛ ⬛ ⬛ ⬛ ⬛
⬛ ⬛ ⬛
A stately 19thC palais, formerly home of a nephew of Franz Joseph. Service is modern and efficient.

MAILBERGER HOF
Annagasse 7 ☎5120641. Map *3D3* ⬛
to ⬛ *40 rms* ⬛ ⬛ ⬛ ⬛ ⬛ ⬛ ⬛ ⬛
An attractive historic building with a lovely courtyard.

NORDBAHN
(2.) Prater Str. 72 ☎21130-0
Fx2113072. Map *4B5* ⬛ *77 rms* ⬛ ⬛
⬛ ⬛ ⬛ ⬛
A fine middle-class hotel near the Prater. The building was the birthplace of Max Steiner, a native of Vienna who made a career in Hollywood as composer of film music for *Casablanca* and *Gone With the Wind.*

PANNONIA INTERNATIONAL
(6.) Matrosengasse 6 ☎59901-0
Fx5976900 ⬛ to ⬛ *214 rms* ⬛ ⬛
⬛ ⬛ ⬛ ⬛ ⬛ ⬛ ⬛ ⬛ ⬛ ⬛
Modern, spotless, efficient, and surprisingly inexpensive pending the settlement of its classification (star-count).

SCHWEIZERHOF
Bauernmarkt 22 ☎*5331931* ℻*630214.*
Map 3D3 ▢ *55 rms* ▢
A centrally located middle-class hotel
with friendly management.

ZUR WIENER STAATSOPER
Kruger Str. 11 ☎*5131274*
℻*513127415. Map 3E3* ▢ *22 rms* ▢
A small family-owned hotel hard by the
Opera.

INEXPENSIVE HOTELS

Vienna's lower-category (2- or 1-star) hotels seem to be geared primarily to guests from the former Eastern bloc countries and the Near East,
and may therefore fail to correspond to the expectations of visitors
from more pampered lands. Usual features include unshaven recep-
tionists, nasty repairmen who keep bursting into your room, and a
gloomy bar full of cigarette-stained formica tables. Still, they can be a
lot of fun if you like having beer with all sorts of people, or if your
interests include cheap Byelorussian radios or Romanian girls.

Those with a literary bent may wish to know that it was at a flea-bitten
hovel near the Südbahnhof, called Hotel Riva, that Franz Kafka met
Milena for the first and only time in his life in 1920. That hotel no longer
exists, and fleas are admittedly rather rare these days, but there are still
enough hotels near the Südbahnhof that Kafka could recognize.

The following four have been checked and found to offer tolerable
standards.

ADLON
(2.) Hofenedergasse 4 (near Praterstern)
☎*266788* ℻*266788116. Map 4B5* ▢
38 rms ☙ ▢
A reasonably well-kept place not far
from the center.

KUGEL
(7.) Siebensterngasse 43 ☎*933355*
℻*931678. Map 3E1* ▢ *to* ▢ *38 rms*
☙
Small, quite clean, and 20 minutes on
foot from the center.

WILD
(8.) Lange Gasse 10 ☎*435174*
℻*433408. Map 3D1* ▢ *14 rms* ☙ ∘ ☙
The cheapest place within walking distance of the center (a few blocks behind
Parliament), yet quite nice and friendly.

ZUR STADTHALLE
(15.) Hackengasse 20 ☎*924272*
℻*924105* ▢ *35 rms* ☙ ☙ ▢ ♿
A place to try when everything else in
town is full.

PRIVATE PENSIONS

Formal pensions are quite similar to hotels, except that they usually
occupy only some floors in buildings shared with other users. It is also
possible to find lodgings at the homes of private individuals on a
bed-and-breakfast basis. This is not always a very attractive option in
the city, but it is possible to discover in the villages some truly pleasant
places to stay on this basis.

The best-established among various bed-and-breakfast referral agencies is **B + B Vienna** *(at (23.) Rieglgasse 47b* ☎ *and* ℻*885219).* They
sometimes offer rooms in the HUNDERTWASSER HOUSE, too (see page 113).

For one enchanting village pension within walking distance of Grinzing,
try **Familie Heim** *(at (19.) Cobenzlgasse 114* ☎*325657, map 1 B3).*

FURNISHED APARTMENTS

Vienna City Apartments *(Marc-Aurel-Str. 7* ☎ *5350365* Fx *5350367,
map 3 C3)* provide fully furnished efficiency (self-catering) apartments
in central Vienna on a daily or weekly basis.

YOUTH HOSTELS

A full listing of youth hostels *(Jugendherberge)* is available from all
tourist information bureaux. An international youth hostel membership
card is necessary to gain admittance. It can be obtained in your home
country or through the **Jugendherbergverband** *(Schottenring 28*
☎ *5335353, map 3 B3)*. Charges vary between AS120 to AS180 per
dormitory bed-and-breakfast, or AS200 to AS400 per private double
room.

City-Hotel   Seilerstätte 30 ☎5128463. Map **3**E3. 170 beds in central
Vienna. Open July to October.

Schlossherberge am Wilhelminenberg   (16.) Savoyen Str. **2**
(train or tram to Ottakring, then bus 46B or 146B) ☎458003-0. Called
Europe's most beautiful youth hostel: a historic castle in a park in the
Vienna Woods. Open March to October.

CAMPING

Five large, well-organized camping places exist within 15km (9 miles)
of the city center in directions to the s and w. Each provides showers,
WCs, electricity, a shop and a café or restaurant, in addition to much
greenery.

Schloss Laxenburg   15km (9 miles) s. Various regional buses from
Bus Terminal near the Hilton. Open April-October ☎(02236) 71333.

Camping Rodaun   10km (6 miles) sw. Take local train from Südbahnhof to Liesing, then bus 60A. Open mid-March to mid-November
☎884154. Map **1**E2.

Wien-Süd   7km ($4\frac{1}{2}$ miles) sw. (23.) Breitenfurter Str. 269. Take
metro U6 or local train to Meidling, then bus 62A. Open June to mid-
September ☎869218. Map **1**E2.

Wien-West I and **Wien-West II**   6km (4 miles) w. (14.) Hüttelberg
Str. 40. Map **1**D2-E2. Take metro U4 or local train to Hütteldorf, then
bus 148 or 152. The two sites are within walking distance of each
other. Wien-West II is open all year.

Eating and drinking

by Nicholas T. Parsons

Viennese cuisine and wine

Until the collapse of the Austro-Hungarian Empire in 1918 there was really no such country as "Austria," merely a collection of territories that comprised some of the most ancient Crown Lands of the Habsburg patrimony. Similarly, it is doubtful whether the concept "Austrian cuisine" has any meaning: all the nine *Bundesländer* or Federal States of the Republic of Austria have their own distinctive style of cooking, although some, like the Tyrol, Styria and Carinthia, are more individual than others.

Most well known of them all is the cuisine of Vienna. Yet it is the most pluralistic, drawing inspiration from national culinary traditions in the old Empire, just as its population once represented an assimilation of the Empire's diverse nationalities.

In the 18thC, Bohemian and Hungarian nobles brought their cooks with them to their magnificent Baroque palaces in the center or at the periphery of the city. The foundations of Viennese cuisine were thus laid, and the versatile dumplings of Bohemia, or the goulash and Debreziner sausages of Hungary, remain faithful Viennese stand-bys.

THE WIENER SCHNITZEL

After the Congress of Vienna in 1814, Southern Slav and Italian influences enriched the kitchens of the middle-class and aristocracy. The most Viennese of all items made a comparatively late arrival on the scene and likewise came from Italy: to Field-Marshall Radetzky, hero of the Italian campaigns of the revolutionary period of 1848-49, we not only owe the most listenable march ever written (Johann Strauss's *Radetzky March*), but also the celebrated *Wiener Schnitzel*.

Of course, this world-conquering Viennese dish, in its pristine form, is actually a *piccata alla Milanese,* a breaded veal cutlet. The Viennese version is more often pork, pounded, turned in flour and salted. After being dipped in egg and breadcrumbs it is fried in butter until golden brown and seasoned with rosemary, sage, lemon and perhaps parmesan. There are of course many subtle variations — in the seasoning, in the way it is fried, and above all in size. Some establishments specialize in trencherman versions with suitably mind-boggling names: for example "cartwheel size"; or even *abortdeckelgross*— the size of a toilet lid!

The Wiener Schnitzel also has its own mythology: the golden brown color is said to recall the "golden Viennese heart"; and some authors claim that the golden sheen is a distant reflection of medieval tradition, whereby food was frequently gilded in the belief that a modest ingestion of real gold was good for the heart. Such musings may indeed seem appropriate, as one tackles a gigantic pork Schnitzel, overflowing the plate on all sides, perhaps in the Wiener Schnitzel Mecca of **Figlmüller** *(Wollzeile 5, map 4D5)*. The Schnitzel should ideally be accompanied by a cold salad of potatoes or tomato and onion, and washed down with a refreshingly tart white wine such as Grüner Veltliner, or with draft beer.

TAFELSPITZ

The fame of the other quintessentially Viennese dish has not traveled the world like the Schnitzel. *Tafelspitz* is a tender cut of boiled beef, served in various forms and with diverse seasonings such as horseradish or a sauce of chives. It is no accident that the shrine where worshipers of Tafelspitz receive their blessings is right next to the Palace of Schönbrunn, at **Hietzinger Bräu** *(Auhof Str. 1, map 1 D3)*.

The Emperor Franz Joseph, hardly an imaginative eater, ritualistically lunched on Tafelspitz every day. The multilayered Civil Service took their cue from the Emperor in this respect, as in all others: in turn-of-the-century Vienna the traditional restaurants were filled at noon with whiskered Franz Joseph lookalikes tucking into their boiled beef.

Unfortunately, the most famous of these establishments no longer exists. It was called Meissl und Schadn and was conveniently situated for politicians and civil servants on the Neuer Markt. There were no less than 26 different versions of Tafelspitz on the menu, which, however, was seldom used. The regulars came in and sat at their usual places, and the waiters knew which type of beef to bring them.

In a later, less secure age, such regular habits proved to have their downside. For it was here, one day in October 1916, that the Prime Minister, Count Stürgkh, repaired for his customary Tafelspitz. Sitting quietly next to him was the son of the Social Democratic leader, a political activist driven to desperation by the appalling slaughter of the war, to which the country's leaders appeared to be cynically indifferent. As the great man was contentedly lighting up a post-prandial cigar, young Adler took out a revolver and shot him dead.

TRADITIONAL CUISINE

Other typically Viennese contributions to the meaty main course include beef goulash, beefsteaks with crispy fried onions *(Zwiebelrostbraten)* and *Beuschel* (offal). Liver is frequently on the menu and almost always good, whether chopped or fried. For obvious reasons, sea-fish dishes are generally confined to the more expensive restaurants or specialist chains like Nordsee. Fresh-water fish, however, are much prized in Central Europe, and one not infrequently encounters the Hungarian *fogosch* (pike-perch).

First courses of a slap-up Viennese meal tend to be strongest in the soup department: beef broth and goulash soup are of course on offer, but so, more interestingly, are *Griessnockerlsuppe* (with semolina dumplings) and *Frittatensuppe* (clear soup with crepes).

The ubiquitous dumpling — made from flour, yeast, or potatoes — is a sort of *leitmotiv* of Viennese cuisine. Noodles or dumplings often appear in the soup, while a variety of excellent dumplings, seasoned with onion, parsley and other herbs, accompany the fillets and stews of the main course; *Buchteln* or *Wuchteln* are yeast dumplings, often filled with plum jam, which make an excellent pudding. Another favorite dessert dumpling, this time made with bread, is the *Marillenknödel,* which has an apricot inside. Nor should you overlook the joys of the *Mohnnudel,* garnished with poppy seed and clarified butter.

Some of this may sound rather heavy, especially by comparison, say, with Italian cuisine. And it is indeed true that for many years Austrian restauranteurs seemed to believe that quantity was really more important than quality.

NOUVELLE CUISINE

That all began to change in the 1970s when Werner Matt from Tyrol arrived at the **Prinz Eugen** restaurant of the Hilton. His great achievement was to answer the need for a lighter style of cooking and to eschew the use of artificial ingredients and deep-freeze products.

Although pot-bellied guzzlers mocked his dainty portions and mourned the absence of cholesterol-saturated recipes, the Matt revolution was not to be stopped, and today there are a number of good restaurants offering a *nouvelle cuisine Viennoise.* They all insist on fresh produce and avoid conserves, deep-frozen materials and excessive use of flour and fat. A welcome consequence has been the gradual disappearance of menus longer than one's family tree and their replacement by a select number of freshly cooked dishes with honest ingredients.

Eating out in Vienna

The increasing liveliness of Vienna is reflected in the number of eating places available, which doubled in the period 1982-86 alone. Many of the new places are so-called *Szenelokalen,* primarily watering holes where light food or snacks may also be served, and where young people hang out in the evenings. Others are establishments devoted to *Neue Wiener Küche;* some of Werner Matt's former pupils have branched out on their own, and their number steadily increases. Then again, there has been a revival in the traditional type of place catering to the Viennese lifestyle of a bygone age. These include the *Beisl* and the coffee house.

BEISELN

Of Yiddish origin, the term *Beisl* implies a convivial, modestly priced locale, often with benches and wooden paneling, where one could repair for a $\frac{1}{4}$ liter of wine or a glass of beer and a steaming plate of hot food. Nowadays the word covers a multitude of sins as well as virtues, and quite expensive restaurants lay claim to the name *Beisl.*

Such places thus run the gamut from modest hostelries in the suburbs, where the local workers eat their Schnitzel and drink their beer, to "in" places in the city center where the Bohemian and intellectual fraternity may be seen displaying their fine plumage. In short, no self-respecting Viennese is without a *Stammbeisl,* a place where he regularly goes to eat and meet his friends, and where the waiters know his caprices.

CAFÉS

Another type of establishment with a long tradition is the café, the apotheosis of which came at the turn of the century, when many people (but especially writers, journalists, artists and the like) took refuge there from dank substandard accommodations and spent most of their waking hours in smoke-filled interiors, drinking coffee and disputing. In the drab postwar era the old-style coffee house looked for a while as if it might die out. But in the last two decades there has been a revival. The engagingly shabby old cafés, for example **Prückel** *(Stubenring 24, map 4D4)* or **Bräunerhof** *(Stallburggasse 2, map 3D3),* are once again full. A new one, **Café Griensteidl,** has arisen on the Michaelerplatz *(map 3D3),* on the site and carrying the name of a famous predecessor. And yet others, such as **Café Diglas** *(Wollzeile 10, map 4D4)* or **Café Central** *(Palais Ferstel, Herrengasse 14, map 3C2),* have been renovated and given a new lease on life.

The café is where you while away your time reading the newspapers provided, nursing one of the dozen or so types of coffee you can order, or simply gazing into space. You can meet friends there for a light lunch or supper, usually at reasonable prices. It is the most flexible of institutions, and there is nothing else quite like it in Europe. Even so, it is not as flexible as it once was: Peter Altenberg, the humorist and chronicler of Viennese life at the turn of the century, was wont to use his café as a bank (a one-sided arrangement in this case), a post office and a study. It was he who characterized the Wiener Café as the place where "one goes to be alone, for which purpose one needs other people around."

KONDITOREI

The *Kaffeehaus* should not be confused with the *Konditorei,* another vital aspect of Viennese gastronomy. These, too, have a long tradition: the most distinguished still advertise themselves as *kaiserlich und königlich* (imperial and royal).

In **Demel** *(Kohlmarkt 14, map 3D3)* or **Heiner** *(Wollzeile 9, map 4D4)* you can enjoy perhaps the most mouth-watering selection of cakes and pastries anywhere in the world. It will include such traditional confections as *Sachertorte* or *Esterhazytorte,* fruit slices, meringue whirls, *strudels* and much else. A visit does nothing for the waistline but everything for the spirit.

HEURIGEN

The true Viennese spirit is most in evidence in the wine taverns, known as *Heurigen,* on the edge of the Wienerwald (the Vienna Woods). These are mostly family-run and offer the current year's wine from the owner's vineyard, which usually backs onto the *Heurige* itself. There are, astonishingly, more than 640 around the outskirts of the capital, 180 of them having their own taverns.

Heurigen serve young, *pétillant* wine from the barrel and also offer a hot and cold serve-yourself buffet including salads, cold meat, roasts and cheese. Most have an attractive garden for sitting out on the long summer evenings or through afternoons in the fall, which is so especially congenial in the Central European climate.

CHARACTERISTIC VIENNESE DISHES

The following dishes frequently appear on menu-cards in Vienna. Where relevant, we give the local names here (German names for similar items are often different, and the Viennese are rightly proprietorial about their dialect; even German guidebooks append a gastronomic lexicon for the bewildered Swiss or German tourist!).

Of course, in luxury restaurants and in *Beiseln* with plenty of tourist custom there will usually be a menu in English, or waiters who speak it; but in more modest establishments and those off the beaten track, you may well be on your own.

Auflauf   steamed pudding
Backhendl   chicken fried in breadcrumbs
Bauernschmaus   mixed meats with dumplings, sauerkraut
Beuschel   chopped offal in sauce
Blaukraut   red caggage
Blunzn   black pudding
Buchteln or *Wuchteln*   yeast dumplings with vanilla sauce or filled with jam

Bummersalat   iceberg lettuce
Debreziner   fatty sausage spiced with paprika
Eierschwammerln   mushrooms
Fasan   pheasant
Faschiertes   minced meat
Fisolen   runner beans (green beans)
(Fleisch)laberln   meat rissoles
Fogosch   pipe-perch ("sander")
Frittatensuppe   clear broth with crepes

Germknödel   yeast dumpling
Grammeln   tallow, usually in
  dumplings
Griessnockerlsuppe   semolina
  dumpling soup
Guglhupf   pound cake
Himbeergrotz   puree of fresh
  raspberries with lard
Hirschragout   venison stew
Jägersalat   salad of Chinese cabbage
Jungfernbraten   loin of pork
Kaiserschmarrn   omelet with
  raisins and plum compote
Kalbsvögerl   knuckle of veal
Karree   shoulder of pork (often
  smoked)
Knödel   dumpling from flour,
  potatoes, bread or yeast
Krautfleckerl   square pasta with
  seasoned cabbage
Krenfleisch   boiled pork with
  grated horseradish
Kuttelfleck   tripe
Lungenbraten   loin of pork
Millirahmstrudel   strudel with
  sweet cheese filling and vanilla
  sauce *(Milchrahmstrudel)*
Mohr im Hemd   steamed pudding
  with chocolate and nuts
Nockerl   homemade pasta
Palatschinken   pancakes

Paradeiser   tomatoes
Perlhuhn   guinea-fowl
Powidl   plum sauce
Rebhuhn   partridge
Rehfilet   fillet of venison
Ribisel   red or black currants
Risipisi   rice with peas
Rollgerstlsuppe   pearl barley soup
Rostbraten   either a roast or a
  pan-fried steak
Schinkenfleckerln   ham with square
  noodles
Schöpsernes   mutton
Schwammerlsuppe   mushroom
  soup
Semmelknöderln   bread dumplings
  with parsley and onion
Serviettenknöderln   similar, but
  differently prepared
Stelze   leg of veal or pork, roast or
  smoked
Tafelspitz   boiled beef
Topfenstrudel   strudel with quark
  and sultanas
Vanillerostbraten   garlic-seasoned
  roast beef
Wiener Schnitzel   fillet of veal or
  pork, breadcrumbed
Zwetschkenröster   plum compote
Zwiebelrostbraten   beef steak with
  crispy fried onions

ETIQUETTE

Once you have mastered the menu, it is not a bad idea to master the local customs. The Viennese are conservative by nature, and establishments that have been run for years in a particular way, offering a particular sort of fare, are not about to change their ways, least of all in order to pander to ignorant foreigners.

An Englishman writing about Vienna has described how he once ordered a gin and tonic with ice in a typical café. "We're out of gin," replied the waiter with some relish, "we don't carry tonic and there's no ice today. But the white wine with soda is nice."

The traditional Viennese head waiter was something of a folk hero, but he was not a man to be trifled with. That old-fashioned breed, all of whom seemed to have stepped out of one of the popular 19thC comedies by Johann Nestroy, or an operetta by Strauss or Kalman, are unfortunately dying out.

Nevertheless, if you want to enjoy the show (never forget that all true Viennese are frustrated actors), there are still such places as **Zur Goldenen Glocke** *(Kettenbrückengasse 9, map 3F2)*, or a café like the **Tirolerhof** *(Tegetthof Str. 8, map 3D3)*, where the service is a performance worth paying for all on its own....

All of which brings us to the delicate matter of tipping. In a café or a modest *Beisl,* the waiter will add up the bill at your table and present the results of his calculations with a flourish, helpfully stating the amount at the same time. If your mathematics and German are up to it, you add on the percentage for the tip to the total and hand him a note, stating what the grand total should be. Ten percent is generally adequate, but if you have sat for a long time in a café and been solicitously supplied with fresh glasses of water at regular intervals, you may think it reasonable to give rather more. Waiters in cafés also have fixed shifts, so that if one should approach you for payment before you have decided to leave, he is not trying to drive you out, merely going off-duty and is obliged to "collect" from all his customers before he goes.

Middle-priced and expensive restaurants are more formal and nowadays often present a computerized bill which shows the Value-Added Tax (*Mehrwertsteuer* in German, shortened to MWST) that has been charged — ten percent on the food, twenty percent on the drink. Hardly any places include a service charge automatically in the bill.

Restaurants in Vienna

All the restaurants described in the following pages have long-established track records. District numbers are not indicated for establishments in the Inner City (1.).

PRICES
Price categories are based on the estimated minimum and probable maximum cost of a full meal for one without drink (as of 1991-92). Prices have tended to rise at least in line with inflation. In some places, the spread between the least and most expensive meal may be even greater than these general guidelines indicate.

Symbol	Category	Current price	(Dollar amount)
▦	very expensive	AS700-1,200	($60-100)
▦	expensive	AS500-750	($40-65)
▥	moderate	AS300-500	($25-43)
▨	inexpensive	AS150-250	($13-22)
▢	cheap	AS80-150	($7-13)

LUXURY RESTAURANTS ▦
A number of the best establishments are located in hotels. Indeed, the five leading hotels in Vienna — the **Bristol**, the **Imperial**, the **Hilton**, the **Inter-Continental** and the **Schwarzenberg** — have five of the best restaurants. They are by no means alone in having impressive cuisines, for the **SAS-Palais**, **Sacher** and **König von Ungarn** provide formidable competition. A handful of independent restaurants for serious gourmets are nevertheless prepared to take on the mighty hotels.

ALTWIENERHOF

(15.) Herklotzgasse 6 ☎*837145* 📠

By general consent, Rudolf Kellner is an exceptional culinary artiste with a feeling for harmony and balance in his cuisine that is only equaled by his imaginative personal touches and almost obsessive attention to detail. Accompanying the dishes, which have a Central European character with added French finesse, is one of the best wine lists in Vienna.

Kellner learned his trade at Maxims in Paris and at the Savoy in London. All this explains why the business does not suffer from being located in the unfashionable 15th District.

KORSO BEI DER OPER

Mahler Str. 2 ☎*51516/51546. Map 3E3* 🆎 💳 💳 💳

The restaurant of the hotel BRISTOL is generally regarded as the last word in Ringstrasse elegance; it is ideally placed for those who accept nothing but the best to hop over from their opera boxes and continue to spoil themselves with Reinhard Gerer's equally creative productions. *Haute cuisine* with a very individual character.

PALAIS SCHWARZENBERG

(3.) Schwarzenbergplatz 9 ☎*784515. Map 4F4* 💳 📠

The use of noble titles having been proscibed by the First Republic, Prince Schwarzenberg likes to describe himself in the Austrian media as "forestry manager and hotelier." As the latter, he had the advantage of the family pile being to hand, and has turned two wings of his palace into a luxury hotel, the jewel of which is the restaurant. You dine looking out onto one of Vienna's most elegant Baroque parks, and will be guaranteed excellent — predominantly Austrian — cuisine. The wine list is distinguished. (See our description of the palace on page 128 and the hotel entry on page 136.)

STEIRERECK

(3.) Rasumofskygasse 2 ☎*7133168. Map 4D5* 🆎 📠

Diplomats are a demanding, not to say spoiled, breed as far as food is concerned, and Steirereck lies on the edge of the embassy quarter. It has a well-founded reputation for superb food. Even the most fastidious are mellowed by offerings such as caviar on red cabbage gelée with a puree of celery and other such star turns of the *Neue Wiener Küche*. Service is especially attentive and friendly, and the wine list, to quote a professional, "will make the heart of every connoisseur beat a little faster."

VIER JAHRESZEITEN

Johannesgasse 28 ☎*7112203. Map 4E4.*

A remarkable combination of flair and daring characterizes the cooking of the Vier Jahreszeiten (Four Seasons), which is to be found in the INTER-CONTINENTAL WIEN hotel. There is a fixed-price lunch available, and an à la carte choice for the evening, which expands on the theme of the seasons. The chef is noted for his fondness for crustaceans, which are otherwise not widely on offer in Vienna. The puddings are exotic and the wine list superb.

EXPENSIVE RESTAURANTS ▥

Many restaurants fall into this category, not a few of them verging on the very expensive. To justify the price, such places should ideally compensate with ambience for any marginal deficiencies in cuisine, or vice versa.

Happily a number of those in Vienna do so, and you leave them without that disagreeable feeling that you should either have blown your savings on a guaranteed gourmet experience, or alternatively have saved yourself much expense and disappointment with a humble but reliable sausage and a beer.

BELVEDERESTÖCKL
(3.) Prinz Eugen Str. 25 ☎ *784198. Map 4F4* AE CO VISA 🚗

The Viennese and international menu is by no means modestly priced, but the bonus is the very attractive garden. In summer it is open from noon to midnight continually, although only a cold buffet can be offered between 3 and 6pm.

DO & CO.
im Haas Haus, Stephansplatz 12 ☎ *5353969. Map 3D3* AE CO CD VISA

The originality of mixing local cuisine with a range of Far Eastern dishes, and throwing in other European delicacies for good measure, pays dividends. The establishment is part of the same gastronomic empire that owns the KERVAN-SARAY, and this has ensured high-quality materials for the chefs to work on. It is situated on top of Hans Hollein's remarkable **Haas Haus**, a complex of shops and offices, completed in 1990 on the city's prime site, next to the cathedral. However, the better views of St Stephen's are to be had from the café on the same floor.

Not far away *(at Akademie Str. 3, map 3E3),* **Do & Co.** has another small restaurant backing onto an exotic delicatessen. There is a very refined short menu that changes daily, and noble wines are — exceptionally in Vienna — available by the glass. This is a daytime locale that closes its doors when the shop does.

ECKEL
(19.) Sieveringer Str. 46 ☎ *323218. Map 1B3* CO 🚗

Eckel is a traditional Viennese restaurant whose dishes, and the number of them on offer, resist the general trend toward *nouvelle cuisine* selectivity. Good cooking, unforced conviviality and an interesting wine list keep the customers rolling out to the 19th District. Seafood wins praise here from the regulars.

HIETZINGER BRÄU
Auhof Str. 1 ☎ *8777087. Map 1D2. No cards.*

In fashionable Hietzing lived the well-to-do civil servants of the Dual Monarchy and others who more or less qualified as such, like Franz Joseph's mistress, Anna Nawoski and her (platonic) replacement, Katharina Schratt. At the nearby **Café Dommayer** (which still exists), Johann Strauss beguiled the local burghers with his waltzes. It is appropriate, therefore, that the shrine for *Tafelspitz* addicts should also be here. For a tantalizing whiff of old Vienna, not to mention the choicest beef in town, this is indisputably the place to go.

KERVANSARAY
Mahler Str. 9 ☎ *5128843. Map 3E3* AE CO CD VISA

A colorful restaurant with a Turkish flavor, but also a range of international dishes. On the first floor is the *Hummer-bar* (Lobster Bar), where you can select your own lobster and watch it being prepared. Many regard this as the best fish restaurant in town.

ZU DEN 3 HUSAREN
Weihburggasse 4 ☎ *5121092-0. Map 3D3* AE CO CD VISA

The enormous *hors d'oeuvres* trolley bursting with *terrines,* goose liver, lobster, calf's brains and all manner of good things set the tone for an enjoyable evening in the graceful surroundings of Zu den 3 Husaren. Perhaps more than in any other Viennese restaurant, the beautifully prepared traditional dishes and the discreetly attentive service here recall the gracious living of a bygone age.

MODERATELY PRICED RESTAURANTS ▥
In this category may be placed many traditional or new *Beiseln,* together with a few places that aspire to more serious cooking, but which have miraculously kept their prices within bounds.

HEDRICH
Stubenring 2 ☎*5129588. Map 4D4. No cards.*

Trained by Werner Matt, Richard Hedrich struck out on his own some years ago and created a small, elegant restaurant that justifiably became something of a cult. You must book, especially at lunchtime, when the *Feinschmecker* (gourmets) from the nearby ministries crowd in. The cuisine is creative and refreshingly light, the wine list well chosen, the service immaculate and the prices surprisingly moderate. They close at 9pm, however.

KUPFERDACHL
Schottengasse 5 ☎*639381. Map 3C2. No cards.*

A pleasant family-run enterprise where many of the more unpretentious Viennese dishes are well prepared. The fish especially attracts universal praise. Modest wine list.

LATERNDL
Landesgericht Str. 12 ☎*434358. Map 3C1. No cards* 🍴

Once a coaching inn, Laterndl retains a good deal of the authentic *Beisl* ambience, reflected also in the colorful style of the service. Seasonal specialties on offer.

OFENLOCH
Kurrentgasse 8 ☎*637268. Map 3C3. No cards* 🍴

Traditional Viennese specialties, decor in the style of the turn of the century and an engagingly presented menu — "The First Viennese Beisl Newspaper." Very fair prices.

OSWALD UND KALB
Bäcker Str. 14 ☎*5121371. Map 4D4. No cards.*

If you want to rub shoulders with Bohemians and intellectuals, who traditionally have a nose for good value in food, this may be the place to go. It keeps appropriate hours for such a fraternity, staying open until 2am (closed for lunch). Cooking with a Viennese and Styrian flavor.

SALZAMT
Ruprechtsplatz 1 ☎*5335332. Map 4C4* 🔲 🍴

Another fashionable "in" place for artists and the like, with a lively bar at the front and cooking with a Mediterranean accent. Nice ambience, fair prices, idiosyncratic decor.

STADTBEISL
Naglergasse 21 ☎*5333507. Map 3C3. No cards.*

One of the old-style *Beiseln*, with a paneled interior, conveniently situated right in the center of town. You can drift in simply for a glass of wine in the mid-afternoon, but their meals are also very honest and good value. Try the venison if it's on.

ZUM HERKNER
Dornbacher Str. 123 ☎*454386. Map 1C2. No cards* 🍴

Toward the end of a long evening's labors the ruddy complexioned Heinz Herkner sometimes emerges from his culinary lair and receives the plaudits of his guests with suitably laconic insouciance. They are no more than his due — the home cooking here is thought by many to be the most genuine in Vienna. Quality folk jostle to get in, precisely because it is *not* a place where one goes to see and be seen, but to be anonymous and informal. The result, hardly surprisingly, is that you must reserve well in advance. The prices are extremely reasonable, and the goose or the pheasant pretty near as good as such things can be.

ZUM SCHWARZEN KAMEEL
Bognergasse 5 ☎*638125. Map 3C3. No cards.*

This is a lunch venue (the restaurant closes at 7pm) and is favored by businessmen, who appreciate the *Jugendstil* decor, the *bonnes bouches* imported from the attached delicatessen, and the really outstanding wines. Those who are in a hurry can eat more cheaply and informally in the delicatessen part, which is surely the most upscale serve-yourself bar in Europe!

151

ZUR GOLDENEN GLOCKE
Kettenbrückengasse 9 ☎ *5875767. Map 3F2* 🆎 💲 🍴
This place is particularly nice in summer, when you can sit out in the garden and enjoy the wall paintings. The head waiter is a card, keeping up a steady stream of flowery compliments and humorous observations. The excellent traditional cooking is moderately priced and there is no reason to venture beyond the excellent house wine.

INEXPENSIVE RESTAURANTS 🔲

Eating inexpensively in Vienna usually means patronizing a *Keller* (wine-cellar), a *Heurige* (wine-tavern on the edge of the Wienerwald) or a coffee house. The attraction for the visitor, apart from price, is that in these locales one is, as it were, doing things the Viennese way, the hallmarks of which are unpretentiousness and conviviality. There is an extensive choice, but obviously the quality of the food can be variable. The following offer a combination of ambience and good value.

FIGLMÜLLER
Wollzeile 5 (in passageway) ☎ *5126177. Map 3D3. No cards.*
A Viennese institution that supplies the largest Wiener Schnitzels you are likely to see, and good open wine from their own vineyard. Usually very crowded, so reservations are advisable. The waiters are famous for their repartee.

Of the wine-cellars, which range from those that offer mostly cold cuts, cheese and so on to those that operate as a normal restaurant, the following, among others, are attractive:

ESTERHAZYKELLER
Haarhof 1. Map 3D3. No cards.
Excellent wines and acceptable hot and cold buffet in the cellar next to the Esterhazy Palace. During the Turkish siege of 1683, the Esterhazy of the day threw open the cellars to the townsfolk, who not only took refuge here from the Turkish cannonballs, but also drank their fill from the barrels.

GIGERL
Rauhensteingasse 3. Map 3D3 🆎 💲 💳 📧 🍴
Hot and cold buffet, vegetable and noodle dishes. Large selection of open Austrian wines, but also some foreign wines by the bottle. This is at the upscale end of the *Keller* range.

URBANIKELLER
Am Hof 12. Map 3C3 🆎 💳 📧
Located in a Baroque patrician house. Viennese cooking. Because of its location, this is a shade touristy, and the presence of *stimmungs musik* makes it no less so. Worth it for sound cooking and attractive surroundings, however.

Many coffee-houses offer a selection of warm dishes. Good value may be had at **Café Diglas** *(Wollzeile 10, map 4D4* 🆎 💲 💳 📧 *)*. Relatively expensive but good are the main courses at **Café Griensteidl** on the Michaelerplatz *(map 3D3)*. The home cooking at the **Café Ministerium** *(Georg-Coch-Platz 4, map 4C4)*, where the civil servants from the neighboring ministries are the *Stammgäste* (regulars), is wonderfully cheap, but best at lunchtime.

CHEAP FOOD 🔲

Cheap eating in Vienna may be divided into the traditional and modern styles. In the traditional category may be placed the ubiquitous *Würstelstände* (sausage stalls), the meaty snacks available at quality butchers and the excellent sandwich bars. In the modern category are the serve-yourself chains, ranging from large establishments with lots of choice to McDonald's. The following should not disappoint.

NASCHMARKT
Schottengasse 1, Schwarzenbergplatz 16 and Mariahilfer Str. 85, all map 3E1.
It is hard to praise this serve-yourself chain too highly for providing a wide range of hot and cold food, wines by the glass and beer on draft, together with a good selection of desserts, snacks, and so forth, not to mention espresso coffee. The interiors are in tasteful late *Jugendstil*, and the back-up service is efficient. Of the three branches, the best is the Schwarzenbergplatz one.

NORDSEE
Kohlmarkt 6, Mariahilfer Str. 34 and 84, Kärntner Str. 25, Neubaugasse 9, all map 3E1; and elsewhere.
A very acceptable selection of hot sea-fish dishes, together with fish-based open sandwiches.

SANDWICHES
Duran & Co *(under the arches at Rotenturm Str. 11, map 3D3)* has a good selection. The most famous place is just off the Graben, the unpronounceable **Trzesniewski** *(Dorotheergasse 1, map 3D3),* which again has a huge selection of open sandwiches with mouth-watering ingredients. Also beer and apple juice.

BUTCHER'S SNACKS
Try the excellent **Ziegler** chain *(branches at Kruger Str. 5 in the city center, map 3D3, at Neubaugasse 7, and elsewhere).* Lastly, two tips for gourmet snacks: the bottom of **Herzmansky's** great store at Mariahilfer Str. 26-30 *(map 3E1)* has various food bars serving fish, instant grills etc.; and just opened opposite **Demel** on Kohlmarkt at #11 *(map 3D3)* is **Demel Vis-à-vis**, for oysters, smoked salmon and other delights, plus a choice of noble wines by the glass.

Austrian wine and the Heurigen scene

Table wine in Austria is likely to be an acquired taste, at least for those brought up on more mellow French, Italian or Californian offerings. In the *Kellern* or *Heurigen*, as also in all but the most expensive restaurants, the open house wine is what people generally like to drink, and that will often be *Heurige* (this year's) wine — the whites usually *herb* (astringently dry) and the reds sometimes rather hard for real pleasure, but, at their best, fruity and refreshing. In summer the custom is to put soda water with the wine, making a *Gespritzter* — the tart whites especially are perfectly pleasant when drunk in this way.

Noble wine is produced in all four of Austria's main wine-growing areas: the **Weinviertel** in Lower Austria, the **Wachau** in the Danube Valley, **Burgenland** in the E, and the slopes of the **Wienerwald**. The

153

classic Austrian grape is the *Grüner Veltliner,* which produces excellent white wine, often served from the barrel. At its best it is fruity, very dry, aromatic and somewhat acidic.

The most aristocratic white wine is the *Rheinriesling* from the Wachau. Of the reds, *Blaufränkisch* and *Zweigelt* are usually reliable, but seldom great. It is worth looking out for *St Laurent,* which is smooth, elegant and fruity.

Austrians are refreshingly free from the higher wine snobbery, but that does not mean they do not know a good wine. Almost any Austrian friend will tell you about (or better still take you to) his favorite *Heurige,* or recommend a *vinothek* that sells a particularly good wine that he has discovered. Open wine is drunk in fractions of a liter — a *Viertel* ($\frac{1}{4}$-liter mug) or an *Achtel* ($\frac{1}{8}$ of a liter).

Those who would like to sample a much greater range of wine types and vintages than is usually available in a *Keller* or a *Heurige* can try out some of the specialist wine-vaults in the city: the **Weinmuseum** *(Weihburggasse 20, map 3 D3)* has some 100 to choose from and serves appropriate snacks. (You can also take out bottles at shop prices.) Opposite the previously mentioned Figlmüller is their wine-bar **Vis à Vis** *(Wollzeile 5, map 3 D3),* with about 40 wines to drink by the glass at any one time, together with Schnapps specialties.

HEURIGEN

The wine-taverns are in the villages on the periphery of the city to the s, the sw, the w and the nw. The most famous of them is **Grinzing** (see page 112), which has inevitably become rather touristified. However, the **Altes Presshaus** *(Cobenzlgasse 15 ☎ 322393, map 1 B3 [AE] [☐] [☐] [VISA] ☻)* has good food and wine, although it is now more of a conventional restaurant than what is understood by a traditional *Heurige.* For that one should visit a village like **Stammersdorf** in the 21st District, which pullulates with tiny inns.

Other colorful places are **Heiligenstadt** (where Beethoven lived — see page 113), **Mauer** in the sw, **Neustift-am-Walde**, and its neighboring village of **Salmannsdorf**.

Out of the 180 *Heurigen* it is rather invidious to pick out any for special mention, but the visitor would be likely to enjoy the old **Beethovenhaus** (Mayer) *(Pfarrplatz 2, Heiligenstadt, map 1 B3 ☻)* and **Fuhrgassl-Huber** *(Neustift-am-Walde 68 ☻).*

Genuine *Heurigen* must follow extremely strict rules: they should offer only wine from their own vineyard (usually the so-called *gemischter Satz,* that is, the product of mixed grape varieties all grown together); and they should stay open only as long as the supply of this year's wine *("Heurige")* holds out.

The locales that are open are indicated by a bunch of pine twigs over the door and a sign with the word *ausg'steckt.* A list of *Heurigen* that are *ausg'steckt* appears in the daily press and also (in some villages) on a mast placed in the main street. Generally the taverns are open between March and October from mid-afternoon to late in the evening, and on weekends also for lunch.

The arts

Classical **music** is the field that comes to mind in connection with Vienna: rightly so, for Mozart's city continues to lead the world of music with a menu of offerings few other European cities can match. Equally prominent is its **theater**, though inevitably limited in its appeal to non-German speakers.

The confidence displayed by its **art galleries** reflects Vienna's newly earned reputation as Europe's most vibrant powerhouse of contemporary plastic arts.

ART GALLERIES

Vienna has more than 150 art galleries, most of them clustered in the Inner City. The best tend to gather around Augustinerstrasse/Dorotheergasse, the BERMUDA TRIANGLE (see page 81), Schönlaterngasse and Franziskanerplatz.

The most comprehensive coverage of current exhibitions is found in the Friday edition of the *Presse*.

ALTE SCHMIEDE
Schönlaterngasse 9 ☎*5128329. Map 4D4.*
An ancient ironsmith's shop, converted some years ago into a modern house of arts. Literary events, music, "artotheque," workshops and snack bar as well as art gallery.

BLAUE-GELBE
Herrengasse 21. Map 3C2.
A leading showplace of conceptual art and photography.

CORSO
Mahler Str. 4 ☎*5139562. Map 3E3.*
Stole the show in 1991 with an exhibition of Anthony Quinn's paintings.

HILGER
Dorotheergasse 5 ☎*5125315. Map 3D3.*
Vienna's arbiter of contemporary art.

NEUE GALERIE
Rotenturm Str. (corner of Rabensteig)
☎*5336131. Map 4C4. Open Mon-Fri 11am-1pm, 3-6.30pm; Sat 10am-1pm.*
Elisabeth Schaumberger has been a trend-setter in the Vienna art scene since the 1970s, and her gallery has promoted such leading Viennese artists as Arnulf Rainer, Pichler and Attersee.

PRISMA
Franziskanerplatz 1 ☎*5128428. Map 4D4.*
Watercolors and "realistic art."

RONDULA
Stephansplatz/Jasomirgott Str. 6
☎*5333424. Map3D3.*
Respected gallery with an international clientele.

WÜRTHLE
Weihburggasse 9 ☎*5122312. Map 3D3.*
A leader in modern classics.

CINEMA

Street posters list all films currently showing, with hours, telephone, metro and tram lines, whether they serve snacks, have air conditioning and so on. *Jugendfrei* or JF means "No kids, please." Note the Teutonic way of showing times: 1/29 means 8.30; 3/410 is 9.45. A majority of films are shown dubbed in German. The *Standard* newspaper lists foreign-language movies separately under *Fremdsprachige Filme.* For information in English, call ☎51450339.

Two cinemas, the **Auge Gottes** *(at (9.) Nussdorfer Str. 75 ☎346344, map3A1)* and **Haydn** *(at (6.) Mariahilfer Str. 57 ☎5872262, map3E1)* have beautifully ornate old-style auditoriums. The **Burg** *(Opernring 19 ☎5870406, map3E3)* specializes in original-version English-language movies.

The distinguished **Österreichisches Filmmuseum** *(Augustinerstrasse 1 ☎5337054-0, map3D3)* has been nominated "one of Europe's most active cinematheques." Its *Invisible Cinema* makes film-viewing a sensuous and moving experience.

The **Viennale**, an internationally renowned film festival, takes place twice yearly in March and April (at the **Urania Theater**) and October (at the **Apollo Theater**). Information and tickets from Urania, Urania Str. 1, A-1010 Wien ☎723484, map **4**C5.

CLASSICAL MUSIC, OPERA

Vienna was the world capital of classical music for 150 years, and it capitalizes mightily on that legacy. There is, on the one hand, a vast industry of crowd-pleasers (Mozart in original costumes, Strauss waltzes in City-Park, the Philharmonic New Year's concert); on the other hand, and perhaps as a reaction, Viennese ensembles have since the 1960s led the worldwide movement toward uncompromisingly academic interpretations of old music.

The Vienna Philharmonic, one of the world's finest orchestras since 1842, usually performs in the "Golden Hall" of the **Musikverein** *(at (1.) Bösendorfer Str. 12 ☎5058190, map3E3)*, which, incidentally, deserves to be visited on purely architectural grounds. The building, which dates from 1870, also features a smaller Brahms Hall and a Chamber Hall.

The **Konzerthaus**, Vienna's second major concert hall, houses the Vienna Symphony Orchestra. It is also used occasionally to stage jazz and pop concerts *(at (3.) Lothringer Str. 20 ☎7124686-0, map4E4)*.

The season at the grandiose **Staatsoper** (see OPERA, page 120) runs from October to June, while in summer chamber productions of — usually — 18thC operas are staged daily in the apt setting of the SCHÖNBRUNN PALACE (see **Schlosstheater** on page 125). The **Volksoper** *(at (9.) Währinger Str. 78, off map3A1)* specializes primarily in operettas and musicals, although it does occasionally make sallies into the realm of more serious music.

In summer, operetta and light opera productions take place at the Stadttheater of **Baden**, a spa town in the Vienna Woods *(reservations in writing from Theaterplatz 7, A-2500 Baden ☎(02252) 48547)*.

Of the dozen or so historic palaces that host the concerts of the Wiener Musik-Sommer, two deserve special mention for their graceful architecture: **Palais Palffy** and **Palais Auersperg** (see pages 79 and 129).

The Vienna Choirboys (see page 97) make concert appearances in a variety of settings, but the best outlet for their ethereal voice is Mass (every Sunday at 9.15am) in the **Hofburg chapel**.

Schubert lovers must note the Schubertiads which take place on Saturday afternoons in summer at **Schloss Atzenbrugg** near Tulln, in the NW Vienna Woods *(for information: Kremser Str. 43, 3452 Atzenbrugg* ☎ *(02275) 235)*.

FESTIVALS

The year opens with the celebrated **New Year's Concert** of the Vienna Philharmonic *(tickets in writing from Musikverein, Bösendorfer Str. 12, A-1010 Wien; do not try less than a year in advance)*. Alternatives for the night of December 31 include the annual performance by the **Vienna Symphony Orchestra** of Beethoven's Ninth at the Konzerthaus, the staging by the **Staatsoper** of Johann Strauss' *Die Fledermaus (tickets from Bundestheaterverband, Goethegasse 1, A-1010 Wien* ☎ *5131513)*, and the annual **Emperor's Ball** in the Hofburg, the top event of Vienna's social calendar *(tickets from WKV, Hofburg, A-1014 Wien* ☎ *5873666-14)*.

The **Wiener Festwochen** bring to town well-known orchestras, soloists and drama groups from around the world *(mid-May to mid-June; program and tickets from Bestellbüro der Wiener Festwochen, Lehargasse 11, A-1060 Wien* ☎ *5881676-0)*. Various shows organized on the "fringe" (such as the "Töne & Gegentöne" festival of exotic and avantgarde music) have lately become livelier than the festival itself.

Just when most concert halls and theaters close down for the dead season of late June to mid-September, the **Wiener Musik-Sommer** opens the otherwise closed gates of various palaces, castles, churches and public gardens to the public. The emphasis is on classical music, and the chance to hear Mozart or Beethoven or Strauss in their original, splendid setting forms one of the great highlights of the Viennese summer. *(Program and tickets from Wiener Musik-Sommer, Friedrich-Schmidt-Platz 5, A-1082 Wien* ☎ *40008400.)*

An outdoor **Jazz Festival** is organized in early July on the Danube Island.

Vienna Ticket Service supplies tickets for the Festwochen and Musik-Sommer as well as all major concerts and musical plays *(write to A-1043 Wien, Postfach 160* ☎ *5879843* Fx *5879844)*.

ROCK

Underneath the profusion of *Heurige* bands and oom-pah jollity, Vienna continues to produce a small quantity of dark, driven and brilliant rock. The great name of the 1970s was Wolfgang Ambros, whose sardonic snapshots of everyday Viennese life *(Es lebe Zentralfriedhof)* shaped the culture of a generation. In the early 1980s, Ronnie Urini was the archetype of the Austrian underground musician. More recently, Markus Spiegel *(Rock me Amadeus)* became the first singer from Austria to achieve international fame.

Large pop events take place at the **Praterstadion** *(map 2 C5)* and at the 10,000-seater **Wiener Stadthalle** *(at (15.) Vogelweidplatz 14* ☎ *9810-0).* The **CA-Zelt**, a circus tent set up within the premises of **UNO-City** *(☎ 5052324, map 2 B4),* and the vast auditorium of the **Austria Center** *(☎ 2369-0),* nearby, host major concerts.

For a listing of rock clubs as well as a selection of jazz and Latin locales, see page 159 in ENTERTAINMENT AND NIGHTLIFE.

SON ET LUMIÈRE

A light and sound show is staged at the **Belvedere** every evening at 9.30pm (May 15-August 31) or 9pm (September 1-30). Tickets can be bought at (4.) Prinz-Eugen-Str. 27 ☎5125685, map 4F4.

THEATER

For two centuries spanning the era from Maria Theresa to Max Reinhardt, Vienna was the home, the shop window and the motor force of German drama. Although no longer considered a vanguard, the Viennese stage still commands immense prestige. Visitors who are able to enjoy the German language have rich pickings at their disposal, from the glamorous (the **Burgtheater, Akademietheater, Theater an der Wien** and **Theater in der Josephstadt**) to the frivolous (**Kleine Komödie, Raimundtheater**), political (**Drachengasse, Schauspielhaus**) and avant-garde (**Graumann, Gruppe 80**).

For those who prefer to stay with English, two Vienna-based expatriate companies offer regular performances:

International Theater and **The Fundus**   Both companies at (9.) Porzellangasse 8 ☎316272. Map 3B2.

Vienna's English Theater   (8.) Josefsgasse 12 ☎4021260. Map 3D1.

Entertainment and nightlife

The café, the restaurant and the *Heurige* (see EATING AND DRINKING) remain the cornerstones of Vienna-by-evening, helping make the city one of the most civilized places in this world. Those who seek harder stuff, whether in alcohol, music or adventure, may find the Austrian capital a little provincial in the range of its offerings.

WALTZING IN VIENNA

Many *Heurigen* feature a house band which will strike up a waltz at the first sight of a tourist bus. But the most popular place to go waltzing or waltz-watching in Vienna remains the garden/terrace of the *Kursalon* in the STADTPARK (see page 123), where an orchestra plays the tunes of Lanner and both Strausses everyday in summer from 4pm *(free entry* ♫ ✹ *)*.

The Danube ship *DDS-Johann Strauss* offers a Walzerkonzert-Café with live waltz music and ballet show, daily at 8.30pm and 10pm, as well as the café-restaurant **Johann Strauss** *(at Schwedenplatz* ☎ *5333163, map 4 C4* ⚞ 💻 ♫ *)*.

The **Rathauskeller** in the City Hall organizes a "Viennese Musical Evening" from Tuesday to Saturday from 8.30pm *(at Rathausplatz, map 3 C2, entry AS102, menu AS306* ⚞ ♫ ✹ *)*.

ROCK CLUBS AND DISCOTHEQUES

The rock equivalent of waltzing-at-Stadtpark is the **Volksgarten Tanz-café** *(in Volksgarten* ☎ *630518, map 3 D2)*, where there is live music and outdoor dancing in summer on Monday, Friday and Saturday from 10pm and on Thursday from 7pm. By far the most popular discotheque for more than 10 years has been the **U4**.

The following include some of the key locales of Vienna's live rock music scene, plus a handful of discos. Check newspapers or the various "program" magazines for daily events.

AFRICAN CLUB
Riemergasse 13. Map 4D4.
Reggae, African soul, disco.

ARENA
(3.) Franzosengraben ☎ *788595.*
Converted from a grimy old factory

building on the edge of Simmering into a concert hall with much atmosphere.

ATRIUM
(4.) Schwarzenberg P. 10 ☎ *5053494.*
Map 4F4.
An "international student disco,"

though the clientele includes a strong contingent of older people. Daily except Tuesday, Wednesday. See also **Papa's Tapas** under JAZZ CLUBS, below.

B.A.C.H.
(16.) Bachgasse 21 ☎*4501970.*
The biggest hit of recent years in the world of avant-garde music, exploring the borderline between jazz and rock.

CAMERA
(7.) Neubaugasse 2 ☎*933218.*
Hard rock and the corresponding clientele.

CHELSEA
(8.) Piaristengasse 1 ☎*485196. Map 3D1.*
Like B.A.C.H., but said to have lost some of its pizazz. Selection of underground magazines from England and the US.

FLEX
(12.) Arndt Str. 51.
A key institution of Vienna's musical subculture.

METROPOL
(17.) Hernalser Hauptstrasse 55
☎*433543.*
Cabaret, theater, literature readings, a bit of Austro-pop, some chansons, soft rock.

MOVE CLUB
(8.) Daungasse 1 ☎*433278.*
Near the university and full of young people. Daily from 9pm.

ROCKHAUS
(20.) Adalbert-Stifter Str. 73
☎*334641.*
Home of Viennese heavy metal.

SZENE WIEN
(11.) Hauffgasse 26 ☎*743341.*
Opened in 1983 as a self-administering commune of politically "engaged" musicians, in Simmering.

TAKE FIVE
Annagasse 3a ☎*5129277. Map 3D3.*
Daily from 10pm.

TIFFANY DANCING
Goethegasse 2 ☎*5878296. Map 3E3.*
Upper crust, in disco terms. Daily from 8pm, Sunday 5pm.

U4
(12.) Schönbrunner Str. 222 ☎*858318.*
Vienna's "in" disco for more than 10 years. Each day of the week features a different DJ — and different musical coloring. Frequent live music concerts. Next door is **U5**: smart bar and video clips.

WAKE UP
Seilerstätte 5 ☎*5121212. Map 4D4.*
Reputedly "Vienna's most beautiful disco."

WUK
See page 59 for details.
The hub of Vienna's underground culture.

JAZZ CLUBS
Vienna is not somewhere that leaps readily to mind when thinking of an original, vigorous jazz scene. Yet the following cafés offer passable fare, and occasionally some memorable bands.
America Latina (6.) Mollardgasse 17 ☎5979269. Mainly Latin jazz.
Andino   (6.) Münzwardeingasse 2. Andean folk groups and salsa.
Jazzland   Franz-Josefs-Kai 29 ☎5332575. Map 4C4. Vienna's jazz classic. Blues, swing and Dixieland groups.
Jazzspelunke   (6.) Dürergasse 3 ☎5870126. Map 3F1. A perennial of the Viennese jazz scene.
Papa's Tapas   (4.) Schwarzenbergplatz 10 ☎650311. Map 4E4. Live blues and boogie combine with an exotic menu and first-rate

drinks. Also part of the same establishment are **Atrium** disco (see page 159) and **Wurlitzer**, in the cellar, which offers jukebox dancing to the music of the 1950s and '60s.

PUBS AND BISTROS

An "In-Treff" is where you go for a drink and a chat at night if your haircut is sufficiently cool and your dress casually fashionable. The coolest and casualest go to the **Bermuda Triangle**, where the bloom of Vienna's post-yuppie generation congregates at night. Sloppier people can try one of the many jolly, musty, *gemütlich* wine cellars which have mushroomed in the vaulted basements of the Inner City's ancient buildings.

BABYLON
(4.) Gusshaus Str. 20 ☎*5054104. Map 3F3.*
100 sorts of beer. Weekdays from 9pm, weekends from 7pm.

BIJOU BAR
(13.) Hietzinger Hauptstrasse 12 ☎*87804 ♥*
The most popular hotel bar in town, in Parkhotel Schönbrunn. Closed Monday.

CHATTANOOGA
Graben 29a. Daily from 8pm ☎*5335000. Map 3D3 ♥ ♥*
Snack bar and garden in front, live music and dancing in the back.

FRAUENCAFÉ
(8.) Lange Gasse 11 ☎*433754. Map 3D1.*
For women only. Daily except Sunday from 7pm.

KRAH KRAH
Rabensteig 8 ☎*5353387. Map 4C4.*
Lively beer-tavern favored by the academic community. Daily from 11am.

LOOS-BAR
Kärntner Str. 10 ☎*5123283. Map 3D3.*
Original Art Nouveau decoration by Adolf Loos; smart clientele. Monday to

Saturday from 8pm, and Sunday from 7pm.

MA PITOM
Seitenstettengasse 5 ☎*5354313. Map 3C3.*
"Designer" underground café. Daily from 5.30pm.

ROTER ENGEL
Rabensteig 5 ☎*5354105. Map 4C4 ♥*
Wine bar with live music: chansons, folk or jazz blues. Monday to Saturday from 3pm, Sunday from 5pm.

SALZAMT
Ruprechtsplatz ☎*5335332. Map 4C4.*
Trendy meeting point of art and culture people, a key attraction of the Bermuda Triangle. Daily from 6pm.

SANTO SPIRITO
Kumpfgasse 7 ☎*5129998. Map 4D4 ♥*
Classical music café. Daily from 5pm.

SCOTCH
Park Ring 10 ☎*5129417. Map 4D4 ♥*
Café by day, cocktail bar after 7pm, disco after 9pm.

WUNDERBAR
Schönlaterngasse 8 ☎*5127989. Map 4D4.*
Daily from 4pm.

SIN

Except in the context of a few distinctly American/international hotels, a **bar** in Austria means a place where barely clad women offer various services to unaccompanied gentlemen. The industry has benefited immensely from the revolutions in Eastern Europe in the quality and quantity of its offerings.

There is no specific district where bars in this sense congregate, although a good many can be found in side streets near the main hotel zones (for example, off Kärntner Str.).

CONTACT BAR
(9.) Alser Str. 18 ☎*4373924. Map 3C1.*
Drinks, sauna, attractive girls in intimate and unsleazy atmosphere.

JOSEPHINE
Sonnenfelsgasse 9. Map 4D4.
Numerous hostesses, cramped premises.

• **Escort services** are advertised in tourist brochures distributed in hotels but *not* in the yellow pages.
• For the bluest **films** try **Rondell** *(at Riemergasse 11, map 4D4)* or **Schubert-Kino** *(at (9.) Währinger Str. 46, map 3B1).*

GAY FACILITIES

ALTE LAMPE
Heumühlgasse 15 ☎*5873454. Map 3F2.*
Café, open daily except Monday from 9pm.

GAY PRIDE PALACE
See page 57 under HOMOSEXUELLE INITIATIVE WIEN.

ROSA-LILA-VILLA
(6.) Linke Wienzeile 102 ☎*568150.*
Café, library, counseling and communication center for gay men and women.

Café Willendorf: daily 7pm-2am. **Café Warmes Nest**: Monday to Friday 5pm-midnight.

RÖMER SAUNA
Passauerplatz 6 (near Maria-am-Gestade)
☎*635318. Map 3C3.*
Sauna, bar, café.

WHY NOT
Tiefer Graben 22 ☎*5351158. Map 3C3*
♥
Café-disco.

GAMBLING
In the former Palais Esterházy is the **Casino Wien** *(Kärntner Str. 41, map 3E3, daily from 3pm):* French and American roulette, baccarat, black jack, poker, red dog, punto banco and machines.

Shopping

Nearly all Western — especially German — brand-names and chain stores are represented in Vienna; meanwhile, Austria's native retail industry lags behind modern Europe in style and pizazz. The most interesting shopping propositions are therefore found where specifically Austrian artistry and traditions make a difference.

One such area is clothing fashions inspired by Austrian folk and hunting costumes *(Trachtenmode)*. Others include various offshoots of old Viennese finery that are now more or less exclusively geared to the tourist market: porcelain and crystal tableware, silver, enamel and petit-point lacework. Another perennial favorite is confectionery, as is only to be expected of the city that just about invented coffee and cake.

Shopping is concentrated in the Inner City, particularly along the **Kärntner Str.-Graben-Kohlmarkt** axis. **Mariahilfer Str.** has all the major department stores and a variety of electronics stores, which flourished after 1989 thanks to booming demand from Eastern European visitors. A glitzy new shopping complex, the **Shopping City Süd**, was recently opened in Vösendorf, just over the southern city boundary.

SHOPPING HOURS
Austria enjoys the most draconian laws governing shopping hours in Europe — stricter, would you believe, than Germany itself. A constitutional controversy has enveloped the subject since late 1990, and there is a slight chance that some life may soon be allowed to seep into the deadly peace of the Viennese after-hours and Sunday.

At present, shops in general open 9am to 6pm on weekdays and until noon on Saturday. In addition, they are permitted to stay open late one day of the week, or to open on Saturday afternoon once a month. Most smaller shops take a break at various times between noon and 4pm.

Only *six* shops in the city have permission to stay open beyond the usual hours for food, stationery, books and tobacco goods. These include one shop each in the main rail stations (everyday until 10 or 11pm) and the **Julius Meinl** supermarket at Opernring 3-5 *(map 3 E3, Mon-Fri until 8pm, Sat until 2pm)*. In addition, some shops in nearby villages that thrive on weekend tourism are allowed to work on Sundays.

TAX
The Austrian Value-Added Tax *(Mehrwertsteuer)* is rated in two bands: 20 and 32 percent. In order to get a refund on items costing more than AS1,000, fill form **U-34** in shops displaying the "Tax Free" sign, have it

stamped at exit Customs, then send it back to the shop to claim any difference from the VAT or sales tax rate in your own country.

ANTIQUES

For low-end antiques try your luck at the **flea market** held on Saturdays from 8am-6pm at the upper end of NASCHMARKT (see page 119). Side streets along Linke Wienzeile upward from the flea market hide many antique stores full of delightful surprises. For expensive stuff, visit the shops clustered behind the Hofburg and around the cathedral.

ALT-WIEN KUNST
Bräuner Str. 11 ☎*5129143. Map 3D3.*
Five-times yearly art and antique auctions. Catalog on demand.

DOROTHEUM
Dorotheergasse 17 ☎*51560-0. Map 3D3.*
The DOROTHEUM is a venerable Viennese institution (see page 80). Daily auctions and direct sale of everything from used junk to high art.

MONIKA KAESSER
Kruger Str. 17 ☎*5122805. Map 3E3.*

A specialist in Jugendstil.

MICHAEL KOVACEK
Stallburggasse 2 ☎*5129954. Map 3D3.*
Superb selection of antique glassware.

W.E.MOSER
(9.) Nussdorfer Str. 72 ☎*3480524. Map 3A1.*
Militaria, antique weapons, medals.

BRÜDER SOFFER
Singer Str. 4 ☎*5124428. Map 3D3.*
Wide selection of antiques.

BOOKS, RECORDS, MUSIC

Go beyond the front department of bookstores, which seem to be devoted exclusively to Franz Joseph and Mozart: you will discover the world of German-language publishing, which will amaze anyone from the English-speaking world with its breadth, sophistication, seriousness and — relative — lack of pulp. Sorry, it's all in German. To find the same level of quality applied to less language-specific fields, try the map shops or record stores.

MUSIKHAUS DOBLINGER
Dorotheergasse 10 ☎*51503-0. Map 3D3.*
Comprehensive collection of sheet music, books on music, and records.

FREYTAG-BERNDT U. ARTARIA
Kohlmarkt 9 ☎*5332094. Map 3D3.*
F&B offer an extraordinary selection of travel books, guides and maps, including a full chest of hiking and mountaineering maps. Artaria, upstairs — formerly publishers of Mozart, Haydn and Beethoven — specialize in art books and music.

GRAMOLA
Look for the CD store at Kohlmarkt 5

☎*5335034. Map 3D3.*
Quite possibly the world's finest retailer of classical music, with a fabulous selection and expert sales help. The sale annex at **Graben 16**, around the corner, carries bargain offers, Pavarotti's Latest and Mozart's Greatest.

HASBACH
Wollzeile 9 and 29 ☎*5128876. Map 4D4.*
Wide selection of antique prints and copperplates.

LÖCKER & WOGENSTEIN
Annagasse 5 ☎*5127344. Map 3D3.*
An antiquarian bookstore specializing in politics, posters and Judaica.

RED OCTOPUS RECORDS
(8.) Josefstädter Str. 99 ☎*4081422. Map 3D1.*
Jazz in every imaginable shape, form, variety and extension. Imports from around the world, including rare and unusual finds.

SHAKESPEARE & CO
Sterngasse 2 ☎*5355053. Map 3C3.*
The best selection of English books to be found anywhere in town. They also present poetry readings and cultural activities.

WOLFRUM
Augustinerstrasse 10 ☎*5125398-0. Map 3D3.*
Austria's sophisticated art publisher: old and new art books, posters, postcards and a wide selection of exhibition catalogs.

FASHION
There are some fine old houses, like the selection listed immediately below. But they are no longer really top-class in international terms. Compare the difference with imports from Britain — for example, at **Ladislaus Hantak** *(Opernring 15, map 3E3)* — or from Italy, such as **D. Linnerth** *(Lugeck 1-2, map 4D4).*

FRED ADLMÜLLER
Kärntner Str. 41 ☎*5126650. Map 3D3.*
Vienna's fashion czar: women's fashions for an elite clientele.

W & A JONAK
Trattnerhof 2 ☎*5339906. Map 3D3.*
International haute couture.

KNIZE & CO
Graben 13 ☎*5122119. Map 3D3.*
Once upon an imperial time, they were personal tailors to His k.u.k. Majesty Franz Joseph. This historic landmark shop was designed by Adolf Loos.

• More interesting in their own class are shops specializing in *Tracht*, or traditional Austrian folk costumes. In the past, when Vienna used to be a fashion capital of Europe, no one but a backward bumpkin would appear in the city wearing a Tyrolean hat or a *Dirndl* . Provincial fashions have since then invaded the capital, and the results can in fact be quite pleasing.

Tracht goes hand in hand with some classy and superbly made outdoors wear: as elsewhere in German-speaking lands, hiking and hunting are taken seriously here and obey an elaborate dress code of their own.

RESI HAMMERER
Kärntner Str. 29-31 ☎*5126952. Map 3D3.*
A former Olympic skiing medalist whose line of sturdy yet elegant outdoors wear has been one of Austria's most successful export items of late.

LODEN-PLANKL
Michaelerplatz 6 ☎*5338032. Map 3D3.*
Vienna's oldest *tracht*-shop.

WANTKY
Main shop: Tuchlauben 18 ☎*630553. Map 3C3.*
85-year-old house with branches throughout the city.

FOOD, CONFECTIONERY AND WINE
Edibles are the one field of consumption in which Vienna still belongs unquestionably in the top league, not far below the unscalable heights of France and northern Italy.

DEMEL
Kohlmarkt 14 ☎*5335516-0. Map 3D3.*
This is the *Café-Konditorei* which has been synonymous with the Viennese tradition of sweetery since its founding in 1776, the year when the United States achieved independence. Each one of their pastries, bonbons, chocolates, pralines, Strudels, *biscottes, Kipferls* and *Gugelhupfe* is a masterwork, as are its packaging and presentation.

DO & CO
Akademie Str. 3 ☎*5126474. Map 3E3.*
Fine delicatessen and imported foods; attached food bar.

MEINL AM GRABEN
Graben 19 ☎*5334586. Map 3D3.*
This is the "exclusive" gourmet outlet of Julius Meinl, Austria's largest supermarket chain.

VINOTHEK ST STEPHAN
Stephansplatz 6 ☎*5126858. Map 3D3.*
Fine selection of Austrian and imported wines.

DAS WEINKELLER
In Döbling, (19.) Osterleitengasse 9 ☎*363115. Map 1B3.*
The wine cellar and sales point of the official Society for the Promotion of Austrian Wines, with 750 varieties of premium wine.

GEBRÜDER WILD
Neuer Markt 10/11 ☎*5122179. Map 3D3.*
Famous gourmet shop with highest-quality foods.

HANDICRAFTS
The post-1960s revival of interest in traditional handicrafts has begun to produce some highly creditable results. The best place to shop for them is the various outdoor handicraft markets, of which the three listed below are particularly lively. They also offer a pleasant atmosphere, with strolling couples and numerous wine and food stalls, allowing a glimpse of Viennese life beyond the usual stereotypes.

DANUBE CANAL PROMENADE
Between Schottenring and Schwedenplatz. Map 3B3-4C4.
Every Saturday and Sunday in summer (from May to September). See also pages 82-83.

SPITTELBERG
Map 3E1.
Every Saturday in summer (from April to November), daily in December.

HEILIGENKREUZER HOF
Map 4D4.
The first Saturday and Sunday in each month from April to November.

• Three specialist shops in the central Inner City also deserve mention:

JOH. BACKHAUSEN UND SÖHNE
Kärntner Str. 33 ☎*514040. Map 3D3.*
Print fabrics with Jugendstil and "Liberty" designs.

NIEDERÖSTERREICHISCHES HEIMATWERK
Herrengasse 6 ☎*5333495. Map 3D3.*
Folk art from the villages of Lower Austria.

ÖSTERREICHISCHE WERKSTÄTTE
Kärntner Str. 6 ☎*5122418. Map 3D3.*
Established in 1903 as part of the previous wave of crafts revival which gripped Europe at the turn of the century, and counting Klimt, Kokoschka, Kolo Moser and Egon Schiele among its guiding spirits, the Austrian Workshops (formerly Wiener Werkstätte) had a seminal influence on 20thC design. The 3-story shop on Kärntner Str. is a cooperative venture embracing several hundred well-known Austrian artisans. Objects in glass, ceramic, enamel, leather and straw.

• Finally, two noteworthy representatives of that typically Austrian handicraft, petit-point lacework:

Berta Smejkal Opernpassage ☎5872102. Map **3E3**.
Maria Stransky Hofburg-Passage 2 ☎5336098. Map **3D3**.

JEWELRY AND CLOCKS
The finest jewelers in Vienna are to be found along Kärntner Str. and Graben. Their emphasis is on the restrained and classical.

HABAN
Branches at Kärntner Str. 2 and Graben 12
☎*5126730, 5121220. Map 3D3.*
A subsidiary of the Swiss jewelers and watchmakers Bucherer.

HELDWEIN
Graben 13 ☎*5125781. Map 3D3.*
Classic jewelry.

HOFER & SOHN
Schulhof 2 ☎*5334577. Map 3C3.*
Hand-made modern and antique clocks, located in the same ancient building as Vienna's Clock Museum (see page 78).

HÜGLER
Freisingergasse 4 (Petersplatz)
☎*5339619. Map 3D3.*
A prominent Vienna jeweler.

KÖCHERT
Neuer Markt 15 ☎*5125828. Map 3D3.*
Jeweler to the royal and imperial court since 1814.

TABLE AND GLASSWARE
The Habsburg court regarded table manners and tableware as matters of the utmost importance. The Viennese aristocracy, and then the Viennese middle class, followed suit. Visit the Imperial SILVER AND TABLEWARE COLLECTION of the Hofburg (see page 100), then see which of the following come nearest.

167

ALBIN DENK
Graben 13 ☎*5124439. Map 3D3.*
Suppliers of porcelain, silverware and glassware to the court, in business since 1702.

AUGARTEN PORZELLAN
Main outlet at Stock-im-Eisenplatz 3 ☎*5121494, map 3D3. Factory sales at Schloss Augarten* ☎*21124, map 2C4. Shops at Mariahilfer Str. 99, map 3E1, and at the airport.*
Europe's second-oldest porcelain manufacturer, a Viennese specialty since 1712.

FISCHER-STURM
Tegetthof Str. 3 ☎*5126924. Map 3D3.*
Table silver and other silver articles that can be engraved with your monogram upon demand.

GMUNDNER KERAMIK
Kärntner Durchgang ☎*5125824. Map 3E3.*

Much-beloved rustic ware from the town of Gmunden in Upper Austria.

JAROSINSKI & VAUGOIN
(7.) Zieglergasse 24 ☎*933388.*
Silversmiths since 1847, still housed in their original Biedermeier-style shop.

LOBMEYR
Kärntner Str. 28 ☎*5120508. Map 3D3.*
Tradition-rich maker of finest crystal and glassware. Representatives of Herend porcelain (from Hungary) in Vienna. Glass museum upstairs.

PAWLATA
Kärntner Str. 14 ☎*5121764. Map 3D3.*
Rich selection of Gmunden ceramics.

THUN-HOHENSTEIN
Wollzeile 26 ☎*5125461. Map 4D4.*
Noble chinaware marketed under the escutcheon of one of Austria's noblest families.

Recreation

Ideas for children

- **BABY-SITTERS:** A service is provided by the **Austrian Academic Exchange Service** (☎ *5873525, round the clock, AS100 per hour plus transportation costs)* and **Babysitterzentrale** (☎ *951135, call Mon-Fri 8am-2pm, AS50 per hour plus transportation costs)*.

- **NURSERY:** The **International Kindergarten Alt-Wien** *(at (7.) Mariahilfer Str. 88a ☎ 930174, map 3 E1)* accepts children up to the age of 12. Cost including meals: AS140 per day.

- **AMUSEMENTS:** For a fun outing that will enchant children and grown-ups alike, go to the PRATER *(map 4 B5-6)*, to enjoy the giant ferris wheel, Lilliputbahn, Planetarium, amusement park and nature park (see page 121), or the **Donaupark** behind **UNO-City** *(map 2 B5)*, where there are playgrounds, table tennis, a rosarium, a bird-watching alley and a mini-train.

- **TOY STORES:** Top rating goes to **Modellbahn-Ecke** *(at (15.) Ölweingasse 21 ☎ 839121, map 1 D3)* with its fantastic collection of model trains. Another fun place for father and son is the **ABZ Scout Shop** *(at (7.) Breitegasse 13 ☎ 935444, map 3 E2)*.

- **PUPPET THEATER:** The **Urania Puppet Theater** mounts frequent shows in winter (October to April) at the venerable Urania Theater *(Julius-Raab-Platz ☎ 726191-0, map 4 C5)*.

- **OTHER IDEAS:** Visits to the NATURAL HISTORY MUSEUM (see page 119), the **Clown and Circus Collection** (see page 132), the SCHÖNBRUNN Zoo (see page 126) and the **Gänserndorf Safari Park** (see page 180) are likely to meet with children's approval. The ART HISTORY MUSEUM and the Museum of Modern Art at LIECHTENSTEIN GARDEN PALACE (see pages 104 and 118) offer various special programs designed for younger people.

Sport and leisure

BIKING

Two **maps** will be great help to those wishing to go biking in Vienna and along the Danube: the *Stadtplan Wien* by Fahrradbüro Wien *(from (4.) Frankenberggasse 11* ☎*658435, map 3 E3)* and the *Donauradweg Passau-Hainburg* by Verlag Schubert & Frantzke in St Pölten. Bicycles can be rented at the following places:

Salztorbrücke   On the Danube Canal ☎4606072. Map **4**C4. April to mid-October Monday to Friday from 9am.

Simmeringer Fahrradstadl   (9.) Ravelin Str. 2 ☎268557. Map **4**D5. March to November daily 9am-8pm.

Schuh-ski   On Danube Island ☎236518-0. Map **2**C4. April to October weekdays after 1pm, weekends from 9am.

Austrian Railways(ÖBB)   Rent touring bikes at nearly all rail stations at AS90 per day. Train passengers pay only half.

BOATING

Scullers and sailboats can be rented at various places along the Alte Donau, including:

Fritz Eppel   (22.) Wagramer Str. 48 ☎235168. Map **2**B5.

Karl Hofbauer   (22.) An der Oberen Alten Donau 184 ☎236733. Map **2**B4. This is also a sailing school.

F.M. Schneider   (22.) Wagramer Str. 48b ☎236782. Map **2**B5.

BOWLING

Brunswick Bowling   (17.) Schumanngasse 107 ☎464361.

Bowlinghalle Prater   (2.) Prater Hauptallee 124 ☎246461. Off map **4**C6.

FLYING

Polsterer Jets   Departures from Schwechat Airport ☎71110-2077. 20-minute overflights of Vienna at AS440 per person, as well as air tours over different parts of Austria.

Ballonsportclub Wien   ☎5878139. Balloon flights over the city at AS10,000 per take-off.

Österreichische Aero-Club   (4.) Prinz-Eugen-Str. 12 ☎50510280. Map **4**F4. Information on hang-gliding, ballooning and other types of flying for fun.

FOOTBALL (SOCCER)

Major games take place at the 63,000-person **Praterstadion**, located about 2.5km (1½ miles) into the Prater *(map 2 C5; metro U3 to Schlach-thausgasse, then bus 80B)*.

GOLF

Golf-Club Wien   (2.) Freudenau 65a ☎2189564. Map **2**D5. Members of any European golf club are admitted for AS450 every day of the week (guests of club members only on weekends).

Colony Club Gutenhof   30 minutes by car to the s of the city in Himberg ☎(02235) 88055-10. AS500 on weekdays, AS650 on weekends.

RIDING
Apply to **Bundesverband für Reiten und Fahren** *(at (4.) Prinz-Eugen-Str. 14/6a* ☎ *5058363, map 4 F4)* for information.

SWIMMING
Many of the 23 districts of Vienna have their own public outdoor or indoor swimming pool *(freibad* or *hallenbad)*, and often both, with sauna, baths and associated facilities. For a particularly attractive outdoor pool try **Freibad Krapfenwald**, which lies on a hill of the Vienna Woods and commands a broad panorama *(at (19.) Krapfenwaldgasse 73* ☎ *321501, map 1 B2, open daily May-Sept)*.

A string of river beaches exists along the Alte Donau and on the Danube Island. The most popular one occupies the island of **Gansehäufel** on the Alte Donau *(map 2 C5; metro U1 to Kaisermühlen, then bus 90A; open daily May-Sept)*.

Topless bathing has become the norm rather than the exception at all beaches and many swimming pools. Gansehäufel features a nudist *(FKK)* beach, too, but the real mecca for Vienna's nude bathing enthusiasts is **Lobau**, a wild area of many ponds and lagoons by the Neue Donau *(map 2 C5; metro U1 to Kaisermühlen, then bus 91A to Roter Hiasl or Panozzalacke)*.

TENNIS
Look in the yellow pages under *Tennisplätze* for a variety of tennis clubs.

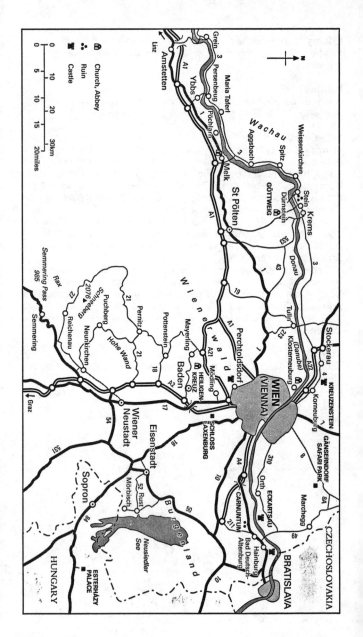

Excursions from Vienna

Lower Austria and the Danube

Small towns of great charm and character fill the landscape around Vienna, giving enormous scope for pleasant weekend excursions. The city itself lies on a physical watershed. To its w are the forested hills of the Vienna Woods, the easternmost spur of the central European massif: in the s, they climb gradually to the Alps; in the n, they squeeze the Danube into a series of gorges of great panoramic beauty. The villages of this part have roots going back to the early Middle Ages, and a strong anchor in German culture and traditions.

In the opposite direction, Vienna marks the boundary of the Pannonian (Hungarian) Plain, a vast and featureless expanse of land stretching as far as the Carpathian Mountains and Belgrade in the e. Historic Hungary (as opposed to the modern state) starts at the river Leitha, less than 10km (6 miles) beyond Vienna's airport; Bratislava, the capital of Slovakia, was once practically a suburb of the imperial city. The countryside here has a distinctly "East European" flavor with its old, dilapidated manorial castles and tiny rural villages huddled in their shadow. The spirit of Maria Theresa hovers in bonbon-colored houses, puff-cream châteaux and bulb-spired churches, all seemingly abandoned to the arms of a gentle decline for the last 100 or 200 years.

PLANNING

Vienna is surrounded by the state of Lower Austria, so it is well worth paying a visit to the **Tourist Office of Lower Austria** *(at (1.) Heiden-schuss 2, between Freyung and Am Hof* ☎ *5333114-34, map 3 C3)* for ideas, brochures and listings.

A variety of packaged excursions are offered by tour operators, with typical tours such as the following (duration and price are quoted as general examples only):

- **VIENNA WOODS SOUTH: Perchtoldsdorf, Mödling, Heiligenkreuz Abbey, Mayerling, Helene Valley** and **Baden.** Attractive landscape, enchanting old villages, good food and wine. Total distance about 70km/44 miles (5 hours, AS400).
- **THE DANUBE:** By land to **St Pölten** ("Austria's Baroque capital") and **Melk,** famous for its spectacular abbey. By boat down the **Wachau** district, with stops at the picturesque medieval village of **Dürnstein** and the historic town of **Krems.** Return by land or boat. Total distance about 180km/112 miles (8 hours, AS900).

- **BURGENLAND: Eisenstadt,** the residence of the Esterházy princes and Joseph Haydn, with the villages of Rust and Mörbisch on Neusiedler See. Might include a visit to either **Wiener Neustadt** or **Sopron,** across the border in Hungary. Total distance without Sopron or Wiener Neustadt: about 140km/87 miles (8 hours, AS900).
- **OTHER OPTIONS:** ‡ A journey along the Danube to **Bratislava,** via the Roman ruins of **Carnuntum** and the walled town of **Hainburg** ‡ A rather quicker visit to the medieval abbey of **Klosterneuburg,** immediately to the N of the city, together with the mock-medieval castle of Kreuzenstein across the river ‡ A tour by car and/or train of the **Semmering** Pass via the Schneeberg valley ‡ A fuller Danube journey, spread over two days, from Vienna to **Linz** and back ‡ The most ambitious, most interesting excursion of all, to **Budapest,** a mere 250km (156 miles) down the river, which forms the subject of the second half of this book.

FOR INDEPENDENT TRAVELERS

By car   Drivers should note the breakdown assistance numbers of Austria's two automobile clubs — ☎120 for **ÖAMTC** or ☎123 for **ARBÖ.** Further useful numbers for German speakers — ☎1583 for snow information ☎1566 for weather (all Austria) ☎1590 for road conditions.

Share-a-ride   For rides to anywhere in the world, including the whole of Austria, make contacts via **Mitfahrzentrale** *(at (5.) Franzensgasse 11 ☎ 564174, map 3 F2).*

By train   Austrian Railways offer various combinations of tickets and reductions to travelers by **train.** The **Rabbit Card (RC Junior** for passengers under 26) allows free train travel within Austria for 4 days at AS950/590. The **Umweltticket** costs AS990 and earns a 50-percent discount on all train tickets for a year. Bicycles are available for rental at most rail stations, and can be returned to any other station; train passengers enjoy a 50-percent reduction. *(For train information ☎ 1717 (24hrs). Reservations: Wien-West ☎56502999; Wien-Süd ☎ 580035638).*

By boat   The **Donaudampfschiffahrtsgesellschaft** (sic — it means the Danube Steamboat Company, abbreviated to **DDSG)** is the semi-monopoly operator of Danube passenger **boats.** Their head office and passenger boat landing are at (2.) Handelskai 265 *(☎ 266536, map 2 C4, metro U1 to Vorgarten Str.).* Rental bikes are also available at some DDSG landings. Major routes (all valid mid-May to late September, some for longer):

- **Upstream,** Vienna to Linz: depart 8am (15 hours); stops at Nussdorf, Greifenstein, Tulln, Krems, Dürnstein, Weissenkirchen, Spitz, Aggstein, Aggsbach, Melk, Pöchlarn, Marbach, Ybbs, Grein, Mauthausen.
- **Upstream,** Krems to Melk: depart 10.30am, noon and 4pm (3 hours).
- **Downstream,** Linz to Vienna: depart 8.05am (12 hours).
- **Downstream,** Melk to Krems: depart 10am, 2pm, 3.30pm (1¾ hours).

- **Downstream** by Vienna-Bratislava hydrofoil: depart 7.30am, 8.45am, 4.45pm, 5pm, 6.45pm (1 hour).
- **Downstream** by Vienna-Budapest hydrofoil or hovercraft: depart 8am, 8.10am, 2.30pm ($4\frac{1}{2}$ hours).

Excursions A to Z

BADEN ☆
25km (16 miles) s of Vienna. Population: 25,000. Train S1, R10 from Wien-Süd; Badener Bahn from in front of the Opera ☎ *code 02252* **i** *Hauptplatz* ☎*86800-310* ᶠˣ*80733* ✗ *May-Oct Mon 2pm and Thurs 10am: meet at* **i**

The sulfurous hot springs of Baden were known since Roman times. They became fashionable in the 18thC (Constanze Mozart was taking the cure in Baden when the composer got ill and died unattended at home), but their moment of true glory came under Franz I of Austria, who made a habit of retiring *aufs Land* to Baden each summer from 1803-34. The dominant note of the town is thus Biedermeier, with variety added by touches of Baroque, late 19thC and Jugendstil. Located in a particularly verdant grove of the Vienna Woods, it continues to be a favorite summer retreat of well-to-do Viennese.

The heart of the resort is naturally the **Kurpark**, the classic feature of every Central European spa, with its shady groves and promenades, elegant casino, Beethoven Temple and obligatory bandstand *(summer evening concerts daily except Mon)*. Dignified — if mildly under-maintained — old hotels, a theater affecting the facade of an Attic temple, and the summer palace of Franz I surround the park.

The town itself is filled with romantic little taverns and ancient village houses turned into stylish boutiques. A **Beethoven Museum** occupies the house where the composer spent his final summers, composing parts of the Ninth symphony and his stupendous last quartets *(Rathausgasse 10* 🖾 *open Tues-Sun 4-6pm, Sat-Sun 9-11am)*. A plaque marks the birthplace of Katharina Schratt, the feisty little actress who was the lifelong companion of Franz Joseph.

BATHS   The thermal waters, emerging at a temperature of 36°C (97°F) from 15 springs, are prescribed for bone and joint ailments. There are three groups of public baths: the **Indoor thermal pool** *(Brusattiplatz 4* ☜ ☼ ➾ *open year-round except part of July, daily 9.30am-9.30pm, but Wed only until 6pm)*, the **open-air thermal pools** *(Helenen Str. 19-21, large pool with sand beach, lawns, table tennis ➾ and café; open May-Sept)* and the **mineral water thermal pools** *(Marchetti Str. 13, lawn, snack bar; open late Apr-early Oct)*. In addition, six hotels possess private pools: **Schloss Weikersdorf**, **Gutenbrunn**, **Herzogenhof**, **Parkhotel**, **Grand Hotel Sauerhof** and **Seminarhotel Baden**.

CASINO   In the **Kurpark**. French and American roulette, blackjack, poker and machines daily from 3pm; baccarat on Wednesday, Thursday, Friday. Bus service to/from Vienna Opera ☎44496.

MUSIC   Operetta classics at the **Summer Arena** early July to mid-September ☎48547. **Beethoven Festival** in mid-September.

GOLF   There are 18-hole courses at **Country Club Brunn/Gebirge** (20km/13 miles) ☎(2236) 31572; **Schloss Ebreichsdorf** (15km/9 miles) ☎(02254) 3888; **Golf Club Enzensfeld** (8km/5 miles) ☎(02256) 812721.

❧ ⊨   **Frauenhof** (*Josefsplatz 3* ☎80666-0 ▭ ☙ ☐ ▣ ⴵ) is a stylish, tradition-rich hotel with one of the prettiest, and best-known, garden-restaurants in town.

The **Grand Hotel Sauerhof** *(Weilburg Str. 11-13* ☎41251-0 🖷48047 ▭ *87 rms* ♈ ☙ ☞ ○ ♈ ♨ ☐ ▣), an impressive Biedermeier palais with a formal park in central Baden, boasts a historic wine cellar, the **Rosenkavalier** restaurant, a beauty farm and thermal bath.

Schloss Weikersdorf *(Schlossgasse 9-11* ☎48301-0 🖷48301-1503 ▭ *75 rms* ☙ *heated* ≋ ☞ ○ ♈ ▣), a luxury hotel in a Renaissance-style château, is located in Baden's most beautiful park. Thermal bath, gourmet food, wine cellar, heated pool.

⌂ ⊨   5km (3 miles) from the town, **Schwalbennest** (☎44315 ▭ *18 rms* ⴵ ☙) is an ivy-covered old village house deep in the woods in Helene Valley. Hearty food, hunters' pub with open fireplace, romantic gardens, thermal whirlpool.

Seminarhotel Baden *(Trostgasse 23* ☎88662-0 ▭ *75 rms* ☙ ≋ ☞ ○ ♈ ♨ ☐ ▣ ⴵ): quiet and classy atmosphere in an attractive street lined with villas; unpretentious luxury, gourmet food, café, thermal bath.

⊨   **Flair** *(Kaiser-Franz-Ring 1* ☎41571, closed Mon), Baden's most elegant restaurant, located in the premises of the gambling casino. Reserve ahead.

Stadtkeller *(Theresiengasse 1* ☎80771) is a historic wine cellar and garden serving local specialties.

Zum Sandwirt *(Weilburg Str. 45* ☎44358, closed Tues) is a rustic cellar offering traditional country fare.

▲   At **Laxenburg** *(see page 183)*.

BRATISLAVA (Czechoslovakia)

54km (34 miles) E of Vienna. Population: 430,000. 4 trains daily from Wien-Süd (70mins); hydrofoil from DDSG - Schiffahrtszentrum (1hr). Group tours organized by CEDOK (at Park Ring 12 in Vienna ☎5120199, map 4D4). Valid passport required (no visa needed for citizens of most Western countries) **i** *Leningradská 1* ☎(0042-7) 333715.

The city known as Pressburg in German and Poszony in Magyar became the capital of Habsburg-controlled Hungary in 1526 and remained the seat of the Hungarian Diet (Assembly of Lords) until 1848. Its cession in 1918 to Slovakia on the strength of its lower-class ethnic majority was a mighty — and never fully forgotten — blow to Hungarian national pride. Since 1989 the city has become the center of Slovak separatist sentiment within Czechoslovakia.

Located on the Danube at the conjunction of three countries, Bratislava is surrounded by an industrial belt of phenomenal ugliness. But inside this shell lies a historic center of great wealth and delicacy — a small replica of Vienna's Inner City, minus the excessive commercialism that can detract from the pleasure of the latter. The replication goes far: Masters Puchsbaum and Pilgram (compare page 93), for example, worked on Pressburg's Gothic Cathedral, whose building history closely matches that of the Stephansdom; at Palais Pálffy *(Jiráskova 10)* Mozart gave concerts; the Palais Grassalkovich *(Mierové namèstie)* was the site of the wedding of Duke Albert of Teschen (see page 74) with Marie-Christine (see page 79), with Haydn directing the music; and the Palais Esterházy once stood on Herrengasse, now rechristened Nálepkova.

A majority of the buildings of the center are historic landmarks. Highlights are the **Old Rathaus** (14th-16thC), now housing several museums; the **Primatial Palace**, a magnificent Neoclassical edifice built in 1778-81 for Prince-Archbishop Joseph Batthyányi; the **Palace of the Royal Hungarian Chamber**, a Baroque masterpiece of Martinelli (1753-56); and the **Academia Istrapolitana**, founded in 1465 by the Hungarian king Matthias Corvinus as one of Europe's leading universities, and subsequently enlarged with many Baroque additions. The most visible landmark of the city, the **castle**, was destroyed by fire in the 19thC and rebuilt as a faithful if somewhat sterile copy in the 1960s.

☞ **Devín** *(Riecna 4* ☎ *330851* ▥ *50 rms),* Bratislava's luxury hotel on the Danube bank; 1950s architecture.
　　Carlton *(Hviezdoslavovo námestie 2* ☎ *331851* ▥ *125 rms),* a pleasant hotel converted from several historic buildings, with a fine panorama of the old city.

▲　**Autocamping Zlaté Piesky** *(Senecká cesta* ☎ *60578).*

CARNUNTUM
*36km (22 miles) E of Vienna. Train S7 from Wien-Nord and Wien-Mitte to Petronell, then 10mins' walk **i** in Petronell* ☎ *(02163) 2228.*

The chief frontier garrison of Roman Pannonia was established early in the 1stC AD at a point where the Amber Road crossed the Danube, connecting Rome with the lands of the Baltic coast. Carnuntum, the civilian city which grew outside the military fortress, had a population of 50,000 when it was overrun by the barbarians in AD395. The excavated Roman ruins are extensive and well presented, though they do not necessarily rank among the world's most exciting Roman monuments. Sights include parts of the **campus** which occupied the site of the village of Petronell (with a **military amphitheater**, c.AD180), as well as a section of the civilian city a short distance to the w, with a larger **civilian amphitheater**, mosaic-paved streets, and the **Heidentor**, a section of a 2ndC triumphal arch.

Petronell offers, in addition, the 17thC château of Counts Traun, built near the ruins of an ancient Roman palace. Nearby **Bad Deutsch-Altenburg**, famous for its sulfurous thermal baths, possesses a museum devoted to the finds of Carnuntum, as well as **Schloss Ludwigstorff**, a Biedermeier gem now used as an Africa Museum. In the village of **Rohrau**, 5km (3 miles) s of Petronell, you can see the charming farmhouse where Joseph Haydn was born in 1732 *(open daily 10am-5pm, except Mon),* and the Baroque castle of the Harrach family where his mother was employed as a cook *(☎ open daily 10am-5pm, except Mon),* which has an important art collection.

DÜRNSTEIN   See WACHAU.

EISENSTADT ☆
52km (32 miles) sw of Vienna. Population: 10,000. Train R11 from Wien-Süd to Ebenfurth, then train or bus i at Rathaus ☎(02682) 2710. Bus 765, 766 to Rust and Mörbisch.

The capital of Burgenland, Austria's easternmost state, merits a visit on account of the impressive palace of the Princes Esterházy, many mementoes of Haydn, their court composer, and an intensely provincial, yet pleasant, historic center. Its rural countryside by appearance and tradition belongs more to Hungary — rather to a Hungary that *might have been* without its 20thC experience — than Austria.

Burgenland was created by the Treaty of Trianon in 1920 out of a sliver of historic Hungary which was granted to Austria partly on ethnic and partly on economic grounds. Its name — contrary to what many guidebooks claim — does not derive from an unusual multitude of castles *(burgen).* The name adopted after 1918 was Vierburgenland, or Fourcastleland, a reference to the four districts of Pressburg, Ödenburg, Eisenburg and Wieselburg, which formed the province. The first of the four (now Bratislava) was claimed by Czechoslovakia, leaving behind Dreiburgenland; the second lost its chief town (now Sopron) to Hungary, so finally it was found safer to drop the number altogether.

The chief sight of the town is **Schloss Esterházy**, a Baroque mansion of royal proportions, which was rebuilt in 1663 by Martino Carlone on the foundations of an earlier medieval stronghold; its Neoclassical rear facade dates from 1797-1805. The palace follows Viennese models, but many "Hungarian" themes are noticeable in its iconography, such as the royal statues lining the front. The splendid **gala hall** has been renamed after Haydn, many of whose works were first performed here *(✗ daily 10am-4pm; concerts every Sat evening May-Sept; biennial Haydn Festival in May and Sept).*

The Esterházys, descendants of the minor Hungarian nobility, rose to power during the Thirty Years' War through their devotion to the Habsburg crown and the Jesuit cause. Their role in re-Catholicizing Hungary and suppressing the revolt of Rákoczi (1703-11) was rewarded with power and wealth second only to the imperial dynasty. The peak of the family's fortunes was reached under Prince Nicholas (1761-90). The reforms of Joseph II threatened Esterházy interests, and the revolution of 1848 destroyed the foundations of their authority. The remainder of Esterházy estates in Austria now belong to Dr. Paul Esterházy, a wine producer.

The charming old garden house on Haydngasse where the composer lived in 1766-78 is now a **Haydn Museum** *(☎ open daily 9am-noon,*

1-5pm). The unusual cave-church at **Kalvarienberg** (Calvary Hill), dating from 1701-7, contains his tomb as well as a series of 260 naive statues depicting the suffering of Christ.

Joseph Haydn (1732-1809) entered the service of Prince Nicholas in 1762, and for nearly three decades composed music for the public and private occasions of the Esterházy household. Pensioned off at the death of the prince in 1790, he settled in the Vienna suburb of Gumpendorf, where he enjoyed great acclaim as Europe's senior musician. In 1796 he re-entered the Esterházy payroll under the new prince Nicholas II, although he continued to reside in Vienna.

☙☱ **Burgenland** *(on Schubertplatz* ☎ *(02682) 5521* ▭ ❧ ☙ ☙ *)* is the top hotel in town, with an attractive gourmet restaurant. Bicycles can be rented.

☙ **Goldener Adler** *(* ☎ *(02682) 2645* ▭ *)*, a nice old building on the main street, with a wine garden and tavern, has been an inn since 1582, and in the same family since 1772.

VICINITY
Two delightful little villages that carefully cultivate the claim that time has passed them by lie within a short drive of Eisenstadt, amid the vineyards covering the slopes near Neusiedler Lake. **Rust**, a quintessentially "Austrian" village with its weatherworn ocher houses, ancient church and myriad wine taverns, is the ideal place for an extended Sunday lunch. **Mörbisch**, only 6km (4 miles) away, presents the very different but equally attractive countenance of an old Croatian farming village with its narrow alleys, flower-covered adobe houses and traditionally-clad women. Its extreme isolation on the edge of the Iron Curtain, which until recently added a certain exotic luster to the name of Mörbisch, is now gone *(Hungarian border open to pedestrians and bikers, 8am-5pm)*, but the village still remains one of the most secluded rural corners of Austria.

Neusiedler Lake forms a popular swimming and water sports destination for the Viennese, though its shallow weedy waters (average depth 70cm/27 inches) are not quite on a par with Waikiki.

☙☱ **Hotel Stadt Rust** *(* ☎ *(02685) 250* ▭ *)*, in the historic center of Rust, is a pleasant, simple place with a good restaurant. An excellent seafood restaurant exists on the lake shore 1km ($\frac{1}{2}$ mile) E of the town center. **Mörbisch** possesses several pensions but no hotel as such.

GÄNSERNDORF   See HAINBURG.

HAINBURG ★
42km (26 miles) E of Vienna. Population: 6,000. Train S7 from Wien-Nord and Wien-Mitte **i** *at Hauptplatz 23* ☎ *(02165) 2111.*
Hainburg, on a beautifully situated hillside on the Danube, was fortified in the Middle Ages as a frontier town of the Holy Roman Empire.

Its 13thC **walls** have survived almost intact, with 12 towers and the massive **Wiener Tor**, a Gothic gatehouse. A ruined 11thC **castle** towers over the town, and numerous handsome burghers' houses give it a deeply historic aspect.

VICINITY

The district between the Danube and the March/Morava — the March-feld — is rich in castles and stately homes, and ripe for touring on a day's drive from Vienna. Two Baroque manor houses call for short detours between Hainburg and Marchegg: **Schlosshof**, a mini-Belvedere designed by Hildebrandt for Prince Eugene of Savoy, and **Niederweiden**, a manor house built by Fischer von Erlach.

Marchegg itself, a sleepy village which was a bigger place than Vienna in the 13thC, has an 18thC château now housing a Hunters' Museum. The beautiful waterside castle of **Eckartsau**, built for the Kinsky family in 1722-32, formed the setting of the final abdication of Karl I from the Austrian throne in 1918. The castle of **Orth**, which goes back to the reign of Maximilian I in the early 16thC, is now a Fishing Museum.

The **Gänserndorf Safari Park**, 3km (2 miles) s of the town of the same name, houses a rich variety of exotic animals roaming semi-freely along a 5km/3-mile-long car route. Children can play with different kinds of baby animals (✱ *open Mar-Oct daily 10am until 3hrs before dark; train S1 to Gänserndorf, then bus ◪ AS135 per person in own car* ☎ *(02282) 7261).*

HEILIGENKREUZ ✰

32km (20 miles) SW of Vienna. Population of Heiligenkreuz: 1,100. Bus from Baden, Mödling and Perchtoldsdorf rail stations **i** *at Gemeindeamt* ☎*(02258) 2286.*
The Cistercian Abbey of Heiligenkreuz ("Holy Cross"), located in a particularly idyllic corner of the Vienna Woods, rivals the more imposing monastic institutions of the environs of Vienna with its tranquility and meditative charm rather than its architectural splendor. The founding of the monastery goes back to St Leopold III (1133), and several of the Babenbergs including Leopold the Virtuous and Friedrich the Quarrelsome have their final resting place in the premises.

The abbey church combines an austere Romanesque nave with an attractive Gothic choir, which has retained its 13thC stained glass windows. The courtyard holds a **Trinity Column**, one of the most elaborate of the hundreds that were erected throughout the empire around the same time as Vienna's plague memorial.

VICINITY

Mayerling, a tiny rural backwater 4km ($2\frac{1}{2}$ miles) sw of Heiligenkreuz, is memorable mainly for the most dramatic event of the closing years of the Habsburg monarchy, the suicide of Crown Prince Rudolph and his girlfriend in 1889. The hunting mansion where the tragedy took place was demolished shortly afterwards and replaced with a small Capuchin convent whose inmates keep a vow of lifelong silence.

Rudolph, the only son of Franz Joseph and Elisabeth, was distinguished for his unusual intelligence and progressive ideas; he was regarded by many as a last hope for the decrepit Habsburg state. His body was discovered on the morning of a convivial day spent with friends, with that of Mary Vetsera, a 17-year-old star of Viennese society. Conspiracy theories kept Europe busy for many years, including a persistent hypothesis that the Crown Prince was murdered because of his involvement in a Hungarian plot against his father's throne.

A deeply romantic route follows the valley of the **Helene** from Mayerling to BADEN.

KLOSTERNEUBURG ★

12km (7½ miles) NW of Vienna. Population: 23,000 **i** *Niedermarkt 19* ☎*(02243) 2038. Suburban train S40 from Franz-Josefs-Bahnhof or metro U4 to Heiligenstadt, then bus* ✗ *of abbey Mon-Sat from 9am-5pm, Sun from 1.30pm until dark* ☎*6375-25.*

The majestic **Abbey** of the Augustinian Canons makes Klosterneuburg, located immediately N of Vienna, a popular goal of excursions.

The strategic site, controlling the last hilly redoubt on the middle Danube, became in c.1100 the seat (*Neuburg* = New Castle) of the Babenberg warlord Leopold III, who was later canonized for his role in conquering and Christianizing Lower Austria. The monastery (*Kloster*) was recorded in existence in 1114. In 1730 Karl VI began the most ambitious building project ever undertaken by a Habsburg at Klosterneuburg, which he planned to convert into a palace-monastery to rival the Spanish Escorial. Although only a small part of his design was actually realized, it gives a good idea of the grandeur of the original conception.

The abbey church dates from the early 12thC, though with Baroque additions; the adjoining Leopold's Chapel houses the chief treasure of the abbey, the so-called **Verdun Altar** (★), a work of vivid color and lunatic craftsmanship consisting of 51 enamel miniatures (1181). **Leopold's Court** forms a highly picturesque ensemble of Gothic and Renaissance buildings, while Karl VI's Baroque complex, with the addition of a Neoclassical wing completed in 1842, constitutes the **Emperor's Court** (*Kaiserhof*). An imperial crown and Austrian ducal hat cap a dome here, one of the many elaborate Babenberg-Habsburg symbols found here.

A series of splendid halls are shown on guided tours: the **Marble Hall** with a mural by Daniel Gran (1749), the **Gobelin Hall**, the Treasure Hall, containing a museum, and the library, with its valuable collection of medieval manuscripts. The **cellar**, which has produced a famous wine since at least the 12thC, possesses a giant vat (*Tausendeimerfassl*) which forms the focus of a wine-soaked celebration on November 14-17, the feast of St Leopold.

VICINITY

The former **Hoffmann Sanatorium**, in the Kierling district of Klosterneuburg, has set up a Kafka Room where the author spent the last days of his life and died in 1921.

A car ferry bears the visitor across the Danube to the historic town of **Korneuburg** (✫), which preserves parts of its walls. Just 3km (2 miles) to the N, **Kreuzenstein** (✫ ◁ᴱ ✗), one of the most perfect medieval castles in Europe, is located on a panoramic promontory.

The original Castle Kreuzenstein was built here around 1120, and destroyed by the Swedish troops of Thorstensson in 1645. The ruins were acquired by the Counts of Wilczek, one of whose number (Hans Wilczek of the Austrian North Pole Expedition — see page 85) rebuilt them in 1879-1908, using original material from all over Europe, into a castle quite as fantastic as Bavaria's more famous contemporary, Neuschwanstein, than which it is even more "authentic" in many details. With its hay-filled courtyard, rusty armor and sooty kitchen (containing a superb collection of original utensils), Kreuzenstein conveys a stronger impression of knightly life than many a "real" castle *(* ▧ *open Mar-Nov daily 9.30am-4.30pm).*

≕ **Tuttendörfl** *(in Korneuburg* ☎ *(02262) 5677, closed Sun and Mon),* a delightful country restaurant on the Danube, serves local specialties.

KREMS ✫
*72km (45 miles) NW of Vienna. Population: 32,000. Train R40 from Franz-Josefs-Bahnhof **i** Kloster Und, Und Str. 6 ☎(02732) 82676. Dominican Abbey-Museum open Tues-Sat 9am-noon, 2-5pm; Sun 9am-noon.*

The attractive town of Krems is set apart from other historic localities of Austria by its predominantly medieval and Renaissance (rather than Baroque) flavor. First mentioned in 995, the town was, in the 11thC, a more important way-station for the Danubian trade than Vienna; the first Austrian coin, the **Kremser pfennig**, was minted here in 1130.

Sights include the **Steiner Tor** city gate (1480, with a Baroque tower of 1765), a colorful **Rathaus** (1548), the Gothic **Spitalkirche** (1470) and **Piarist church** (1475-1520), and numerous **burghers' houses**, of which the Gozzo House (c.1260), Sgraffito House (c.1560) and Gögl House (12th/15thC) deserve mention. The former **Dominican Monastery** (1236, with 18thC additions), now revived as a museum and cultural center, encloses a handsome Gothic courtyard.

Stein, the equally historic twin of Krems, lies 2km (1¼ miles) to the W on the Danube bank. Among its monuments are a richly decorated Imperial Toll House (1536), the mighty Tithe House of the bishops of Passau (1293), and the churches of St Nicholas (1263) and Frauenberg (12thC). The former **Und Monastery**, halfway between Krems and Stein, has been converted into a wine house where you can taste, buy or enjoy a variety of local wines.

�@✔ ≕ Ideally located for a Sunday's lunch excursion from Vienna, Krems and Stein possess a large number of restaurants with a pleasant ambience and/or gourmet fare. The best cuisine is found at the **Gourmet-Hotel Am Förthof** *(in Stein* ☎ *(02732) 83345* ▯ *to* ▥ *).* For the loveliest garden, try **Hotel-Restaurant Alte Post** *(on the main street of Krems* ☎ *(02732) 82276* ▯ *no cards),* whose arcaded courtyard dates from the 15thC.

❧ **Gasthof Jell** *(Hoher Markt 8-9* ☎*(02732) 82345* ▢ *)* is one of many inexpensive, charming family-owned pensions in Krems.

═ Mautern, across the river, boasts a regionally famous restaurant: **Landhaus Bacher** *(* ☎*(02732) 2937).*

VICINITY
Krems marks the lower end of the **Wachau,** a panoramic stretch of the Danube (see under DÜRNSTEIN). Located 10km (6 miles) s of the town is the Benedictine abbey of **Göttweig** (◀∈ ═▄ ⚔), on a wooded hill commanding the Danube. Its origins go back to 1074; the monumental Baroque structure that exists now was started in 1718 to the design of Hildebrandt, and left unfinished when Joseph II dissolved the monastery in 1782. Notable features include the Gothic/Baroque church, the Grand Hall with its frescoed ceilings (1731), four imperial apartments, and a richly ornamented library.

LAXENBURG ★
15km (9 miles) s of Vienna **i** *Schlossplatz 8* ☎*(2236) 71101. Train R61 from Südbahnhof to Laxenburg/Biedermannsdorf. Bus from 3., Marxergasse 4-6. Franzensburg open Easter through Oct daily 10am-noon and 2-5pm.*
One of the handsomest of the many imperial summer palaces and the finest example of 19thC "romantic" landscape gardening in Austria, Schloss Laxenburg remains relatively undiscovered by tourists. The complex consists of **Altes Schloss,** built in the 14thC and altered in 1682, now housing a film museum, and **Neues Schloss,** which was built for Maria Theresa in 1752 and served as the residence of Karl I in 1916-18.

Located on an islet in an artificial lake in the park is **Franzensburg** (★), a mock-medieval castle built in 1798-1836 for Franz I of Austria. An unexpectedly interesting museum in the castle displays artwork from various Austro-Hungarian palaces, as well as imperial memorabilia like some cookie cutters that belonged to Maria Theresa.

Not far from the palace at Laxenburger Str. 365 is Vienna's vast and colorful **Wholesale Flower Market** *(retail sales after 9am).*

MAYERLING   See HEILIGENKREUZ.

MELK ★
84km (52 miles) w of Vienna. Population: 6,000. Train from Wien-West; DDSG passenger boat from Vienna (depart 8am, arrive 4pm). See under WACHAU for other boat information **i** *Rathausplatz* ☎*(02752) 2307. Abbey open Mon-Sat 9-11am and 1.30-5pm, Sun 10-11am and 1.30-5pm* ⚔ *every hour.*
The Benedictine Abbey of Melk, whose imposing mass looms over the historic town of the same name, is one of Europe's most important

183

works of Baroque architecture, and one of the most majestic sights along the course of the Danube. The abbey church, a work of Jakob Prandtauer, is certainly the most extravagant of Austria's many Baroque churches.

The castle of Melk (from a Slavic word meaning "Frontier") served as the seat of the Babenbergs for a half-century after 976. In 1089 it became the first nucleus of a fortified Benedictine monastery. The current buildings date wholly from the reconstruction carried out in 1702-36 by Prandtauer and Josef Munggenast.

The origins of the monastery are associated with St Koloman, a Slavic prince who evangelized the pagans of the Danube region in the 9thC and was killed in Melk as a spy. The annual market of Melk is held on his feast day on October 13.

The abbey is visited on guided tours, which take visitors through the prelature (ceiling fresco by Paul Troger), emperors' rooms, **marble hall** (Troger fresco, *The Triumph of Moderation*), a terrace with a fine panorama of the Danube, and the magnificent **library**. The **church** is decorated with frescoes by Rottmayr and paintings by Rottmayr and Troger.
SPORT   Bicycle rental at the rail station, ferry landing and tourist bureau. Horseback riding at **Schloss Albrechtsberg** *(☎(02754) 6170)*. Fishing information from **Marktgemeinde Leiben** *(☎ 7287)*.

☜ ═ **Stadt Melk** *(Hauptplatz 1 ☎(02752) 2475* ⒻⓍ*(02752) 247519* ▯▯ *16 rms* ⒜⒠ ⓒⓄ ⓋⒾⓈⒶ Ⓨ ▭ ⬲*)*, a charming old-timer on the main square of town with an imposing view of the abbey, serves good food.
    Goldener Ochs *(Linzer Str. 18 ☎(02752) 2367* ⒻⓍ*(02752) 23676* ▯ *35 rms* ⬥ ⒜⒠ ⓒⓄ ⓒⓄ ⓋⒾⓈⒶ *)* has a wine cellar.

▲   **Kolomaniau** *(☎3291)*, beside the DDSG ferry landing.

VICINITY
Melk stands at the conjunction of **Nibelungengau** and WACHAU, two highly panoramic sections of the Danube. **Schallaburg**, one of the finest Renaissance mansions of Austria, is located 5km (3 miles) s of the town *(open late Apr to early Nov daily 9am-4pm, concerts in summer)*; a marked hiker's path leads to the castle through attractive countryside. The parish church of **Mauer**, 10km (6 miles) E of Melk, possesses a splendid wood-cut altar of the year 1515.

MÖDLING ★
15km (9 miles) sw of Vienna. Population: 19,000. Train S1, S2, R10 from Wien-Süd.
This delightful Biedermeier village in the Vienna Woods, renowned for its wines, has a documented history going back to 904, although an Avar settlement is known to have existed earlier at the site. It became a popular resort in the 1810s, when its summer residents included Beethoven (the **Beethoven House** at Hauptstrasse 79 has an arcaded Gothic courtyard), Schubert, Grillparzer and Waldmüller. Much later, Schönberg developed his theory of 12-tone harmony at his house on

Bernhardgasse, while his student Alban Berg lived a few doors down the street. A stroll through the picturesque lanes of Mödling today reveals the **Ducal Court** (15thC), **Rathaus** and **St Othmar's Church** (both 16thC), many old burghers' houses and quaint wine taverns.

🏠 ⊨ **Rosen-Hotel Mödling** *(Guntramsdorfer Str. 10a* ☎ *(02236) 85123* 🞮 *(02236) 5970689-89* ⬚ *50 rms* ❧ ❦ ⚅ ▣ *)* is a comfortable, peaceful hotel, at the edge of vineyards.

⊨ **Mödlinger Kobenzl** *(in Jubiläumspark* ☎ *(02236) 888525, closed Mon),* a lovely country house/wine tavern/restaurant; **Admiral Tegetthof** *(Schiller Str. 90* ☎ *(02236) 880033, open Tues-Sat 7pm-4am),* a restaurant-steakhouse with live Austrian music and dance.

NIBELUNGELAU   See STRUDENGAU AND NIBELUNGELAU.

PERCHTOLDSDORF ☆
12km (7½ miles) sw of Vienna. Population: 16,000. Train S1, S2, R10 from Wien-Süd **i** *Marktplatz 11* ☎ *(0222) 867634-0.*
The best time to visit this historic market town just outside Vienna is on a summer evening, when the mighty **Watch Tower** (1521) and Baroque **Trinity Column** (1713-14) are illuminated, and the scores of wine gardens come to life with a jolly informality more easily associated with the trattorie of an Italian town.

On a hill high above the town is the 12thC castle of **Liechtenstein**, which lent its name to a princely family, which in turn named a sovereign state (see page 81). The castle has been restored to its medieval shape *(*✦ *open Apr-Oct Mon-Fri 9.30am-5pm, Sat-Sun 10am-6pm),* and the 18thC château at its foot is now a hotel and seniors' home.

✦ ⊨ **Gartenhotel Central** *(on Marktplatz* ☎ *(0222) 860223* ⬚ *55 rms* ❧ ⚅ *).*

⊨ All *Heurigen* in town are listed and illustrated on a public billboard at Altort. One of the better-known restaurants is the **Jahreszeiten** *(* ☎ *(0222) 864763).*

SANKT NIKOLA   See STRUDENGAU AND NIBELUNGELAU.

SANKT PÖLTEN ☆
60km (37 miles) w of Vienna. Population: 50,000 ☎ *code 02742* **i** *at Rathaus* ☎ *53354. History Museum open Tues-Sat 10am-5pm; Sun 9am-noon (* ☎ *2531).*
The capital, since 1986, of Lower Austria campaigns hard to promote the image of a Baroque-yet-upbeat city, but at heart it remains a sleepy provincial town — and a charming one, at that. The historic center dates almost wholly from the 17th and 18thC, with many Baroque frills, but on a scale more modest — and more pleasant — than Vienna.

A walk along Domplatz, Klostergasse, Kremsergasse, Rathausplatz, Linzer Str. and Riemerplatz reveals a Romanesque **cathedral** with a Baroque interior (renovated by Prandtauer; murals by Altomonte and Daniel Gran), **Franciscan** (Rococo, 1779) and **Carmelite** (Baroque, 1707) churches, the **City Hall** (Renaissance, 1591), the **Institute of English Maidens** (a girls' school founded in 1707), and a Jugendstil **Synagogue** (1912), now converted into a cultural center. Various monuments, including a palais on Rathausplatz, bear the name and arms of Counts Montecuccoli, a leading family of the Habsburg monarchy.

SPORT   18-hole golf course (par 73) at Schloss Goldegg ☎(02741) 7360. AS350 weekdays, AS450 weekends.

☜ ⊒   St Pölten offers a range of accommodations: one luxury hotel, the **Top-Hotel Metropol** (☎(in Vienna) 551645 ▦ to ▦ 100 rms ⊒ ☒ ▭ ❒); a dozen or so small, family-run inns, such as **Gasthof Seeland** in Waitzendorf (*Goldegger Str. 114* ▭ *40 rms* ⊒ ☎62461 ☒6246188); and a **youth hostel** (*Kranzbichler Str. 18* ☎63010).

▲   At Ratzendorf Lake, the **"Mega-Fun Freizeitpark"** (☎51510 ☙ ☙ ☀), with all facilities.

SEMMERING ◄€
91km (57 miles) sw of Vienna **i** *Kurwervaltung* ☎(02664) 326.

The Vienna Woods climb steeply to the first peaks of the Alps a short distance s of Vienna; the Hohe Wand (1,132m/3,714 feet), Schneeberg (2,076m/6,811 feet) and Rax (2,007m/6,585 feet) lie within an hour's drive of the city. An autobahn leads to the mountain pass of Semmering (985m/3,232 feet), while a highly scenic secondary road loops around the three peaks via Neunkirchen, Puchberg, Pernitz, the Klostertal, Reichenau and Semmering.

It is possible to drive to the summit of the **Hohe Wand** from the village of Maiersdorf, while an extremely quaint cogwheel railway huffs its way up from Puchberg to within 280m (919 feet) of the summit of the **Schneeberg** (*May-Oct at 8.55am and 11.40am; 80mins' duration; AS88*).

Semmering, the principal resort of the region, is imbued with an atmosphere of 19thC opulence. Its history is closely associated with the Semmering railway, which opened in 1848 as Europe's first alpine railway, and the railway hotel, a fairy-tale castle built in 1879, which marked Semmering's coming of age as the fashionable summer outing of the Ringstrasse era.

▣   The legendary **Südbahnhotel**, with its gables, turrets, courtyards and half-timbered halls nested in a wooded hillside, is now — sadly — in private possession. The best hotel in Semmering these days is **Panhaus** (☎(02664) 8181 ▦ 75 rms), a graceful turn-of-the-century establishment.

Villages in the region are rich in idyllic country hotels. A particularly nice one is **Pension-Gasthof Flackl** (☎(02666) 2291 ▭), a rustic but comfortable Alpine farmhouse in Reichenau.

SOPRON (Hungary) ★

70km (44 miles) sw of Vienna. Population 57,000. Frequent trains from Wien-Süd via Wiener Neustadt (80mins). Valid passport required (no visa needed for citizens of most Western countries) i Ögabona tér 8 ☎(99) 12040.

Sopron (Ödenburg in German), architecturally one of the most interesting towns in Hungary, is located within 7km ($4\frac{1}{2}$ miles) of the Austrian border and an hour's drive of Vienna. The strong flow of tourism from Austria, attracted by the low price of most goods and services as much as the sights, has made the town the first in Eastern Europe to have a branch of Marks and Spencer.

Sopron was ceded to Austria by the Treaty of Trianon in 1920 but opted to rejoin Hungary by a plebiscite held in December 1921.

The historic center, in part still surrounded by walls, offers no major individual sight but many handsome specimens of Austro-Hungarian provincial architecture and a pleasant, tranquil atmosphere. The finest building in town, the former **Palais Esterházy**, is now a museum devoted to mining.

❧ **Pannonia**, a stately 19thC edifice — the best hotel in town.

VICINITY

The **Esterházy Palace** in Fertöd (27km/17 miles w on the highway to Györ, then 3km/2 miles N), often called the Hungarian Versailles and comparable in magnificence only with the Schönbrunn and Belvedere palaces, was built in the 1760s for Prince Nicholas (Miklós) Esterházy.

Its decades of glory were 1770-90, when Haydn directed at least one new opera each month and Maria Theresa was among the guests. Damage in World War II and decades of neglect have now reduced it to a forlorn shell of its former self, but somehow it continues to make a more powerful impression than the well-oiled tourist palaces w of the border *(open in summer daily except Sun 8am-noon, 1-5pm).*

STRUDENGAU AND NIBELUNGENGAU

85km (53 miles) w of Vienna (at Melk). Left bank drive Melk-Dornach: 51km (32 miles). Bridges below Dornach, Ybbs, Melk. Car ferry at Marbach and Pöchlarn. DDSG passenger boat stops at Grein, Ybbs, Marbach, Pöchlarn, Melk.

At Dornach the Danube enters a gorge with a wild appearance and sharply rising hills hemming the view on both sides; below Persenbeug/Ybbs the landscape becomes tamer, with vineyards rather than steep forests covering the banks. Both districts, called Strudengau and Nibelungengau, respectively, are quite as picturesque as the WACHAU in natural panorama and historic sights, but receive far fewer tourists.

The Nibelungen saga, whose popularity in German culture is comparable to that of the King Arthur story in English, is based on the wars between the Burgundians and the Huns in the 5thC. Part of the story concerns the revenge of Kriemhild upon the Nibelungen warriors who served King Gunther, the murderer of her husband Siegfried. Many landmarks of the middle Danube figure prominently in the epic.

187

SIGHTS AND PLACES OF INTEREST

Following the course of the river, one sees **Schloss Wallsee** opposite Dornach, a private residence belonging to a cadet branch of the Habsburgs, the Salvator-Habsburg-Lothringen family; here the American General Patton and the Soviet Marshall Tolbuchin met in 1945 to celebrate victory.

Ardagger Abbey consists of a Romanesque basilica (1049) with Gothic and Baroque additions. **Grein** (✪) is a pleasant town with a 15thC hilltop castle (now a Boat Museum) and many 16thC houses; the Rathaus contains a delightful little Rococo theater from 1790, the oldest in Austria.

The vicinity of **St Nikola** and **Sarmingstein** is arguably the most scenic stretch of the Strudengau. At **Freyenstein** are the ruins of the largest castle along the entire course of the Danube: legend has it that Nöck, the Lord of the Danube, lurks here in the depths of the river, and emerges to despoil virgins.

Ybbs, one of the oldest towns of Austria, has a gloomy medieval mien, while **Pöchlarn** has an attractive position; its ruined castle was the earliest power base of the Babenbergs in the 10thC. The Expressionist painter Oskar Kokoschka was born in Pöchlarn in 1886 *(house and documentation center open Wed-Sun 10am-noon, 2-5pm)*.

On the opposite bank, a steep road leads up to the hilltop village of **Maria Taferl**, which commands a memorable view over the Danube; the icon of Maria Dolorosa in Prandtauer's dainty Baroque church here is an important object of pilgrimage.

A pleasant country road continues from this village to **Artstetten** (there is a shorter road from Kleinpöchlarn), which deserves a detour on account of the country mansion of Archduke Franz Ferdinand. This houses a highly interesting collection of memorabilia pertaining to the man whose assassination in Sarajevo was the immediate cause of World War I *(▨ open Apr-Oct daily 9am-5.30pm)*.

◆▾ In Grein: **Goldenes Kreuz** *(☎ (07268) 316 ⓕ(07268) 316-8 ▢ to ▢ 22 rms ▣ closed Nov to mid-Dec)* is a pleasant, unpretentious old hotel on the village square.

◆▾ ⇶ In Pöchlarn: **Moser** *(☎ (02757) 2448 ⓕ(02757) 2833 ▥ 32 rms ♥ ⇙ ✿ closed Jan)* serves good food. Pets and bikers are welcome.

In Maria Taferl: **Krone** and **Kaiserhof** *(☎ (07413) 6355 ⓕ(07413) 635583 ▥ 56 rms ⇙ ✿ ♈)* are old-fashioned twin hotels in the village center, with a magnificent view, large, grassy gardens, miniature golf, an indoor pool and a whirlpool.

▱ ⇶ In St Nikola: **Donau-Hof** *(☎ (07268) 8107 ▥ ♥ ≋ ⇙ ✿ ♈)* has wonderful views over the Danube.

▱ In Ybbs: **Villa Vogelsang** *(☎ (07412) 4681 ▥ 5 rms ♥ ▢)* is a lovely villa by the river, run by a friendly family. Excellent comfort; bicycles can be rented.

Gasthof Gressl *(☎ (07413) 372 ▢ 4 rms ♥)* is a pleasant place at the edge of the forest.

⇶ **Villa Nowotny** *(in Ybbs ☎ (07412) 2620)*.

WACHAU ★

85km (53 miles) w of Vienna (at Melk). Left bank drive Melk-Krems: 60km (37 miles). Bridges at Melk and Mautern/Krems. Car ferry at Spitz and Weissenkirchen. DDSG passenger boat stops at Melk, Aggsbach, Aggstein, Spitz, Weissenkirchen, Dürnstein, Krems.

Between the historic towns of **Melk** and **Krems** the Danube traverses the Wachau, a scenic region of steep hills, vineyards and romantic castles. In the 9th and 10thC, this was the home territory of the frontier lords of the Eastern March, which in time formed the nucleus of the duchy, the empire and the republic of Austria.

SIGHTS AND PLACES OF INTEREST

Small wine-growing villages succeed each other regularly on either bank, each with its ancient church, flower-potted taverns and meticulously maintained nature-hiking trails. **Maria Laach**, high in the hills on the left bank, attracts pilgrims with its miracle-working icon of the Virgin with six fingers. **Willendorf**, an otherwise insignificant place, was where the so-called Venus of Willendorf, one of man's oldest known works of art, was discovered in 1909. **Weissenkirchen**, maker of some of the best Austrian wines, possesses several vintner's courts of great charm, dating from the 16thC.

A spectacular castle soars above a bend of the river at **Aggstein** (◀€); now a moss-covered ruin, it once used to be the base of robber knights who would block the Danube with chains to extract a ransom from passers.

Dürnstein (★ ◀€), easily the most picturesque of the region's villages, stands on a bluff rising sharply from the riverbank, its narrow medieval lanes perpetually thronged with sightseeing groups from Vienna. The main landmark of the village is the blue-and-white Baroque **church** (1721-25) of the former Augustinian Abbey, which stands next to the ruins of a medieval monastery, now partly converted into a hotel. The dainty 17thC château of the Starhemberg family has also become a hotel.

Rising above the village are the ruins of the castle of Kuenringburg, where Richard the Lionheart of England is said to have been kept a prisoner in 1192-93.

▱ ▭ **Schloss-Hotel Dürnstein** *(* ☎ *(02711) 212* ⊠ *(02711) 351* ▥ ◀€ ❦ *indoor and outdoor* ≋ ♥ ○ ♆ ≋ AE ⊙ ⊙ VISA *open late Mar to early Nov)* is a Baroque gem, not too large nor too luxurious, on a lovely terrace above the Danube. Built in 1626 and acquired by Count Starhemberg shortly thereafter, it boasts the best gourmet restaurant within a wide radius.

▱ **Richard Löwenherz** *(* ☎ *(02711) 222* ▥ *50 rms* ◀€ ❦ ≋ AE ⊙ VISA *)*, a tastefully appointed, comfortable hotel, occupies part of the ruined Gothic convent in the heart of the village. Its beautiful terrace restaurant, overlooking the river, has an excellent selection of wine. The hotel has a fine lawn.
Sänger Blondel *(* ☎ *(02711) 253* ▯ *16 rms* ⊙ VISA *)*, a lovely inn and *Heurige*, in another part of the abbey ruins, is smaller and less expensive than the above.

Budapest

Culture, history and background

Capital of the Hungarian Republic. City constituted in 1873 by the union of Buda, Pest and Óbuda.
Municipal area: 525 square kilometers/203 square miles.
Population: 2.1 million.
Altitude at river bank: 96 meters/315 feet.
Religion: Roman Catholic; Lutheran and Reformed minorities.
Language: Hungarian (Magyar).

Budapest was built into one of the most beautiful cities of Europe in a short yet intense burst of creative activity spanning the half century from the 1860s to the eve of World War I. For a brief golden age it was the "Paris of the East," a city of stately vistas, sparkling nightlife, good wine and beautiful women. The vigor of its intellectual life was felt by all, though shielded from the rest of the world by the obscurity of the Hungarian language.

Similarly, in the run-up to World War II, while the rest of the continent reeled in a maelstrom of socialism and National Socialism, Budapest stood alone with its unflinching devotion to the old-fashioned values of a gay, irresponsible and irredeemably romantic gentry.

That *belle époque* Budapest was buried in ash in the 40-odd years of war and communism. Its people rose up in revolt, were defeated, and became resigned to a life of drab clothes and dispirited cynicism. Buildings turned black with soot and crumbled; the baths, among Europe's greatest monuments to public extravagance, were invaded by vulgar plastic and the smell of cheap soap. Western tourists came on state-organized tours to images of gypsy violinists churning tunes of irresistible frenzy; they found instead state employees peddling choreographed "folklore."

The revolution of 1989-90 has begun miraculously to recover the spirit of Budapest from under decades of debris. Few European nations seem capable of matching the average Magyar's innate gallantry, that singular mix of verve and romanticism, sophistication and naivety, which so enchanted the visitors of the turn of the century: and already it has begun to transform the city in ways that would have been unimaginable only a few years ago. The excitement of revival alone (combined, it is true, with the ever-present shadow of economic disaster) makes a fascinating experience, and many visitors will find Budapest, with its sloppy but eager charm, a more lovable place than the impeccably packaged attractions of tourist Vienna.

History: an overview

HUNGARY

The Hungarian Plain was invaded by various tribal groups of Turkic, Celtic, Germanic and Slavic origin before the arrival of the Magyars. The Magyars (Hungarians), an Uralic people distantly related to the Turkish nomads of Central Asia, swept across Europe in the 9th and 10thC. They adopted a sedentary way of life and the Christian religion toward the year 1000.

The Hungarian kingdom, whose origin is traditionally dated from the coronation of St Stephen (István) in the year 1000, flourished in the late Middle Ages. Its collapse in 1526 under Turkish onslaught left Hungary divided between the Ottoman and Habsburg empires, with a third part forming the buffer principality of Transylvania.

Austria succeeded in bringing all three parts under its rule between 1683 and 1711. But attempts to assimilate Hungary into a unified Austrian empire failed in the face of mounting Hungarian nationalism. By the Compromise of 1867 Hungary became a near-independent kingdom under the Habsburg crown. It declared its independence in 1918.

Historic Hungary as it existed for some 900 years before World War I covered a much larger territory than today, stretching from the Adriatic into the confines of Poland and Ukraine. A hereditary Hungarian nobility ruled over this broad zone of ethnically mixed and largely peasant population, exercising a feudal constitution whose roots lay in the Magyar conquest and in royal charters of the Middle Ages.

Hungarian nationalism was born as a movement of the ruling class. Its growth provoked the subject nations of Hungary into nationalist sentiments of their own, so that when Hungary became independent in 1918, its move was followed by the secession of two-thirds of its provinces. Transylvania was taken over by Romania, Slovakia followed the Czechs into Czechoslovakia, Banat (Voivodina) was annexed by Serbia, while Croatia joined it in newly created Yugoslavia. Additional chunks of land went to Poland, Ukraine, Austria and Italy. Hungary's refusal to accept its dismemberment was a major source of European instability during the interwar period, and resulted in the country's (partial) collaboration with Nazi Germany in World War II.

Hungary was occupied by the Soviet army in 1945 and came under a one-party dictatorship in 1948. Democratic government was re-established in 1990.

BUDAPEST

Budapest was created in 1873 by the union of two cities of dissimilar character, Buda and Pest, along with a third of lesser importance, Óbuda. Buda, which grew from its walled core on a steep hilltop on the right bank of the Danube, was a historic and conservative town with a heavily German population. Pest, formerly a modest place on the flat left bank of the river, became the birthplace of modern Hungarian culture in the first half of the 19thC and grew into a world-class city in the second half of the same century.

Óbuda ("Old Buda"), under the name of **Aquincum**, had been an important frontier stronghold of Roman Pannonia. Legend made it also the residence of Attila the Hun, though with few facts in its support.

Buda was first fortified in the 1240s and became the capital of the Hungarian kingdom in the 14thC. It remained the chief city of Turkish Hungary, but war and pillage had reduced it to a derelict shell by the time the Austrians took the town in 1686. What remained of it was rebuilt and resettled by German colonists, who formed the dominant element of Buda until the end of the 19thC and remained an important factor of its population until 1945.

The growth of **Pest** (pronounced *Pesht*) began in the 1780s when the Habsburg Emperor Joseph II transferred the administrative capital of Hungary from Pozsony/Bratislava to here. It passed an important milestone in 1808 with the founding of the City Embellishment Committee, which planned many of the city's landmark monuments, and another in 1839 with the commencement of the Széchenyi Chain Bridge, the first to connect the two banks of the Danube. After 1848 Pest overtook Buda as the richer and more dynamic half of the twin cities.

In 1918 Budapest was transformed from the center of a great multinational state into the overgrown capital of a small and impoverished country. Large parts of the city, including almost all of its famous riverfront, were destroyed in 1945 in the course of battles between the German and Soviet armies. Although much effort has been put into restoration since the war, the effects of both tragedies remain palpable today.

Landmarks in Budapest's history

See LANDMARKS IN VIENNA'S HISTORY on page 31 for further details of the two cities' mutual history.

HUNGARY BEFORE THE MAGYARS

12BC-AD395/433: Roman rule in Pannonia (right bank of the Danube). "Barbarian" tribes of Celtic, Germanic and Scythian origin beyond the Danube (Transdanubia). **376**: Gothic hordes cross the Danube, displaced by the invading Huns.

395-402: Goth revolt followed by the invasion of barbarian tribes. Roman frontier collapses; Roman civilians abandon Pannonia. **433**: Pannonia formally ceded to Attila the Hun. **454**: Huns retreat from Europe after Attila's death. Goths in Pannonia; Gepid kingdom in Transdanubia. **527**: Langobards invade Pannonia. **568**: Avars, a nomadic Asian people, invade eastern-central Europe (main base in Pannonia). Slavic auxiliaries settle many parts of the Avar kingdom.

791-805: Charlemagne destroys the Avar kingdom. Slavic tribal states (Moravians, Bulgars) on the Hungarian plain.

THE MAGYAR KINGDOM

1st Millennium BC: Magyars, a nomadic people, migrate from the w

Siberian steppe (N Ural Mountains) into the Volga basin. **c.AD700**: A branch of the Magyar nation migrates to the Don-Dniepr region (N of the Sea of Azov). **c.890**: Displaced by Pechenegs and Bulgars, the Magyar tribes begin a vast migration westward.

896: Under the leadership of Árpád, Magyars occupy the Hungarian plain. **900-955**: Magyar raids into Italy, Germany, France, Spain, Constantinople lay waste large parts of Europe. **955**: Otto I of Germany defeats the Magyars near Augsburg, thus saving Christendom. End of Magyar conquests. **972-997**: Settlement and Christianization of Magyar tribes under prince Géza.

1000: Coronation of Géza's son István (Stephen), the first Christian ruler and patron saint of Hungary, takes place at Esztergom on Christmas day. Royal crown, sent by Pope Sylvester, symbolizes the Hungarians' entry into the European family of nations. **1038**: Death of István without an heir triggers a period of turmoil. Anti-Christian risings of tribal chieftains. Royal power consolidated by Lászlo I (Ladislas, 1077-95), Kálmán (1095-1116) and Béla III (1172-96). **1222**: The Golden Bull of András II (Andrew) confirms the rights and privileges of the Hungarian nobility, forming the basis of Hungary's feudal constitution until modern times.

1241-42: Mongol invasion devastates Hungary. Reconstruction under Béla IV (1235-70): fortified towns built, in part repopulated with German settlers. **c.1242**: First fortification of Buda Hill. **c.1255**: Construction of the Matthias Church in Buda.

1301: Death of András III ends the native Árpád dynasty. In the following period, various European princes are elected King by the Hungarian nobles. **1308-42**: Golden age of Hungarian feudalism under Károlyi Robert I (Charles Robert) of Anjou. Royal seat moved from Székesfehérvár to Buda. **1342-82**: Lajos I (Louis) of Anjou grants city privileges to Buda and builds a royal palace on Castle Hill. **1387-1437**: Zsigmond (Sigismund) of Luxemburg king of Bohemia and Hungary; elected Holy Roman Emperor in 1410.

1446-58: János Hunyadi, a Transylvanian lord, elected regent: the first native ruler of Hungary in 150 years. Twice defeated by the Turks, he triumphs over them at Nándorfehérvár (Belgrade) in 1456. **1458-90**: Cultural and political peak of the Hungarian kingdom under his son Mátyás (Matthias) Corvinus, who maintains a brilliant Renaissance court in Buda. **1514**: Peasant rebellion of György Dósza spreads with Turkish support.

1526: Battle of Mohács: Hungarian army destroyed by the Turks; Lajos II (Louis) killed on the battlefield. Ferdinand of Habsburg claims the royal title and invades Western Hungary; Hungarian nobles elect János Zapolyai, a Turkish puppet. **1541**: Turks occupy Buda on the death of Zapolyai. Hungary divided into three parts: a Turkish province in the center and s (capital: Buda), a Habsburg-controlled "kingdom" in the w and N (capital: Pozsony/Bratislava), and the semi-independent principality of Transylvania in the E.

TURKS AND HABSBURGS
1541-1697: Perpetual warfare devastates western and central Hungary, while Hungarian culture stays alive in Calvinist-Lutheran Transylvania.

1605: István Bocskay, elected prince of Transylvania, fights Austria with his *haiduk* irregulars; he is crowned King of Hungary by the Sultan. **1618-29**: Gábor Bethlen, prince of Transylvania, allies with the enemies of Austria during the Thirty Years' War, fighting to liberate Austrian-held Hungary. **1635**: Jesuits open Hungarian University in Nagyszombat (Trnava in Slovakia). **1671**: Conspiracy of Hungarian magnates (Miklós Zriny, Ferenc I Rákóczi) against Austrian rule is crushed with extreme cruelty; Protestant worship is banned in Habsburg Hungary, Protestant churches are closed and members are persecuted. **1676**: Imre Tököly, a Protestant lord, organizes a force of *kuruc* irregulars to fight Austria. **1682**: Tököly crowned King of Hungary by the Sultan; he joins the Turkish siege of Vienna the following year.

1683: Austrian counterattack after the failure of the Turkish siege. **1686**: Buda captured in September. **1687**: Golden Bull rescinded, Hungarian monarchy made hereditary in the house of Austria. **1694**: Tököly defeated but escapes to Turkey. **1697**: Final Turkish defeat at Zenta. By the Treaty of Karlowitz (1699) all of historic Hungary comes under Habsburg rule. Plunder, colonial policy and forced Catholicization lead to **1703-11**: the Hungarian War of Independence under Ferenc II Rákóczi. Rebels approach the suburbs of Vienna, but are defeated by Prince Eugene of Savoy. Rákóczi takes refuge in Turkey. **1711**: Treaty of Szatmar: Hungary loses its independence, but retains feudal rights.

1740: Hungarian nobles agree to support Maria Theresa in the War of Austrian Succession in return for confirmation of their privileges. **1781-84**: József (Joseph) II introduces radical reforms to Hungary: the Hungarian crown is abolished, feudal privileges curbed, a centralized civil service introduced, and German is made the sole official language. Administrative capital of Hungary is transferred to Buda/Pest, away from the feudal Diet in Pozsony. **1790**: Lipót II (Leopold) withdraws many of Joseph's reforms, reinstating Hungarian privileges. **1795**: Nationalist conspiracy of Hungarian "Jacobins" led by Ignác Martinovics is crushed by police.

c.1820-48: "Reform Period": revival of Hungarian national sentiment, and Hungarian culture among liberal intelligentsia in Pest. The leading reformist is Count István Széchenyi. **1839-49**: Construction of the Chain Bridge on the Danube becomes a symbol of national aspirations.

1848, March 15: Revolution breaks out in Pest. August-October: The Hungarian movement takes a radical-nationalist turn under the leadership of Lajos Kossuth. **1849**, January: the Austrian army under Windischgrätz captures Buda/Pest. Kossuth declares independent Hungarian government in Debrecen. August: the Russian army comes to Austria's aid. October: Hungarian independence crushed, and its leaders executed in Arad (Oradea, Romania). **1849-66**: Period of sharp repression.

1867: "Compromise of 1867", negotiated by moderate nationalists Ferenc Deák and Gyula Andrássy, grants full autonomy to Hungary with a separate parliament and government in Buda/Pest. Ferenc József I (Franz Joseph) is crowned King of Hungary in Buda's Royal Castle. **1873**: Budapest is formed by the union of Buda, Pest and Óbuda. **1896**: Celebration of the 1,000th year of Hungarian conquest marks the high point of an era of progress and prosperity. **1897-1907**: The collapse of the Austro-Hungarian customs union leaves Hungary effectively independent of Austria.

INDEPENDENT HUNGARY

1918, October 31: Revolution in Budapest brings Count Mihály Károlyi to power. November 11: Karl I deposed in Vienna; Austria declares itself "a constituent part of Germany." November 16: Hungary declares independence. Czech, Serbian and Romanian troops occupy parts of Hungary. **1919**, March 21: Károlyi is forced to resign as the Bolshevik-inspired "Republic of Councils" under Béla Kun takes power in Budapest. Civil war with the "White" troops of Admiral Miklós Horthy. August 1: Kun overthrown by invading Romanian army. November: Horthy enters Budapest and launches "White" Terror.

1920: The Trianon Peace Treaty creates a severely truncated Hungary, divesting 60 percent of its territory and 64 percent of its population. 33 percent of ethnic Hungarians remain in Czechoslovakia, Romania and Yugoslavia. Hungary proclaimed a kingdom with Horthy as Regent; the throne remains vacant. **1920-31**: Conservative/gentry governments of Prime Minister István Bethlen. **1932-35**: Pro-Nazi shift under Prime Minister Gyula Gömbös.

1939-44: Hungary in uneasy alliance with Nazi Germany, receiving parts of Slovakia (1939), Transylvania (1940) and Yugoslavia (1941) as reward. **1942**: Prime Minister Pál Teleki commits suicide after an unsuccessful move to end the German alliance. **1944**, March: German troops occupy Hungary. October: Horthy deposed by Germans after he attempts to declare armistice. Pro-Nazi Arrow-Cross Party institutes a regime of terror; widespread Jewish deportations. December: Soviet troops invade Hungary. **1945**: Intense fighting in Budapest between the Red Army and the Reichswehr (December 24-February 12) leaves the city in ruins.

1945-49: Communist Party entrenched in power despite poor showing (17 percent) in 1945 elections. Smallholders' Party compromised; Socialists forced to merge with CP (1948). New constitution names Hungary a People's Republic (1949).

1948: Lászlo Rajk, the independent-minded CP leader, purged by pro-Moscow faction after show trial (executed in 1950). **1948-56**: Stalinist dictatorship of Mátyás Rákosi. Widespread purges and executions in 1949-53.

1956: Hungarian Uprising. October 23: Student demonstrations lead to a general insurrection in Budapest. November 4: Soviet crackdown leaves thousands killed. Imre Nagy, the revolution's leader, arrested and executed.

1956-88: János Kádár's rule. Initially despised as a Soviet puppet, Kádár introduces a relatively open economy ("goulash socialism"), which turns Hungary into the most prosperous of Eastern Bloc countries.

1988, May: Kádár deposed; Károly Grosz named CP Secretary General. September: Political parties permitted. Over 30 parties emerge in four months. **1989**, June: Massive rally in Budapest commemorates Imre Nagy and the martyrs of 1956. August: Grosz deposed by the CP's reformist wing. CP renamed "Socialist Party" and agrees to hold free elections and permit free travel to Austria. September-November: Wave of East German defectors leads to the collapse of the Berlin Wall.

1990: March: Hungarian Democratic Forum gains a decisive victory in the first free elections since 1945; Socialists (ex-CP) obtain 11 percent. József Antall (HDF) prime minister. Árpád Goncz of the Free Democratic Party elected president.

A history of revolutions

Few symbols capture the history of a nation as succinctly as the Millennium Monument, an altar of vast and solemn dimensions which was raised in Budapest in 1896 to commemorate the first 1,000 years of Hungarian history. Its procession of 14 statues was originally designed to represent the great and good among Hungary's kings: nine rulers of the medieval kingdom, whom nationalist enthusiasm had rescued from their semimythical obscurity, followed by five Habsburgs, the ancestors of Franz Joseph, who was present in person to inaugurate the monument.

Visitors today do not see the latter five. They have been replaced by the statues of five national heroes, leaders of the centuries-long struggle for Hungarian independence. All five (Bocskay, Bethlen, Tököly, Rákóczi and Kossuth) distinguished themselves by leading rebellions against foreign — Habsburg — rule, fighting with singular verve and gallantry. And all were defeated, dragging the nation down a path of untold disaster.

OLD REVOLTS

There were no less than six Hungarian revolts against Habsburg rule between 1605 and 1711. In each case the rebellion was led by leading nobles of Hungary's hereditary aristocracy, often with a Transylvanian background, and often under the banner of Protestantism; in many cases they received Turkish support. The last and greatest was the revolt of **Ferenc II Rákóczi**, hereditary lord of vast sections of Eastern Hungary, whose volunteer army succeeded in maintaining Hungarian independence for eight years (1703-11) in large parts of the country.

Rákóczi's mother, Helena Zriny, had defended the ancestral castle of Munkács (now Munkacevo in Ukraine) against the Austrians in 1688. Young Ferenc (1676-1735) entered Habsburg service after her defeat, and was schooled by Jesuits in Prague and Vienna. Arrested in 1701 for his involvement in a French-inspired conspiracy, he managed to escape to Poland, whence he returned to his paternal lands to launch a freedom struggle. The final 24 years of his life was spent as an exile in Turkey.

By the Peace of Szatmar in 1711, Hungary bowed to the Habsburg crown, keeping in return its ancient feudal constitution, its Diet (Parliament) and the privileges of its landed nobility. The reforms of Maria Theresa, which created a modern imperial administration beyond the reach of local lords, did not touch the Hungarian lands. Joseph II's more radical approach, which regarded Hungarian separatism as an archaism serving the interests of the landlord class alone, provoked a mutiny in the Diet and had to be recalled hastily.

The full Hungarian reaction to Joseph's reforms, however, came from an unexpected quarter: in 1795, a group of young noblemen led by **Ignác Martinovics** (1755-95) launched a movement that was inspired by the French Revolution, and used the themes of modern nationalism (liberty, progress, motherland and language) to combat foreign domination for the first time in Hungarian experience. Although their conspiracy was nipped in the bud by Austrian police, it lit a fuse which would continue to burn until 1848.

1848

The cultural and intellectual rebirth of Hungary occurred in the first half of the 19thC, particularly in the so-called Reform Period that followed the 1820s. The towering personality of this period was Count **István Széchenyi** (1791-1860), who advocated a liberal program of economic and cultural progress that looked to England as its model. His achievements included the founding of the National Museum, the National Library and the Academy of Sciences, the construction of the first bridge across the Danube between Buda and Pest, the introduction of railways and steam shipping into the country, and various projects to improve Hungarian banking, agriculture, horse breeding, publishing and typography.

A more radical approach was represented by the lawyer-journalist-politician **Lajos Kossuth** (1802-94), a fiery orator who claimed that no progress was possible without independence. The revolution that broke out in March 1848 in response to the events in Paris and Vienna at first brought together different strands of nationalist opinion. But the early collapse of the revolution in Vienna allowed Kossuth's fanaticism to gain the upper hand.

Elected Regent by the government of a Hungary declared independent, Kossuth traveled the country rousing the people to arms in a hopeless struggle against Austrian forces. When the movement finally collapsed in October 1849, the entire political and intellectual leadership of Hungary was executed (Lajos Batthyányi, Pál Esterházy), killed in action (Sándor Petőfi), imprisoned, exiled (József Eötvös) or forced underground (Gyula Andrássy, Mihály Táncsics). Széchenyi became deranged and ultimately committed suicide. Kossuth continued to exercise his rhetoric in exile in Turkey, England and the United States until his death in Turin in 1894.

A new factor came to the fore in the course of the disaster of 1848: the fact that the overwhelmingly non-Magyar majority of Hungary's population did not necessarily share the goals and sentiments of Hungarian nationalism. The initial military challenge to the revolution was organized by Jellacic, the commander of Croatia, a province of the Hungarian crown. This lesson was not lost on the Habsburg government, which devoted its policies in the following decades to cultivating the loyalties of the non-Magyar peoples of Hungary — the Slovaks, Croats, Serbs,

Romanians and Ruthenians — who began voicing their national demands with a discreet wink from Vienna.

1918

Under the Compromise of 1867, Hungary experienced the period of greatest prosperity and progress in its modern history. The Magyar upper class seemed reconciled to its role as one of the two "ruling nations" of the Dual Monarchy, while also cultivating the nationalist symbols and rhetoric of 1848. These grew acute in reaction to the growth of Lueger's brand of German nationalism in Vienna, and came to a head over the issue of the German alliance in World War I.

It was Count **Mihály Károlyi** (1875-1955), a left-liberal politician who led the parliamentary faction opposed to Germany during the war, who finally realized the 400-year-old dream of Hungarian independence. The dream, however, turned quickly into nightmare as neighboring countries, championing the rights of Hungary's subject nationalities, proceeded immediately to invade two-thirds of the historic kingdom. Deprived of the Habsburg shield, Hungary now lost nearly all of its industry and mineral sources, its most fertile agricultural land, and some of the most emotionally charged localities of its national history.

Károlyi was expelled within months by a Bolshevik-inspired coup which installed a Republic of Councils under **Béla Kun** (1886-1939). This in turn collapsed only 133 days later while pursuing the mad dream of reconquering Slovakia against the opposition of the victorious Entente. Budapest eventually fell to the anti-Bolshevik volunteer army of Admiral Miklós Horthy.

For the next quarter-century the country was plunged into a world of hopeless anachronism, recoiling from the catastrophe of 1918 and imagining only scapegoats where the world saw clear cause and effect. Károlyi, the "Red Aristocrat," was branded a traitor and forced to live in exile. He came back as an elder statesman in 1945, but became quickly disillusioned with the creeping Stalinist terror and went abroad again in disgust over the Rajk trial in 1949.

1956

The worst era of Stalinism was followed after 1953 by a period of relaxation, which was cultivated by a group of moderate Party leaders around Prime Minister **Imre Nagy** (1896-1958). The expulsion of Nagy in 1955 signaled a return to a harder line.

A modest student demonstration on October 23, 1959 was the spark that lit a revolution which would astonish the world with the ease by which it overturned the communist autocracy. The demonstration was suppressed forcibly. Over the next two days, the enraged inhabitants of Budapest took over the streets, destroying symbols of the regime, overthrowing the colossal statue of Stalin, and lynching suspected members of the secret police.

Nagy was hurled back into office on October 24. On November 3, Cardinal Mindszentyi, the primate-archbishop of Hungary who had been released from jail a few days earlier, made a broadcast speech announcing the dissolution of the socialist system and advocating the restitution of nationalized properties. The Hungarian army under General Pál Maléter joined the rebels on the same day.

In military terms, however, the revolution was doomed from the start. Soviet tanks rolled into Hungary on November 4, and needed but two days to establish full control over the country. Some 3,000 people lost their lives in desperate resistance, and 200,000 Hungarians fled the country. Nagy took refuge in the Yugoslav Embassy, but was arrested three weeks later when he left the compound on false assurances of safety. After a secret trial in Budapest, he was executed on June 16, 1958.

1989-90

The bloodless revolution which brought the People's Republic to an end has so far been exceptional for its lack of emotional drama and a hero-leader. The old regime permitted limited forms of private enterprise after 1982, and tolerated an increasingly bolder margin of political liberties after 1985. In 1988 it introduced a reform package which envisaged the establishment of multiparty democracy in the long run.

The transition, however, went faster than planned. Given a modicum of freedom, the Hungarian people refused to grant any further residue of authority to the Communist Party. Opposition coalesced in 1988 around environmentalist protests against the projected Nagymaros Dam on the Danube. From early 1989 onward there were increasingly vocal demands to honor the memory of Imre Nagy and other martyrs of 1956, who were finally cleared of all charges and given a heroes' reburial on June 16, 1989 in what turned out to be the emotional high point of the transition.

June 16 was the regime's deathblow. Shortly afterward, following secret talks with Germany and Austria, the Hungarian government agreed to open its borders with the West. The resulting stampede of Eastern Europeans seeking to emigrate led to the collapse of the Berlin Wall on November 10 and 11 and of the Czechoslovak regime a week later.

In the Hungarian general elections held on March 25, 1990, the reform wing of the former Communist Party received only 11 percent of the votes, while the hard-line faction failed to elect any candidates. The victor was the Democratic Forum, the main opposition movement, which adopted a platform of populist and nationalist themes and received most of its support in the countryside. The Free Democrats came second, stressing civic liberties and a liberal economy. They were allied with *Fidesz*, the Young Democratic Party, which restricted its membership to persons younger than 35 and attracted lively interest among urban voters.

Art and architecture

For all its fragments of older history, Budapest is a city of the 19thC —
of one sharply defined age of glory, to be exact, which only lasted from
1867 to 1918. What remains of art and architecture older than that are
either the disjointed relics of a distant past, unearthed and embalmed
in the search for authentic Hungarian roots, or modest, provincial re-
flections of the imperial culture of the Habsburg capital. What comes
after 1918 is largely a tale of woe. In between the two lies a dazzling
outpouring of art and wealth and excellence, the like of which few
European cities have witnessed in so short a time scale.

The population of Budapest grew from 54,000 in 1799 to 280,000 in
1867 and 1 million in 1913, as the city transformed itself from a sleepy
backwater into the most dynamic and hopeful of Europe's capitals. Its
growth was steered by an extraordinary sense of national pride, which
never wavered from the confident belief that the capital of reborn
Hungary should be the most beautiful in the world, and was fed by the
vast quantities of wealth that poured in from the provinces.

By the end of the century Budapest had the largest parliament building
and stock exchange in the world, and a royal palace that was one of
Europe's most spectacular (although lacking a full-time king to accom-
modate). The capital was built at a time when palaces and churches no
longer provided the chief outlet for architectural talent (as they had in
the 18thC), but when the average citizen still aspired to the style and
accouterments of the gentle life (unlike the 20thC).

The most lavish care was thus spent on the most commonplace details
of the city: its avenues (such as Andrássy Avenue), squares (Szabadság
Square), apartment houses (Kodály körönd buildings), hotels (Gellért),
baths (Széchenyi), fairground pavilions (Vajdahunyád Castle), lookout
terraces (Fishermen's Bastion) and insurance company headquarters
(Gresham, New York) are all examples of this characteristic approach.
The result was a city that formed, as a whole, a great, Eclectic monument
to 19thC architecture. As one author puts it:

"The sheer quantity of Eclectic buildings provides a feeling of unity
absent elsewhere.... Whereas in other cities the excellence of individual
buildings dominates the urban scene, in Budapest the urban entity
amounts to much more than the sum of its parts: the macroform of the
city has become a work of art."

Here is a brief summary of Budapest's artistic and architectural legacy.
The chronological order inevitably gives more weight to some periods
than is justified by what is actually there to see.

THE OLD KINGDOM *(1000-1541)*

Little survives from the time before the Turkish conquest. Some houses
in the Castle district of Buda retain parts and details of their original
13th/14thC predecessors, and the interesting displays at the Budapest
History Museum do convey an image of the city's medieval past.

Under the Angevin dynasty (1307-82), and again in the era of Matthias
Corvinus (1458-90), the Hungarian royal court belonged firmly with the

mainstream of European culture, producing — or at least importing — some of the finest art of the time. The collection of medieval altarpieces at the National Gallery, and a remarkable series of Gothic statues that were found buried in the royal palace grounds (now at the Budapest History Museum), provide a glimpse of that era of distant splendor.

TURKISH *(1541-1686)*
A major legacy of the century-and-a-half of Ottoman dominion in Hungary was the culture of **public baths**, which subsequent ages retained and developed into one of Budapest's leading urban assets. Four of Budapest's historic baths date wholly or in part from the Turkish era.

Another Ottoman relic is the attractive mausoleum of Gül Baba, a Muslim dervish of the 16thC. Unlike many other Hungarian towns (such as Pécs or Eger), however, Budapest has not preserved a Turkish mosque.

BAROQUE *(1686-1780)*
The architecture of the Baroque in Hungary was, with few exceptions, a provincial reflection of Vienna's time of glory. In Budapest the period is represented by several modest churches (St Anne, the University Church of Pest, Tabán Parish Church), many civilian houses in the Castle district of Buda, and Antonio Martinelli's massive hospital for war veterans (now the Municipal Hall) in Pest.

Two great aristocratic houses elsewhere in the country — the Esterházy Palace in Fertöd, near Sopron, and the manor house that Hildebrandt built for Prince Eugene in Ráckeve — belong among the best specimens of the Habsburg Baroque, while the town of Tata, w of Budapest, is distinguished for its many buildings designed by Jakob **Fellner** (1722-80), a leading master of the style in Hungary.

CLASSICISM *(1760s-1848)*
The Classicizing manner arrived in Hungary toward the end of the reign of Maria Theresa and under that of Joseph II (cathedral and triumphal arch in Vác), though it took firm root only in the first decade of the 19thC. The first significant work of the period was the Calvinist church of Debrecen (1803), whose starkly rational lines represented a break with the Catholic-dominated tradition of the Baroque.

The turning point, however, came with the establishment in 1808 of the City Embellishment Committee of Pest, which endowed the new national capital with monuments in the simple and elegant manner of Classicism. Many buildings of this period were destroyed in the flood of 1838 or pulled down in the building fury of the end of the century. One edifice that survives is the National Museum, a work of Mihály **Pollack** (1773-1855), who designed many of the early landmark buildings of Pest. Another major figure of the period was József **Hild** (1784-1867), who created countless buildings in Pest and directed the reconstruction of the Basilica of Esztergom.

ROMANTICISM *(1848-1870s)*
The patriotic fallout from the revolution of 1848 prompted Hungarian

203

architects, like painters, writers and musicians, to initiate a search for specifically "Hungarian" forms of expression. The trend emerged most forcibly in the 1850s, in the "Romantic" school of Frigyes **Feszl** (1821-84: Vigadó Concert Hall, the Great Synagogue of Pest), although its ideas continued to have influence in the following periods too.

Feszl sought solutions in Moorish, Oriental and Byzantine themes, and devised a language of grand gesture and wild flourish that would remain a distinctive mark of Hungarian architecture through its richest era. Eclectic designs of the 1870s and '80s often turned to the symbolism of ancient Magyar tribal warriors, while the Hungarian version of Art Nouveau derived inspiration from the forms and colors of Hungarian folk art.

ECLECTICISM *(1867-1918)*

The Eclecticism of Budapest was less historically inclined than Vienna's Ringstrasse school, and less restrained in both budget and imagination. The Compromise of 1867 allowed Hungarian nationalism to keep the rhetoric of 1848 alive while burying its ancient feud with the House of Habsburg; so the architects of the era happily crossed the subdued elegance of Maria-Theresa Baroque with paprika-laden Magyar exuberance in designing a palace for their absentee king. Imre **Steindl** joined a Gothic body with a Renaissance dome, Byzantine mosaics and leaping Magyar horsemen to produce the Hungarian Parliament, one of the world's most spectacular parliament houses.

Parliament Building

The leading architect of the Eclectic style was Miklós **Ybl** (1839-1902), whose predominantly neo-Renaissance designs included much of the Royal Palace, the Opera, the Basilica of St Stephen, and many buildings along Andrássy Avenue. Several of Ybl's projects were carried out after his death by Alajos **Hauszmann**, who also designed several of the finest buildings of the period (Ethnographical Museum, New York Palace, "Strozzi Palace"). A third architect of grandiose manner and great mastery of detail was Ignác **Alpár**, who created the Stock Exchange, National Bank, and that epitome of historical Eclecticism, Vajdahunyád Castle.

Hungarian painting of the second half of the 19thC remained preoccupied with the melodramatic language and historical themes of nationalism. Major painters of the period were Mihály **Zichy** (1827-1906), Viktor **Madarász** (1830-1917), Bertalan **Székely** (1835-1910), and above all Gyula **Benczúr** (1844-1920), whose *Recapture of Buda Castle from the Turks* (1896) represented the culmination of the historical school. The best-known painter of the period, Mihály **Munkácsy** (1844-1900), combined realistic themes with a solemn and theatrical manner, while Pál **Szinyei Merse** (1845-1920) developed his personal variant of "Impressionism" around the same time as, but independently from, the French Impressionists.

ART NOUVEAU AND MODERNISM *(1896-1918)*

The idiosyncratic Hungarian version of Art Nouveau/Jugendstil/Secession took its cue from the designs of Ödön **Lechner** (1845-1914), the most original Hungarian architect of the turn of the century. Lechner's seminal work was the Town Hall of the southern city of Kecskemét (1896), which employed the colorful motifs of Hungarian folk art with great abandon. His subsequent buildings included the Postal Savings Bank and the Museum of Applied Arts in Budapest, both of which made use of the distinctive ceramics manufactured by the famous Zsolnay porcelain factory.

Several prominent buildings of the period (Gresham Palace, Gellért Hotel) combined the vocabulary of Art Nouveau with the grandiloquence of the Eclectic style, while the apartment buildings of Béla **Lajta** (1875-1920) achieved a rare level of refined elegance.

Notable among the various artistic tendencies that emerged around the turn of the century was the **Gödöllő School**, named after a small town E of Budapest that became the home of a group of painters (Aladár Körösfői Kriesch, Sandor Nagy and others) influenced by the British pre-Raphaelites and the Arts and Crafts movement.

INTERWAR YEARS *(1918-1944)*

Vienna fell into bleak despondency after the debacle of World War I, while Budapest held on to the ghost of past grandeur for another quarter of a century. The modernistic nihilism of the 1920s and '30s was thus hardly able to gain a foothold in Hungary.

Two leading schools in the Horthy years were the so-called National Romantic ("Folkloristic Modern") School, which grew out of Art Nouveau (an example is the Calvinist Church on Gorkij fasor), and the Neo-Neo-Baroque, which combined nostalgia for a richer past with the ruder forms of the 20thC (Corvin Cinema; new wing of the Széchenyi Baths).

CONTEMPORARY TRENDS *(from 1945)*

The art and architecture of the 1950s was confined to the rigidities of the Stalinist orthodoxy (Óbuda Party Headquarters at (III.) Flórián tér; MOM Cultural Center at (XII.) Csörsz u.), while the 1960s and '70s introduced those of the international style. The more colorful designs of Post-Modernism arrived in Budapest in the late 1980s (International Trade Center on Bajcsy-Zsilinszky út; Taverna Hotel).

Practical information

On-the-spot information

ORIENTATION
Budapest is divided into 22 **districts** *(kerület)*. District V. is the inner city on the Pest side. It is surrounded by districts XIII., VI., VII., VIII. and IX., which in part also belong to central or "downtown" Pest. District I. covers the Castle district and Víziváros (Watertown) section of Buda. Districts II. and XII. include the well-to-do hill suburbs of Buda, while district III. contains the small, self-contained core of Óbuda, surrounded by industrial suburbs.

The 4-digit **postal code** indicates city districts by its middle 2 digits. Thus Budapest-1053 is in district V. and Budapest-1221 in district XXII.

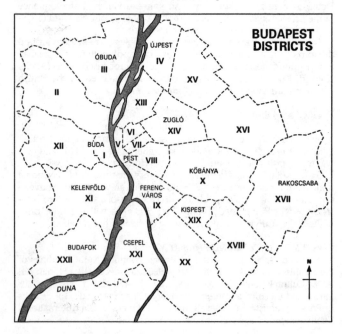

Our **maps** provide considerable detail of the metropolitan (greater) Budapest region (map **5-6** on pages 208-9) and central Budapest (map **7-8** on pages 216-17). We also include a map of the metro system, on page 212.

More detailed maps of the city have been issued by Falk and Hallwag. The most useful map of the city so far, however, is that published locally by the mapmakers Cartographia, which indicates city districts in different colors and includes all bus and tram routes.

TOURIST SERVICES

The central office of **Tourinform**, the official tourist information bureau, is located at (V.) Sütő u. 2, just off Deák tér ☎117.2200 ꬵ117. 9578, map **8**D4.

IBUSZ, the Hungarian state travel company, offers a full range of services including information, guided tours, hotel arrangements, money exchange, car rental and sale of theater tickets. The IBUSZ **main office** in (V.) Petőfi tér *(map 8E4)* is open round the clock and also acts as agents for **American Express** in cashing checks in emergency and refunding travelers' checks *(☎ 118.5707 ꬵ 117.9099)*. IBUSZ **branch offices** exist at both terminals of the airport (open daily 7am-9pm), the international boat pier (open daily 7am-9pm) and the lobbies of all major hotels (Mon-Sat 8am-8pm, Sun 8am-noon).

The offices of **American Express** are located at (V.) Deák Ferenc u. 10 *(☎ 117.3539/251.5500 ꬵ 251.5220, map 8D4)*. Services include sightseeing tours, hotel reservations, foreign exchange, air tickets and cardmember services.

A number of private tourist agencies can be found in the vicinity of Váci u. and near the main rail stations; examples are **Legenda** *(XI. Fraknó u. 4 ☎ 117.2203)*, **Primatour** *(V. Károlyi Mihály u. 17 ☎ 117.4983, map 8E5)* and **Travel Plus** *(V. Apáczai Csere János u. 3 ☎ 137.3373, map 8D4)*. They offer a wide range of tours and provide hotel and room reservation service.

Sightseeing buses operated by various firms depart from Erzsébet tér in Pest *(map 8D4)* and from Szent György tér on Castle Hill *(map 7D2)*.

Boat tours of the city start from the Danube embankment at Vigadó tér. For information contact any **IBUSZ** office or the Hungarian shipping company **MAHART** *(at (V.) Belgrád Rakpart Boat Station ☎ 118.1704, map 8E4)*.

PUBLICATIONS

The *Daily News/Neueste Nachrichten,* published in English and German Tuesday to Saturday, carries local and international news, a listing of foreign-language films and classified advertisements. The newer *Budapest Week* covers similar ground with somewhat greater sophistication. The quarterly *Hungarian Travel Magazine* publishes feature articles and travel news of considerable interest.

Danubius Radio, broadcasting in German on 103.3 MHz in Budapest and on 100.5 MHz in Western Hungary, has a deserved reputation as the

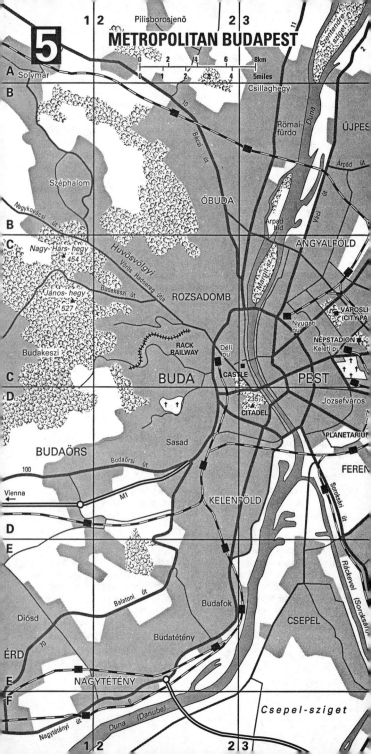

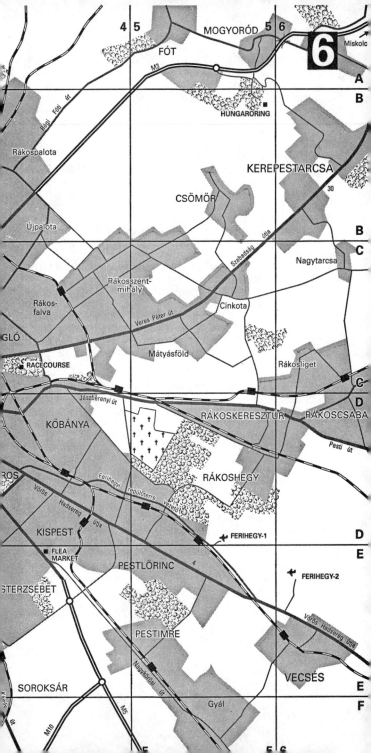

best foreign-language news and music outlet to emerge in post-liberation Eastern Europe.

International newspapers are now available at many newsstands in central Budapest. Further reading matter can be found at the **Foreign Language Bookshop** on Váci u. *(map 8 D4)* and at the **British Council Library** located in the British Embassy *(at (V.) Harmincad u. 6, map 8 D4, open Mon-Fri 10am-12.45pm, 2.30-5pm)*.

MONEY AND BANKING

Money can be exchanged officially at nearly all hotels, IBUSZ offices and banks. Banks stay open 9am to 5pm on weekdays. Theoretically, you may reconvert unused forints into hard currency up to a legal limit of half of the total amount you officially bought, with a maximum of $100; in practice it is all but impossible.

The easiest way to transfer cash from abroad is through **American Express** *(office at Deák Ferenc u. 10, off Vörösmarty tér, map 8 D4)*. See page 18 for details of the **MoneyGram®** service.

Contact the main IBUSZ office at Petőfi tér for any problems connected with charge and credit cards. See also MONEY on page 17.

POST AND TELEPHONE

The **main post office** is located at (V.) Petőfi Sándor u. 13 *(map 8 D4)*. The international telephone and telex center is on the same street at #17-19. There are 24-hour post offices near the West Station *(Nyugati pu. VI. Erzsébet körút, map 8 B5)* and East Station *(Keleti pu. VIII. Baross tér, map 5 C3)*.

The Hungarian telephone system does not yet meet internationally accepted standards, although with sufficient patience it is quite possible to get through to most numbers. **Public telephones** operate on 5, 10 and 20 forint coins, though you may still find old (gray) phones that work on a single 2 forint coin. **Directory assistance** in English is available on ☎117.2200, from 7am to 8pm. Note that formerly 6-digit telephone numbers in Budapest have been converted to 7-digit numbers with the addition of a 1; newer numbers start with 2.

For **international calls** dial 00, wait for the tone, then proceed with the country code, the local code (without a zero) and the number. Calls to the US and Canada, including collect and charge/credit card calls, can be made through the AT&T operator: dial 00, wait for the tone, then 360111. The country code for the UK is 44.

Long-distance calls within Hungary are made by dialing 06, then the area code and number.

BUSINESS SERVICES

Hungarian Chamber of Commerce   (V.) Kossuth Lajos tér ☎153.3333 [Fx]153.1285. Map 7 B3. With more than 2,500 member businesses, this is the chief source of business information in Hungary. Friendly staff, speaking most European languages. Large database, investment counseling, numerous publications. Information office open weekdays 9am-3pm.

American Chamber of Commerce in Hungary   Dózsa György út 84/a ☎142.8752 ⨳122.8890. Off map **8B6**. Association of 200 American businesses in Hungary. Publications, job bank, consultations by appointment. Open for nonmembers 9am-noon.

International Executive Service Corps   (II.) Csalogány u. 23-25 ☎ and ⨳201.6809. Map **7B2**. Association of retired US corporate executives on volunteer advisory projects.

AMI Business Center   (I.) Fő u. 14-18 ☎201.4616 ⨳201.4564. Map **7C3**. A full range of office services, translator/interpreters, offices for rent short- or long-term.

LANGUAGE INSTRUCTION

Hungarian Language School   (VI.) Szinyei Merse Pál u. 1 (at Kodály körönd) ☎112.2382. Map **8B6**.

IHSL   (II.) Bimbó út 7 ☎115.5275. Map **7A2**. Six-week intensive Hungarian-language courses.

CONSULATES

Australia   (VI.) Délibáb u. 30 ☎153.4233/153.4577. Map **8B6**.

Canada   (II.) Budakeszi u. 32 ☎176.7711/176.7312.

UK   (V.) Harmincad u. 6 ☎118.2888. Map **8D4**.

USA   (V.) Szabadság tér 12 ☎112.6450. Map **8C4**.

RELIGIOUS SERVICES

The British Church   (VI.) Vörösmarty u. 51. Map **8B5**. Shared on alternating Sundays by the Anglican community (first and third Sunday each month) and the Scottish Mission (second and fourth Sunday of each month). Services are held at 11.30am in both cases.

International Baptist Fellowship   (II.) Tapolcsány u. 7. Sunday morning and evening worship ☎165.1081. Off map **7A1**.

International Church of Budapest   At Buda Cultural Center, (I.) Corvin tér 8. ☎136.4518. Map **7C2**. English-language worship at 10.30am every Sunday.

Krisztus király kápolna   (VIII.) Reviczky u. 9 ☎118.3686. Map **8E5**. Masses held in English on the last Sunday of every month at 11.30am.

The **Jewish community** in Budapest can be contacted at (VII.) Síp u. 12 ☎142.1335, map **8D5**.

Getting around in Budapest

PUBLIC TRANSPORTATION

Metro   See map page 212. The three **metro** (subway/underground) lines intersect at the busy junction of Deák tér. A fourth line is under construction. The ancient Yellow Line (#1) which runs along Andrássy útja has the distinction of being the oldest in continental Europe. The Hungarian words for subway are *metró* or *földalatti*.

BUDAPEST metro

KEY

▬	M1
▬	M2
▬	M3
○	Interchange with other lines

M2 **Déli pályaudvar** *(South Station)*

Moszkva tér

Batthyány tér

M1 **Vörösmarty tér**

DANUBE

Kossuth Lajos tér

Arany János utca

Nyugati pályaudvar *(West Station)*

Lehel tér

Dózsa György út

DUNA

Újpest-Városkapu

Gyöngyösi út

Forgách utca

Árpád-híd

M3 **Újpest-Központ**

M1 **Mexikói út**

Széchenyi fürdő

Hősök tere

Bajza utca

Kodály körönd

Vörösmarty utca

Oktogon

Opera

Bajcsy-Zsilinszky út

Deák ferenc tér

Astoria

Ferenciek tere

Kálvin tér

Ferenc körút

Klinikák

Blaha Lujza tér

Keleti pályaudvar

Nagyvárad tér *(East Station)*

Népliget

Ecseri út

Pöttyös utca

Határ út

Népstadion

Pillangó utca

M2 **Örs Vezér tere**

M3 **Kőbánya Kispest**

M4 **Bocksai utca** ◄ ▬ *under construction*

212

Buses   The double-length Ikarus buses are as much a symbol of
Budapest as the double-deckers were of London: they belch prodigious clouds of black diesel fumes and turn the sharpest corners thanks
to their bellows-shaped soft bellies. Buses with a red number serve the
same route as those with the identical number in black, but skip most
stops along the way. Buses with an **E** following their number provide
nonstop service between two terminals. The Hungarian for bus is *busz*
(pronounced *booss*).

Trams and trolleybuses   Trams *(villamos)* run along the most important thoroughfares. The trolleybus *(trolibusz)* system is quite small
but is undergoing expansion. Keep in mind that bus (blue) tickets are
not valid on trams and trolleybuses.

Maps   Our metro map (opposite) shows the complete system. The
standard Cartographia city map indicates all metro, bus, tram and trolleybus lines.

Tickets   Urban transportation tickets are sold in metro stations (at
the regular booth until 7pm, thereafter only in a night office) and most
tobacconists. Metro, trams and trolleybuses share a common (yellow)
ticket costing F12 as of 1992, while the bus (blue) ticket costs F15.
There also exists a day ticket valid for all branches of urban transportation, as well as a reduced-rate day ticket which cannot be used on
buses. Tickets cannot be purchased in the vehicle, so it is important to
keep a sufficient supply on hand. They must be validated as you board,
either by an on-board ticket man or a ticket automat.

Night services   A sign at every bus, tram and trolley stop indicates
when the last vehicle starts from the terminus on that line, usually
between 11pm and midnight. A small number of buses and trams
serving central routes operate all night. The metro runs between
4.30am and 11pm.

TAXIS

At F26 per kilometer (thus rarely more than F300 for a ride in the city),
taxis are a remarkably inexpensive way of getting around Budapest. Be
warned, however, that many "pirate" cabs operate with homemade
meters, and that they charge anywhere between double and treble the
normal fare.

TRAINS

Budapest has three major rail stations, called *palyaudvár* (abbreviated
pu.) in Hungarian:

- **West Station** (Nyugati pu.): (VI.) Téréz körút at Marx tér. Map **8**B5.
  Metro 3 (Nyugati pu.). Trains to Debrecen, Kecskemét, Szeged,
  Moscow.
- **East Station** (Keleti pu.): (VIII.) Baross tér/Thököly út/Kerepesi út.
  Map **5**C3. Metro 2 (Keleti pu.). Trains to Győr, Sopron, Vienna,
  Miskolc, Warsaw.
- **South Station** (Déli pu.): (I.) Magyar Jakobinusok tere/Alkotás u.
  Map **7**D1. Metro 2 (Déli pu.). Trains to Pécs, Veszprém, Balaton,
  Szombathely, Zagreb; some trains to Győr-Vienna.

Four **suburban rail** (HÉV) lines serve towns in the immediate vicinity of the capital. The yellow metro/tram ticket is valid within city boundaries. HÉV terminals are located at:

- (I.) Batthyányi tér. Map 7C3. Trains to Szentendre.
- (XIV.) Örs vezér tere. Trains to Gödöllő.
- (IX.) Boráros tér. Trains to Csepel Island.
- (IX.) Kvassay Jenő út. Trains to Ráckeve.

INTERCITY BUSES

Passenger buses to most points in Hungary depart from the intercity bus terminal in Erzsébet (formerly Engels) tér *(map 8D4)*. Buses to a number of destinations in the Buda Hills and points farther west, on the other hand, depart from Moszkva tér in Buda *(map 7B1)*.

Emergency information

HEALTH
Ambulance ☎04 or 111.1666 (English and German spoken).
Dental emergencies The Dental Surgery Clinic at (VIII.) Mária u.
52 *(map 8 E6)* operates 24 hours ☎133.0189.
First aid and emergency transportation is available to foreigners free
of charge. All other medical expenses will be charged, although costs are
considerably lower than in Western countries. By agreement between
Hungary and Britain, UK residents can receive free emergency health
care and emergency dental treatment in Hungary.

CAR BREAKDOWNS
The **International Car Emergency Center** of the Hungarian Automobile Club provides 24-hour emergency assistance in English and
German at ☎252.8000. **Budasegély**, a private organization, has a
reputation for being faster and more efficient in providing breakdown
assistance. Their number is ☎188.6201 or 180.3996.

AUTOMOBILE ACCIDENTS
In the event of an accident, call **Hungária Biztosító** *(☎252.6333,
Mon, Thurs 7.30am-7pm, Tues, Wed 7.30am-4pm or ☎183,6527 Fri
8am-3pm)*, the public insurance company which handles all insurance
matters involving foreigners.

ILLEGAL PARKING
Cars parked illegally are towed to the **Szent István park**. Call
☎157.2811 for information.

OTHER EMERGENCIES
Fire ☎05 or 121.6216; no English spoken.
Police ☎07; some English spoken. In case of theft or a complaint
it is best to report to Central Police Station Reports Office.
(Rendőrfőkapitányság Panaszfelvétel) at (V.) Deák Ferenc u. 16-18
☎112.3456, map 8D4. Open 24 hours.
Lost and found (V.) Erzsébet tér 5 ☎117.4961, map 8D4. For
property lost on public transport: (VII.) Akácfa u. 17 ☎134.4787, map
8D6.
In case of major emergencies including loss or theft of passports you
are recommended to notify the consulate of your home country.

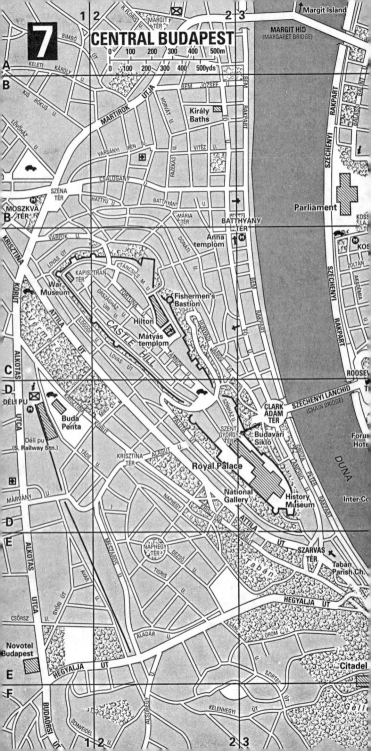

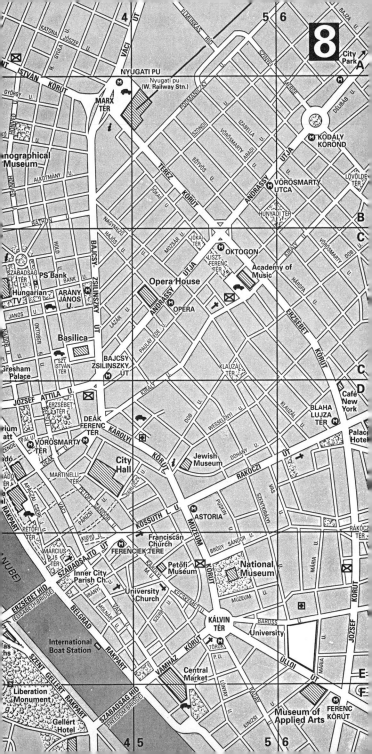

Planning and walks

Many streets in Budapest which had been renamed under the People's Republic have reverted to their former names since 1990. The following is a selected list of the main changes:

Old name	New name
Beloiannisz u.	Zoltán u.
Dimitrov tér	Vámház tér
Engels tér	Erzsébet tér
Felszabadulás tér	Ferenciek tere
Guszev u.	Sas u.
Lenin krt.	Téréz krt. (Marx tér to Királyi u.)
	Erzsébet krt. (Királyi u. to Blaha Luiza tér)
Majakovszkii u.	Király u.
Münnich Ferenc u.	Nádor u.
Népköztársaság utja	Andrássy útja
November 7 tér	Oktogon
Rosenberg házaspár u.	Hold u.
Rudas Laszlo u.	Podmaniczky u.
Tanács krt.	Károlyi krt.
Tolbuhin krt.	Vámház krt.

- Marx tér and Moszkva tér retain their names as of 1992.

When and where to go

The seasons of Budapest are not much different from those of Vienna, except that cold days arrive a little earlier in October and depart a bit earlier in April. The liveliest popular celebration is the **Corpus Christi** procession, which occurs in May or June and culminates with a huge fireworks display. Also interesting are the national holidays of **March 15** and **October 23**, which are celebrated with far greater drama and ceremony than in nations that hold a more jaded view of history.

Budapest is really two cities. Each has a different atmosphere and architectural character, and in each case the overall beauty of the urban picture provides the chief source of attraction, rather than any particular monument or museum. The thing to do, in other words, is to put on a pair of sturdy shoes and go walking.

Buda, the older city, offers a relatively compact area to explore — the Castle Hill and Royal Palace — which can be toured in as little as half a day. **Pest**, the 19thC city, extends wider, with most of its points of interest spread along the Danube Embankment, Váci Street, Szabadság Square and Andrássy Avenue.

The enchanting vista of the **Danube** is available from many vantage points in the city, but undoubtedly the best way to enjoy it is to take a leisurely boat tour along the river. Finally, no visit to Budapest should be considered complete without a call at one of the historic **baths**, perhaps the Gellért or Széchenyi.

A 2-day sightseeing program in the Hungarian capital might then be:
DAY 1
• Castle Hill of Buda: Matthias Church, Fishermen's Bastion, Royal Palace. Gellért Hill (Citadel). Gellért Baths. Evening promenade along and around Váci Street.
DAY 2
• Sightseeing tour by boat. Parliament, Szabadság Square, the Basilica, Andrássy Avenue to City Park. Museum of Fine Arts. Vajdahunyád Castle. Széchenyi Baths.

With more time on your hands, the following might well head the list: the central **covered market**, the **National Museum**, a stroll along the **Grand Boulevard** (Ring Avenue), the park on **Margaret Island**, the **tomb of Gül Baba** and the Roman ruins of **Aquincum**.

Walking tours

The Buda side of the city offers two clear-cut zones — Castle Hill and the district of Víziváros, along Fő u. — that reward strolling, while Pest spreads its attractions evenly over a much wider area. A good reference point likely to be the starting and end point of many sallies into the city (though not of the walking plans proposed here) is **Vörösmarty Square**, which lies at the center of the Inner City (Belváros) of Pest: it is closed to traffic, abuts the main shopping and promenading alley of the city (Váci St.), lies within shouting distance of all three metro lines and many of the biggest hotels, and enjoys one of the best coffee-houses of Budapest (the **Gerbeaud**).

One of the great fascinations of walking in Budapest is to explore the magnificent apartment buildings of the turn of the century, monuments that straddle the line between public and private, and so promise — and often yield — the exquisite pleasures of discovering something hidden and uncommon. They often wear a face of grime and fallen plaster, dusty behemoths of past luxury. Many have an interior courtyard where the signs of decline and poverty come out in much sharper focus, and the smells and textures of rot predominate. Make sure you walk into them: your reward may be a gateway of the most coquettish Art Nouveau, a Baroque stairway of stupendous dash, floor works of astonishing superfluity, the overthrown statue of a goddess, or the proud escutcheon of some noble family long since vanished in who knows which of the two world wars, several economic collapses, countless persecutions and grinding stagnation of this century.

Each of the following two itineraries covers a length of 12-15km (about 7 to 9 miles) and can easily be accomplished in 6 to 8 hours.

WALK 1: CENTRAL BÚDA AND CENTRAL PEST

Start at the Pest end of the Elisabeth Bridge, maybe at the Inner City Parish Church, walking away from the river toward Ferenciek tere. A quick detour right on Károlyi Mihály u. and Eötvös Loránd u. will permit a look at the **Franciscan Church of Pest** and the impressive buildings of the **Eötvös University**; but the more interesting sights are on VÁCI STREET, to the left, which you can reach via Kigyó u. Follow this main shopping and tourist street of Budapest to Vörösmarty tér, pausing for a coffee and cake at the legendary **Café Gerbeaud**.

Now turn W toward Vigadó tér to admire the **Vigadó Concert Hall** as well as the classic panorama of the DANUBE EMBANKMENT which opens up at this point. Continue upriver to Roosevelt tér, and go across on the **Széchenyi Chain Bridge**, the oldest of Budapest's eight bridges.

Immediately across the bridge at Clark Adam tér is the base station of

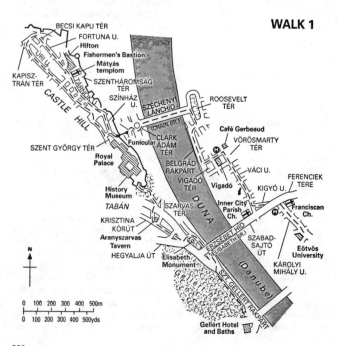

the funicular which will take you up to the CASTLE HILL of Buda, the oldest and in many ways the most attractive part of the city. Turn right at the top, following Szinház u. and Tarnok u. to Szentháromság tér (Trinity Square), which is dominated by MATTHIAS CHURCH (Mátyás Templom), a centerpiece of visitor's Budapest. Behind the cathedral is FISHERMEN'S BASTION, offering a superb panorama over the river, and the **Hilton**, which incorporates the ruins of a medieval church.

Follow Fortuna u., one of the two main streets of old Buda, as far as Becsi kapu tér, then double back along Úri u., the other main street, all the way back s to Szent György tér, the terminus of the funicular as well as the main entrance to the ROYAL PALACE. The various museums in the palace will require a minimum of 2 hours to explore.

Thereafter, continue through the lobby of the Budapest History Museum to the rear gardens of the palace, where a pathway continues downhill through the park and historic district of **Tabán**, back to the **Elisabeth Bridge**, your starting point for the day.

Before crossing back to Pest, however, walk on s another 10 minutes along the foot of GELLÉRT HILL to what might very well be the most unforgettable experience of the day, and end your walk with a relaxing bath amid the Art Nouveau splendor of the GELLÉRT BATHS.

WALK 2: ALONG THE DANUBE AND ANDRÁSSY AVENUE

Start at Clark Adam tér, on the Buda side of the Széchenyi Chain Bridge, turning N on Fő u., the main street of the district of Víziváros. At BATTHYÁNYI SQUARE, visit the attractive old **Church of St Anne**, and take in the fine vista of the **Parliament** across the river. Continue N along the riverbank (Bem Rakpart) toward the **Margaret Bridge**.

At the foot of the bridge, a small side loop will bring you to one of the more unusual corners of old Buda. Follow Frankel Leo út to Török u., then turn left and immediately right to arrive at Gül Baba u., a steep alley which seems to have changed little since the time of the Turks. Climb it to the upper end and turn left to visit the Tomb of GÜL BABA, a Turkish saint. Then follow Apostol u. back to the bridge.

Now cross over to the Pest side, resisting the temptation to get off the bridge to explore the shady walks of MARGARET ISLAND. Turn right on Széchenyi Rakpart, noting the big white building which until lately was the Hungarian Communist Party headquarters, and proceeding on to the PARLIAMENT, which deserves a full loop around its huge mass to savor its wealth of architectural detail. The **Ethnographical Museum** opposite, on Kossuth Lajos tér, is worth a visit for its impressive interior.

Following this, take Alkotmány u. left and Honvéd u. right to emerge on SZABADSÁG TÉR (Liberty Square), one of Budapest's most monumental public spaces. Observe the massive building of the **Hungarian TV**, formerly the Budapest Stock Exchange, on the E side of the square, then, if you are interested in Art Nouveau architecture, cross W and walk a half block over to Hold u. to see the **Postal Savings Bank Building**.

Continue on Bank u. to Bajcsy-Zsilinszky út, turn right, and walk until you get to the BASILICA of St Stephen, the largest and most ostentatious church of Budapest. It is entered from Szent István tér on the W.

WALK 2

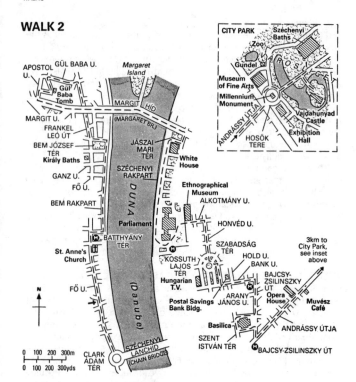

ANDRÁSSY AVENUE, the heart and soul of turn-of-the-century Budapest, demands a good hour to explore its majestic 3km (2-mile) course: break it if you wish with a coffee or snack at one of the stately old cafés along the way, perhaps the **Művesz** or **Lukács**.

The CITY PARK (Városliget), which terminates the boulevard, is also crowded with attractions. Start at the MUSEUM OF FINE ARTS, Budapest's response to Vienna's Art History Museum, then check if there is anything interesting on at the **Exhibition Hall** across Hősök tere. Now enter the park, past the extravagant MILLENNIUM MONUMENT, which summarizes the first 1,000 years of Hungarian history, cross the bridge, then veer right to admire **Vajdahunyád Castle**, a delightful architectural pastiche which combines every known style of building in European history.

The SZÉCHENYI BATHS, just a short walk across the park, offer even greater pomp and luxury than the Gellért, and thus call for a visit. Younger members of the group might prefer the zoo and amusement park nearby. Conclude with a dinner at **Gundel**, one of the few happy places in this world where a true gourmet meal costs less than $20.

Sights and places of interest

Introduction

The **churches** of Budapest are of mostly secondary interest, and the one **palace**, a work of misplaced vanity, is more imposing than beautiful. Instead, Budapest has an **old town** of quaint and provincial charm (CASTLE HILL) and many **public buildings**, **shopping arcades**, **company palaces**, **museums** and **apartment houses** of magnificent ostentation. The best of these are found along ANDRÁSSY AVENUE, VÁCI STREET, SZABADSÁG SQUARE, and to a lesser extent the GREAT BOULEVARD.

Four **museums** are of considerable, if not overwhelming, interest: the MUSEUM OF FINE ARTS, the NATIONAL MUSEUM, the National Gallery and the Budapest City Museum (the last two being located in the ROYAL PALACE). Two others, the Ethnographical Museum and the Museum of Applied Arts, deserve to be visited mainly on their architectural merits.

Various **vantage points** on Castle Hill (FISHERMEN'S BASTION, Tóth Árpád sétány, the ROYAL PALACE), GELLÉRT HILL (Citadel) and the more distant BUDA HILLS reveal the relatively complex layout of the right bank. The left bank is entirely flat and lacks any corresponding features to help grasp its geography.

The **baths** of Budapest, one of the city's most idiosyncratic attractions, we list under a separate heading following the main alphabetical list of other sights.

MUSEUM OPENING TIMES
With few exceptions, the standard opening hours for all museums are 10am-6pm in summer (April to September) and 10am-4pm in winter (October to March), closing on Mondays. The typical entrance charge is F20 (25 US cents), and even that can be saved on Tuesdays when every museum in Hungary can be visited free.

HOW TO USE THIS SECTION
In this chapter, look for the ★ symbol against the outstanding, not-to-be-missed sights. The ☆ symbol indicates sights we consider particularly to merit a visit if you are in the neighborhood. Places of special interest for children (♣) and with outstanding views (◀€) are also indicated. For a full explanation of symbols, see page 7.

Some lesser sights do not appear under their own headings but are included within other entries: if you cannot find them readily within the text, look them up in the INDEX.

Bold type is generally employed to indicate districts, buildings or other highlights.

Places mentioned without addresses and opening times are often described more fully elsewhere in this chapter. Check whether they are **cross-references**, which are in SMALL CAPITALS. If they are, they have their own heading and description.

In this alphabetical section, districts are indicated in bold parentheses — e.g., **(III.)** and **(VI.)** — preceding the address, map reference, opening times etc.

Budapest's sights A to Z

ANDRÁSSY AVENUE (Andrássy útja) ★
(VI.) Map 8C4-A6. Metro 1 (stops at Deák tér, Opera, Oktogon, Vörösmarty u., Kodály körönd, Bajza u., Hősök tere). Buses 1 and 4 run the length of Andrássy útja.

Budapest's response to Vienna's Ringstrasse and the Parisian Champs-Elysées stands out for its architectural extravagance, which qualifies it as one of Europe's most impressive urban thoroughfares. The boulevard was laid out in 1872 and was fully developed by the end of the 1880s.

The original name of Sugárút (Radial Road) was changed several times to reflect the prevailing political winds: thus Andrássy in the 1890s, Stalin after 1948, the Hungarian Youth for a few days in 1956 and the People's Republic (Népköztársaság) under Kádár's regime all lent their name to the avenue, which reverted to its late 19thC name of Andrássy útja once again in 1990.

The eponymous Count Gyula Andrássy (1823-90) was condemned to death *in absentia* for his involvement in the revolution of 1848 and forced to hide for 8 years. Pardoned in 1857, he went on to become the co-architect, with Ferenc Deák, of the Compromise of 1867. Subsequently he served as prime minister of Hungary from 1867-71 and foreign minister of Austria-Hungary from 1871-79. His intimacy with Empress-Queen Elisabeth has been the subject of historical romance.

Gyula Andrássy Jr, his son, was the last foreign minister of Austria-Hungary, and as such negotiated the surrender of 1918.

Sights and places of interest
Andrássy útja is split into three nearly equal portions by the spacious circuses of the Oktogon and Kodály körönd. It starts with a magnificently ornate urban artery as far as the Oktogon, continues with a somewhat more restrained, tree-lined section of middle-class apartments, and culminates in a stretch of stately detached villas and embassies leading up to the CITY PARK (Városliget). The 120 or so buildings along the way form a unique showcase of Eclectic architecture of the 1870s and '80s.

The most important edifice in the first part of the boulevard is the **State**

Opera (Állami Operaház) at #22 *(map 8 C5)*, which was built by Miklós Ybl in 1875-84 with the explicit intention of matching and surpassing its rival in Vienna — a goal many consider it more than achieved. The auditorium, decorated with a massive fresco and several hundred statues, is regarded as one of Europe's most beautiful *(only group 𝄡 outside performance times, via TIT ☎ 1431360)*. Statues of Franz Liszt, the composer, and Ferenc Erkel, the first director of the Opera, stand outside the main entrance.

Liszt composed an orchestral work for the opening night of the Opera in 1884, which was rejected because it employed the *Rákóczi March,* an inflammatory nationalist tune. Gustav Mahler directed the Budapest Opera for 3 years prior to his appointment at Vienna.

The Neo-Renaissance building facing the Opera at #25 is the **State Ballet Institute** *(map 8 C5)*, built in 1883. The entrance halls and courtyards of many buildings in the vicinity deserve exploration on account of their extremely rich (if often dilapidated) detailing. Of especial note are **#10** (sculptured lampposts), **#12** (frescoes in the courtyard), **#29** (Művész café with a splendid interior), **#39** (the Divatcsarnok Department Store, with Art Nouveau murals dating from 1909 in its interior hall) and **#47** (outstanding gateway).

Notable for less pleasant reasons is **#60**, the secret police headquarters of the Stalinist period where countless people were bundled in to face interrogation, some of whom never left again. In **#67**, the palatial residence where Franz Liszt held court in the last 7 years of his life (1879-86) and organized the Hungarian Academy of Music, there is a Liszt Memorial Room containing the composer's original furniture *(open Mon-Fri noon-5pm, Sat 9am-1pm, closed Sun)*.

The **Academy of Fine Arts** *(Képzőművészeti Főiskola 69, map 8 B5)*, a Neo-Renaissance work of 1877, is among the most extravagant buildings on Andrássy útja. The **Lukács café** at #70 *(map 8 B5)*, rich with literary associations and renowned for its excellent pastry, is furnished with museum pieces of the turn-of-the century.

Kodály körönd *(map 8 B6)*, one of the most elegant spaces in Budapest, is circled by four apartment buildings of outstanding monumentality, one of which, #89-91, was the home of the composer Zoltán Kodály until his death in 1967: it now forms a museum.

The former **Palais Pallavicini** at #98 *(map 8 B6)*, now houses an engineering company, though it is possible to visit its rich Neo-Renaissance courtyards. A particularly fine Art Nouveau villa at **#101** is employed as the Press House, while #103 houses an interesting **Museum of East Asian Art** *(Chinese section at Gorkij fasor 12, map 8 B6; standard opening hours)*.

At #102 is the (ex-Soviet) **Russian Embassy** *(map 8 B6)*, much diminished in political stature these days.

The metro line #1 which runs beneath Andrássy útja was inaugurated in 1896 as Europe's second-oldest underground line after London's; it originally bore the name of "the Franz Joseph Underground Railway." A **Metro Museum** *(entrance through the Deák tér station, map 8 D4 ✱)* has been set up in an unused portion of the line.

AQUINCUM

(III.) Map 5B3. Suburban rail from Nyugati (West) Station. Museum 🏛 *Roman Baths* 🏛 *both standard opening hours. Hercules Villa* 🏛 *open Tues-Fri 10am-2pm, Sat-Sun 10am-6pm, closed Mon.*

Considerable sections of the ruins of the ancient Roman city of Aquincum have come to light in recent years in various parts of the suburb of Óbuda (Old Buda), approximately 6km (4 miles) N of the center.

The military garrison of Aquincum, the chief Roman base on the Pannonian frontier, was established early in the 1stC AD. A civilian city of perhaps 40,000 grew near it in the 2nd and 3rdC, and was abandoned by Roman citizens around the year 400. There is reason, but no hard evidence, to believe that Attila the Hun took up residence in this former Roman capital in the final part of his reign, and that the legendary Etzelburg (Attila's Castle) of the Nibelungen Lied was situated here.

A good starting point for exploring the antiquities of Óbuda is Flórián tér, the right-bank end of the Árpád Bridge. The underpass here contains the entrance of the ruined **Roman Baths**, whose excavation in the 1780s was the earliest archeological project to be undertaken in Hungary. A short walk N to Meggyfa u. leads to the foundations of a 3rdC residence, dubbed the **Hercules Villa** on account of the mosaics decorating its floor, depicting the Greek hero rescuing Deianeira from a centaur.

The main body of the ruins is located about 3km (2 miles) farther N on the Szentendre road *(bus 42 or 134).* The field of excavation contains the remains of public baths, houses, a marketplace, an early Christian church and a Temple of the Unconquered Sun, as well as the **Civilian Amphitheater**, which lies outside the excavation zone across the rail line. The **Museum** in the archeological zone is notable for an unusual water-organ of the Roman period and a fine bas-relief of the Persian sun-god Mithras wearing a Phrygian cap, plunging a dagger into a bull's throat.

Vicinity

A small section of old Óbuda has been lovingly restored in recent years, forming a pleasant oasis in the midst of an otherwise dreary part of the city. The historic area is focused around Fő tér, immediately E of Flórián tér; its centerpiece is **Palais Zichy**, an 18thC mansion where concerts are given in summer.

Two restaurants of old-fashioned charm, the **Postakocsi étterem** *(III. Fő tér 2)* and **Kéhli vendéglő** *(III. Mókus u. 22; see WHERE TO EAT)*, are nearby.

BASILICA (Szent István templom)

(V.) Szent István tér. Map 8C4. Metro 1/2/3 to Deák tér.

Budapest's most grandiose church was modeled in part on the Basilica of St Stephen, the coronation church of Hungarian kings in Esztergom. The original Neoclassical design of József Hild (1851) was altered with a number of Eclectic details by Miklós Ybl, who directed the construction in 1867-91. The 96-meter/315-foot-high dome was modified after its first version collapsed in 1868, and the church was finally conse-crated in 1906 with Franz Joseph in attendance. The church holds 8,500 people and is the largest in Hungary.

An open-air mass was held in front of the Basilica on August 20, 1988 on the occasion of the 950th anniversary of the death of King Stephen. Attracting a crowd of 50,000, this became a milestone in the series of events leading to the collapse of the communist regime.

The iconography of the church revolves around St Stephen, the first king of Hungary, and the Virgin Mary, who became the patron of Hungary when the king, having lost his son Imre in a hunting accident, placed his crown under her protection (rather than seek the help of various rival clans or the support of the German Emperor). The **right arm of St Stephen**, the holiest relic of the Hungarian Catholic church, is kept in a side chapel where it can be seen by activating a coin-operated case. The back of the church, facing Bajcsy-Zsilinszky út, is lined with an elegant Ionic colonnade with the statues of the Twelve Apostles.

Endre Bajcsy-Zsilinszky (1886-1944), after whom this street is named, was a leader of the Hungarian resistance during World War II. He was executed by the Nazis on Christmas Day, 1944.

BATTHYÁNYI SQUARE (Batthyányi tér)
Map 7B2-3. Metro 2 to Batthyányi tér.

The main square of the Buda district of Víziváros (Watertown) com-memorates Count Lajos Batthyányi (1806-49), the scion of one of Hun-gary's oldest landed families, who became the prime minister of the revolutionary regime of 1848 and was executed after its defeat. From here there is a splendid view of the PARLIAMENT across the Danube.

The principal feature of the square is the **Church of St Anne** (Anna templom) *(map 7C2)*, loved by many as the prettiest of Budapest's Baroque churches. Built in 1740-62, it was fully restored after suffering heavy damage in World War II. The statues in the high altar (1773) represent the presentation of Mary by her mother, St Anne, in the Temple of Jerusalem. The adjoining vicarage houses the **Angelika**, one of Buda-pest's more attractive cafés.

The square is flanked on the w by a **Market Hall** with lively vegetable stands downstairs and an ABC supermarket upstairs. Two doors up at #4 is the former **White Cross**, a Rococo structure from the 1770s, said to have numbered among its guests the philanderer Giacomo Casanova (hence the name of the bar on the ground floor) and the emperor Joseph II. The N side of the square is occupied by the former Franciscan Abbey. Adjoining it is the Baroque **Church of St Elisabeth**, formerly known as the Franciscan Church. Dating from 1731-57, it has statues of St Francis and St Anthony of Padua on its facade.

The statue in front of the Franciscan Abbey belongs to Ferenc Kölcsey (1790-1838), the poet of the Hungarian national anthem. Engraved on the base are his immortal verses:

"Look forward and/Face the present wisely;/Work, create,
enrich: thus our/Fatherland will prosper and advance."

Three blocks N on Fő u. stands the forbidding mass of the **Military Courthouse** *(#70-78, map 7B2)*, used as a security headquarters and prison by both the Gestapo and the Stalinist regime of Rákosi. Here in 1958 Imre Nagy and other leaders of the 1956 uprising were condemned to death in secret trial. Next to the Courthouse across Kacsa u. are the KIRÁLY BATHS, the most "Turkish" of Budapest's thermal facilities.

BELVÁROS   See under PARLIAMENT, SZABADSÁG SQUARE and VÁCI STREET.

BUDA HILLS
(II./XII.) Map 5C1-2. Metro 2 to Moszkva tér; then walk to Cogwheel Railway terminus on Szilágyi Erzsébet fasor, or take bus/tram 56 to Hűvösvölgy (lower terminus of the Pioneer Railway).

The western approaches of Buda are covered with pleasantly wooded hills, which provide the inhabitants of the capital with many favorite spots for weekend relaxation, and coveted residential neighborhoods.

In the prewar period a majority of the population of the hills were German. Their memory lives on in some names (thus Svab hegy, "Swabian Hill"), in the architecture of old country houses, and in the traditional country restaurants scattered throughout the area.

A good way to explore the Buda Hills is to take the ancient **Cogwheel Railway** (Fogaskerekű vasút) which climbs from the vicinity of Moszkva tér to the summit of Széchenyi hegy *(❋ ◁€ from 427m/1,400 feet)*, offering many splendid views and attractive villas along the way. The **Pioneer Railway** (Úttörővasút ❋), named after the official children's organization whose members operate the line, continues from the summit, via János hegy (529m/1,735 feet), the highest point in Budapest, to the popular excursion area of Hűvösvölgy ("Cool Valley").

The summit of the nearest hill, **Martinovics hegy** (257m/843 feet), offers a surprisingly attractive natural environment almost directly above Moszkva tér, one of Budapest's busiest intersections.

CASTLE HILL (Várhegy) ★
(I.) Map 7C1-D3. Bus 116 from Március 15 tér, or bus 16 from Erzsébet tér ❋ Cable car (Budavári sikló) operates 7.30am-10pm except 2nd and 4th Mon each month.

The fortified old town of Buda occupies the summit of a steep hill 2.5km (1½ miles) long but only 200 to 500m (220 to 550 yards) wide, overlooking the Danube from a height of 60m (197 feet). The southern outcrop carries the massive body of the ROYAL PALACE; the remainder forms a historic district of outstanding charm whose understated small-town manner contrasts strongly with the imperiousness of 19thC Pest.

History
The hill was inhabited from prehistoric times, but it was only after the Mongol invasion of 1241-42 that a walled town came into existence.

This became a permanent royal seat and received a city charter under Lajos I (1342-82). Under Turkish rule the Castle district was reserved for the Muslim population of Buda, whose massacre and flight during the Austrian conquest (1686) opened the way for the resettlement of the town by a German-speaking colony. As late as 1851 German was the language of more than 80 percent of the population of Buda. Street names, which were in German, were Magyarized by municipal decree in 1847 and again in 1873.

The southern half of the district adjoining the ROYAL PALACE saw some of the severest fighting of the Battle of Budapest, and remains riddled with gaps where buildings destroyed in the war have not been re-erected. Restorations carried on continuously since 1945 have turned the northern half, on the other hand, into one of Europe's most attractive collections of historic urban architecture.

Sights and places of interest

The center of the old town is **Trinity Square** (Szentháromság tér) *(map 7C2),* which is adorned with a rather provincial **Plague Column** from 1713. The Neo-Gothic MATTHIAS CHURCH stands between the square and the **Fishermen's Bastion** (Halászbástya) *(☆ ◁€ , map 7C2),* one of Budapest's leading tourist attractions. The mock-medieval bastion of white limestone, which was built in 1890-1905 for purely decorative purposes, offers one of the finest panoramas of the city, with a view extending over the Danube and the roofs of Pest.

Its name derives from a tradition which holds that the defense of this part of the wall was as-

Fishermen's Bastion

signed to the fishermen's guild in the Middle Ages. On its northern end the bastion abuts the **Hilton Hotel** *(map 7C2),* an undistinguished specimen of 1970s functional architecture, which was permitted to invade the remnants of a medieval Dominican church and an 18thC Jesuit college as a token of the "liberalism" of the late János Kádár's regime.

The historic houses lining the four principal lanes of the Castle district, Táncsics Mihály u., Fortuna u., Országház u. and Úri u. (Lords Lane; *Herrengasse* in German), obtained their present appearance largely in the aftermath of 1686, although many of them have origins going back to the 14thC. Many possess a sign that indicates either the trade or the coat-of-arms of the original owner.

One of the oldest is the **Red Hedgehog House** (Vörös sünház) at

Hess András tér *(map 7 C2)*, marked with a sign that accounts for its name; it was built in 1390 and housed a popular inn through a large part of its history. Táncsics Mihály u. 5 was built in 1808 as a jail, whose inmates at various times included the peasant revolutionary Mihály Táncsics (1799-1884) and the national hero Lajos Kossuth.

The 18thC house at Táncsics u. 26 contains a **Jewish Prayer House** from the 14thC *(map 7 C2, Jewish Museum open Tues-Fri 10am-2pm, Sat-Sun 10am-6pm, closed Mon)*. In Becsi kapu tér (Vienna Gate Square), #7 is a medieval building renewed in 1807 and decorated with statues of a whole pantheon of Classical Greek and Roman worthies. It was the home earlier this century of the writer-historian Count Lajos Hatvany; Thomas Mann was his guest here on several occasions.

Kapisztrán tér, named after the Italian friar who goaded János Hunyadi into his crusade against the Turks, is dominated by the former Nándor Barracks (1847) which now house a **Museum of Military History** (Hadtörténeti múzeum) *(map 7 C1, standard opening hours)*. Behind it stands a memorial to Abdurrahman Pasha the Albanian, the last Turkish governor of Buda, who fell on this spot in 1686.

The **Tower of Mary Magdalene** *(map 7 C2)*, facing the barracks on Kapisztrán tér, is the lone surviving fragment of the former Franciscan Church of Buda, the only church devoted to Christian worship in the Castle district under Turkish rule.

At Fortuna u. 4, the former Fortuna Inn, which gave its name to the street, has been transformed into an altogether charming **Shop and Tavern Museum** (Magyar Kereskedelmi és Vendéglátóipari múzeum) *(map 7 C2, standard opening hours)*, whose displays include the mold for an historic Easter bunny.

A particularly attractive ensemble is formed by Orságház (Parliament) u. 18, 20 and 22, three houses that were rebuilt in 1771 on the basis of medieval originals. The historic **Golden Eagle Pharmacy** at Tárnok u. 18 *(map 7 C2)*, has been preserved as a museum *(standard opening hours)*, while the former **Buda Town Hall** (Budai Városháza) on Szentháromság tér *(map 7 C2)*, a Baroque structure from the early 18thC, now houses a Linguistic Research Institute. Next to the latter stands the **Ruszwurm Café/Pastryshop**, a perfect Biedermeier period-piece, which has been in business continuously since 1837.

The limestone floor of the Castle district is riddled with an extensive network of **underground passages** which were used for defensive purposes on various occasions, most recently by the German troops defending the Hill against Soviet assault in February 1945. A small part of the labyrinth, decorated with wax figures illustrating the more lurid aspects of Hungarian history, can be visited through Úri u. 9, where an Italian entrepreneur has operated since 1986 the first privately owned **museum** in Hungary (Budavári Labirintus) *(map 7 C2 ☀ 10am-6pm daily ⇥ noon-8pm ☿ 9pm-2am ✿)*.

Vicinity

The **Vérmező** ("Blood Meadow") *(map 7 C1-D2)*, a park below the w flank of the Hill, obtains its name from the execution of Ignác Martinovics and his "Jacobin" friends, which was carried out here in 1795.

Tabán *(map 7E2-3)*, the low-lying area between the s slope of Castle Hill and GELLÉRT HILL, was originally a disreputable slum of Serbs, Greeks, Turks and Gypsies, which was transformed in the 19thC into the celebrated "Budapest Grinzing" where generations of poets, bohemians and hedonists found inspiration in wine taverns set among vineyards and apricot groves. It was cleared off on hygienic grounds in the 1920s, leaving behind a sterile park and only a few old buildings to recall the former atmosphere of Tabán. These include the **Tabán Parish Church** (St Catherine of Alexandria, built 1728-36), the **Aranyszarvas** ("Golden Stag") **Restaurant**, and the house of the poet Benedek Virág (1754-1830).

An attractively restored 18thC house nearby houses the **Semmelweis Museum of Medical History** *(map 7D3, standard opening hours)*. Ignác Semmelweis (1818-65), one of the founders of modern immunology, was called "the savior of mothers" for his discovery of the causes of childbirth fever. He was born and died in this house, although his medical career was made in Vienna.

A small park at the bottom of the Tabán below the ramp of the Elisabeth Bridge contains a **Monument of Queen Elisabeth** *(map 7E3)*, depicting the only member of the Habsburg family to have commanded genuine affection in the Hungarian half of the realm. Elisabeth (Erzsébet in Magyar), the wife of Franz Joseph, learned to speak Hungarian, struck up close friendships with leading Hungarian figures, and took an active part in promoting the Compromise of 1867. Her statue was erected in 1932 after many delays caused by political bickering. It was removed from its original stand on the Pest side of the bridge in 1953, at the height of the Stalinist terror, and reinstated quietly on this spot in 1986.

CENTRAL MARKET (Központi vásárcsarnok) ★
(IX.) Vámház körút 1-3. Map 8E5-F5. Tram 2, 47, 49. Bus 1. Open Mon 6am-5pm; Tues-Wed 6am-6pm; Fri 6am-7pm; Sat 6am-3pm. Closed Thurs; Sun.
The main produce, flower, fish, meat and dairy market of Budapest stood out as an oasis of color and private initiative in the dead decades of communism: Margaret Thatcher was one of countless visitors who chose to be photographed buying paprika in the Central Market. Commercial life has now returned to the streets of Budapest, but the market continues to fascinate the visitor with its intoxicating wealth of aroma, noise, color and movement.

The market occupies a gigantic cathedral-like structure 150m (492 feet) long, the largest of five similar market halls built in 1896. Many of the marketeers are peasant women of the provinces, who are said to pay exorbitant sums for the right to rent a stall in the prestigious Central Market. The flower section is dominated by gypsies, while sellers of traditional embroideries tend to be ethnic Hungarians from Transylvania.

An underground **canal** formerly allowed river barges to bring their wares directly into the market hall. The entrance of the canal can be seen on the Danube quay near the Matróz Csárda restaurant.

There are plans for the restoration of the market that would involve its closing down for several years, although they had not yet been put into effect as of early 1992.

Other markets

The other old market halls of Budapest are located at (III.) Hold u. 13 *(map 8 C4)*, (VI.) Hunyadi tér *(map 8 B5)* and (VIII.) Rákóczi tér *(map 8 D6)*. The one at (VII.) Klauzál tér *(map 8 C5)* has been successfully converted into the glossiest supermarket in town by the Skála store chain.

A very popular outdoor market is held daily at **Lehel**, between Váci út and Lehel u. behind XIII. Élmunkás tér *(metro 3 to Élmunkás tér)*.

CITY PARK (Városliget)
(XIV.) Map 5C3. Metro 1 (Hősök tere, Széchenyi fürdő).

ANDRÁSSY AVENUE concludes at Városliget, a large and well-maintained park containing several of Budapest's principal sights. The main entrance of the park at Hősök tere centers on the MILLENNIUM MONUMENT, which is flanked by the MUSEUM OF FINE ARTS and the Exhibition Hall. Points of interest within the grounds include the SZÉCHENYI BATHS, the most extravagant of Budapest's thermal establishments, and **Gundel**, the leading gourmet restaurant of the city since 1869 (see EATING AND DRINKING).

The **Municipal Zoo**, housed in a turn-of-the-century complex, is currently being renovated to improve conditions for its 4,000 occupants. Near it are a permanent **Circus** and a rather run-down **Amusement Park** (Vidámpark) *(open Apr-Sept)* with a vast slot-machine hall. The artificial lake behind Hősök tere becomes, in winter, a popular open-air **skating rink** (✱).

The chief attraction of the park, however, is **Vajdahunyád Castle** (✰ ✱ ▧ *open Tues-Sat 10am-5pm, Sun 10am-6pm, closed Mon)*, a fairy-tale fortress which brings together four major architectural styles of European history to produce a delightful ensemble. The castle was designed by Ignác Alpár as a temporary display for the 1,000th-year celebrations of 1896, then rebuilt in permanent form in 1904. The main part (Romanesque) is a faithful copy of part of the original Vajdahunyád Castle in Transylvania (Hunedoara in Romania); to this are added a Gothic chapel, a Renaissance court and a Baroque mansion, all built with a remarkable precision of detail. The castle houses an **Agricultural Museum** (Mező gazdasági múzeum) *(standard opening hours)*, documenting such matters as pig and poultry breeding, historic animals and agricultural machinery.

A statue outside the museum depicts Anonymus, the first chronicler of medieval Hungary. For obvious reasons he is represented without a face.

The **Petőfi Sport Hall** and Youth Center, just beyond the castle, opened in 1985 and has since grown into a stronghold of Hungary's lively rock and pop scene (see THE ARTS).

The statue of George Washington, located nearby, was erected with funds donated by the US Hungarian immigrant community in the early 20thC.

In the SE corner is a **Museum of Transport** *(Városliget körut 11, open 10am-6pm, closed Mon ✽)*, whose exhibits include bridges, motorcycles, airplanes, ships, cars and trains. Farther on is a small **Garden for the Blind**, where fragrance is all-important.

DANUBE EMBANKMENT ★
Map 7A3-8F5 ◁€

The panorama of Budapest at the Danube embankment has long been one of Europe's classic sights. In the 1920s it prompted Jules Romains to write, "Budapest forms one of the most beautiful cityscapes that exist along a river, probably the most beautiful in Europe." In 1988 it was placed by UNESCO on the World Heritage list of protected monuments.

Yet the full beauty of the waterfront did not survive the destruction of World War II. Virtually every building along the banks was demolished in the battles of January and February 1945, and although many have since been restored to their old, sumptuous facades, there remain many gaps and several unfortunate pieces of postwar urbanism to mar the otherwise enchanting vista. Among sights lost forever is the elegant lineup of hotels and cafés along the edge of the Inner City of Pest — the celebrated Corso (Dunakorzó), whose tree-lined front was a staple of yesterday's postcard-Budapest.

All four of the great Danube bridges that existed then (there are 8 now) were blown up by the Germans in a desperate effort to slow the Soviet advance. Perhaps the most famous of them, the **Széchenyi Chain Bridge** (Lánchíd), was launched in 1839 under the guidance of Count István Széchenyi, the Great Reformer, as the first major public project of the reawakening Hungary. It was designed by William Clark, an Englishman, and constructed by Adam Clark, a Scottish engineer unrelated to him. Their work became a defiant symbol of Hungarian national aspirations, surviving an unsuccessful Austrian attempt to destroy it in 1848.

The **Margaret Bridge** (Margit híd) was commissioned shortly after the Compromise and the unification of Buda and Pest, and completed in 1876. The **Liberty Bridge** (Szabadság híd), originally named after Franz Joseph, was inaugurated in 1896 on the occasion of the Millennium celebrations; the silver rivet which the kaiser drove in still bears the royal initials, although his name was erased from the map of the city after Hungary declared its independence in 1918. However, his assassinated wife, after whom the **Elisabeth Bridge** was named (Erzsébet híd, completed 1903), had a sufficient store of Hungarian sympathy to keep her memory alive after independence. Her bridge was the last to be rebuilt after the war, opening again only in 1963.

One landmark, the **Vigadó** concert and reception hall *(map 8D4)*, remains to impart a feeling of the old Corso. This unique and lively mix of Romantic and national-Hungarian architectural styles was designed by Frigyes Feszl in 1858-65. It reopened in 1980 after a 35-year reconstruction (see THE ARTS).

Three modern hotels, the **Duna Inter-Continental**, **Forum** and **Atrium Hyatt**, have replaced the legendary lineup of the Hungaria, Bristol and Carlton, whose tree-lined riverbank promenade once formed the heart of the Corso. Another grandly convoluted reminder of the past still stands on Roosevelt tér: **Gresham Palace** *(map 8C4)*, the Art Nouveau headquarters of a British insurance company, built in 1907. Part of it was recently converted into Budapest's top gambling casino.

Roosevelt tér carries a memorial plaque extolling Franklin D. Roosevelt for "helping the triumph of freedom and democracy" by his role in World War II. Not far from it, a furious crowd hacked to death Count Lemberg, the Austrian commissioner, in September 1848. In 1867 Franz Joseph chose the same spot, in a gesture of reconciliation, for his coronation as King of Hungary.

FISHERMEN'S BASTION   See under CASTLE HILL.

GELLÉRT BATHS (Gellért fürdő)   See under BATHS.

GELLÉRT HILL (Gellért hegy)
(I./XI.) Map 7F3-8F4 ◁€ *Bus 27 to summit.*

The steep dolomite rock that drops to the Danube at the foot of the Elisabeth Bridge is named after St Gellért (Gerald), an Italian divine who was sent to aid King Stephen in his campaign to convert the Magyars to Christianity, and was martyred 8 years after the death of the king by being cast into the river at this spot. The **Gellért Monument** (1904) *(map 7E3)*, shows the saint holding the cross over a heathen Magyar. It is dwarfed by the **Liberation Monument** (Felszabadulasi Emlekmű) *(map 8E4)*, at the summit of the hill, which commemorates the liberation of Budapest by Soviet troops at the end of World War II.

The powerful **Citadel** (Citadella) of Buda, which crowns the hill, was erected after the suppression of the Revolution of 1848-49 by the Austrian army in order to keep CASTLE HILL under artillery cover; it was symbolically demolished in parts when it came under Hungarian control in 1894. One of the finest panoramas of the city is obtained from its ramparts.

Three of the historic baths of Budapest, the Rudas, Rác and GELLÉRT (see under BATHS) are located at the foot of the hill on its N, NE and SE flanks, respectively.

GREAT BOULEVARD (Nagykörút)
Map 7A3-8F6. Trams 4, 6 and bus 12 run the full length of Nagykörút. Metro lines: 3 to Nyugati pu. and Ferenc körút/Üllői út, 1 to Oktogon, 2 to Blaha Luiza tér.

The circular boulevard encompassing central Pest, the longest thoroughfare of the city, was laid out at the same time as ANDRÁSSY AVENUE but took longer to complete (from 1872-1907). It is lined with an almost unbroken line of turn-of-the-century apartment buildings, which create one of Europe's longest processions (4.1km/2½ miles) of 19thC Eclectic architecture. With a few exceptions, however, the architecture of the Great Boulevard does not compare with Andrássy útja for either grandeur or exuberance.

The boulevard is split into five sections named after four members of the Habsburg dynasty — Ferenc (Franz I of Austria), József (Joseph II), Erzsébet (the wife of Franz Joseph), Téréz (Maria Theresa) — and Szent István, the first king of Hungary. The third and fourth sections carried the name of Lenin until 1990.

Most of the buildings follow a standard interior division, with spacious middle-class apartments on the street side and smaller ones, frequently with a shared bathroom, in the back. Most have two staircases, one for the residents and another for servants and tradesmen. Nearly all were nationalized under the old regime, and await privatization now.

A prominent landmark of the southern arc of the boulevard is the **Museum of Applied Arts** (Iparművészeti múzeum), on the corner of Ferenc körút/Üllői út *(map 8 F6)*, an unusual product of the 19thC project to create a specifically Hungarian architectural style. Ödön Lechner's design (1893-96) combines Victorian, Moorish and Turkish elements to yield an interesting, even attractive whole. The museum itself *(standard opening hours)* was the second of its kind in the world after London's Victoria & Albert Museum.

Not far from the museum, on Kisfaludy köz, is the **Corvina Cinema** *(map 8 F6)*, which was the scene of the fiercest fighting during the 1956 uprising. The area farther N as far as **Rákóczi tér** has some notoriety as Budapest's center of low-class prostitution, a trade said to be connected with the presence of a Gypsy neighborhood on the back streets to the E.

József körút 5 (off Blaha Luiza tér) is the headquarters of the *Népszabadság* ("People's Freedom") daily newspaper, the former Communist Party Central Committee organ which has successfully transformed itself into Hungary's most respected independent newspaper.

Erzsébet and Téréz körút present a series of splendid facades, which make this part visually the finest stretch of the Great Boulevard. The most spectacular of all (indeed, arguably, of all Budapest) is the **New York Palace** at Erzsébet körút 9-11 *(map 8 D6)*, a fantastically overwrought building erected in 1895 as offices for an American insurance company. The coffeehouse on its ground floor, which has regained its historic name of **Café New York** after being called "Hungaria" through the Cold War years, is memorable for its preposterous wealth in marble and bronze and crystal decoration. Having been a bastion of Budapest's literati in the early decades of the century, and a potato store and shoe store in the heroic years of the People's Republic, it is now making a comeback as an intellectual trend-setter and tourist attraction.

A similar revival of the memories of Budapest's *belle époque* is noticeable at the **Grand Hotel Royal** at Erzsébet körút 49 *(map 8 C6)*, which was the largest hotel in the Austro-Hungarian Empire when it opened in 1896. It has recently undergone restoration to remove its ugly postwar accretions.

Near it, at the corner of Király u. and Liszt Ferenc tér, stands the magnificent Art Nouveau building of the **Academy of Music** (Zeneművészeti Főiskola, 1907) *(map 8C5)*, Budapest's principal philharmonic hall. Another impressive facade, a replica of Florence's Palazzo Strozzi, is at Téréz körút 67, off the Oktogon; this was built in 1884 for Count Batthyányi, and now serves as the most popular venue in town for weddings.

The **West Railway Station** (Nyugati pályaudvar) *(Téréz körút 55, map 8B5)* was built in 1874-77 by the Eiffel Company, designers of the famous tower in Paris. The area around it has become a hub of commercial enterprise in post-reform Hungary. The **Skála Metro Department Store** *(map 8C5)*, a success story of the 1980s described by TIME *Magazine* as the "Marks and Spencer of the East," has recently been supplemented by the **Spot Hypermarket**. Nearby is the largest **McDonald's** branch in Eastern Europe.

GÜL BABA
(II.) Türbe u. Off map 7A2. Standard opening hours.
One of the few architectural relics of the 150 years of Turkish occupation in Budapest is the **Tomb of Gül Baba**, a Muslim holy man ("Father Rose") who is said to have taken part in the conquest of the city in 1541 and who later planted a rose garden on the hill that bears his tomb. His small octagonal mausoleum dates from 1548 (it was used as a Christian chapel for a period, and restored to its original condition in 1961), and commands a pretty panorama of the Danube. No less interesting is **Gül Baba utca**, a modest cobble-stoned street leading up to the tomb, which appears to have been completely bypassed by the urbanizing rush of the past two centuries.

Rose Hill (Rózsadomb) *(map 5C3)*, which inherits its name from Gül Baba's garden, was an exclusive suburb of the 1920s, and came back into fashion in the 1980s with Budapest's new middle class of entrepreneurs and younger professionals. Its tree-shaded streets present an odd mix of wealth and hasty improvisation.

KIRÁLY BATHS (Király fürdő)   See under BATHS.

MARGARET ISLAND (Margit sziget)
(XIII.) Map 5C3. Pedestrian access from Margaret and Árpád Bridges; bus 26 and 26A from West Train Station; access from Árpád Bridge to the parking lot. Sightseeing tours by microbus from the parking lot Sat-Sun 10am-6pm (May-Sept). Bicycle rental at parking lot.
A highly attractive and peaceful park occupies Margaret Island, an alluvial deposit on the Danube measuring 2.5km by 500m (1½ miles by 550 yards). A tour of the island on foot or by bicycle takes 2 hours, although it can easily and enjoyably be stretched into a half-day's leisurely exploration.

In the Middle Ages the island was named the Isle of Hares. It obtained its present name from a daughter of King Béla IV, who was committed at the age of 9 to the Dominican convent on the island, fulfilling a vow of her father's who had sworn to sacrifice a daughter to God if Hungary survived the Mongol invasion of 1241-42. Many miracles were attributed to St Margaret, who was canonized in 1943.

The Turks called the island the Isle of Girls, not — as many local guides claim — because it contained a harem, but because of the convent which continued to exist through the 16thC. The island was acquired early in the 19thC by the Habsburg palatine, the representative of the crown in Hungary, and turned into a hunting preserve. The city purchased it from Archduke Joseph in 1908.

The most interesting historical sights on the island are the ruins of the **Dominican Convent**, which in its 13thC heyday was one of the most powerful institutions of the Hungarian kingdom, and those of a **Franciscan Church** of the late 13th/early 14thC. Additional features include the **Palatine Baths**, two modern hotels (the **Grand Ramada** and **Thermal**: see WHERE TO STAY) with attached thermal facilities, an open-air theater, a botanical garden containing many exotic species, a Japanese rock-garden, an animal park, and a 170-year-old **Musical Fountain**, which is a faithful copy of the Roman water-organ seen at the AQUINCUM Museum.

MATTHIAS CHURCH (Mátyás templom) ★
(I.) Szentháromsag tér. Map 7C2.

The main church of historic Buda — the Church of Our Lady (Nagyboldogasszony-templom), commonly called the Matthias Church in honor of the 15thC king — may disappoint architectural purists by its polychrome interior and what John Lukacs, in his book *Budapest 1900,* calls its "unhappy combination of somber dark spaces and sometimes strident colors." It nevertheless attracts masses of admiring visitors.

The church we see now was built virtually from the ground in 1873-96 by the architect Fritz Schulek in a particularly romantic Hungarian version of the Neo-Gothic. Its history, however, goes a long way back. The original church built here in 1015 was destroyed by the Mongols in 1241. A second church that came into existence in the 1250s served as the parish church of medieval Buda's German community; it underwent expansions in the 15thC under King Matthias Corvinus, who celebrated here both of his marriages (to Catherine Podiebrad and Beatrice of Aragon).

The Turks who captured Buda in 1541 converted the church into a mosque (Büyük Cami, or Great Mosque), using it as a Muslim place of worship until 1686. Next came the Jesuits, who carried out extensive renovations in the Baroque style. Franz Joseph was crowned King of Hungary here (hence its third name, Coronation Church); shortly afterwards the old church was pulled down to make way for an enlarged structure.

The church was the setting of a singular incident in the year 1302. During the political turmoil that followed the death of András III, the last king of the Árpád dynasty, the citizens of Buda gathered here to excommunicate Pope Boniface VIII for preferring Charles Robert of Anjou for the throne of Hungary against King Wenceslas of Bohemia, the favorite candidate of the locals. The protest failed, however, and Charles Robert received the crown of St Stephen in the same church 7 years later.

The main portal of the church is modern, but the **Mary Portal** adjoining the s tower dates from the original 13thC building and is decorated in the interior with parts of 14thC frescoes. The frescoes and mosaics of the interior of the church itself are largely the work of Bertalan Székely, and combine Art Nouveau sensibility with a manner reminiscent of the British pre-Raphaelites. A large equestrian statue of **King Stephen** by Alajos Stróbl (1906) stands between the church and FISHERMEN'S BASTION.

MARKETS   See CENTRAL MARKET.

MILLENNIUM MONUMENT (Milleniumi emlékmű)
(XIV.) Hősök tere. Metro 1 to Hősök tere.

The Millennium Monument, the culmination of ANDRÁSSY AVENUE, was commissioned in 1896 in connection with the 1,000th-anniversary celebrations of the Magyar conquest. The design submitted by György Zala and Albert Schikendanz was modified several times between 1896-1929 and was altered yet again after 1945 to remove all positive references to the Habsburg dynasty. It epitomizes Hungarian history with great expressive economy (see page 198 of A HISTORY OF REVOLUTIONS).

The monument forms a solemn national altar embracing **Heroes' Square** (Hősök tere). Its centerpiece is a 36m (118-foot) pillar, surmounted by Archangel Gabriel holding the crown of St Stephen and rising above the equestrian figures of Árpád and the six legendary Magyar chieftains who accompanied him in the conquest of Hungary. A double colonnade forms a semicircle crowned with allegories of War and Peace at its midpoint, and at either end there are paired figures: Work and Prosperity; Knowledge and Glory. Statues of 14 leading figures in Hungarian history line the colonnade with a bronze relief under each statue illustrating his famous deeds. These read in part:

- István receives the crown from the pope in the year 1000.
- Lászlo I saves a maiden from an attacking Cuman [Cumans, a nomadic Asian people, raided Hungary in the 11thC].
- Kálmán forbids witch-burning.
- András II leads a Crusade to liberate Jerusalem.
- Béla IV rebuilds the country after the Tatar [Mongol] assault.
- Charles Robert mints coins in the Florentine fashion. [The modern Hungarian forint was modeled on Charles Robert's coinage.]
- Lajos I enters Naples in 1348.
- János Hunyadi stops Turkish expansion with his victory at Nándorfehérvár.
- King Mátyás meets his scientists.

- Gábor Bethlen concludes an alliance with the Czechs in 1620. [The Bohemian revolt against the House of Habsburg, which precipitated the Thirty Years' War, was defeated at the Battle of White Mountain in 1620.]
- Bocskay's soldiers fight the emperor's men.
- Imre Tököly's *kuruc* fighters defeat pro-Austrians in 1676.
- Ferenc Rákóczi is greeted by Támás Esze on his return to Hungary. [Rákóczi returned after escaping from Austrian jail in 1703 to start the struggle for independence. Esze was a serf whom Rákóczi ennobled as a reward for his loyalty.]
- Lajos Kossuth calls the Lowlanders to arms.

The last five figures were installed after World War II to replace the original statues of Habsburg rulers Ferdinand I, Karl VI, Maria Theresa, Leopold II and Franz Joseph.

A **Memorial of the Unknown Hungarian Soldier** was added to the monument after 1945. The Lenin Monument, which used to stand on Dózsa György út behind the Exhibition Hall, has been removed. It had been erected to replace the colossal Stalin, whose overthrow by a celebratory crowd had formed one of the stock images of the Uprising of 1956.

A mass ceremony was held at Heroes' Square on June 16, 1989 to honor Imre Nagy and other leaders of 1956 who were given a hero's reburial on that day, the 31st anniversary of their execution. The event was attended by a crowd of 100,000. It was regarded by many as the moment of final psychological victory for the popular opposition that eventually toppled the communist regime.

MUSEUM OF FINE ARTS (Szépművészeti múzeum) ★

(XIV.) Hősök tere. Metro 1 to Hősök tere 🚇 Open daily 10am-6pm ✗ in English daily at 10.30am.

The main repository of non-Hungarian painting in Budapest, the Museum of Fine Arts is one of the leading art collections of Central-Eastern Europe. A large part of the museum's holdings derive from the collections of the Esterházy family, which were acquired by the state in 1871.

Nearly all major painters of the European tradition are represented, though it may be fair to say that — with the notable exception of a half-dozen first-rate El Grecos, and perhaps Lucas Cranach the Elder's extraordinary *Salome* — they contain few masterpieces of unequivocal worth. A further point of regret is the condition of both the museum and its contents. Many of the paintings are in need of restoration, a fact which becomes especially clear by comparison with a recently restored Tiepolo, leaping forth with color amid a row of black-brown canvases.

The museum was designed by Albert Schikendanz and Fülöp Herzog and completed in 1906. The high relief over the architrave of the main portal is a copy of the w pediment of the Zeus Temple at Olympia, and represents the battle of Centaurs and Lapiths. The same architects created the **Exhibition Hall** (Műcsarnok) which stands across Heroes' Square. It houses a program of temporary exhibitions.

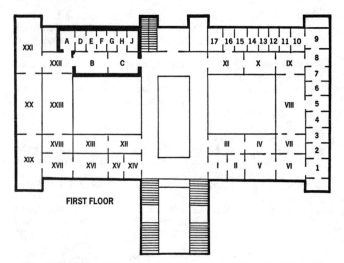

FINE ARTS MUSEUM: KEY   I-VIII and 1-5 Italian Masters   **X-XIII and 6-17** Dutch and Flemish Masters   **XIV-XVII** Spanish Masters   **XVIII-XX** German Masters   **XXI** Austrian Masters   **XXII** English Masters   **XXIII** French Masters   **A-J** 19thC Collection

The **Old Masters Gallery** on the first floor is organized, as at Vienna's Kunstgeschichtliches Museum, according to national schools. Highlights include some particularly fine works by Bellini, Correggio, Brueghel, El Greco, Dürer, Altdorfer, Cranach and Constable, as well as works by Titian, Raphael, Giorgione, Rubens, Rembrandt, Murillo, Velázquez, Goya, Gainsborough and others.

The Austrian collection (**Room XXI** on our plan) is memorable for the unexpected brilliance of the Baroque masters Altomonte, Gran, Troger and Maulbertsch. The 19thC Gallery (**rooms A-J** on our plan), which temporarily hosts some of the 20thC classics as well, holds several excellent pieces by Corot and Delacroix and a wealth of works by each of the main Impressionists.

The lower level of the museum is devoted to several specialized collections, which are currently in the course of major reorganization. Hall 1 houses a small **Egyptian Collection**. Two halls normally devoted, respectively, to **Classical** and **Modern European Sculpture** are now filled with contemporary works recently donated by various American museums, which seem to attract considerably more popular interest than the magnificent **Collection of Prints and Drawings** displayed in Hall 3. The center of gravity of the latter is formed by the odd and extravagant art of the court of Rudolph II (1576-1612), among which the copperplate prints of Adrian de Vries *(Mercury and Psyche; Rape of the Sabine Women)* and Bartholomaeus Spranger stand out with their morbid and convoluted imagery.

NATIONAL MUSEUM (Nemzeti múzeum)

(VIII.) Múzeum körút 14-16. Map 8E5 🔲 *Standard opening hours.*

The National Museum, devoted to the mementoes of Hungary's past, was built in 1837-47 as a symbol and embodiment of the national reawakening. The main promoter of the idea was Count István Széchenyi, the reformer, whose own family collection of historic manuscripts, documents and coats of arms formed the basis of the museum. More than a mere display case, the museum was regarded as a repository of the nation's collective spiritual heritage. It was thus on the steps of the museum that the young poet Sándor Petőfi chose to call the nation to rise against the Habsburg oppressor on March 15, 1848, igniting the revolution that would turn into a national struggle of liberation. His gesture is re-enacted each year on the anniversary of the event.

The chief treasury of the museum since 1978 has been the **Apostolic Crown of St Stephen**, the sacred symbol of Hungarian kingship. The crown, made of gold and surmounted with a cross that stands askew, was

St Stephen's Crown

sent by Pope Sylvester II to Stephen (István) when he was crowned first king of Hungary in AD1000. Its gold-and-enamel circlet was a subsequent gift from a Byzantine emperor, presented at a time when the Eastern Empire competed with the West for the loyalties of the Magyar state.

For 918 years the crown was worn by the rulers of Hungary, including many (but not all) of its Habsburg monarchs. After the destruction of historic Hungary in World War I, it continued to act as a symbol of Hungarian national aspirations, representing Hungary's claims to the surrendered Transylvanian, Slovakian and Croatian lands.

In 1945 it was spirited out of the country by Hungarian Nazis in advance of the Soviet occupation, and eventually came into the possession of the US Army, which transferred it to Fort Knox and refused to yield it for the following 33 years.

It was a goodwill gesture by President Jimmy Carter that at last returned the crown to Hungary in 1978. Since then, the crooked cross of St Stephen has begun to reappear on badges, flags, buttons and broadsheets as the sentimental reminder of a royal — and greater — Hungary.

The remainder of the museum is divided into sections illustrating, respectively, the history of the peoples of Hungary from the Paleolithic to the Magyar conquest, and the history of Hungary from the conquest up to 1849.

The highlight in both sections are two dazzling **Treasury Rooms** devoted respectively to gold objects from the pre- and post-conquest periods. Various charts and maps illustrate such arcane yet interesting subjects as the military organization of Roman Pannonia, the extent of Magyar raids in medieval Europe, and the structure of the Magyar tribal state.

PARLIAMENT (Orságház) ★
(V.) Kossuth Lajos tér. Map 7B3 ✗ by application (☎112.0600 or via travel agencies).

The vast Neo-Gothic mass of the Hungarian Parliament (illustrated on page 204) forms one of the chief features of the Budapest cityscape, occupying a broad and stately frontage along the DANUBE EMBANKMENT. Architect Imre Steindl's masterpiece was inspired by London's Houses of Parliament, reflecting the Anglophile sentiment then prevalent in the country. When completed in 1902, it claimed the distinction of being the largest parliament building in the world.

The Hungarian Diet (Estates) grew from the assemblies of early Magyar chieftains, and acquired a formal charter by the Golden Bull of 1222; it thus rivaled the British Parliament as one of Europe's oldest representative institutions. Pozsony (now Bratislava in Czechoslovakia) was its "temporary" seat from 1526 onward. A resolution was passed in 1843 to transfer the assembly to Pest, but the events of 1848 delayed the move until 1861/67. Parliament played an active political role from 1867 to 1918, had a more marginal position between 1919 and 1944, and was reduced to a rubber-stamp existence from 1948 to 1989.

The building is 268m (879 feet) long, 90m (295 feet) high at the top of the central dome, and contains 691 rooms. There are 88 statues on the exterior and many more inside.

Patrick Leigh Fermor described the building in 1934: "Built at the turn of the century and aswarm with statues, this frantic and marvelous pile was a tall, steep-roofed Gothic nave escorted for a prodigious length by medieval pinnacles touched with gilding and adorned with crockets; and it was crowned, at the point where its transepts intersected, by the kind of ribbed and egg-shaped dome that might more predictably have dominated the roofs of a Renaissance town in Tuscany, except that the dome itself was topped by a sharp and bristling Gothic spire. Architectural dash could scarcely go further."

Vicinity

The main entrance of the Parliament is on **Kossuth Lajos tér**, a broad space dominated by the monuments of Ferenc Rákóczi and Lajos Kossuth, the leaders of Hungary's two failed wars of independence (see pages 198 and 199). A small park to the N holds the statue of Mihályi Károlyi, the architect of Hungary's independence in 1918 (which led to the loss of two-thirds of the country). The statue in the park directly opposite to the S is that of Attila József, the greatest Hungarian poet of the 20thC (he was a communist who, despairing of Stalin's excesses, committed suicide in 1937).

The E side of Kossuth tér is taken up by the stately buildings of the Ministry of Agriculture and the **Ethnographical Museum** (Néprajzi múzeum) *(map 7B3-8B4* 🚾 *standard opening hours)*. The latter deserves a visit to view its magnificent interior, one of the most impressive achievements of Eclectic architecture in Budapest. Its splendor — and the vast mural of *Justitia* decorating the ceiling of the main hall — point to the fact that the building, a work of Alajos Hauszmann (1896), was originally designed to serve as the Supreme Court. Apart from its permanent collections, the museum distinguishes itself with daring and original exhibitions, which in recent years included a provocative documentary of daily life under the People's Republic.

A most elegant apartment building illustrating the Neo-Neo-Baroque style of the 1920s occupies the N side of Kossuth tér. A short distance farther N is the apartment block Balassi Bálint u. 7 *(map 7B3)*, which served as the residence of American diplomats during the days of the old regime; the **Szalai Pastry Shop** here had a legendary reputation as one of the few private confectioners to survive the era of nationalizations.

Farther on at the corner of Margaret Bridge stands the so-called **White House** *(map 7A3)*, which until 1990 housed the Central Committee of the Hungarian Communist Party (now parliamentary offices).

ROYAL PALACE (Várpalota) ★
(I.) Map 7D2-3. See under CASTLE HILL for transportation. All museums 🚾 *with standard opening hours.*

The vast silhouette of the Hungarian Royal Palace, combining Austrian Baroque and the Hungarian nationalist style of the late 19thC, crowns the southern prominence of Buda's Castle Hill, rising powerfully over the Danube panorama. The palace was completed in 1905 for the occasional visits of the monarch, who in fact resided in Vienna, and became redundant when the monarchy disappeared 13 years later. It now houses three museums, the national library, and some offices.

History
The first royal residence on Castle Hill was possibly erected by Béla IV around 1250, although no trace of this structure has been found. A royal castle came into existence in the 14thC under the Angevin kings Charles Robert and Lajos. It was rebuilt and expanded by Matthias Corvinus (1458-90), under whose reign the royal court of Buda became an important cultural and political center of the early Renaissance. The Corvinian Library which was assembled here became in later centuries one of Europe's most important sources of valuable manuscripts.

The palace was the residence of the Turkish pasha during the Ottoman centuries, and was completely destroyed during the capture of the city by Austrian forces in 1686. A small Baroque residence replaced its ruins under Karl VI (1719). This was rebuilt on a wider scale under Maria Theresa (1748), and served as the home of the Palatine, the representative of the dynasty in Hungary. One of its early occupants was Duke Albert of Saxe-Teschen, the founder of Vienna's Albertina.

Plans to build a new palace were launched in accordance with the historic Compromise which restored the Hungarian crown in 1867. The

243

project of Miklós Ybl, carried through by Alajos Hauszmann after his death, adopted the flashy style of Hungarian nationalist architecture for the front section of the palace facing the Danube, while the back incorporated Maria Theresa's Baroque palais and mirrored it in another wing (Wing A) in the same style that Franz Joseph insisted on having.

The Royal Palace was completely burned out during the street battles of 1945. The restoration of some sections was only completed in the 1970s.

Sights and places of interest

A **Statue of Turul**, the legendary eagle who gave birth to the father of Árpád, the leader of the Magyar conquest, spreads its wings over the outer gate. The helmet of a Magyar warrior is said to be the inspiration for the strangely shaped **main cupola** of the palace. The terrace in front of the main entrance, by contrast, carries a **Statue of Prince Eugene of Savoy**, the man whose victories brought Hungary under Habsburg dominion.

National Gallery (Nemzeti galéria)

The central section of the palace (Wings B, C and D) is devoted to the works of Hungarian artists through the ages. The **first floor** of the National Gallery possesses an excellent collection of late-medieval altarpieces and a section of Baroque painters, but its focus is overwhelmingly on Hungarian painting of the 19thC. The dominant theme of this can be expressed as "tragic patriotism."

The styles evolve from the early Romanticism of Károly Kisfaludy and the Neoclassical historicism of Bálint Kiss, through the nationalist fervor of the post-1848 generation (Bertalan Székely, Gyula Benczúr, Mór Than), to the Impressionism of Pál Szinyei Merse. A whole wing is devoted to the solemn and theatrical work of Mihály Munkácsy (1844-1900), the principal Hungarian painter of the late 19thC.

The **second floor** exhibits the works of 20thC painters of the period until 1945. Highlights here include the "pre-Raphaelite" works of the so-called Gödöllő school (such as Aladár Körösfői Kriesch and Sándor Nagy) and the highly personal style of Tivadar Csontváry Kosztka (1853-1919).

The works of contemporary artists of the post-1945 period are displayed on the **third floor**. The **crypt** of the National Gallery contains the tombs of the Habsburg Palatines, which fall rather short of the splendor of their Viennese cousins.

Modern History Museum (Legújabbkori Történeti múzeum)

Wing A of the Royal Palace, which formerly housed the Museum of the Working Class Movement, now hosts various temporary exhibitions pending the discovery of a more permanent role.

Budapest History Museum (Budapesti Történeti múzeum) ★

This interesting and attractive museum occupies the palace of Maria Theresa (Wing E), which replaced the core of the original medieval castle. The main collection documents the history of the city through lucid maps and well-organized exhibits. The more fascinating part, however, is the basement, where large sections of the medieval palace have been brought to light in the course of restoration works carried out since the war.

Some ten underground halls and galleries have been restored to their original condition, and include the vaulted Treasurer's House, where Matthias Corvinus spent some time as a prisoner of King László V prior to supplanting him as king, and the Gothic Hall, which possibly belonged to the queen's apartments. Exhibited here is the prize possession of the museum, a collection of some 50 medieval statues, which are considered among the finest specimens of Gothic sculpture in Europe.

The statues bear the influence of the Burgundian school, and reflect the French lifestyle of the court of Louis of Anjou (1342-82); one commentator describes them as "dandies of the trecento." They appear to have been removed in the course of a general renovation around 1410, and were discovered more or less inadvertently in 1974.

Adjacent to the museum is the **Széchenyi National Library** (Wing F), which owes its foundations to the great reformer, Count István Széchenyi, and contains about 2 million volumes. The secluded medieval gardens and courtyards behind the palace are accessible through the museum *(Mar-Oct only);* a walkway leads through them to the district of Tabán on the s flank of the hill (see under CASTLE HILL).

SZABADSÁG SQUARE (Szabadság tér) ★
(V.) Map 8C4. Metro 2 to Kossuth tér, 3 to Arany János u. Bus 15.

Some of the most opulent architecture of Budapest's turn-of-the-century *belle époque* is concentrated around Szabadság tér (Liberty Square), a broad and elegant space in downtown Pest.

The name of the square carries an oblique reference to the giant army barracks *(Újépület),* a hated symbol of Habsburg domination, which used to stand on this site until 1897. The square, and the park that forms its center, were created in 1902.

The dominant feature of Szabadság Square is the **Hungarian Television Building** (Magyar Televízió-MTV), an early Art Nouveau structure of phenomenal ostentation. Its career began in 1895 as the Budapest Stock Exchange (architect Ignác Alpár), the largest bourse in the world of its time, although its volume of trade hardly qualified as world class. Facing it across the park at Szabadság tér 8-9 is the equally impressive headquarters of the **Hungarian National Bank** (Nemzeti Bank), a work by the same architect from the year 1901.

The **US Embassy** at #12 carries a plaque commemorating the long residence here of József Cardinal Mindszentyi. A prelate of Old Testament vehemence, he was imprisoned by the Stalinist regime of the 1950s. Liberated in 1956, he was compelled to seek refuge in the US Embassy during the Soviet invasion, and was not allowed to leave until 1971. In 1990 his body was transferred from the Vatican to the crypt of the cathedral of Esztergom.

245

The statue in front of the embassy is of US General Harry Bandholtz. As an officer of the Allied peace-keeping force in 1919, Bandholtz is said to have saved the collections of the National Museum from marauding Romanian soldiers by pursuing them with a dogwhip.

Behind the embassy at Hold u. 4 can be seen the headquarters of the **Postal Savings Bank** (Magyar Postatakarék), a work by Ödön Lechner, which is regarded as the one of the finest Art Nouveau buildings of Budapest. Four large apartment blocks dating from the same era, of great elegance of form but various degrees of decrepitude, form the broad northern arc of Szabadság tér. At their center stands a **Soviet Army Memorial**, dating from 1945.

SYNAGOGUE

(VII.) Dohány u. 2-8. Map 8D5. Open to visitors Mon-Fri 10am-1pm. Closed Sat, Sun.
The Great Synagogue of Pest, the largest Jewish temple in Europe, was built in a striking Neo-Oriental style in 1844-59. Its triple naves are capable of accommodating some 3,000 worshipers.

The synagogue was originally surrounded by an enclosed court of residences. Theodor Herzl, the founder of the Zionist movement, was born in the complex (a memorial tablet commemorates him), though his family migrated to Vienna when he was young. A **Holocaust Memorial** installed in 1989 in the back yard of the synagogue marks the mass graves dug during the German occupation of 1944-45.

In 1944 Budapest's Jews were forced into a hastily created ghetto in preparation for mass deportation, which never took place. Many were nevertheless killed in random murders or through starvation. The efforts of the Swedish diplomat Raoul Wallenberg to save the lives of individuals and delay their deportation have been widely documented. A statue of Wallenberg was erected in 1987 on (II.) Szilagyi Erzsébet fasor, near Moszkva tér, and a street in district XIII. bears his name.

The Jewish population of Budapest, which amounted to 5 percent of the total before World War II, has declined to about 10,000, or 0.5 percent.

SZÉCHENYI BATHS (Széchenyi fürdő)   See under BATHS.

VÁCI STREET (Váci utca) ★
(V.) Map 8D4-E5. Metro 2 (to Vörösmarty tér), 1,2,3 (to Deák tér), 3 (to Ferenciek tere).
Váci u. (Vác Street, from the northern town of that name) forms the main axis of **Belváros**, the Inner City of Pest, and is the principal shopping street of Budapest. In the pedestrian-only segment between Vörösmarty tér and Szabadsajtó út, Hungary's market and tourist revolutions can be observed in their most tangible forms.

The street is usually occupied by a colorful lineup of peasants exhibiting their lacework and other folkloric crafts to the floating shoals of tourists. Shops — many now in private hands — overflow with the arts and antiques and sausages of Hungary for sale to plastic-carded visitors. Others, notably the **Adidas Shop** at #24, whose queues of expectant customers became a famous sight of Budapest in their own right in 1990-91, and the **McDonald's** franchise nearby, peddle the exotica of the West to the eager natives. Newspaper stands carry a full range of Western tabloids, whose possession was a matter of criminal offense a few years ago. The youth of Budapest shuffle listlessly between the Vörösmarty Monument and the trendy snack bar of **Hotel Taverna**. The Post-Modern colors and textures of the latter (dating from 1987) compete with the **International Trade Center** across the street in breathing the style of the late 1980s into the staid 19thC grace of Váci u.

Vörösmarty tér *(map 8D4)*, named after the Romantic poet Mihály Vörösmarty (1800-55) whose statue stands at its center, marks the N end of the street. Here are **Café Gerbeaud**, a Budapest institution since 1884, and the **Luxus Department Store**, once the personification of consumer luxury in the people's republic, now eclipsed by the Western brand names sprouting all around it. The large modern building on the w side of the square houses, among others, the head offices of **Hungaroton**, the world's leading producer of inexpensive records.

An outline on the sidewalk at the corner of Váci u. and Türr István u. shows the site of the old Váci kapu (Vác Gate), which was demolished in 1789, at the earliest stage of Pest's growth into a significant city. The lavish **Bank Palace** *(map 8D4)*, which adjoins it (1915) is a work by Ignác Alpár, the architect of the National Bank and the Stock Exchange (see under SZABADSÁG SQUARE). Piarista u. *(map 8E4)* perpetuates the memory of a Piarist school that used to exist at the site of the present Russian bookstore; a statue of St Joseph Calasanta, the founder of the Piarist order, decorates the arch over the street.

The massive building of the **Arts Faculty** of Eötvös Lórand University (1917) is seen next to it on the s. Behind it, at the foot of Elisabeth Bridge, stands the **Inner City Parish Church** (Belvárosi Plébániatemplom) *(map 8E4)*, the oldest building in Pest. The church combines a Baroque (early 18thC) front half with a Gothic (15thC) chancel, and sits over the partly unearthed ruins of the small Roman stronghold of Contra-Aquincum, the oldest ancestor of the city of Pest.

Vicinity

The complex intersection around Ferenciek tere, at the southern end of the pedestrian area of Váci u., contains several impressive buildings. The twin **Klotild Palaces** (1902) *(map 8E4)*, named after a Habsburg archduchess who originally owned them, flank Szabadsajtó út, the extension of Elisabeth Bridge. They now house, respectively, a gambling casino and a retail outlet of the famous Herend porcelain factory.

At Ferenciek tere 5 is the main entrance of the mammoth Neo-Venetian shopping arcade and office complex of **Párisi Udvar** (1911) *(map 8E4)*, with elevator shafts shaped like Gothic chapels and phone-booths imitating small Indian palaces. Facing it at the SE corner of the square is the Baroque **Franciscan Church of Pest** (1743) *(map 8E5)*, carrying a plaque marking the catastrophic flood of 1838.

Török Bank: detail of Art Nouveau mural

Károlyi Mihály u., which branches off here to the s, is sprinkled with the buildings of the Eötvös University, among which the newly renovated Neoclassical edifice of the **University Library**, the dark and vast mass of the Neo-Baroque **University Church** and the imposing **Rectorate** next door stand out.

The Hungarian University was founded by Jesuits in 1635 in Nagyszombat (now Trnava in Slovakia), moved to Buda in 1777 and then to Pest in 1784. Loránd Eötvös (1848-1919), after whom the present institution is named, was a physicist who discovered the torsion pendulum. He was a son of Baron József Eötvös (1813-71), novelist, a leader of the 1848 revolution, and a founder of the modern Hungarian educational system.

Several buildings of interest surround the traffic-choked area at Martinelli tér, one block off Váci u. to the E *(map 8 D4)*. Chief among them is the **Török Bank** building at Martinelli tér 3, whose gable bears a striking Art Nouveau mural depicting Hungaria surrounded by angels and shepherds (illustrated above). The **Servite Church** on the s side of the square hides an attractive Baroque interior (1732) behind a 19thC facade. Városház u., which branches off here, is dominated by the enormous frontage of the **Municipal Hall** (Polgármesteri Hivatal), designed by Antonio Martinelli as a veterans' hospital (early 18thC), and the largest Baroque building in Budapest.

VAJDAHUNYÁD CASTLE   See CITY PARK.

VÖRÖSMARTY SQUARE   See VÁCI STREET.

The Baths of Budapest

The sulfurous mineral waters of Budapest were already known in Roman times, although it was in the Turkish period that public baths became a trademark of the Hungarian capital. There are now more than a dozen of them scattered throughout the Buda (right) side of the river.

Four (Császár, Király, Rác and Rudas Baths) date from the Turkish era. Others represent a full range of architectural styles from the Baroque (exterior of Rác), Classical (Lukács, exterior of Király), Eclectic (Széchenyi) and Art Nouveau (Gellért) to modern (Margitsziget Thermal Hotel) and Post-Modern (Aquincum Thermal Hotel). The temperature of their waters varies from 22˚C to 76˚C (72˚F to 169˚F). The sources are so rich that parts of the city receive hot mineral water on tap.

Two baths in particular, Széchenyi and Gellért, stand out for their extravagant palatial architecture. With the smells of sulfur and must that permeate their interior, and the aura of slow and insidious decay that has been allowed to take them in its grip, they make for some of the most memorable images of a visit to Budapest.

The facilities offered vary from bath to bath, but basic features are shared by all. Visitors are first directed to a cubicle where they deposit their clothes and cover themselves with a meager cloth. Next are one or more indoor hot pools, sometimes supplemented with extra-hot basins, sweating rooms and saunas. Széchenyi and Lukács offer outdoor hot pools where groups of half-submerged and floating men can be seen playing water chess in every sort of weather. Gellért possesses mudbaths in its sub-basement. Massage is available on a fee plus tip basis, and an entire menu of therapeutic services is at the disposal of bathers.

Gellért, the most expensive establishment of all, charges F120 ($1.50) for entry and F100 for a massage. Other baths cost as little as half this price.

GELLÉRT HOTEL/BATHS ★

(XI.) Kelenhegyi út 4 (Buda end of Szabadság Bridge). Map 8F4. Open Mon-Sat 6.30am-8pm; Sun 6.30am-1pm. Closed 4th Wed every month.
One of the most spectacular Art Nouveau buildings in Budapest, built on the very eve of World War I as a kind of swansong for Budapest's *belle époque,* houses both the thermal hotel and the baths (which have a separate public entrance) of Gellért. The cool elegance of the blue mosaic pools contrasts starkly with the peeling plaster of the halls and the decrepit old ladies who attend to the ticket booths.

KIRÁLY BATHS ★

(II.) Fő u. 82-86. Map 7B2. Open Mon-Sat 6.30am-7pm; Sun 6.30am-1pm (Tues, Thurs and Sun for women, rest of the week for men). Closed 1st Thurs every month.
The inner core of these baths survives more or less as the Ottoman Turks built it around 1570, including the typically Turkish dome of the central pool, while the exterior was Europeanized in 1826 with the

addition of an Ionic facade. The name (*király* = "king") comes from a certain König family which owned the establishment in the past century.

LUKÁCS BATHS

(II.) Frankel Leó út 25-27. Off map 7A2. Baths open Mon-Sat 6.30am-8pm; Sun 6.30am-1pm (Mon, Wed, Fri for women, rest of the week for men). Closed 3rd Tues every month. Swimming pool open Mon-Sat 6am-8pm; Sundays to 7pm in summer, 1pm in winter (men and women).

Lukács Baths date in their present form from the 19thC, while the next-door **Császár Baths** are a relic of the Turks. They offer a pleasant environment shaded with ancient plane trees, and a wall covered with votive tablets placed by people who were cured by the medicinal waters.

SZÉCHENYI BATHS ★

(XIV.) Állatkerti körút (in Városliget). Map 5C3. Baths open Mon-Sat 6.30am-8pm; Sun 6.30am-1pm. Outdoor pool open Mon-Sat 6am-7pm; Sundays to 7pm in summer, 4pm in winter.

The main part of the baths consists of a palace of fantastical if decayed luxury, combining 19thC Eclecticism with Art Nouveau details (1909-13). The three outdoor pools are also accessible through the much less impressive N wing, which was added in 1927 in the Neo-Neo-Baroque style popular at that time. The water temperature of the two big pools is 27°C (81°F); that of the small one is 38°C (100°F).

Széchenyi Baths

Where to stay

Anyone who has been a tourist in the countries of the ex-socialist bloc will not need many words to conjure the special atmosphere of State Tourist Authority hotels; anyone who hasn't could probably never understand.

It is not that these hotels are particularly bad: all of them, in fact, manage to stay just above a basic line of acceptability, if only grudgingly. They are never really dirty, although they look so; the personnel is rarely hostile, although they prefer to keep dangerously near the line. There is a slightly menacing air of mystery which one can never really dispel (where did the receptionist vanish? who locked the restaurant at dinner time? why does the waitress sob?), and one always half suspects the whole thing will shut down for good the moment one departs.

To be sure, Budapest's hotels have been the best of the lot (much better than Romania's, for example), and the improvement in the last decade or so has been phenomenal.

The number of available rooms, for one thing, has gotten quite satisfactory, and new hotels are going up at a dizzying pace (a new luxury hotel, the **Aquincum Thermal Hotel**, opened its gates between the writing of this text and its final editing, and another, the **Kempinski**, will have opened shortly after we go to press). Old hotels have been undergoing massive facelifts, updating their fixtures and management, often in partnership with Western hotel chains, and in many cases stripping the ugly accretions of the 1960s and '70s to revert to their prewar appearance.

Privatization is planned for the future. As of this writing, however, three state-owned conglomerates (**Danubius**, **HungarHotels** and **Pannonia**) own almost all hotels of any size in Hungary. Owner-operated private hotels do not yet exist, and private pensions (all 17 of them, with a total capacity of some 250 rooms) are far from meeting the demand.

PRICES
Hotel rates have gone up as fast as the modernization, but they still lag 20 to 50 percent below comparable prices in Vienna. A double room in a comfortable hotel just under the luxury class rarely costs more than F10,000 ($130), including all the usual extras. Pensions charge around F2,000 ($26) for a double room with private bath/shower.

Our price categories follow, as in Vienna, the cost of a **double room** with private shower or bath, inclusive of breakfast and all expenses. Prices used as the basis of comparison were valid for the **winter season** of 1991-92. A surcharge of up to 20 percent should be expected in peak season in most hotels below the luxury class. We use approximately the same price bands as in Vienna, with the result that no hotel in Budapest qualifies in the "very expensive" (over $270) category.

Symbol	Category	Current price	(Dollar amount)
▥	expensive	F12,000-20,000	($160-270)
▱	moderate	F7,000-11,999	($95-160)
▭	inexpensive	F4,000-6,999	($55-95)
▢	cheap	under F4,000	(under $55)

The Hungarian tourist authorities classify hotels with a star system ranging from 5 stars (luxury-class) to 1 star (rock-bottom). Prices follow star count quite closely.

LUXURY HOTELS (5 stars)

A slew of new luxury hotels is expected to open in the 1990s, starting with the afore-mentioned Kempinski, which goes into operation in 1992.

All luxury hotels possess one restaurant or more, a café, a bar, live music/dancing, conference rooms, private garaging, and facilities for handicapped guests. As in this category of hotels in Vienna, the absence of certain symbols does *not* imply any lack of these standard facilities. All of the following offer internationally accepted high standards.

AQUINCUM THERMAL HOTEL

(III.) Árpád Fejedelem u. 94 ☎188.6360
🖷168.8872. Map 5B3. 312 rms ▥ ☀ ✆ ▢
Budapest's newest luxury hotel — as of 1991 — occupies a bold Post-Modern complex on the Danube, next to the old section of Óbuda, a stone's throw from the archeological zone of Aquincum. Under Swiss management in joint venture with the Danubius group, it features natural thermal baths, a Turkish bath and therapeutic services. Non-smokers' rooms. Business services.

ATRIUM HYATT

(V.) Roosevelt tér 2 ☎138.3000
🖷118.8659. Map 8D4. 356 rms ▥ ☀ ✆ ▢
The top attraction of the Hyatt is a 10-story-high inner atrium with hanging gardens and a suspended propeller airplane. Directly on the Danube embankment in the heart of Pest.

DUNA INTER-CONTINENTAL

(V.) Apáczai Csere János u. 4 ☎117.5122

🖷118.4973. Map 8D4. 340 rms ▥ ☀ ✆ ▢
Next to the boat departure point, with all rooms overlooking the Danube and a splendid view of the Royal Palace of Buda.

HILTON

(I.) Hess András tér 1-3 ☎175.1000
🖷156.0285. Map 7C2. 323 rms ▥ ☀ ✆ ▢
A modern building of the 1970s in the center of the historic district of Buda, located between the Matthias church and Fishermen's Bastion, and incorporating the ruins of a medieval church and a Baroque abbey (see page 229). Has its own gambling casino and magnificent open-air auditorium, and some of the best shops in Budapest in the lobby arcade.

THERMAL 🖿

(XIII.) Margitsziget ☎132.1100. Map 5C3.
206 rms ▥ to ▥ ☀ ✆
Massage and medical facilities.
Located in the midst of the splendid old

park of Margaret Island, the Thermal combines the functions of spa, medical sanatorium, public bath and luxury hotel, in a modern building dating from 1979. The **Grand Ramada Hotel** (4 stars) stands next door, with a subterranean connection giving access to the thermal baths.

MEDIUM-TO-BETTER HOTELS (4 or 3 stars)

All of the following have at least one restaurant and a bar/café.

AGRO (formerly **Normafa**) ⌂
(XII.) Normafa u. 54 ☎*175.4011*
🖷*175.6164. 149 rms* ▣ ❧ ≈ ⌖ ⚘
☛ ⚘ ⚐

On Svab Hill with an unparalleled panorama of the Danube and the hills, clean air and a good restaurant. "Central Europe's only swimming with an ozone cleaning system" is their proud claim.

ALBA
(I.) Apor Péter u. 3 ☎*175.9244*
🖷*175.9899. Map 7D3. 95 rms* ▣ ➟
⚐ ▣ ☐

The brand-new Budapest branch of the Austrian hotel chain faces the green flank of the Castle Hill on a calm side street off the embankment of the Danube. All-white interiors create a light, airy, modern ambience.

BÉKE RADISSON
(VI.) Téréz krt. 43 ☎*132.3300*
🖷*153.3380. Map 8B5. 238 rms* ▣ *to*
▣ ⚐ ≈ ☛ ☀ ⚘ ⚐

Originally opened as the Hotel Britannia in 1912, the Béke ("Peace") reopened after extensive modernization in 1985 as one of the top hotels in Budapest. Mosaics and mural paintings by Jenő Haranghy depict scenes from Shakespeare's plays. The café is steeped in history as a headquarters for the rightist officers who dominated political life in the 1920s. In the basement, the *Orpheum* recaptures the spirit of old Budapest music halls.

ERZSÉBET
(V.) Károlyi Mihály u. 11-15 ☎*138.2111*
🖷*118.9237. Map 8E5. 123 rms* ▣ ⚐
A modern, comfortable, family-style hotel in central Pest, rebuilt in 1985 to replace the old Hotel Erzsébet, a landmark building dating from 1872. Named after the beloved queen of Franz Joseph.

FORUM
(V.) Apáczai Csere János u. 12-14
☎*117.8088* 🖷*117.9808. Map 7D3. 400 rms* ▣ ➟ ⚐ ≈ ☛ ☀ ⚘ ▣ ☐ ⚐

Opened in 1981 as the third of the three grand hotels on the Danube embankment of Pest. Slightly less luxurious than the Atrium Hyatt and Duna Inter-Continental, it surpasses them with its careful attention to detail: extra pillows, complimentary shaving razors, altogether charming personnel. Boasts the elegant **Silhouette** restaurant and the CAFÉ WIEN (see page 260).

GELLÉRT
(XI.) Szent Gellért tér 1 ☎*185.2200*
🖷*166.6631. Map 8F4. 235 rms* ▣ ♫ ⚐
⚐ ≈ ☀ ⚘ *Thermal bath, mudbath and medical facilities* ⚐

A magnificent domed hall in elaborate Art Nouveau, built over one of the fanciest of Budapest's baths, with a whiff of sulfur and decay haunting its corridors (see page 249). Each room is individually designed. One of the best restaurants in town.

GRAND HOTEL ROYAL
(VII.) Erzsébet krt. 47-49 ☎*153.3133*
🖷*142.1122. Map 8C6. 366 rms* ▣ *to*
▣ ♫ ⚐ ⚐ ➟ ☀ ⚘ ⚐

Once the grandest of Budapest's grand hotels, modernized in the 1960s and partly restored to its antique pomp more recently (see page 235). The cast-iron statues of the facade were imported from Paris. The main ballroom is converted into a cinema.

KORONA
(V.) Kecskeméti u. 14 ☎*117.4111*

🖼138.4258. Map 8E5. 433 rms ▥ to ▥ ⬤ ♊ ⛟ ☃ ☀ ❤ □ ⛴
A very modern hotel with large, comfortable and airy rooms, and an excellent international restaurant. A huge selection of cable channels is available on TV. In a central location, but triple windowpanes keep out the noise.

NEMZETI (NATIONAL)
(VIII.) József krt. 4 ☎133.9160. Map 8D6. 79 rms ▥ ☃
The National underwent a major facelift in 1991, restoring its magnificent blue and whipped-cream Neo-Baroque facade, bringing its interior up to date and transforming the quality of service from second- to first-world standards. Metro station underneath.

NOVOTEL CENTRUM
(XII.) Alkotás u. 63-67 ☎186.9588 🖼166.5636. Map 7E1. 324 rms ▥ ☘ ⬤ ♊ ⛟ ☃ ☄ ☀ ❤ Bowling □

A comfortable modern high-rise hotel located on the main thoroughfare of Buda. One of the best restaurants in Budapest, with a slight French accent.

PENTA
(I.) Krisztina krt. 41-43 ☎155.6333 🖼155.6964. Map 7D1. 395 rms ▥ ⬤ ♊ ⛟ ☃ ☄ ☀ ❤ □
An efficient modern hotel right next to the South Rail Station.

TAVERNA
(V.) Váci u. 20 ☎138.4999 🖼118.7188. Map 8D4. 224 rms ▥ ⬤ ♊ ⛟ ☃ ☄ ☀ ❤ Bowling □ ⛴
A tastefully modern building in the midst of Váci u., the main pedestrian-only shopping and crowd-watching alley of central Pest. Food for all occasions is available here: a gourmet restaurant, a German wurst-and-beer tavern, a Viennese café and a popular hamburger parlor.

INEXPENSIVE HOTELS (2 stars) and PENSIONS
Some inexpensive but wholly acceptable hotels and about a dozen private pensions ranging in size from 3 to 40 rooms are concentrated along the main connector road (Budaörsi út) leading from the Vienna motorway to the city center.

BARA PANZIÓ
(I.) Hegyalja út 34-36 ☎1853445. Map 7E2. 21 rms □ ⬤
The last pension on the Vienna route before entering the Elisabeth Bridge. A nice, friendly place combining two garden houses via a long underground tunnel. Hearty restaurant.

CINEGE PANZIÓ ⌂
(XI.) Csipke út 4 ☎175.7260. 40 rms □ ⬤ ♒ ⛟
A large pension deep in the suburban villa-district of Szabadság hegy (Buda Hills).

CITADELLA ⌂
(XI.) Gellérthegy, Citadella sétány ☎166.5794. Map 7E3. 15 rms □ ☰ ♊
Located in the grim chambers and case-

ments of the old fortress on the summit of Gellért Hill, this small hotel is attached to a vast and popular restaurant which makes a virtue out of candlelight and Gypsy music.

PANORÁMA (formerly Vöröscsillag) ⌂
(XII.) Rege út 21 ☎175.0522 🖼175.0416. 41 rms ▥ ☄ ☰ ❣ ☃ ⛟ ☀
Located high in the Buda Hills, with an excellent panorama over the city, this makes a good base for nature hikes and cross-country ski tours. There are also bungalows and a camping site and a good choice of restaurants.

WIEN
(XI.) Budaörsi út 88-90 ☎166.5400. Map 5D2. 110 rms ▥ ☰ ❣
This high-rise hotel (the only one in the

area) is directly on the edge of the city near the motorway exit, and not far from the center, either. It's a clean and efficient place full of bus groups and tourists traveling by car from every land in Europe and Asia.

FURNISHED APARTMENTS

The **Rubin Apartment-Hotel** *(at (XI.) Dayka Gábor u. 3* ☎ *166. 6811* [Fx] *166.5193* ⇥ 👪 🍴 *)* can arrange long- and short-term leases, as well as office facilities.

YOUTH HOSTELS

The **Expresz Travel Agency** takes care of all matters concerning youth hostels. It is best to make both advance reservations and same-day bookings through them. There is a 24-hour Expresz office in the East Station *(Keleti pu., map 5 C3)*. Their central office (**Expresz Központi Iroda**) is at (V.) Semmelweis u. 4 ☎117.6634, map 8D5.

Budapest has three year-round youth hostels and many others that operate in summer only. They charge the equivalent of $3 to $10 per night per bed.

Hotel Expresz   (XII.) Beethoven u. 7-9 ☎175.2528. 120 beds. $6.
Hotel Ifjúság   (II.) Zivatar u. 1-3 ☎115.4260. Map 7A2. 400 beds. $10. Good Danube view.

PRIVATE ROOMS

The principal marketplace for private rooms (paying guest service) is the 24-hour **IBUSZ** office at (V.) Petőfi tér 3 ☎118.5776, map 8E4. Various other travel agencies also handle rooms. Typical rates are in the neighborhood of F1,000 ($13) per room excluding breakfast; a 30 percent surcharge is usually added for a stay of less than 4 days.

CAMPING

For camping information apply to the **Hungarian Camping and Caravanning Club** *(at (IX.) Kálvin tér 9,* ☎ *118.5259, map 8E5)*. Camping in the wild is not permitted in Hungary.
Hárshegy   (II.) Hárshegyi út 5-7 ☎115.1482. Open May 1 to October 15. Picturesque site amid much greenery. Bungalows. 3-star category.
Római Fürdő Camping   (III.) Szentendrei út 189 ☎168.6260. Map 5B3. Open May 1 to October 15. The largest camping site in Budapest, with space for 1,300 tents. A short distance beyond the Aquincum archeological zone in Óbuda.
Tündérhegyi (Feeberg) Camping   (XII.) Szilassy út 8. No ☎ Open all year. A small and attractive place with a beautiful location, in a nature reserve in the Buda Hills.

Eating and drinking

The foundations of Hungarian cuisine were mostly determined by the agrarian traditions of "Greater Hungary" (which included present-day Slovakia, part of northern "Yugoslavia" and Transylvania), although there are also pronounced German, Italian and even Turkish influences.

A hundred years ago the famous cooks of Budapest's *belle époque* turned to Hungarian peasant cooking for inspiration. Their major discovery was the *rántás*, a thick sauce of wheat flour fried in pork lard which forms the base of many classic Hungarian dishes, among them the ubiquitous *gulyás*. Another rural import was the liberal use of paprika, the fiery red peppers grown around Szeged and Kalocsa in the southern Great Plains. The predilection for sour cream *(tejföl)* was shared with other nations of Eastern and Central Europe.

Gulyás (pronounced *gouyash,* not "goulash"), which has become synonymous in many a foreign mind with Hungarian food, is a pot-soup made of potatoes and whatever else is at hand (meat, dumplings and vegetables), then thickened with roux and sour cream and flavored with paprika. It is often eaten as a main course, followed by a substantial dessert. *Halászlé* is a fish equivalent.

The thick meat stew that often goes abroad under the name of "goulash" is known here as *pörkölt,* and is specified as *disznó-* (pork), *marha-*(beef), *borjú-*(veal) or *birka-*(mutton) *pörkölt,* depending on the kind of meat used. *Paprikáscsirke* (chicken paprika) is the same thing made with chicken joints, while *rácponty* (Serbian carp) uses fish instead of meat. Boiled potatoes, *nokedli* (gnocchi) and sour cream traditionally accompany all stews.

Other Hungarian specialties include *töltött paprika,* peppers stuffed with minced pork and spices and served with tomato sauce, and *töltött káposzta,* the ultimate pot-meal made of soured cabbage, meatballs, sausages, tomato sauce and sour cream. *Fazék velőcsonttal* (marrow-bone pot) is a delicious if somewhat indelicate dish that involves hunting chunks of marrow out of a piece of broken bone. *Meggyleves,* a sweet soup made of sour cherries, is drunk cold as a refreshing starter. *Gundel palacsinta* (Gundel crêpe) immortalizes a legendary master of Hungarian cuisine in walnut-stuffed and chocolate covered desserts, served flambé in brandy.

Restaurants in Budapest

Budapest possesses some 5,000 eating establishments, ranging from market stalls to jacket-and-tie gourmet restaurants, and including many places of considerable charm and excellent cuisine. The range of selection is rather narrow — few restaurants venture outside the traditional Hungarian kitchen — but what exists is interesting enough to support without tedium many days of eating out.

Many restaurants are state-owned, though the best are already privatized; and large public catering companies still monopolize the supply system. Private entrepreneurs were allowed to lease restaurants from the state from the early 1980s onward, so Budapest already had a livelier and more sophisticated restaurant scene than other cities of the ex-socialist bloc at the time of great change. Things can only improve in the 1990s.

The worst thing about eating out in Budapest is Gypsy music. This is for some reason assumed to please tourists (Hungarians themselves avoid it), so every restaurant where a tourist is likely to wander is infested with bands of strummers playing mercilessly away at *Ochi chornia* and the *Blue Danube*. Tip them, and they'll never leave your table until you are fiddled to death; try to ignore them, and you'll be cut to pieces with the most tragic look of woe and reproach that Snubbed Art did ever muster.

PRICES
The upside is prices. F250 ($3.50) is often enough for a simple lunch at a decent Budapest tavern. F1,000 ($13) will buy a full 3-course dinner with wine and dessert in a good restaurant, and with F1,600 or so ($22) it is possible to have a no-holds-barred feast at **Gundel**, the top restaurant in town. As the Viennese price categories are mostly irrelevant here, we use the following bands to classify Budapest's restaurants:

Symbol	Category	Current price	(Dollar amount)
▥	expensive	over F1,000	(over $13)
▥	moderate	F600-999	($8-13)
▥	inexpensive	under F600	(under $8)

All prices refer to a full dinner for one with wine, dessert and coffee, including tax and tips. Tips, though not mandatory, do in practice bring a smile into waiters' eyes.

RESTAURANTS: HUNGARIAN CUISINE
These restaurants stand out by the quality of their cooking. In atmosphere they range from high-brow to simple and bohemian.

As is often the case, some of the best restaurants in town are those of the great hotels. The restaurant of the **Atrium Hyatt** has a well-earned reputation as a gourmet haven. Its chef, István Lukács, is a nationally renowned cook with countless books on gastronomy and numerous awards to his credit. His gold medal-winning entry at the latest Frankfurt Gastronomy Olympics: larded boar roast with wild berry sauce.

Equally prominent are the restaurants of the **Novotel** (chef Sándor Varga; his recent creation: quail stuffed with almonds and hazelnuts) and the **Gellért**. The roof restaurant of the **Duna Inter-Continental** enjoys a spectacular view over the river. The Hotel **Taverna** offers good fare for every taste (restaurant, cellar tavern, café-confectionery, fast-food parlor) at a very convenient location on Váci Street.

ARANYSZARVAS (Golden Stag)
(I.) Szarvas tér 1 ☎*175.6451. Map 7E3*
🎴 ♪ *Open 5pm-midnight.*
Thus historic tavern/restaurant is the only one to survive in the former fun-and-wine district of Tabán, just below the southern tip of the Royal Castle. Gypsy music in abundance.

BOSZORKÁNYTANYA (Witch's Den)
(III.) Pacsirtamező u. 36 ☎*168.9413. Map 5B3* 🎴 *Open noon to midnight.*
A friendly, informal, youthful place in Óbuda (near the right-bank foot of Árpád Bridge) with a creative menu and excellent kitchen. No tourists — but German is spoken.

GUNDEL
(XIV.) Városliget, Állatkerti út ☎*122.1002. Map 5C3* 🎴 *Open noon-4pm, 7pm-midnight.*
János (Johannes) Gundel, a Bavarian, started the restaurant in 1869 inside the then-new City Park; his son Károly developed the recipes that made it a world-famous embodiment of Hungarian cuisine. Try the Ligeti veal scallops, Gundel sirloin fricassé, pork steak Vajdahunyád, and above all the Gundel *palacsinta*. Cheap socialist-municipal décor contrasts with smooth and classy service. Dress code is enforced. Outdoor garden in summer.

KÉHLI VENDÉGLŐ
(III.) Mókus u. 22 ☎*188.6938* 🎴 ♪
Hard to find in an unlikely corner of Óbuda, but very much worth the try: an unpretentious place with no visible effort at classiness, often filled with noise and cigarette smoke, but a treasured haven of Budapest's connoisseurs of good food and easy atmosphere. Garden, dens and cellars, unobtrusive music. Sample their Sizzling Pot with Marrow-Bone, What Sindbad Ate on

Margaret Island, and Bear Sole Magyar-kút Style.

KISBOJTÁR (Little Shepherd)
(XIII.) Dagály u. 17 ☎*129.5657* 🎴 *Open noon-11pm. Closed Sun.*
An altogether delightful little restaurant specializing in home-style cooking with a rural bent.

KISKAKKUK (Little Cuckoo)
(XIII.) Pozsonyi út 12 ☎*1321732. Map 7A3* 🎴 *Closed Sun evening.*
A small place with a simple, somewhat run-down atmosphere. It has become something of a Budapest attraction with its superb cooking and extraordinarily rich menu: more than 100 main courses with many entirely original items, unusual wild game dishes and even a few Italian specialties. Try their wild duck on apple, or boar ribs in sour cherry sauce. Fast and friendly service. Near the Pest end of Margaret Bridge.

KOSSUTH MUSEUM SHIP
On the Danube in front of the Forum Hotel. Map 7D3 🎴 ♪ *Open noon-midnight. Museum open 10am-6pm.*
A one-time luxury cruise ship, recently converted into a **Danube Shipping Museum** with two successful restaurants (**Erzsébet** and **Lánchíd**) and a cocktail bar.

LÉGRÁDI TESTVÉREK (Légrádi Brothers)
(V.) Magyar u. 23 ☎*118.6804. Map 8E5* 🎴 ♪ *Closed Sat; Sun.*
The ambience: slightly faded old-time luxury, with real silver cutlery, Herend porcelain and antique furniture. The clientele: a mixture of visiting businessmen, the local new rich, and old ladies in 1940s hats. The menu: classic, restrained, and widely recognized as one of the best in Budapest.

NÁNCSI NÉNI (Granny Náncsi)
(II.) Ördögárok út 80 ☎*176.5809* ▯▯ ▱▱
▨▨ ↷ *Open noon-9pm. Closed Sun evening.*
A lovely garden restaurant tucked away
in the woods of Buda Hills, until recently run by Granny Nancsi in person,
a proud relic of the old Swabian/Ger-
man colony of Buda. German cuisine;
huge, hearty menu.

NEW YORK
(VII.) Erzsébet krt. 9-11 ☎*122.3849. Map
8D6* ▮▮ ▱▱ ▨▨ ▱▱ *Café 9am-10pm,
restaurant 11.30am-3pm and
6.30pm-midnight.*
One of Budapest's most venerable
cafés, located in a spectacular turn-of-
the-century building, although the extravagant décor is made absurd by the
cheap imitation-leather bar and regula-
tion-dressed waitresses. The restaurant,
added recently, is a frightful tourist trap
with less-than-excellent food and waitresses who are graceless even by ex-socialist standards. Go for the ambience,
but stick to the café/confectionery. (See·
also page 235.)

PIKKELY HALÁSZCSÁRDA
(I.) Iskola u. 29 ☎*135.6828. Map 7B2* ▯▯
Open daily 10am-10pm.
This small, unpretentious restaurant re-
nowned for its seafood dishes is espec-

ially recommended for its fish soup.
Near Batthyányi tér.

ROBINSON
(XIV.) Városliget, Állatkerti krt ☎*142.3776.
Map 5C3* ▮▮ *Open noon-3pm, 6pm-
midnight.*
A café/restaurant/tea garden situated
on an islet within a pond in the City
Park, with swans floating all over the
place. It rivals GUNDEL in class and
cuisine, though not in tradition. Worth
a try is their Robinson *palacsinta*,
which replaces Gundel's walnuts and
chocolate with fresh fruit salad and vanilla sauce.

SZINDBÁD
(V.) Markó u. 33 ☎*132.2966. Map 8B4*
▮▮ *Open Mon-Fri noon-midnight; Sat-Sun
6pm-midnight.*
A true gourmet restaurant with a small
but excellent menu. Good wine and
some of the best food in Budapest.

VADRÓZSA (Wild Rose)
(II.) Pentelei Molnár u. 12 ☎*135.1118.
Map 5C2* ▮▮ *Closed Mon.*
One of Budapest's trendiest restaurants,
located in a garden villa in suburban
Rózsadomb, is favored by diplomats
and yuppies. Fish and game specialties
are accompanied by piano music.

RESTAURANTS: INTERNATIONAL AND SPECIALIZED
AMERICAN: **Fehér Bölény** (The White Bison) at (V.) Bank u. 5
☎112.2825. Map 8C4 ▮▮ Closed Mon. A dozen kinds of steaks, all
thick and juicy. A stone's throw from the American embassy: the cur-
rent president and Stars and Stripes are on the counter.
CHINESE: **Vörös Sárkány** (Red Dragon) at (VI.) Andrássy út 80
☎131.8757. Map 8B6 ▮▮
  China Palace at (VIII.) Üllői út 6 ☎114.1094. Map 8E5 ▮▮
FRENCH: **Le Jardin de Paris** at (I.) Fő u. 20 ☎201.0047. Map 7C3
▮▮ Quaint Biedermeier building painted in Maria-Theresa yellow. Live
jazz every evening from 8pm.
GREEK: **Görög Taverna** at (VII.) Csengery u. 24 ☎141.0772. Map
8C6 ▯▯
ITALIAN: **Marco Polo** at (V.) Vigadó tér 3 ☎138.3925. Map 8D4
▮▮ A very classy modern establishment owned by an Italian entrepre-
neur, reputed to import his meat daily from Italy.
RUSSIAN: **Bajkál** at (V.) Semmelweis u. 1-3 ☎117.6839. Map 8D5
▮▮ A charming place with folk-art displays and excellent food.

TRANSYLVANIAN: **Csendes** at (V.) Múzeum krt. 13 ☎117.3704.
Map **8E5** ▯
VIENNESE: **Bécsi Liesinger Söröző** at (V.) Eötvös Loránd u. 8
☎117.4504. Map **8E5**. A beer cellar serving huge portions of excellent
Viennese fare, much frequented by members of the university community.
VEGETARIAN: **Vegetárium Étterem** at (V.) Cukor u. 3 ☎138.
3710. Map **8E4** ▥ Open noon-10pm. The only one in Budapest, a welcome break from the calorie-rich meats and starches of the Hungarian
kitchen.

FAST FOOD

As of 1992 there is a **McDonald's** near the West Station *(Nyugati pu.,
map 8B5)* and another on Váci u. *(map 8D4)*, a **Burger King** in the
Oktogon *(map 8C5)*, and a **PizzaHut** at the corner of Király u. and the
Great Boulevard *(map 8C5)*. No doubt there will be more by the time
we go to press.

The local version of a fast-food parlor is called a *kifőzde* or *étkezde:*
a tiny kitchen-shop with shared tables, serving whatever the cook feels
like making for the day — often such things as tripe or tongue.

Cafés and confectioners

Budapest shares the coffeehouse culture of Vienna in full. More than a
place to have coffee and cake, the café is a social club and a public
institution. Every self-respecting café has its regular customers and
semi-resident intellectuals, and older ones boast of legendary times
when their tables served as the birthplace of literary movements, artistic feuds and political conspiracies. A collection of newspapers and
periodicals is sometimes at hand, and patrons can stay as long as they
wish once they have ordered a cup of coffee.

The decoration of some of the better-established cafés matches the
best of Vienna in elegance and splendor. At F100 for a large cappuccino
and the best cake, they represent about the most inexpensive whiff of
luxury one could expect to encounter in Europe.

ANGELIKA
(I.) Batthyányi tér 7. Map 7B2.
An old-fashioned café in a relatively
quiet corner of Buda, which was recently refurbished with no great improvement.

CAFÉ WIEN
*(V.) Apáczai Csere János u. 12-14. Map
7D3.*
The most successful — and most popu-

lar — of the many hotel cafés is located
in the hotel FORUM.

GERBEAUD
*(V.) Vörösmarty tér 7. Map 8D4. Closed Sat
afternoon, Sun.*
Budapest's best place to see and to be
seen since it was taken over by Emil
Gerbeaud, a Genevan, in 1884. The
decoration is sumptuous — but some
habits die hard: the telephones never

work, and the regulation state-employee waitresses will only let their attention stray after 20 minutes of wild hand-waving. Heavenly pastry, however, is worth the calisthenics: try their *dobos torte* and *diplomata puding*.

LUKÁCS
(VI.) Andrássy útja 70. Map 8B5.
Magnificent fixtures, good confectionery — a Budapest classic.

MINIATŰR PRESZÓ
(II.) Rózsahegy u. 1. Map 7A2. Closed Sun.
An old-fashioned, stately place in Buda with some of the best waiters in town.

MŰVÉSZ ("Artist")
(VI.) Andrássy útja 29. Map 8C5.
A small, intimate, rich café boasting one of the most opulent interiors in Budapest.

NEW YORK
(VII.) Erzsébet krt. 9-11. Map 8D6.
One of the most tradition-rich cafés of Budapest recently regained its original name after several decades under the name of Hungaria. See also pages 235 and 259.

RUSZWURM
(I.) Szentháromság tér 7. Map 7C2.
Founded in 1827 and in continuous operation ever since in its perfect little Biedermeier house. A favorite of tourists. Maybe they enjoy the Bolshie waitresses.

Drinking

A bar/pub/bistro specializing in wine is called *borozó* and one whose point of gravity is beer is called *söröző*. The former, modeled largely on the Viennese *heurige,* is far the more popular.

The best-known Hungarian wine is the **tokaji**, a dry white which comes from only 28 villages in the Tokaj district of NE Hungary. The *Tokaji aszú*, a sweet dessert wine made from grapes left to rot on the vine, is the noblest of the lot and can be obtained in delicatessen. Its cousins include the *Szamorodni*, the *Hárslevelű* and the *Furmint*, these two latter being dry whites if drunk on their own.

Westerners commonly suppose that the most popular red is the *Egri bikavér*, a wine of extremely full body, as implied by its name ("bull's blood of Eger"). This popularity is in fact the product of shrewd marketing allied to general Western ignorance of Hungarian wines. More interesting are the *Villány* wines.

Beer drinking has a lesser tradition in Hungary, though its arrival in the country as a serious alternative to wine dates back to the 19thC. The Kőbányai brewery is the biggest in Hungary, selling brands such as *Világos* (the cheapest), *Korona* and *Jubileum* (the best).

Pálinka, a murderous spirit distilled from apricots *(barackpálinka),* cherries *(cseresznyepálinka)* or other fruits, is the national liquor.

ARANYSZARVAS PINCE
(I.) Szarvas tér 2. Map 7E3.
Historic "heurige" beside the restaurant of the same name (see page 258) in Tabán, the hillside below the Royal Castle.

BALLANTINES CLUB
(VI.) Andrássy útja 19. Map 8C5. Open Mon-Fri from 9am, Sat-Sun from 6pm.
Exclusive place with wide selection of whiskeys. After 9pm, it's open for members only, including prominent figures

of the local Anglo-American community.

BROADWAY DRINK BAR
(VI.) Nagymező u. 49. Map 8B4. Open Mon-Fri 9am-1am; Sat-Sun from 4pm.
One of the first modern cocktail bars in Budapest, opened by two young entrepreneurs.

FREGATT SÖRÖZŐ
(V.) Molnár u. 26. Map 8E4.
The only successful "British" pub in Budapest — and quite possibly in all Eastern Europe. Pub food and occasional live jazz.

GÖSSER SÖRPATIKA
Off Váci u. (V.) Régiposta u. 4. Map 8D4.
A popular place. Gösser is the Austrian brand of beer that is served, and the name means "beer pharmacy."

GRINZINGI
(V.) Veres Pálné u. 10. Map 8E4.
Jolly atmosphere, with hard-boiled eggs and sandwiches to accompany good wine. Centrally located but not touristy.

HALÁSZBÁSTYA (Fishermen's Bastion)
(I.) Halászbástya ☎ 156.1446. Map 7C2.
The elegant bar of the HILTON hotel, with live music and dancing.

OTARD DRINK BAR
(V.) Kristóf tér 3. Map 8D4.
"Possibly the most expensive place in town," as they disarmingly claim. French brandies.

TOKAJI BOROZÓ
(VI) Andrássy útja 20. Map 8C5.
Full selection of Tokay wines, next to the Opera.

The arts

The bilingual monthly called *Programme in Ungarn/in Hungary* is distributed in hotel lobbies. The *Daily News* and the Entertainment Guide of the *Budapest Week* are also good sources of information about cultural activities, music and film. Tickets to most events can be obtained through **IBUSZ** or private travel agencies, or through one of the many ticket agencies that exist in downtown Pest.

ART GALLERIES

Képcsarnok, the cooperative association of Hungarian artists, dominates the exhibition and marketing of art in the country, with a good dollop of kitsch thrown in. They have five galleries in Budapest and a particularly important one in nearby Szentendre.

Csók István   (V.) Váci u. 25 ☎118.2592. Map **8D4**.
Csontváry   (V.) Vörösmarty tér 1 ☎118.4594. Map **8D4**.
Derkovits   (VII.) Téréz körút 9 ☎142.0754. Map **8B5**.
Medyánszky   (V.) Károlyi körút 26 ☎117.5983. Map **8D5**.
Pór Bertalan   (VIII.) József körút 70 ☎114.0225. Map **8E6**.

The **Szentendre Art Gallery** *(Szentendre, Fő tér 20 ☎(26) 10139, closed Mon)* exhibits work by some 60 painters from the artists' colony in Szentendre.

Other galleries include:

Knoll   (VI.) Liszt Ferenc tér 10. Map **8C5**. The most modern and professional of Budapest's galleries, owned by a Vienna gallery of the same name. Expert information on the Hungarian and East European art market.

Műgyűjtők Galériája   (V.) Kossuth Lajos u. 12 ☎117.6579. Map **8D5**. Closed Saturday and Sunday. Auctions and direct sales of traditional Hungarian art.

Na-Ne Gallery   (IX.) Lónyáy u. 41. Map **8F5**. A closed group of avant-garde designers.

CINEMA

Many foreign films are shown in the original version with Hungarian subtitles. A full listing of foreign-language movies with commentary, times and addresses is given in the *Budapest Week*.

CLASSICAL MUSIC AND OPERA

Opera performances by the National Opera Company take place at the **Operaház** *(at (VI.) Andrássy útja. 22 ☎115.3017, map 8 C5; see page*

225), as well as the smaller **Erkel színház** *(at (VIII.) Köztársaság tér 30* ☎ *133.0540, off map 8 D6)*.

The **Budapest Chamber Opera**, the latest addition to Budapest's musical life, came into existence in 1991 with an impressive roster of supporters, which includes Otto von Habsburg, Elisabeth Schwarzkopf and Dietrich Fischer-Dieskau. Its repertory focuses on authentic performances of pre-classical pieces, which are staged at the **Arany János színház** *(at (VI.) Paulay Ede u. 35* ☎ *141.5626, map 8 C5)*.

Budapest's lively operetta tradition lives on at the historic **Vigadó**, which is also called the Redoute, or Municipal Concert Hall *(at (V.) Vigadó tér 2* ☎ *118.9903, map 8 D4)*, and the **Fővárosi Operettszínház** *(at (VI.) Nagymező u. 17* ☎ *112.6470, map 8 C5)*.

The main venue for orchestral concerts is the **Zeneakadémia** or Academy of Music *(at (VI.) Liszt Ferenc tér 8* ☎ *142.0179, map 8 C5)*.

The **Vigadó** also offers a program called "the Budapest Experience," involving operetta excerpts, folklore and dance *(at (V.) Vigadó tér 2* ☎ *118.9903, map 8 D4)*. Reservations through **Vigadó-Profil GMK** *(at (V.) Vörösmarty tér 1* ☎ *117.6222, map 8 D4)*.

FESTIVALS AND FESTIVITIES

The main event of the year is the **Budapest Spring Festival**, held over ten days in March, with a lesser counterpart in the **Budapest Art Weeks** of September and October. However, neither offers that much to get excited about.

Concerts and various performances are staged in July in outdoor theaters on Margaret Island, the Dominican Courtyard of the Hilton and elsewhere in town.

By far the most exciting traditional celebration is held — with a huge religious procession, and fireworks display — on **Corpus Christi**, which falls on a Thursday in late May or early June. Fireworks go off also on August 20 (officially Constitution Day, in reality the feast of St Stephen, the founding father of the Hungarian kingdom) and December 31.

FOLKLORE

The movement to revive and perpetuate the traditional music and dances of the Hungarian countryside remains extremely popular with the urban youth of Budapest. There are folk-dancing performances every Tuesday and Wednesday from 6 to 10pm in the **Municipal Cultural Center** *(Fővárosi Művelődési ház, XI. Fehérvári u. 47* ☎ *181. 1360)* and every Saturday starting at 7pm in the **MOM Cultural Center** *(XII. Csörsz u. 18* ☎ *156.8451, map 7 E1)*.

The first part of each performance is devoted to teaching the intricate steps of various Hungarian folk dances.

LASER THEATER

A highly popular show of fantastic laser and music effects is staged in the cupola of the **Planetarium** in People's Park *(at (X.) Népliget, map 5 D3)*. The hour-long performances begin at 6.30 and 8pm on Monday, Thursday, Friday and Saturday.

ROCK, JAZZ

Rock arrived in Hungary in the mid-1960s and quickly established itself as the cultural expression of a younger generation dissatisfied with the banalities of the old regime. Of the three legendary groups of that era, one — Omega — still exists today, and can periodically be heard in the context of the musical productions of the **Vígszínház** *(at (XIII.) Szent István krt. 14, map 8 A4)*.

Heavy metal was the wave of the 1970s, punk that of the early '80s. Great open-air rock concerts turned the slopes of Castle Hill into a showcase of Budapest's youth culture from 1982-85; they were banned after 1985, but found a new venue in the Metropolitan Youth Center (Petőfi Csarnok), which opened in the City Park in the same year.

Petőfi Csarnok *(at (XIV.) Zichy Mihály u. 19 in Városliget, map 5 C3)* remains the most important outlet for Budapest's rock music scene, with several groups giving live performances daily (10am to 10pm). Those with the largest following include Omen, Bonanza Banzai, R-Go, Korál, Éva-Neoton and Első Emelet. The Hobo Blues Band has grown into a star phenomenon with its proclaimed mission to introduce the rhythm-and-blues of the 1950s into Hungary. An extremely popular disco night is organized at Petőfi Csarnok every Saturday.

Expo 25, named after Pavilion 25 in the Budapest Expo, features the most popular DJs in Budapest through the week, with live groups on Saturday night. The dance floor at (X.) Albertirsai köz, Hungexpo Fair Site, entry II, accommodates 1,000 couples.

KEK, the student club of the Agricultural University, is another lively center of Budapest's younger generation. Rock groups and disco are featured every Saturday evening, while jazz performers play from 8pm on Wednesdays *(at (XI.) Villányi u. 35)*.

The **Benkó Dixieland Band** has been a household name in the Hungarian jazz world for more than 20 years. Their humble club *(at (IX.) Török Pál u. 3, map 8 E5)* is crammed to capacity every Wednesday from 6pm, although, sadly, music has to stop at 9.30pm sharp.

Much newer is the **Merlin Jazz Club** *(at (V.) Gerlóczy u. 4 ☎ 117.9338, map 8 D4)*, which features some of the best Hungarian groups. Two sets are performed nightly at 10pm and midnight, and groups change every third night. A light dinner is served.

International and Hungarian rock opera hits are performed at the beginning and end of each month at the **Thalia Theater** *(at (VI.) Nagymező u. 22, map 8 C5)*.

THEATER

The **International Merlin Theater** opened in 1991 as part of an arts complex which also includes a jazz club (see above), restaurant, drama school and exhibition gallery, declaring war on "the idea that the mysterious Hungarian soul cannot be understood by foreigners." It stages plays by classical and contemporary Hungarian writers in English translation. Tickets are available at the box office *(at (V.) Gerlóczy u. 4 ☎ 117.9338, map 8 D4)* or through American Express *(at (V.) Gerlóczy u. 4 ☎ 117.9338, map 8 D4)*.

Entertainment and nightlife

It is customary to debunk Budapest nightlife as "provincial" and "nothing to write home about," but word has begun to go around that it may be livelier, at least, than stolid Vienna. The rock and jazz scene is decidedly more exciting than the other city on the Danube, the variety shows less subject to Catholic inhibitions, the gambling dens more numerous, and all those Romanian girls who could never get a visa to Austria take care of the rest.

DISCOS
See the previous chapter under ROCK AND JAZZ for additional opportunities to go disco dancing. Other popular places include the following.

LEVI'S 501
(VI.) Nagymezö u. 41 ☎ *132.3857. Map 8C5.*
Elegant disco-bar upholstered in blue denim.

MARGITHÍD
(V.) Szent István krt. ☎ *.112.4215. Map 7A3.*
One of the biggest discos, open daily to 4am.

MEDITERRANEAN CLUB DISCO
(I.) Alkotás u. 63-67 ☎ *166.8007. Map 7E1.*

In the Bowling Beerhall of the Novotel. Expensive and classy. Open Thursdays only.

ROCK CAFÉ
(VII.) Dohány u. 18. Map 8D5.
A cramped cellar lined in giraffe skin, with a motorcycle coming out of the front wall. English DJs, live bands.

VÉN DIÁK
(V.) Egyetém tér 5 ☎ *119.4603. Map 8E5.*
Popular and crowded place favored by students of the Eötvös University.

NIGHTCLUBS AND VARIETY SHOWS8
Many beer halls *(söröző)* offer some form of live music, usually jazz, to enhance the general jolliness. A dozen houses specialize in old-fashioned floor shows with go-go girls, striptease, crooners, comedians and all. A selection of the best:

ASTORIA
(V.) Kossuth Lajos u. 19 ☎ *118.6351. Map 8D5.*
Bold erotic show somewhat at odds with the old-fashioned ambience of the

hotel Astoria. Closed Monday.

BÉKE ORPHEUM
(VI.) Téréz krt. 97 ☎ *132.3300. Map 8B5.*

A smart night spot in the BÉKE RADISSON hotel. Dinner is served after 9pm, with a floor show after 10.45pm. Closed Sunday.

CASANOVA PIANO BAR
(I.) Batthyányi tér 4 ☎*135.8320. Map 7B2.*
Casanova himself is said to have stayed here when the place was an inn.

FORTUNA
(I.) Hess András tér 4 ☎*175.6857. Map 7C2.*
In a historic cellar with Gothic vaults.

Jazz, a dance floor and a midnight revue.

MAXIM VARIETÉ
(VII.) Akácfa u. 3 ☎*122.7858. Map 8D6.*
International shows at 8pm and 11pm, in the Hotel Emke. Closed Sun.

MOULIN ROUGE
(VI.) Nagymező u. 17 ☎*112.4492. Map 8C5.*
Revues that hark back to an earlier, more glamorous era, in a ridiculously ornate turn-of-the-century theater. The show starts at 9pm.

SIN
The bars of international hotels are the traditional haunts of Budapest's *belles de nuit,* who are said to be under intense competition lately from visiting Romanian colleagues. Those who cannot afford hard-currency prices patronize the sleazier establishments around (VIII.) Rákóczi tér *(map 8 D6-E6).*

GAMBLING
Casinos Hungaria, a subsidiary of Casinos Austria, was launched in 1981 with the casino in the Buda Hilton. It now operates two other gambling casinos in town (the **Gresham Palace** and the **Schönbrunn Casino Boat**) and several others around the country. Rivals have arrived on the scene more recently.

HILTON
(I.) Hess András tér 1-3 ☎*175-1001. Map 7C2. Open 5pm-2am.*
French and American roulette, blackjack, machines. Maximum stake: DM5,000.

IMPERIAL CASINO
(V.) Szabadsajtó út 5 ☎*118.2374. Map 8E4* ⚌ *Open noon-5am.*
Retaining the glamorous Art Nouveau décor of the former Belvárosi Café, this is a long-established Budapest institution. French and American roulette, blackjack, poker, red dog. Maximum stake: DM1,000.

Shopping

Handicrafts are taken seriously in Hungary, and include many items of genuine beauty made with care. Herend porcelains are highly valued by many buyers. And one does occasionally come across antiques of good value.

Apart from these, the main selling point when it comes to Hungarian products is their low cost. Prices of foodstuffs, clothing and most other items are between a third and two-thirds lower than those in the West, prompting hordes of Austrians to descend on Budapest each weekend to do their routine shopping. Very often, however, the quality gap is as great if not greater than that in price, and one does often hear the woeful tales of would-be bargain hunters who end up with wads of unspent forints in their pockets.

Standard working hours for most shops are 9.30 or 10am to 6pm on weekdays, and 9 or 9.30am to 1pm on Saturday. Many shops stay open on Thursday until 8pm. Sunday closing laws are relatively relaxed.

Hard-currency shops, where the happy few could once buy the wonders of the West for valuable marks and dollars, have become history as of the end of 1991.

ANTIQUES

A state monopoly called BÁV is the sole distributor of all antiques sold through state shops. Their largest outlet is the **Antiquaries' Central Store** *(at (V.) Múzeum körút 15 ☎ 117.3514, map 8 E5)*. The antiques store at (V.) Szent István krt. 3 *(map 7 E3)* often carries a particularly good selection of period furnishings and paintings. The **Konsumturist** shop at Andrássy útja 29 *(opposite the Opera, map 8 C5, closed Sat)* specializes in engravings, sculptures, small items of furniture and coins.

The smaller antique stores sprinkled through the Castle district and around Petőfi Sandor u. and Király u. deserve browsing through, though the chances of discovering something of unusual value is rather slender.

Budapest's **flea market** is held daily except Sunday *(Mon-Fri 8am-4pm, Sat 8am-3pm)* in the Ecseri bazaar which lies along (XX.) Nagy-körösi út *(map 6 D4; bus 54 from Boráros tér)*.

BOOKS AND MAPS

The **Könyvesbolt** (Bookshop) at Váci u. 32 *(map 8 D4)* has the largest selection of books that might be of interest to a foreign reader, in Magyar as well as other languages. The **Antikvárium** shops at Váci u. 28 and 75 *(map 8 D4 and 8 E4)*, Múzeum krt. 15 *(map 8 E5)* and Károlyi

Mihály u. 3 *(map 8E5)* sell second-hand and antique books, mostly in Magyar but also in German and other languages.

Cartographia, one of Europe's largest publishers and packagers of maps, has its retail shop at (VI.) Bajcsy-Zsilinszky út 37 *(map 8C4)*. It offers a wide selection of maps, including many unusual ones rarely found in the West.

DEPARTMENT STORES
Department stores are a good bet for seekers of bargains in clothing, shoes, gifts and home accessories. **Skála Metró**, the first large semi-private company that was launched in the 1980s, offers the widest choice, while the state-owned **Luxus** has successfully renewed itself and remains the classiest. A half-dozen department stores are ranged along Rákóczi út between the inner Ring and the Great Boulevard.

Corvin   (VIII.) Blaha Lujza tér 1-2 ☎133.4160. Map 8D6.

Csillag   (VII.) Rákóczi út 20-22. Map 8D5.

Fontana   (V.) Váci u. 16 ☎138.2013. Map 8D4.

Luxus   (V.) Vörösmarty tér 3 ☎118.2277. Map 8D4.

Skála Metró   (VI.) Marx tér. Map 8B4.

Sugár Shopping Center   (XIV.) Örs vezér tér.

FOOD
Supermarkets and grocers generally open at 6 or 7am and stay open until 7 or 8pm on weekdays. "Non-stop" (i.e., 24-hour) food shops, an increasingly popular phenomenon, include the **Metro Center** supermarket at (VII.) Dohány u. 22 *(map 8D5)*, **Montazs** at (V.) Október 6 u. 5 *(map 8C4)* and **Nonstop bolt** at (V.) Irányi u. 5 *(map 8E4)*. The **Mozaik** shop at (V.) Múzeum krt. 27 *(map 8E5)* carries a good selection of Hungarian wines and stays open 24 hours Tuesday to Saturday (closed all day on Sunday and Monday).

The best selection of local and imported foods is found at **Skála Csarnok**, a beautifully restored old market hall at Klauzál tér *(map 8C5)*.

HANDICRAFTS
Hungarian folk art is mass-produced by craftsmen working all across the country on "authentic" patterns supplied by a national company, which markets the product through a network of folk art shops in Budapest and elsewhere. The colorful peasants who tout their wares oh-so-sweetly along Váci u. are employees of the same state company. Kalocsa embroidery is the most popular item with tourists, followed by lacework, earthenware, leather goods and wood carvings.

The main folk art and home-craft shop is called **Népművészeti és Háziipari Szövetkezet** and is located at Váci u. 14 *(☎118.5840, map 8D4)*.

A handicrafts market is held at **Petőfi Csarnok** *(in Városliget, map 5C3)* every Saturday and Sunday morning. A livelier one shapes up in the town of **Szentendre** (see EXCURSIONS) on summer weekends. Bargaining is essential, and the crucial trick is to avoid being taken for a German — they are invariably overcharged.

MUSIC

Hungary has long been a worldwide supplier of reasonable-quality records (LPs, CDs and tapes) at discount prices. The **Hungaroton** shop at Vörösmarty tér 1 *(map 8 D4)* has the largest selection of records in town, covering classical, rock, jazz and folklore.

The **Amadeus CD-shop**, which opened up in 1991 around the block at (V.) Szende Pál u. 1 *(map 8 D4)*, carries a full range of imported and Hungarian CDs with a classical bias. A good choice of original Hungarian rock and jazz can also be found in the **Hungaroton** shop at (V.) Martinelli tér 2 *(map 8 D4)*.

PHILATELY

The best philatelist in town is located at (VI.) Oktogon 3 *(entrance at Andrássy útja 51, map 8 C5, closed Sat)*.

PORCELAIN

The main retail outlet of the famous **Herend** porcelain factory is located at (V.) Kigyó u. 4 *(☎ 118.3712, map 8 E4)*. The small antique and craft stores of the Castle district are often a good source of rare, unusual and discontinued pieces valued by collectors.

Fimcoop studióbolt at (V.) Apáczai Csere János u. 7 *(☎ 118. 3912, map 8 D4)* is the retail outlet for several of Hungary's lesser-known porcelain factories.

Recreation

Ideas for children

- CITY PARK (Városliget) accommodates an excellent **zoo**, a rather unsophisticated **amusement park**, a permanently resident **circus**, a **boating lake** in summer that becomes a **skating rink** in winter, a fairy-tale **castle**, an **agricultural museum** full of stuffed farm animals and the like, and a **museum of transport** *(all map 5 C3)*.

- Another interesting museum of transport is the **Metro Museum** at Deák tér station *(map* **8**D4*)*.

- Children love climbing to high places, particularly by exotic methods of transportation. The ascent to CASTLE HILL by cable car, and the fine panorama from the **Fishermen's Bastion**, can be combined to make an exciting day's outing. While there, braver youngsters will enjoy the somewhat gruesome historical waxworks set up in the underground catacombs *(entrance at Úri u. 9)*.

- Other high places with sweeping views include GELLÉRT HILL, with its powerful citadel, and the BUDA HILLS (see below).

- More expensive rides that will certainly appeal to children include a boat trip along the Danube, or, in Buda, a ride in a horse-drawn cab *(fiacre)*.

- The **Pálvölgyi Dripstone Cave** *(at (III.) Pálvölgyi köz)* is an impressive sight for children and adults alike.

- A day trip to the BUDA HILLS offers a pleasant interlude from the city. The **Cogwheel Railway** climbs to one summit with splendid views, and from there another can be reached via the **Pioneer Railway**, which is operated by children. Within the hills there is also a game reserve with a 5km (3-mile) **nature trail**.

- Puppets transcend language barriers. The national **puppet theater** (Állami Bábszínház) performs regularly at (VI.) Andrássy útja 69 *(map 8 B6)*. Call ☎142.2702 for information.

- The spectacular hour-long **laser show**, performed several times each week at the Planetarium in People's Park *(at (X.) Népliget, map* **5**D3*)*, will delight technologically-minded children.

Sport and leisure

BILLIARDS
Billiárd Fél 10   (VIII.) Mária u. 48. Map **8E6**.
Billiárd Salon   (XII.) Krisztina körút 15. Map **7C1**.

BOWLING
Bowling   (V.) Szende Pál u. 1. Map **8D4**.
Teke Csárda   (VIII.) Bezerédy u. 7.

CYCLING
The leaflet *Cycling in Hungary* contains valuable information about regulations, routes and Customs formalities. Cyclists are barred from the Chain Bridge, the Castle Hill tunnel, motorways (freeways) and the connector road to the airport. A **rent-a-bike** shop exists at (I.) Hunyadi János út 4 *(☎ 116.8835, map 7C2)*.

FISHING
Apply to the **Hungarian Anglers' Association** (Magyarországos Horgász Szövetség) at (V.) Október 6 u. 20 *(☎ 132.5315, map 8C4)*.

RIDING
Pegazus Tours specialize in equestrian tourism *(at (V.) Károlyi Mihályi u. 5 ☎ 117.1644, map 8E5)*. Horseback-riding facilities *(Lovarda)* are available at (VIII.) Kerepesi u. 7 and (II.) Ady-liget, Petneházy rét *(bus #63 from Hűvösvölgy)*.

SWIMMING
* **Csillaghegyi Strand** at (III.) Pusztakúti út 3 *(map 5 B3)*. Open and covered pools, sauna, modest hotel. Part of the hillside is devoted to nudists. HÉV suburban rail to Csillaghegyi stop.
* **Palatinus Strand** on Margaret Island *(map 5 C3)*. Accommodates up to 10,000 people at a time. Seven pools, artificial waves, water chute, children's play area. A 15-minute walk from Margit híd, or take Bus 26 from Marx tér.
* **Római Fürdő** at (III.) Rozgonyi Piroska u. 2 *(map 5 B3)*. Established in Roman times: fragments of ancient ruins recall their erstwhile presence. HÉV suburban rail to Római Fürdő stop.

Information about nudist beaches can be obtained through the **Naturists' Federation** (Naturisták Szövetsége) (XIII.) Kárpát u. 8.

TENNIS
There are public tennis courts at (I.) Tabán/Krisztina körút *(map 7E3: in the park)*, (I.) Tigris u. 65 *(map 7E2)* and (II.) Szamos u. 2.

WATER SPORTS
Canoes, kayaks and camping equipment can be rented from **Ezermester** in (III.) Hajógyárisziget and **Sports Facilities Company** at Frankel Leó út 35 *(☎ 115.0639, off map 7A2)*.

Excursions from Budapest

Nearly all points in Hungary lie within a 3-hour drive of Budapest, so you can cover the whole country in a series of excursions from the capital. Four Hungarian cities stand out for their historic character and wealth of sights: **Eger** with its great castle and picturesque streets, **Debrecen** with the memorials of its Protestant past, **Pécs** with its pleasant mixture of Turkish and Baroque monuments, and **Veszprém** with its impeccably preserved 18thC core. **Lake Balaton** has long been the most popular holiday destination in the land because of its mixture of attractive landscape, historic towns and swimming opportunities.

If you have at least 2 days to spare, an excellent tour of the Hungarian countryside, combining 3 major points of interest in SW Hungary, is suggested in the following round trip of about 600km (375 miles):

- Start by driving to Veszprém, stopping along the way to look around **Székesfehérvár**, then continue to the N shore of **Lake Balaton**, touring the **Tihany Peninsula** and perhaps making a detour inland to **Sümeg**. One of several good places near the lakeshore for spending a night is **Keszthely**.
- Next, proceed along the S shore of the lake: go as far as you like, for there are no less than six possible routes S when you decide to continue toward **Pécs**.
- The 200km (125-mile) drive back from Pécs is featureless, so stay to enjoy that historic town late into the day, even, perhaps, until the evening meal.
- You can follow the same itinerary by train or — better — by public bus; but your schedule will be tighter, and it might be wise to allow 3 days.

For those who wish to stay nearer Budapest, the Great Bend of the Danube offers a series of memorable places within a radius of 60km (38 miles): **Szentendre**, which is easily the most attractive village in Hungary, as well as the stupendous fortress of **Visegrád** and the archiepiscopal cathedral of **Esztergom**. Nearly every travel organization in the capital offers bus and/or boat tours combining these three. Visitors who prefer to strike out on their own could organize an itinerary as follows (total length as described: 120km/75 miles):

- Start by driving along the right-bank drive to **Szentendre**
- Cross by ferry to **Vác**
- Continue on the left bank to **Nagymaros**

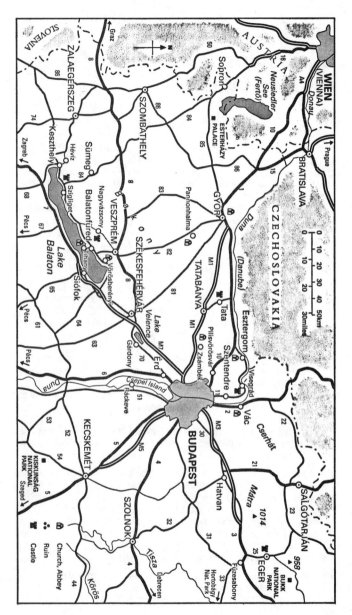

- Cross back at **Visegrád**
- Proceed on the right bank to **Esztergom**
- Return by the inland route (Route 10) via **Pilisvörösvár**

Finally, three localities merit at least a stopover along the route from Budapest to Vienna:

- The village of **Zsámbék**, for its ruined medieval church
- The town of **Tata**, for its graceful Baroque architecture
- The city of **Győr**, for its considerable historic heritage.

Sopron, on the alternative route to and from Vienna, was described earlier in this book under EXCURSIONS FROM VIENNA (see page 187).

LAKE BALATON ★

100 to 160km (63 to 100 miles) sw of Budapest. Frequent trains from South Station (Déli pu., map 7D1). Buses from Erzsébet tér, map 8D4. M7 motorway to Siófok, or Route 70 via Székesfehérvár **i** *in most towns around the lake. The lake is crisscrossed by ferries at many points.*

The largest lake in central Europe (with a surface area of 600sq.km/230 square miles) lies in a landscape of wooded hills thickly dotted with the villages, churches, castles and abbeys of — predominantly — the 18thC. Its shores are lined with the leisure facilities and summer homes of Hungary's middle classes.

Lake Balaton tends to get extremely crowded on summer weekends. During the summer season, it is wise to avoid the M7 motorway southbound on Friday evenings and northbound on Sunday evenings.

Most of Lake Balaton's history is concentrated along the N shore, while the S shore is occupied by an unbroken string of beach colonies, mostly of recent origin. The towns of **Siófok** on the S shore and **Balatonfüred** (★) on the N shore form the nodal points of vacation activity.

The **Tihany Peninsula** (★), which forms a national park and open-air museum, is distinguished by its former Benedictine Abbey, whose graceful Baroque church contains the virtuoso woodcarvings of Sebastyén Stulhof *(organ concerts on Tues and Wed)*, and a delightful ex-fishing village of unusual folk architecture. **Vörösberényi** possesses a remarkable fortified church from the 13thC, while **Szigliget** offers a château of the Esterházy family and the medieval castle of Lengyel.

Keszthely (★), perhaps the most graceful of the lakeshore towns, has an outstanding **Festetics Mansion** (1745), a Baroque jewel housing the 50,000-volume Helicon Library. Not far from the town is **Hévíz** (★), a spa based around Europe's largest thermal lake characterized by a fascinating atmosphere of *fin de siècle* elegance gone to seed.

Vicinity

A 22km (14-mile) drive N from Szigliget is the historic town of **Sümeg** (★) where the ancient mansions of a half-dozen noble families stand side by side in the center, radiating the unspoiled air of a 19thC provincial town. **Nagyvázsony**, a sleepy market town 14km (9 miles) inland from Zánka, attracts many visitors with its medieval castle and the Baroque/Classical **Zichy Mansion** *(a 4-day festival of chivalry is held here in July)*.

✎   There are hotels in some 25 towns along the lakeshore, and the whole Lake Balaton region has the greatest number of private pensions and campsites in Hungary. One of the best hotels is **Erika** *(2 stars)*, on Tihany Peninsula *(☎ (in Budapest) 864.8644* Fx *864.8646* ▥ *15 nicely furnished, air-conditioned rooms* ⇌ ♪ ⛴ *)*, open year-round.

The best hotel in Keszthely is **Hullám** *(3 stars)*, on the waterfront *(☎ 12.644* ▥ ⇌ ⛴ *)*. The **Helikon Tourist Hostel** *(Honvéd u. 22* ☎ *11.242* ▭ *)* presents a less expensive alternative.

DEBRECEN ☆

245km (153 miles) E *of Budapest. Population 217,000* i *Hajdú Tourist, Kálvin tér* ☎ *(52) 15.588. Express or local train from West Station (Nyugati pu., map* 8B5*). Bus from Erzsébet tér, map* 8D4*. Route 4 via Szolnok.*

The second-largest city in Hungary has a distinguished history as a stronghold of Protestant (mainly Calvinist, some Lutheran) culture and anti-Habsburg sentiment. The principal monument in the city is the **Calvinist Church** (Nagytemplom), one of the major works of Neo-classical architecture in Hungary (1803-23).

Near the church is the **Reformed College**, founded in 1538 (the current buildings are early 19thC) and through the centuries an important source of reformist and nationalist ideas. Also nearby is the **Déri Museum**, the most important collection of Hungarian art outside Budapest *(standard opening hours)*.

Hajdú County, of which Debrecen is the center, gave its name to the *hajduk* guerrillas who fought against the Austrian forces in the 17thC. The word is still used as "bandit" in most Balkan languages.

✎   **Arany Bika** ("Golden Bull", 3 stars), a stately Art Nouveau edifice with a modern wing added, is Debrecen's best hotel *(Vörös Hadsereg u. 11-15* ☎ *(52) 16.777* Fx *12.709* ▥ *268 rms* ⇌ ♪ ♈ ⛢ ⚐ *)*.

EGER ☆

130km (81 miles) NE *of Budapest. Population 67,000* i *Eger Tourist, Bajcsy-Zsilinszky u.* ☎ *(36) 11.724. Train from East Station (Keleti pu., map* 5C3*); change in Füzesabony. Bus from Erzsébet tér, map* 8D4*.*

Located in a sunny valley between the Mátra and Bükk mountains, full of narrow, winding, stepped streets and colorful architecture, and producing some of the best-known wine in the country (Egri Bikavér, "bull's blood of Eger"), Eger is one of the more pleasant Hungarian towns in which to spend a day.

A magnificent **castle**, whose heroic defense against the Turkish siege of 1552 formed a memorable chapter in Hungarian history, overlooks the town from a height. It encloses a 15thC **Bishop's Palace** used as a museum *(open Tues-Sun 9am-5pm, closed Mon)*, another museum dedicated to István Dobo, the commander of 1552, and a series of underground tunnels.

Other monuments in town include a 17thC Turkish **minaret**, several substantial Baroque buildings (Archbishop's Palace, Lyceum, County Hall, Minorite Church, St Anne's Church), and a massive Neoclassical **cathedral** designed by József Hild.

✥   The **Park Hotel** *(3 stars)* is located at the edge of the city park at Klapka u. 8 (☎(36) 13.233 ▥ 27 rms ⚏ ♫ ⛾ ⚘ ⚞ ⚘ ☼).

Unicornis *(1 star)* is centrally located on Kossuth út between the main square and the foot of the castle (☎ *(36) 12.886* ▱ *47 rms* ⚏).

ESZTERGOM ✪
64km (40 miles) N of Budapest on the right bank of the Danube. Population 33,000 i *Komturist, Széchenyi tér 13* ☎*(33) 22.484. Bus from Erzsébet tér, map 8D4. Route 11 from Óbuda.*

Already a key stronghold in the era of Celtic tribes and Roman legions, Esztergom became the seat of Hungarian kings in the mythic times of the 10thC and remained so until the Mongol destruction of 1241. The first Christian temple of Hungary was erected here in the reign of Prince Géza, the father and predecessor of St István, and since the turn of the millennium this has been the seat of the archbishop-primate of the Hungarian Catholic church.

The great **fortress** of Esztergom, a linchpin of the Turkish control of Hungary, girds the steep prominence that marks the start of the narrows of the Danube Bend. It fell to Habsburg arms in a famous battle in 1683 that became the opening sally of the war of reconquest. Today only parts of it survive.

An archiepiscopal **Basilica** (✪) was built within it in the 10thC, and rebuilt in 1195 and again after 1242. It disappeared during the period of Turkish rule. Its third reconstruction as Hungary's most grandiose church was started in 1822 and completed, after many delays, in 1856. József Hild was the architect of its Neoclassical design, whose prominent features are a gigantic Corinthian portico and a 72-meter (236-foot) dome.

The most interesting feature of the church's interior is the **Bakócz Chapel** (1511), an altar of red marble that is counted among the finest artworks of the Hungarian Renaissance. The **Crypt** contains the tombs of the archbishops of the Hungarian church, including Joseph Cardinal Mindszentyi, who died in exile in 1975 and was buried here in 1990. The **Treasury** *(*▩ *open Tues-Sun 10am-4.30pm, closed Mon)* contains an interesting miniature model of the church.

Béla III (1172-96), who directed the most important phase of the construction of the original Basilica, was brought up as a prince of the Byzantine imperial court. He pursued a pro-Byzantine policy at a time when the conflict between the crusading West and the beleaguered East was at its sharpest. During his reign and throughout the early part of Hungarian history, "blandishments from the East as well as the West flickered over the great Hungarian Plain with the ambivalence of a mirage" (Patrick Leigh Fermor). Making a subtle reference to that past are the oversized figures of saints Jerome, Ambrose, Augustine and Gregory, the four founding fathers of the Western (Roman Catholic) as opposed to the Eastern (Greek Orthodox) church, who support the cupola of the present Basilica.

The **Castle Museum** *(open Tues-Sun 9am-4.30pm, closed Mon)* occupies the partly reconstructed ruins of the royal palace of Esztergom and contains a collection of archeological fragments and documents. **Szent Támás Hill**, which can be seen to the SE of Castle Hill, carries a chapel dedicated to the English martyr St Thomas à Beckett.

The **town** of Esztergom is situated some distance to the s of both hills and contains several attractive 18th and 19thC buildings.

☛ **Esztergom Hotel** *(3 stars* ⌂ *)*, located on Prímás Island, is the best in town *(* ☎ *(33) 12.883* ▢ *36 rms* ═ ✿ *)*. **Fürdő** *(2 stars)* is based on a natural thermal source and possesses medical facilities *(* ☎ *(33) 11.688* ▢ *91 rms* ═ ⋔ ✿ ⛄ *)*. **Volánturist** *(1 star* ⌂ *)* occupies an attractive park by the river *(* ▢ *35 rms* ═ ✿ *)*.

There are numerous private pensions and two campsites in Esztergom.

GYŐR ☆

124km (77 miles) w of Budapest. Population 130,000 **i** *Aradi Vértanúk útja 22* ☎ *(96) 11.557. Trains from South Station (Déli pu., map **7**D1) and East Station (Keleti pu., map **5**C3). Bus from Erzsébet tér, map **8**D4. Situated on M1 motorway half-way between Vienna and Budapest.*

Too often overlooked on the journey from Vienna to Budapest, Győr justifies a visit to see its attractive historic core, hidden away within a dreary industrial shell. The town, under the German name of Raab, was once a key stronghold of Habsburg Hungary in the time of the Turkish wars. It thus has a more continuous architectural legacy than other Hungarian cities that spent the same period under Turkish rule.

The main sights are concentrated in **Káptalandomb** (Chapter Hill), a fortified hill dominating the confluence of the Rába river and the Moson Danube, and **Széchenyi tér** (☆), the main square of the old town, which lies near the base of the hill. Located on the former is a massive Gothic **cathedral** (☆) carrying traces of its 13th, 15th, 17th and 19thC reconstructions. Its interior stands out for a series of excellent frescoes by Maulbertsch (1781) and a magnificent reliquary **bust** of St Ladislas, king of Hungary (c.1400).

Near the church on Gutenberg tér stands the **Ark of the Covenant** (☆), a splendid example of Baroque convolution, attributed to Fischer von Erlach.

Széchenyi tér is surrounded by one of Hungary's most homogenous ensembles of Baroque architecture. It includes: a **Jesuit church** dedicated to St Ignatius Loyola (1641); the historic **Széchenyi Pharmacy** (1667), founded by Bishop György Széchenyi, an ancestor of the Great Reformer; an **Esterházy Mansion** (1770s); the so-called **Iron Beam House** *(Vastuskózbáz 4, modern art collection within)*, which contains an analogue of Vienna's Stock-im-Eisen; and the residence of the abbots of Pannonhalma (1742), which now houses a **History Museum**. At the center of the square stands an attractive **Column of the Virgin Mary**, erected in 1686 as a thanksgiving for the defeat of the Turks.

The Mary Column and various artworks in the Loyola Church bear the signature of Count Leopold Kollonitsch. As Catholic bishop of Raab and Wiener Neustadt, Kollonitsch was the architect of the violent persecution of Hungarian Protestants following the rebellion of 1671. His inquisitorial zeal led to the emergence of *kuruc* ("crusader") guerrilla bands, who found their leader in Prince Imre Tököly. In turn, Tököly was instrumental in goading the Turks into the ill-fated adventure of 1683.

🕭 Győr has two good hotels and several lesser establishments serving mainly traffic in transit from Vienna to Budapest: **Klastrom** *(3 stars; Fürst u. 1* 🕿*(96) 15611* Ⓕⓧ*27030* ▯▭ *42 rms* ⥤⥥ ❖*)* and **Rába** *(3 stars; Árpád u. 34* 🕿*(96) 15533* ▯▭ *to* ▥▥ *170 rms* ⥤ ⴲ ♱ ⴴ *)*. **Aranypart** *(1 star* ▱ *)* occupies a pleasant green site by the riverside *(Áldozát út 12* 🕿*(96) 26033* Ⓕⓧ*26442* ▯▭ *43 rms* ⥤ ⴲ ⴲ ⴴ water sports, fishing).

Vicinity

The **Benedictine Abbey of Pannonhalma** (Pannonhalmi Apátság), situated 20km (13 miles) SE of Győr, has been one of the most powerful institutions of the Hungarian Catholic church since the reign of Prince Géza in the late 10thC. It was one of the few monastic institutions in Hungary to survive the antireligious measures of the 1950s. The Romanesque buildings date from the 13thC. The Neoclassical library building, which houses an important collection of manuscripts, was added in the early 19thC *(open for visits Tues-Sat 8.30am-5pm, Sun 10.30am-5pm, closed Mon)*.

KECSKEMÉT

81km (51 miles) SE of Budapest. Population 105,000 **i** *Pusztatourist, Szabadság tér* 🕿*(76) 29.499. Train from West Station (Nyugati pu., map 8B5); suburban train from Kőbánya (map 6D4). The M5 motorway runs to within 10km (6 miles) of Kecskemét.*

Situated in the heart of the vast and featureless plain of Hungary, the *puszta,* Kecskemét has become a favorite destination of organized tours that profess to introduce visitors to the "Hungarian experience." Various folkloric events and horse-riding shows are organized in the **Kiskunság National Park**, which spreads over five enormous tracts of rural land.

The town is distinguished by several highly colorful examples of the folkloristic Art Nouveau architecture from the turn of the century. Notable among them are the **Town Hall** (1896), a pioneering work by Ödön Lechner, and the even bolder **Cifrapalota** ("Ornamental Palace," 1902), which now houses a museum of local art.

Other museums in town are a **Museum of Naïve Art** (🔲 *standard opening hours),* which occupies a house dating from c.1730, and a

Museum of Hungarian Folk Textiles (☒ *open Wed-Sun 9am-5pm, closed Mon-Tues),* located in a Baroque beerhall dating from 1793.

✍ Kecskemét offers four hotels of "quality" class (two are listed below), a couple of private pensions, and — so far — nothing in between.

Aranyhomok *(3 stars; Széchenyi tér 3* ☎ *(76) 20.011* ▯ *113 rms* ≡ ☎ ☂ ♫ ✌) is a large hotel in the town center.

Szauna *(3 stars; Sport u. 3* ☎ *(76) 28700* [Fx] *22.729* ▯ *38 rms* ≡ ☂ ☎ ☎ ☀ ☂ ☎) is a modern resort hotel with thermal facilities, situated by a reservoir outside the town.

PÉCS ☆

195km (122 miles) s of Budapest. Population 110,000 **i** *Mecsek Tourist, Széchenyi tér* ☎ *(72) 14.866. Train from South Station (Déli pu., map **7**D1). Bus from Erzsébet tér, map **8**D4. M6 motorway to Siófok, then turn s; or Route 6 via Érd.*

Pécs was one of the leading cities of Hungary in Turkish times, when its population consisted of Turks, Greeks, Bosnians and Serbians. Two **mosques** survive from that period, which are unique as Muslim monuments converted into the Baroque style: Gazi Kasim Pasha Mosque, now the Central Parish Church, and Yakovali Hasan Pasha Mosque, the former church of St John of Nepomuk.

Also of interest are various Roman relics (notably a 4thC **Early Christian Mausoleum** on Szent István tér), several houses dating from the medieval and Turkish periods, the usual complement of Baroque churches (notably the **Franciscan Church** on Sallai u., 1720s), an **Episcopal Palace** (1852) in the Romantic style, and a neo-medieval **cathedral** (1891).

Worth a visit too are the **Csontváry Museum**, dedicated to the work of one of Hungary's most original artists *(Janus Pannonius u. 11-13, standard opening hours),* and the **Zsolnay Ceramics Exhibition**, displaying the distinctive products of the Pécs-based porcelain factory whose designs have influenced Hungarian architecture for the past century *(Zsolnay Kerámia Kiállítása, Káptalan u. 2, standard opening hours).*

The **Mecsek Hills** rising on the N side of Pécs contain popular nature trails, lakes and several historic castles.

✍ **Pannónia** *(3 stars)* is the largest and newest hotel in town *(Rákóczi út 3* ☎ *(72) 13.322* ▯ *113 rms* ≡ ♫ ✌ ⇌).

RÁCKEVE

*48km (30 miles) s of Budapest. HÉV suburban rail from (IX.) Soroksári út (map **5**D3). Route 51 to Kiskunlacháza, then turn w.*

This pleasant small town near the s end of Csepel Island contains the Baroque **Château of Prince Eugene of Savoy** (1702-22), a work by Lukas von Hildebrandt, the same architect who designed the Belvedere in Vienna for the conqueror of Hungary. The estate, which was allowed to deteriorate after 1918, is now fully restored and functions as an architects' recreation center. There is a restaurant in the cellar.

Also interesting is the **Serbian Orthodox Church**, built in Gothic style in 1487 for a colony of Serbian refugees (*Rác* in Magyar) who settled in the town in the 15thC.

Keve *(2 stars* ☎ *(26) 85.047* ⬛ *36 rms* ═ ❧ ⚭*)*, on the riverbank.

SZÉKESFEHÉRVÁR

62km (39 miles) sw of Budapest. Population 110,000 **i** *Albatours, Szabadság tér 6* ☎*(22) 12.494. Train from South Station (Déli pu., map* **7D1**). *Bus from Erzsébet tér, map* **8D4**. *M7 motorway, or Route 70 via Érd.*

Székesfehérvár (meaning "Royal Whitecastle"; in Latin, *Alba Regia;* in German, *Stuhlweissenburg*) was after Esztergom the second seat of the medieval Hungarian kingdom. It was the burial site of King Stephen and his son Imre, and the traditional place for the coronations, marriages and burial ceremonies of the Hungarian kings.

Today, all that remains to bear witness to that era of former glory is the **Field of Ruins** (the Romkert, behind the Episcopal Palace on Széchenyi tér), which comprises the foundations of the medieval cathedral of St Stephen (at one time the final resting place of no less than 37 Hungarian kings), and the Gothic **Chapel of St Anne** (c.1470).

The new **cathedral** dates mainly from the 1750s. Two other Baroque churches (**St Nepomuk** and the **Carmelite Church**, both 1750s) also deserve notice.

Alba Regia *(3 stars; Rákóczi u. 1* ☎ *(22) 13.484* ⬛ *112 rms* ═ ♈ ♫
❧*).* **Magyar Király** *(2 stars; Március 15 u. 10.* ☎*(22) 11.262* ⬛ *57 rms* ═*).*

Vicinity

Lake Velence (Velenceitó), 10km (6 miles) to the E, is a popular destination for excursions from Budapest. **Velence**, an attractive village, occupies a pleasant site on vine-covered slopes, while **Gárdonyi** is being developed as a resort town.

═ The **Vörösmarty Cellar** *(under the Vörösmarty Theater on Marcius 15 u.)* serves local wines and Hungarian specialties.

SZENTENDRE ★

20km (13 miles) N of Budapest on the right bank of the Danube. Population 20,000 **i** *Dunatours, Bogdányi u.* ☎*(26) 11.311. Suburban rail from (l.) Batthyányi tér, map* **7B2**. *Route 11 from Óbuda (Szentendrei út). Bus and boat excursions in summer.*

With its narrow uneven streets, colorful houses and quaint squares, Szentendre is generally reckoned to be Hungary's most attractive village. Being so near to Budapest, it endures a steady stream of day visitors in summer, but outside the high season the village presents a sleepier aspect than would ever be imaginable in a place of similar charm anywhere in Western Europe.

Szentendre, which was named after St Andrew, was settled from 1686 by a colony of Serbian refugees from the Ottoman Empire. It went on to become the most important center of Serbian culture in the Habsburg lands, playing a crucial role in the diplomatic and commercial initiatives of the empire within the Balkans. Its population was enlarged with additional Balkan communities, such as Greeks, Albanians and Dalmatians, who enjoyed much wealth and influence in the cosmopolitan atmosphere of pre-independence Hungary. Today, dwindling bands of their descendants retain their ancestral traditions here in Szentendre.

Six of Szentendre's seven churches were built in the 18thC by the Serbian community; four still serve the Orthodox rite, and two have been converted, respectively, to Catholic and Reformed use. The most elaborate is the so-called **Belgrade Church** (1764), which served for a century and a half as the episcopal seat of the Serbian Orthodox church of Hungary. It possesses some fine examples of Rococo woodcarving. The **Blagovestenska Church** (1754) at Fő tér is also worth a visit to view its limewood iconostasis.

An interesting **Collection of Serbian Ecclesiastical Art** is housed in one of the buildings of the former episcopate, and a Serbian festival is held every year on August 19 at the **Preobrazenska Church** (1746). The modest **Catholic Parish Church** is of medieval origin, though it was altered in the 18thC to serve the Dalmatian community of Szentendre.

Szentendre, having lost its economic and political significance at the time of independence, was then "discovered" by a colony of artists who transformed the village into a mecca of Hungarian art. Today, many of Hungary's leading painters and sculptors, and many others of somewhat less talent, continue to work in Szentendre. The **Artists' Colony**, established in 1928, is located on Ady Endre u.; its gallery is considered the most influential outlet of current art in the country.

Other galleries and museums in town display permanent collections by some of the major names in modern Hungarian art, notably **Károlyi Ferenczi** (1862-1917) and his children, **Béla Csóbel** (1883-1976), **Margit Kovács** (1907-77) and **Jenő Kerényi** (1908-75).

The top hotel is **Danubius** (2 stars; Ady E. u. 28 ☎(26) 12.511 ≡ ❀ ⚘). Szentendre also offers a half-dozen attractive pensions located in old village houses.

Bárcsy Fogadó (Bogdányi u. 30) is a charming, traditional inn and tavern.

Vicinity

Located in the hills a short distance NW of Szentendre is an **Open-air Ethnographical Museum** (Szabadtéri Néprajzi múzeum or Skanzen ★), which brings together specimens of traditional rural architecture — houses, farmsteads, a village church — from various regions of Hungary (open Apr-Oct Tues-Sun 9am-5pm ✗ in English available through travel agencies in Szentendre).

TATA ★

70km (44 miles) w of Budapest. Population 26,000. Trains from South Station (Déli pu., map 7D1) and East Station (Keleti pu., map 5C3). Bus from Erzsébet tér, map 8D4. M1 motorway.

Near the Vienna-Budapest motorway, lying between two small lakes that envelop the town center on two sides, the historic town of Tata makes an enjoyable short visit.

The town owes its wealth of Baroque buildings to Jakob Fellner (1722-80), a Moravian architect who was active here for most of his life. His works include the main **church** on Kossuth tér and the **Esterházy Mansion** nearby; the latter earned a footnote in history for having been the residence of Franz I of Austria when he fled in 1809 from Napoleon.

The **Old Castle** (Őregvár ★), of mighty and medieval aspect, which stands surrounded by a moat in the center of the town, was originally built in the 15thC for King Sigismund. The existing structure is a work of the late 19thC, undertaken to honor a visit by Franz Joseph. The castle houses a museum of ceramics (**■** *standard opening hours*). Two other Baroque buildings designed by Fellner hold a museum devoted to the German ethnic minority (which once formed the dominant element of Tata) and another dedicated to the history and art of butchery.

VÁC

33km (21 miles) N of Budapest (left bank of the Danube). Population 36,000. Train from West Station (Nyugati pu., map 8B5). Bus from Erzsébet tér, map 8D4. Route 2 from Marx tér (Váci út, map 8B4).

Vác is a quiet and unassuming town, with few reminders of the time, during the Middle Ages and through the Turkish period, when it rivaled Buda in size and importance. Its principal monuments are a **cathedral** (1763-77) and a **triumphal arch** (1764), both by Isidore Canevale, notable for being two of the earliest Neoclassical monuments in the Habsburg Empire. The former is decorated with frescoes by Maulbertsch; the latter honors Maria Theresa and bears portraits of the empress, her husband and their children.

The **State Prison**, which stands next to the arch and dates from the same era, was used to incarcerate many prominent political offenders of the Horthy regime and the Stalinist period.

VESZPRÉM ★

*115km (72 miles) sw of Budapest. Population 66,000 **i** Balatontourist ☎(80) 26.277. Hourly train from South Station (Déli pu., map 7D1). Buses from Erzsébet tér, map 8D4. M7 motorway, or Route 70 via Érd.*

The entire old town of Veszprém is a protected area whose main thoroughfare, Vár utca, lined with an unbroken sequence of mostly Baroque buildings, is hailed as the most enchanting street in Hungary.

The entrance to the historic Castle district is marked by a **Fire Tower** (Tűztorony) of medieval origin, whose long career included a period as a Turkish minaret. Notable buildings along Vár u. include a historic fire-station (#1, 1814), with a statue of St Florian, the patron saint of firefighters; the former Piarist school (#8 and 10); the Piarist Abbey (#12) and church (1836); the Baroque Bishop's Palace (#16, 1767); the medieval **Gizella Chapel**, which contains 13thC frescoes in the Byzantine manner; the Baroque Franciscan Church and Abbey (#33); and the Baroque **Cathedral of St Michael** (1723).

Veszprém Hotel *(2 stars)* is the best hotel in town *(Budapest u. 6 ☎ (80) 24.876 76 rms).*

VISEGRÁD

*41km (26 miles) N of Budapest (on the right bank of the Danube). Train from West Station (Nyugati pu., map **8**B5) to Nagymaros (on the left bank), then car/passenger ferry across the river (continuous service). Bus from Erzsébet tér, map **8**D4. Palace open Tues-Sun 9am-5pm; closed Mon. Citadel open daily 10am-6pm.*

The ruined **fortress** of Visegrád stands on the pinnacle of a steep hill rising over the Great Bend of the Danube, while the tiny village below on the riverside holds the ruined but partly reconstructed remains of the legendary **castle** of the medieval Hungarian kings.

Both date from the Mongol invasion of 1241. But it was Charles Robert I who first turned Visegrád into his royal residence (c.1316). Later, Matthias Corvinus rebuilt the castle into what one papal legate described as "an earthly paradise." A dazed traveler of the quattrocento eulogized it as a place of "magnificent and spacious halls, beautiful windows, terraced gardens and splashing fountains." Corvinus' palace was later buried by debris washing down the hillside. It lay there, utterly forgotten, until 1934, when it was rediscovered by archeologists under a layer of earth.

In 1335 Visegrád was the site of one of the most famous summit meetings in European history, which brought together Charles Robert of Hungary, John of Bohemia and Casimir of Poland in a far-reaching alliance against Vienna. In February 1991, the leaders of democratic Hungary, Czechoslovakia and Poland chose Visegrád for their summit meeting, which produced wide-ranging agreements.

The fortress is accessible from the village by a steep and exhausting climb, which is rewarded with an extraordinary panorama. The best distant view of the fortress itself can be obtained from the village of **Nagymaros** across the Danube.

ZSÁMBÉK

*28km (18 miles) W of Budapest. Bus from (I.) Széna tér, map **7**B1. M1 motorway to Vizimalom, then 8km (5 miles) N. Also secondary road via Budakeszi.*

The ruined hulk of the **Romanesque church** of Zsámbék, one of Hungary's most remarkable medieval monuments, stands a short distance above the village. The triple-nave church was built in 1220-58. Like many others of its era it was endowed by the local lordly dynasty — in this case the counts of Ainard, who were of French origin.

The languages in a nutshell

GERMAN
The German language as spoken in Vienna bears the same relationship to the German of Germany as Oxford English does to American. The many peculiarities of Viennese idiom are an infinite source of amused admiration for visitors down from the north. Austria's history has made its vocabulary susceptible to Italian and French influences, while the language of the street contains many Slavonic, Hungarian and Yiddish terms.

PRONUNCIATION
The pronunciation of German is generally more predictable than English and more logical than French.

- Words are **stressed** much more strongly than in English. The stress falls on the stem syllable, which, with nouns and verbs, is generally the first.
- The simple **vowels** A, E, I, O, U represent one basic sound each. They can, however, be short or long.
- The **umlaut** (as in ä, ö, ü) signifies a dropped E after A, O or U (ä = ae, ö = oe, ü = ue). These rather un-English sounds can be pronounced:

Ä (short)	*e* as in *hen*
Ä (long)	*ay* as in *say*
Ö	*er* as in *herb*
Ü	*ew* as in *dew*

- **Diphthongs** (composite vowels) are straightforward:

AI, EI	*i* as in *eye*
AU	*ow* as in *cow*
ÄU, EU	*oi* as in *noise*

- Most **consonants** present no problems. Exceptions are:

C	alone or before E, I: *ts* as in *bets*
CH	hard *h*, but not quite a Scottish *ch*
CHS	*x* as in *ax*
J	*y* as in *yes*
S	normally *z* as in *zip*
	s as in *sip* at the end of word
	sh as in *ship* before K,P,T at beginning of word
SS	*s* as in *sip*
SCH	*sh* as in *ship*
TSCH	*ch* as in *chip*
V	*f* as in *fat*
W	*v* as in *vat*
Z	*ts* as in *bets*

WRITTEN GERMAN
All substantives (nouns) in German are written with an initial capital letter. The archaic German script form of ss (ß) can still be seen.

GRAMMAR

German nouns are masculine, feminine or neuter. The definite article (*the*) is accordingly *der* (m.), *die* (f.) or *das* (n.). The article for the plural of all three genders is *die*.

Depending on their role in a sentence, noun endings can vary (nominative, accusative, genitive or dative case). This yields a total of 24 possible variations (3 gender x 4 cases x singular/plural). The indefinite article (*a/an*) is equally complex.

Here is the present tense of the verbs *to be* (I am, you are, he/she/it is...) and *to go* (I go...):

	to be *(sein)*	to go *(gehen)*
ich	bin	gehe
du	bist	gehsth
er, sie, es	ist	geht
wir	sind	gehen
ihr	seid	gehet
Sie	sind	gehen

HUNGARIAN

Hungarian, like Finnish, Esthonian and several tribal languages spoken in northern Russia, belongs to the Finno-Ugri family, which bears practically no relationship to other European languages. The Roman alphabet has been used since the Middle Ages, but many idiosyncracies make its pronunciation treacherous for the non-Hungarian speaker.

PRONUNCIATION

Hungarian **vowels** are short or long. An accent (as in á, é, ú) indicates that the vowel is to be pronounced long. The stress is almost invariably on the first syllable of a word.

The pronunciation of **A** is most problematic. Whereas *A* (short) is pronounced like an English *o* as in *hot*, *Á* (long) is similar to long *a* as in *far*. E/É, I/Í, O/Ó, U/Ú present fewer problems. Ö and Ü (both short) are pronounced like the German equivalents; Ő and Ű, both unique to Hungarian, are longer versions. There are no diphthongs in Hungarian.

The following **consonants** and consonant pairs deserve notice for their unusual pronunciation:

C	*ts* as in *pets,* except in CS
CS	*ch* as in *chip*
CZ	(historic spelling) same as C
G	hard *g* as in *go,* except in GY
GY	*j* as in *jeep*
J	*y* as in *yes*
LY	*y* as in *yes*
S	*sh* as in *ship*
SZ	*s* as in *sip*
ZS	French *g* as in *garage*

GRAMMAR

Hungarian has no grammatical gender. The indefinite article *a* is used

286

far more sparingly than in English. A characteristic of the language is its tendency to add strings of suffixes to a word to modify its meaning, creating such tongue-twisters as *legeslegmegszentségteleníthetetlenebbül* ("in a way that is most impossible to desecrate").

Another feature is vowel harmony, which causes suffixes appended to a word to adapt their vowel to the final vowel of the word. Thus the plural suffix can take the forms -ak, -ek, -ok or -ök depending on the final syllable it is added to: *férfi,* pl. *férfiak* (men); *könyv,* pl. *könyvek* (books); *állam,* pl. *államok* (states); *ötvös,* pl. *ötvösök* (goldsmiths).

Key words in three languages

English / German / *Hungarian.*

REFERENCE WORDS

Monday / Montag / *hétfő*
Tuesday / Dienstag / *kedd*
Wednesday / Mittwoch / *szerda*
Thursday / Donnerstag / *csütörtök*
Friday / Freitag / *péntek*
Saturday / Samstag / *szombat*
Sunday / Sontag / *vasárnap*
One / eins / *egy*
Two / zwei / *két/kettő*
three / drei / *három*
four / vier / *négy*
five / fünf / *öt*
six / sechs / *hat*
seven / sieben / *hét*
eight / acht / *nyolc*
nine / neun / *kilenc*
ten / zehn / *tíz*
eleven / elf / *tizenegy*
twelve / zwölf / *tizenkettő*
thirteen / dreizehn / *tizenhárom*
twenty / zwanzig / *húsz*
thirty / dreissig / *harminc*

fifty / fünfzig / *ötven*
hundred / hundert / *száz*
thousand / tausend / *ezer*
England / England / *Anglia*
English (lang.) / Englisch / *angolul*
English (person) / Engländer(-in) / *Angol*
American / Amerikaner(-in) / *amerikai*
Austria / Österreich / *Ausztria*
Austrian (person) / Österreicher(-in) / *osztrák*
German (lang.) / Deutsch / *németül*
Hungary / Ungarn / *Magyarország*
Hungarian (lang.) / Ungarisch / *magyarul*
Hungarian (person) / Ungar(-in) / *magyar(-nő)*
Mr. / Herr / *úr*
Mrs. / Frau / *asszony*
Gents / Herren / *férfi(ak)*
Ladies / Damen / *női/nők*

BASIC COMMUNICATION

Yes / Ja / *igen*
No / Nein / *nem*
Thank you / Danke (schön) / *köszönöm*
Please / Bitte (schön) / *kérem*
Excuse me / Entschuldigung / *bocsánat*
Good day / Guten Tag / *jó napot, jó*

napot kívanok
Good morning / Guten Morgen / *jó reggelt*
Good evening / Guten Abend / *jó estét*
Good night / Gute Nacht / *jó éjszakát*
Good bye / Auf Wiedersehen / *A viszontlátásra*

The informal **German** expressions of greeting, *Servus* ("[your] servant" — Austrian only) and *Grüss Gott* ("God greet" — Austrian/Bavarian), are used far more often in Austria than the standard *Guten Tag* ("good day"). *Tschüss* ("bye") is what friends say upon departure. The **Hunga-**

287

rian *szia* (pl. *sziasztok*) means both "hello" and "bye" depending on the situation. *Szervusz* (pl. *szervusztok*) is also used in both senses.

yesterday / gestern / *tegnap*
today / heute / *ma*
tomorrow / morgen / *holnap*
hour / Stunde, Uhr / *óra*
day / Tag / *nap*
week / Woche / *hét*
month / Monat / *hónap, hó*
year / Jahr / *év, esztendő*
here / hier / *itt*
there / da / *ott*
nice, beautiful / schön / *szép*
good / gut / *jó*
well / gut / *jól*
bad / schlecht / *rossz*
big / gross / *nagy*
small / klein / *kis*
hot / heiss / *forró, meleg*
cold / kalt / *hideg*
quick / schnell / *gyors*
slow / langsam / *lassú*
expensive / teuer / *drága*
cheap / billig / *olcsó*
far / fern / *távol, messze*
near / nah / *közel*
right / rechts / *jobb*
left / links / *bal*
and / und / *és*
but / aber / *de, pedig*
or / oder / *vagy*
very / sehr / *nagyon*
what / was / *mi*

when / wann / *mikor*
why / warum / *miért*
where / wo / *hol*
who / wer / *ki*
entrance / Eingang / *bejárat*
exit / Ausgang / *kijárat*
pull / ziehen / *húzni*
push / drücken / *tolni*
open / geöffnet / *nyitva*
closed / geschlossen / *zárva*
I don't know. / Ich weisse nicht. / *Nem tudom.*
I don't understand. / Ich verstehe nicht. / *Nem értem.*
My name is... / Ich heisse... / *A nevem...*
Do you speak English? / Sprechen Sie Englisch? / *Beszél angolul?*
I am American (fem.)/English (fem.) / Ich bin Amerikaner(in)/ Engländer(in). / *Amerikai/ angol vagyok.*
Have you any ... ? / Haben Sie ...? / *Van ... ?*
How much is this, please? / Wieviel kostet das, bitte? / *Mennyibe kerül?*
What time is it? / Wie spät ist es? / *Hány óra van?*
That's OK. / (Alles) in Ordnung. / *Jól van.*

BASIC WORDS
name / Name / *név*
book / Buch / *könyv*
music / Musik / *zene*
center / Zentrum / *központ*
house / Haus / *ház*
child / Kind / *gyermek*
friend (m.) / Freund / *barát*
friend (f.) / Freundin / *barátnő*
money / Geld / *pénz*

pharmacy / Apotheke / *gyógyszertár, patika*
hospital / Spital (Austr.) / *kórház*
physician / Arzt / *orvos*
town / Stadt / *város*
capital / Hauptstadt / *főváros*
garden / Garten / *kert*
hill / Berg, Hügel / *hegy*
rain / Regen / *eső*
water / Wasser / *víz*

TRANSPORTATION
airport / Flughafen / *repülőtér*
bicycle / (Fahr)rad / *bicikli*
boat / Schiff / *hajó*
bus / Autobus / *busz*
cab driver / Taxifahrer / *taxisofőr*
car / Auto, Wagen / *autó*

rail station / Bahnhof / *pályaudvar (pu.)*
railway / Eisenbahn / *vasút*
ticket (fare) / Fahrkarte / *menetjegy*
ticket (entry) [for comparison] / Eintrittskarte / *belépőjegy*

street / Strasse, Gasse / *utca*
road / Strasse, Weg / *út*

station / Station / *állomás*
taxi / Taxi / *taxi*

POST/TELEPHONE
airmail / Luftpost / *légiposta*
letter / Brief / *levél*
phone number / Telefonnummer / *telefonszám*
postcard / Postkarte / *képeslap*

post office / Post / *posta, posthivatal*
stamp / Briefmarke / *bélyeg*
telegram / Telegramm / *távirat*
telephone / Fernsprecher / *telefon*

FOOD
hungry / hungrig / *éhes*
meal / Essen / *étel*
breakfast / Frühstück / *reggeli*
delicatessen / Feinkost / *csemege*
restaurant / Restaurant / *étterem*
tavern / Gasthaus / *vendeglő*
beerhall / Bierstube / *söröző*
winehall / Weinstube / *borozó*
Cheers! / Gesundheit! Prosit! / *egészségére!* (formal)/ *egészségedre!* (informal)
drink / Getränk / *ital*
soft drinks / Alkoholfreies / *üdítő italok*

meat / Fleisch / *hús*
veal / Kalb / *borjú*
chicken / Hahn / *csirke*
fish / Fisch / *hal*
fruit / Obst / *gyümölcs*
salt / Salz / *só*
vegetable / Gemüse / *zöldség*
potato / Kartoffel / *burgonya*
bread / Brot / *kenyér*
egg / Ei / *tojás*
butter / Butter / *váj*
honey / Honig / *méz*
cheese / Käse / *sajt*

SHOPPING
bookstore / Buchhandlung / *könyvesbolt*
shop / Laden, Geschäft / *üzlet, bolt*
shopping / Einkaufen / *vásárolni*
department store / Kaufhaus / *áruház*
gift / Geschenk / *ajándék*
grocery / Lebensmittel / *élelmiszer*

jeweler / Juwelier / *ékszerbolt*
leather / Leder / *bőr*
market / Markt / *vásár*
supermarket / Supermarket / *közért*
gold / Gold / *arany*
shirt / Hemd / *ing*
shoe / Schuh / *cipő*

AT THE HOTEL
bath / Bad / *fürdőkád*
bed / Bett / *ágy*
bill / Rechnung / *számla*
hotel / Hotel, Gasthof / *hotel, szálloda*

pension / Pension, Privatzimmer / *panzió*
room / Zimmer / *szoba*
shower / Dusche / *zuhany*

SIGHTSEEING
art / *Kunst* / *művészet*
church / Kirche / *egyház, templom*
castle / Burg, Schloss / *vár*
city, town / Stadt / *város*
city hall / Rathaus / *városháza*
cross / Kreuz / *kereszt*
king / König / *király*
emperor / Kaiser / *császár*
forest / Wald / *erdő*

court(yard) / Hof / *udvar*
monument / Denkmal / *emlék, műemlék*
gate / Tor / *kapu*
island / Insel / *sziget*
palace / Palast, Schloss / *palota*
queen / Königin / *királynő*
tower / Turm / *torony*
village / Dorf / *falu*

289

Index

Page numbers in **bold** refer to main entries. *Italic* numbers refer to illustrations and maps.

INDEX OF PLACES

VIENNA INDEX

BUDAPEST INDEX

American Express Travel Guides

spanning the globe....

EUROPE
Amsterdam, Rotterdam
  & The Hague
Athens and the
  Classical Sites ‡
Barcelona & Madrid ‡
Berlin ‡
Brussels #
Dublin and Cork #
Florence and Tuscany
London #
Moscow & St Petersburg *
Paris #
Prague *
Provence and the
  Côte d'Azur *
Rome
Venice ‡
Vienna & Budapest

NORTH AMERICA
Boston and New
  England *
Los Angeles & San
  Diego #
Mexico ‡
New York #
San Francisco and
  the Wine Regions
Toronto, Montréal and
  Québec City ‡
Washington, DC

THE PACIFIC
Cities of Australia
Hong Kong & Taiwan
Singapore &
  Bangkok ‡
Tokyo #

*   Paperbacks in preparation   #   Paperbacks appearing January 1993
‡   Hardback pocket guides (in paperback 1993)

Clarity and quality of information, combined with outstanding maps — the ultimate in travelers' guides